The Blitzkrieg Myth

Also by John Mosier

The Myth of the Great War

The Blitzkrieg Myth

How Hitler and the Allies Misread the Strategic Realities of World War II

JOHN MOSIER

HarperCollins*Publishers*

HarperCollins books may be purchased for educational, business, or sales promotional use. For information, please write: Special Markets Department, HarperCollins Publishers Inc., 10 East 53rd Street, New York, NY 10022.

FIRST EDITION

Designed by Sarah Maya Gubkin

Printed on acid-free paper

Library of Congress Cataloging-in-Publication Data is available upon request.

ISBN 0-06-000976-4

03 04 05 06 07 ❖/RRD   10 9 8 7 6 5 4 3 2 1

Men prefer one great lie to a mass of small truths.

—ALEXANDER PUSHKIN

CONTENTS

ILLUSTRATIONS

Maps

Photographs

ACKNOWLEDGMENTS

The genesis of this book began more than thirty years ago. I was thinking about it and researching it even as I was writing another book, *The Myth of the Great War.* Consequently I am indebted to many of the same institutions and individuals for their help. The archivists and curators at the National Archives (Washington, D.C.), the Austrian Army Museum (Vienna), the Imperial War Museum (London), and the Bavarian Army Museum (Ingolstadt) were all unfailingly helpful. The exhibits at the U.S. Army's Aberdeen Proving Ground were invaluable. The support offered by Patricia Doran of the J. Edgar and Louise S. Monroe Library of Loyola University in New Orleans has been exemplary.

Mary McCay, who succeeded me as chair of the Department of English at Loyola, was not only supportive but instrumental in obtaining release time for me so that I could finish the manuscript. In Washington, D.C., Albert and Annick Casciero were kind enough to put me up—and to put up with me—over the course of my many visits to the National Archives, and to take time out from their own work to lend their photographic skills.

Scores of other people, mostly readers of my earlier book, took the time to write or call me and give me their own views on both world wars. I found their insights stimulating and rewarding, and their moral support most helpful. There are far too many of them for me to attempt even a partial list, but I cannot help but name John Stacy (formerly captain, Eighty-second Airborne), who, together with his lovely wife, Mary Ann, often extended his hospitality.

I've been very fortunate to have the boundless energy and enthusiasm of my agent, Jim Hornfischer, and the editorial services of my wife, Sarah Spain Mosier. And last but not least, I've benefited from the ideas as well as the editing skills of my editor at HarperCollins, Cass Canfield, Jr. Without him this book would never have been written.

The Blitzkrieg Myth

INTRODUCTION:

NEW THEORIES OF WARFARE

Their ideas are prefabricated. Experience teaches them nothing.
—ALBERT SCHWEITZER

T his book, the result of a quarter century of research and reflection, demonstrates that traditional accounts of the Second World War are seriously flawed. The fundamental error is this: in the 1920s two new theories of warfare were postulated, most notably by the English armored officer J. F. C. Fuller and the Italian aviator Giulio Douhet. Over the course of the next decades these theories—or their key portions—were adopted almost universally by military and political leaders and by historians and military analysts. The resulting ideas, identified as Blitzkrieg and airpower, are now universally accepted, not merely as important concepts in modern warfare—which they certainly are—but as assumptions defining how the war was fought and why one side was successful and the other not. Douhet and Fuller—and their apostles—reworked the evidence to support their arguments. As this book explains, their ideas were mostly incorrect, but all accounts of the Second World War accept their assumptions.

Although both Douhet and Fuller pretended to be rigorous and scientific theorists, their ideas, far from being borne out by what happened in the First World War, are almost completely contradicted by it. It follows, therefore, that those historians who have accepted their ideas as holy writ give a highly misleading picture of the war.

Not as to the actual outcomes: in this regard the Second World War is entirely different from the First, whose results were at bottom paradoxical and inconclusive. In an earlier book I argued that the military lessons of the Great War were mislearned. The Allies were largely ineffective militarily, the Germans largely victorious, even though they ultimately lost the war. In this book my critical focus is on the reasons given for the various defeats and victories, since the end results are clear: During 1939 and 1940, seven nations officially admitted their defeat by Germany; in May 1945 Germany officially admitted its own defeat and surrendered. Its cities were in ruins, its national territory occupied. There is no ambiguity there at all. The problem arises when we begin to consider how these defeats came about. My argument is that evidence demonstrates that these defeats were not primarily the result of new ideas about warfare but the result of traditional factors: politics and strategy.

The implications of this argument are fundamental for military history. It is almost universally accepted, for example, that the construction of the Maginot Line was an exercise in near futility that revealed the defeatist, retrograde thinking of the French. However, the facts reveal this to be a misperception of the realities of the 1920s and the 1930s. During the 1930s German military engineers presided over the construction of elaborate and extensive defensive positions, both east and west, almost exactly comparable to what the French had planned the decade before. Surprisingly little is known about the nature and extent of these fortifications, whose details (for the eastern frontier) did not begin to emerge until after the collapse of Communist Poland.

The assumption that the Maginot Line was uniquely French, and that it tells us something about France, is simply not true. The evidence shows that the Germans went through the same discussions the French did, that Hitler himself took a keen interest in what was being built, and that one of the key officers involved, a young major on the newly reformed general staff, was none other than Erich von Manstein, generally—and correctly—regarded as one of the Wehrmacht's most successful commanders and the alleged architect of some of its greatest offensive victories. To understand what happened in this war, one must begin with an explanation that embraces the facts as they are known to exist, not as several generations of analysts have wished them to be.

The other point made by this book is no less fundamental: That is the argument that the airpower theories of men like Douhet, and the Blitzkrieg theories of men like Fuller, are at bottom the same thing, the difference being only in the mechanism used (tanks as opposed to planes). Both proposed to strike directly into the heart of the enemy, to win the war in one swift and decisive stroke. For want of a better term, I have employed the word *breakthrough* to describe this idea, which came to dominate both the direction of the war and what has been written about it since.

The point of this book is that accounts of this war, as of the one preceding it, are based on a slowly collapsing paradigm that is riddled with anomalies and contradictions—too dependent on the suppression of evidence—to be accepted as a satisfactory explanation of the phenomenon itself. British historians of the First World War produced a gripping and absorbing account of how the war was won. The only thing wrong with it was that little of it was actually true. Through repetition they came to think that it *was* true, and to explain away any evidence to the contrary by mystifying the facts and hiding primary causes in a forest of secondary ones. In the Second World War partisans of national interest have largely (although in the United States not entirely) been replaced by adherents of the two theories, but the end result is the same sort of tale with all the same problems: It makes for a gripping story, but most of it isn't true.

The basic ideas of my narrative are simple, although its implications are not. The structure is divided into three parts: The first explains what these new theories of warfare were, and shows why they were largely, although not entirely, incorrect. The second explains how the two chief European powers, France and Germany, prepared for a future war. Not by devoting their defense budgets to tanks and planes but by building fortifications. The third, by far the longest section, reexamines the campaigns of the war in Western Europe in the light of what the first two sections establish as the historical truth.

In researching my earlier book on the Great War, I noticed two significant facts: first, that German losses in combat were substantially lower than those of their adversaries, generally in the neighborhood of two and even three to one; and second, that most of the casualties in the war were caused not by rifle bullets (as had been the case in all previous modern wars), but by shellfire from guns. These two facts led me to an investigation of German artillery, since it appeared that here was one important reason for the casualty imbalance.

By their very nature the instruments of modern warfare are complex technical devices. Yet without understanding the why and how of their basic functions, one can hardly judge the theories of their use that dominated military thinking in the decades before 1940. The old cliché that those who do not understand history are doomed to repeat it is nowhere more applicable than in the study of warfare in this century. That alone justifies the necessity of combining the technical and the general, the practical and the theoretical, so that this account of combat in the Second World War goes beyond a simple recitation of the conventional wisdom on the subject—for, as we shall see, at every turn the conventional wisdom is hardly sustained by what actually happened on the battlefield.

After 1942 the Germans, having enjoyed absolute air superiority in their earlier campaigns, failed signally to appreciate the realities of armored warfare without it. Their technical expertise in one area blinded them to the underlying reasons for their own success, a theme that this book expounds on at length. None of the specialists who planned for this war, or the military leaders who directed it once it began, seems to have had any real sense of the events that had gone before. Thus we find Patton, far and away the most literate and historically astute of all the major commanders, completely bogged down in precisely the same theater of operations—Lorraine—in which he had fought in the First World War. Of all the senior allied commanders, he should by rights have been the most aware of the difficulties involved in dislodging German infantry from fortifications.

The explanation for these failures, I believe, lies not so much in the personal or professional inadequacies of the commanders but in their conversion to theories of armored warfare that were in themselves mostly erroneous. Significantly Montgomery, generally the most cautious and conventional of all the senior commanders, alone seems to have grasped the realities of the modern battlefield. But even there, with Operation Market-Garden, the attempt to leapfrog into Germany by dropping airborne troops all along the key route through the Netherlands, we see the same failure: on the one hand the belief that armored units could cut swiftly through opposition, and on the other an obvious ignorance of just how costly the invasion of the Netherlands had been for German airborne units in May 1940.

These simple comparisons suggest the principle that underlies this history: Cross-comparisons spread over the course of the war—and over the course of the century—allow us a much more profitable understanding of what actually happened than do the specialized studies of one isolated offensive, weapon, or idea.

NOTES

1. As quoted by Alain Peyrefitte, *The Trouble with France*, trans. William R. Byron (New York: New York University Press, 1986), 12. The "they" are the French, but in context the quotation is perfectly applicable to the military theorists being discussed.

1.

War as Pseudoscience: 1920–1939

Nothing is more dangerous in war than theoreticians.
—MARSHAL PÉTAIN[2]

The Second World War was the complete opposite of the First. In the latter, Allied propagandists had been free to weave their fables, unchecked and unquestioned. The result was a highly consistent series of myths that foundered not because of any real internal inconsistencies but because they were based on a series of palpable untruths, facts about relative losses of men and territory that could ultimately be verified or proved false.

This was not possible in the Second World War, in which, from the very first, many of the claims of the combatants were subject to verification. Americans listening to William Shirer's censored broadcasts from Berlin in 1939–40 received a surprisingly coherent and in many respects truthful account of what was happening—even under the worst censorship it far exceeded what had been available in 1914–15. Moreover there were men in Great Britain who had bitter memories of how their government had managed the truth. When, in 1940, the government attempted to lay all the blame for the collapse on the hapless Belgians,

Adm. Sir Roger Keyes stood up in the House and exposed the government's efforts for what they were—an attempt to find a scapegoat to cover up its own ineptitude. Like all slanders, bits and pieces of this one stuck, but the myth of how Belgium betrayed the Allied cause and brought it to ruin was quickly shattered.

It was precisely the lack of any central coherent myth to recast the narrative of World War II that made all the various accounts so full of internal contradictions and anomalies. It was easy to see that, but the very incoherence of the narrative of the war made it difficult to piece together what had actually happened.

The explanation is that military theory between the wars was dominated by the work of airpower enthusiasts and apostles of armored warfare. In both cases and in every country, the theoreticians resorted to rewriting the history of the Great War to vindicate their theories about how wars should be fought. When the Second World War actually broke out on September 1, 1939, both the military theorists and the propagandists of the combatants produced converging explanations of what had happened.

The invasion of Poland provides a perfect example. Hitler's propagandists were eager to portray the Polish offensive as a terrifying German military triumph that glorified not only the achievements of the Luftwaffe, which from the first had been regarded as the most National Socialist of the services, but would glorify those achievements in such a way as to cower everyone else into submission.

The airpower enthusiasts and armored apostles were only too delighted to shape the Polish campaign so that it justified their emphasis on armor and airplanes. To the followers of Giulio Douhet (and to the airmen in the United States and Great Britain who hit on these same ideas independently) the Polish campaign was proof positive that the side that lost command of the air would be quickly destroyed—from the air. The misleading and simplistic belief that Warsaw was destroyed by the Luftwaffe was thus turned into a great symbol with all sorts of layers: on one level it represented the barbarism of Hitler's ideas, on another it served as a sort of dissuasive bogeyman for timid Frenchmen and Englishmen. And on still another level it supported the arguments that more money needed to be spent on airplanes instead of other areas of national defense.

Since Poland had even fewer tanks than it had planes, much the same process occurred. The German successes, insofar as they were not exclusively caused by airplanes, were attributed to the fact (in reality not particularly true) that they deployed tanks en masse, organized as armored divisions. An army with no armored divisions was helpless in the face of this onslaught.

However, the primary reasons for Poland's defeat were strategic, not tactical. When Erich von Manstein dissected the causes of Poland's defeat, his concluding sentence was that "Poland's defeat was the inevitable outcome of the Warsaw government's illusions about the actions its allies would take, as well as of its over-estimation of the Polish Army's ability to offer lengthy resistance."[2] As we shall see, even this oversimplifies the situation considerably, but then Manstein, a keen supporter of Hitler, forbore to do more than briefly mention Poland's other strategic difficulties.[3]

The point is not to deny the importance either of technology or tactics on the battlefield, but simply to say that the fundamental error lies in elevating those two components above all other concerns. The Polish government believed, with justification, that it had a guarantee from both France and England to begin offensive operations against Germany if that country attacked Poland. If Poland's army could hold out for two weeks, the Allied attack would force Germany to reallocate its army and air force to the defense of its own territory. That these agreements were actually made, and were not simply some illusion on the part of the Polish government, is incontrovertible. So is the fact that on September 14, 1939, Poland still had substantial armies in the field and was in control of a surprisingly large amount of its national territory. So although tactics and technology played an important part in the defeat, they were by no means the primary causes. In a war that pitched its army against Germany's and the Soviet Union's, Poland would have lost, whether the Germans deployed tanks and airplanes or not.

The Blitzkrieg as an Idea Both True and False

As the Germans occupied northern France and what we now call Benelux, demolished Yugoslavia and then Greece, and routed the Soviet armies in the summer of 1941, Allied analysts insisted that the cause was simple. The Germans were using a radically new kind of warfare, for which the vague and mystical word *Blitzkrieg* was simply a convenient shorthand.

To demystify the concept, and for want of a better term, we can speak of this new idea as that of the *breakthrough,* a term that in the military sense was probably first defined by the U.S. Army to denote a penetration through the depth of the defensive position, a penetration that theorists like J. F. C. Fuller had argued was only possible using masses of tanks operating under an aerial umbrella which involved command of the air.

During the Second World War, both sides pursued the idea of the breakthrough. An almost blind adherence to the concept, coupled with a refusal to examine the mounting contrary evidence, bedeviled Allied strategy from the North African landings on through the end of the war. It explains both why a prudent and experienced general like Montgomery would mount disastrous offensives like Goodwood in July and Market-Garden in September 1944 and why official U.S. Army doctrine was that tanks would not actually fight enemy tanks (and thus there was no need for a high-velocity main gun capable of destroying the enemy's main battle tank with one shot).

I have used the term *blind adherence* because, at the highest levels, it certainly seems to be a fair characterization. Neither the armored apostles nor the airpower enthusiasts modified their views as a result of the experiences of the war. In this they were quite like Hitler, who—if we are to believe Manstein—failed to learn from Poland's strategic failures and apply the lessons to German defensive operations.[4] Instead Hitler would demand that his beleaguered troops go over to the offensive. In August 1944 they were to cut through the hinge between the British and American forces and destroy them; in December 1944 they were to do the same thing only on a grander scale, aiming at Antwerp. Whatever chance Hitler had of fighting the war to a stalemate of any sort died in those two offensive operations.

But Hitler was hardly the only major figure in the war to ignore the facts of the situation. Despite the horrific losses of German airborne units in their assaults on the Netherlands and Crete, the Allies repeated the same mistake, operating under the mistaken belief that airborne deployments would make the breakthrough an accomplished fact. But this was to be a war in which hardly anyone seemed to have learned anything at all. Senior British and American air force leaders were still insisting that bomber offensives could win the war outright as late as the summer of 1944. And as late as December 1944, American experts were still refusing to equip American tanks with a high-velocity gun, despite the fact that the Germans and the Russians had been deploying such weapons for several years.

Perhaps more troubling, senior commanders were judged not on the traditional basis for success—low casualties and high achievements—but on the extent to which they were willing and able to carry out these ambitious deep penetrations that had been determined to be the only successful way to conduct operations on the battlefield. Indeed, the vastly inflated reputations of both Patton and Rommel are almost totally a function of their successes in directing such operations.

Doubtless some readers will be delighted to hear the achievements of Rommel and Patton questioned, others will be simply surprised, and a few will be distressed. The purpose here is not a reevaluation of their careers but to suggest how our perceptions have been so decisively shaped by the blind acceptance of the breakthrough theory of military operations. Both men were first-rate commanders whose abilities had already been established, albeit at lower levels, on the battlefields of the Great War. Their fame in the next one, however, is more a function of the need to have great leaders whose ideas fit the current paradigm than of their actual achievements.

This mention of personalities suggests, however, the importance of the idea, as it allows us to see in a much different light the notorious conflicts that plagued the Allies. As is well known, there were serious divisions in the Allied command: disagreements based on national rivalries (British versus American), disagreements based on interservice rivalries (air force versus army), and disagreements based on personalities (Eisenhower and Montgomery). These personality problems have proved a vast and fruitful area for biographers, and as biographers have produced some of the most readable and serious work in recent military history, there is an almost inevitable tendency to see things through the prism of personality.

But the basic Allied conflict in the fall of 1944 was not primarily a function of personality clashes or national or service rivalries. Montgomery, no less than Patton or Bradley or Harris or Spaatz, was entirely dominated by the desire to defeat Germany. The real conflict was between Eisenhower (supported by his immediate superior, Marshall) and the senior Allied commanders, who, regardless of their nationality or branch of service, were convinced that the only proper way to win the war was to throw all the Allied resources into one powerful offensive operation. "Let us assemble a powerful force of forty or fifty divisions and strike into the heart of Germany," Montgomery pleaded.[5] The problem, of course, was that Churchill, Bradley, and Patton all had similarly convincing proposals, and the bomber barons, the commanders of the American and British strategic air forces, had their own ideas.

The received wisdom on this issue often seems to parallel Montgomery's frustrations: Rather than making a decision in favor of option A, B, or C, Eisenhower simply let every option be exercised. The consequent weakening of the Allied efforts through dispersion made an extension of the war into 1945 inevitable.

But Eisenhower had a great advantage as a senior commander of a great coalition: He had never been in combat; he had never held any meaningful battlefield command. His military experience in the U.S. Army had been exclusively that of a staff officer, and one whose duties were mostly concerned with the higher levels of strategic planning. His appreciation of how to fight the war, therefore, was far removed from the actual battlefield.

In fact, his plan of 1944, usually called the "broad front" strategy, was pretty much the same plan that the Germans had used in September 1939, May 1940, and June 1941: a massive attack on a broad front that simply overwhelmed the enemy's defenses. Given superiority in resources, the great advantage to this approach was that it had worked before.

The problem with what was being proposed by the advocates of the breakthrough approach was that their ideas couldn't possibly work. Patton and Bradley wanted to attack up into the Saar, and Montgomery wanted to attack into the Ruhr. Subsequently all three—and their many defenders and apologists—marshaled impressive evidence to demonstrate that if only this had been done, the war would have been over in a few short months.

The problem is that in each case the operation was mounted, and in each case it failed. It is customary to say that it failed because of a lack of resources caused by Eisenhower's unwillingness to support the most sensible plan. Thus Montgomery wasn't given enough troops to make his breakthrough operations successful, and Patton wasn't given enough gasoline for his. What this overlooks is the fact that the Germans, despite Hitler, were very adept at switching their forces around to counter Allied moves. In effect the more resources the Allies threw into any one operation, the more resources the Germans switched over to counter that attack. Claims that any one offensive, conducted with overwhelming force, would have been successful, are thus fatally flawed. They all ignore the most obvious counter: The Germans would simply have matched the Allied buildup, as they did in the First World War, and as to a certain extent they were able to do on the Eastern Front.

Nor is this purely theoretical. Throughout 1944 the Germans did precisely that—despite Allied command of the air, the Germans were able to filter reinforcements into Normandy and contain the American and British troops for months. Allied planners for Normandy were uncomfortably aware of the need to capture Caen (or, more precisely, the territory adjacent to the city, which could be used for airfields) at the very start of the landings. It was hardly a coincidence that the Germans had the resources in place to defend the city, and that they continued to switch forces there as Montgomery tried a variety of attacks designed to seize it. With variations, this pattern continued.

A common thread that runs through all these operations is a certain obliviousness to the reality of a successful defense. Although this is often put down to intelligence failures, in every case an investigation into the situation reveals that reasonably accurate intelligence existed and was passed on. The Allies certainly knew the whereabouts of the German divisions around Caen, for example. But the information was simply ignored. Out of ineptitude? No, because by 1944 it was basically an article of faith that all breakthrough operations succeeded, regardless of the forces arrayed in defense.

Nor was it solely a function of ground warfare planners. The bomber barons motored on with an even more marked disconnect from the realities of bomb damage assessment. As late as the summer of 1944, they still believed that the two competing and curiously complementary theories of strategic bombing employed by the British and the Americans would of themselves win the war outright—ignoring all the abundant evidence to the contrary.

Thus in less than a quarter century the pendulum had swung from the insistence that in modern warfare the defense was all powerful to its exact opposite. In neither case were there many facts to support the dominant idea, but neither governments nor theorists need evidence. Governments have a disturbing tendency to manufacture it, and theorists an equally albeit less dangerous tendency to suppress it whenever it conflicts with their ideas. In the idea of the breakthrough, both were at work.

What is needed is not more and better facts but more rigorous and coherent accounts that use the facts already at our disposal. That is the account this book attempts to provide. Having said that, let me enumerate a few stipulations as to what this book is *not* about. It is not a comprehensive account of the entire war, because, as A. J. P. Taylor rather puckishly noted, "the problem with the Second World War is not so much how did it begin but when did it begin. The Second World War was not some precise, sudden event like the First. . . . Suppose you said that a declaration of war indicates that the world war has started, then you would have to go back to 1932."[6] Taylor was correct; this was a war that comprised many wars. In some measure it is thus an event closer to what is called in America the French and Indian War—a series of interrelated conflicts fought in a variety of different places.[7]

Instead this is an account of the crucial parts of the ground war in Western Europe, for the reason—which seems to me self-evident—that it was there, in 1939, 1940, and 1944, that the conflict between the Western democracies and Hitler was resolved. On the ground, and not in the air, on the sea, or through economic or political means. The Allies did not beat Hitler because of their strategic air force. Indeed, as this account makes clear, to a certain extent, the prevailing notions of airpower held by the leaders of the Allied air forces impeded rather than caused victory. Nor did the Allies win because of their superior economic power, their political acumen, or their command of the sea. Clearly all these were factors. However, the decisive factor, the most important one, was what happened on the ground. And that is what this narrative is about.[8]

The German Problem

A final point has troubled me greatly these past decades. It was very clear that both the Germans and the Russians had tough and well-equipped armies. The problems afflicting the West before the war had little effect on the military preparedness of these two powers. Both fought tenaciously for years. Although not a great deal was known about the Soviet military (save for the propaganda emanating from the Soviet Union), the Allies had dissected the German military in great detail, and there was near unanimous agreement as to its excellence.

The extent to which German officers, especially senior commanders, knew what Hitler was doing and agreed with it is a difficult issue to resolve in any satisfactory way, and it is quite understandable why military historians would feel it was an issue that could easily be separated out of their accounts of the war. Understandable and defensible but ultimately wrong. It seemed to me that these accounts had fallen into a sort of moral confusion, in which the authors, perhaps without even realizing it, were inclined to gloss over the wickedness of the two dictatorships and emphasize the faults of the democracies.

In *Spandau: The Secret Diaries*, Albert Speer, while insisting that he was not guilty of the crimes attributed to him, nevertheless observed that he felt himself guilty in another, more profound, way. His presence, his abilities, enabled and empowered Hitler: "and yet—I drove with Hitler under those streamers and did not feel the baseness of the slogans being publicly displayed and sanctioned by the government. Once again: I suppose I did not even see the streamers . . . it even seems to me that my own 'purity,' my indolence, makes me guiltier."[9] Whether for that sin or for others, Speer did penance. There is no senior German commander any less guilty than Speer, and most are considerably more so. In any event, all of them were Hitler's enthusiastic supporters.[10]

The Breakthrough Breakthrough

During the First World War an officer in the Royal Tank Corps, Maj. J. F. C. Fuller, had already developed a blueprint for successful offensive operations, which he initially called Plan 1919. Fuller, surveying the experiences of the British Expeditionary Force (BEF), reasoned that true breakthroughs were impossible with foot soldiers. The pace of their advance was far too slow. While the infantry laboriously crossed the cratered terrain of the battlefield, the enemy could establish a new defensive position, transporting its reserves into place using railroads or trucks, and thus capitalizing on the slow speed of an infantry advance. Moreover, Fuller argued that in an infantry attack there was an inherent tendency for the attackers to move inward rather than outward. So the area behind the enemy's initial positions, instead of becoming larger, would inexorably shrink.

To Fuller, who had planned the tank offensive at Cambrai in November 1917, this was a basic law, just like the law of gravity, and he saw the tank as the solution to the failure of the Allies either to engage in a successful battle of rupture or in one of annihilation. His idea, schematically rendered in a diagram that has been reproduced in virtually every book written about armored warfare, had an elegant simplicity: A great army of tanks would break through the enemy lines. Unlike the infantry the tanks would be able to overpower static defensive positions, crush barbed wire, and blow up the automatic weapons positions that had been the nemesis of Allied infantry. And, unlike the foot soldier, the tank's speed would enable it to thrust deep into enemy lines, achieving penetrations so deep that the rupture could never be sealed.

Indeed, this deep and rapid penetration made the plan so distinctive that it was no longer simply a means of achieving a rupture. The new aim, Fuller hypothesized, was to strike deep through the enemy position, piercing its defenses and attacking its soft and unprotected rear positions. Here is his summary:

> In 1918 I substituted another plan, which was accepted by Marshal Foch for the 1919 campaign. Instead of launching frontal attacks against the enemy's front, it was decided to launch it against his rear—his command and supply system—by suddenly and without warning passing powerful tank forces, covered by aircraft, through his front. Next, directly paralyzation of his rear had disorganized his front [sic], to launch a strong tank and infantry attack of the Cambrai pattern against that front. Thus, what twenty years later became known as the "Blitz" attack was born; and had the war continued into 1919, seeing that the Germans had no properly ordered antitank defense, these tactics would have produced even more startling results than they did in 1939–1940.[11]

This statement is probably the single most important paragraph in the military history of the twentieth century. To say that Fuller's idea took hold is an understatement. By the summer of 1940, after Poland and the fall of France, it had the status of sacred doctrine.

This was an entirely new idea, completely different from the idea of the battle of rupture, as Fuller's first two sentences make clear. It was the difference between a boxing match and a fencing bout. The rupture battle was like a boxing match: In a series of mighty blows, you drove your opponent up against the ropes, and ultimately, one punch would flatten him. To continue the analogy, that final punch was the battle of annihilation. Fuller's plan was the strategy of the fencer. Instead of trying to smash in the enemy's defensive positions, you aimed for the one deep thrust that would disable him completely. Not a slash, but a thrust whose deadly power was a function of the depth of penetration.

Fuller's idea, then, was not simply about how to win the battle using a different mix of forces, but rather an idea which substituted an entirely new objective, the breakthrough. Fuller realized it was a new idea; his disciples and students during the interwar years realized it was a new idea; and when the war broke out, it became the received wisdom. The Germans were successful because they had studied Fuller's ideas and applied them. The Allies were unsuccessful because they had ignored Fuller's ideas and stuck to their old ways, planning to fight classical battles of annihilation, or aiming for a victory that could be achieved using the Delbrückian idea about a strategy of exhaustion.

It was a British idea, but only the Germans had learned how to apply it successfully. If the Allies were to win, they would have to employ the same technique, and this became particularly true when the United States entered the war and Allied planners began to consider a series of successive invasions of Europe, in which they would be on the offensive and the Germans on the defensive. The key to success would be to land and then push armored columns in deep, as Montgomery charged his field commanders during his pep talks for the Normandy offensive.

Pushing armored and mechanized columns in hard and deep was what Patton was all about; it was how the war in the desert had been fought. In short, it was the only proper way to conduct ground operations, and when the events of May 1940 were discussed, the French were roundly condemned for squandering their armor, for using it in "penny packets," to employ a British phrase that has become common in such discussions.

Fuller's ideas spread rapidly. Although initially ignored in his own country, his works were required reading in the Czech and Soviet armies, while both German and French tank experts took it to heart: Denis Daly, the British military attaché, has testified to hearing Heinz Guderian discourse on Fuller at length well before the war.[12] Fuller was indeed an almost unique figure: an officer with experience in the field; a formidable theorist and historian, and a voluminous writer. To several generations of forward-thinking officers, this was an irresistible combination. His ideas had been tested on the field of battle and found to work, a claim that was helped immensely by the interpretations of military history in Fuller's many postwar writings. Between the wars (and to a certain extent even after 1945) Fuller was probably the most read military analyst in any language, and certainly the most prolific. Certainly no one who read Fuller could miss his main point: Future wars would be decided by fleets of tanks mounting powerful armored thrusts deep into enemy-held territory.

Instead of a battle of rupture or annihilation, there would be a new type of battle, the breakthrough, in which hordes of tanks would strike deep into the soft rear of the enemy and paralyze its command and control facilities, bringing a quick end to its ability to wage war. Any other notion was simply the result of a resolute clinging to tradition, of a refusal to understand that war was a science.

So far as ground warfare went, Fuller's ideas reigned supreme. All the French and German theorists studied his writings carefully. Their ideas did not take root immediately, and in Great Britain they took root hardly at all. But Fuller's Plan 1919 became the controlling paradigm for effective ground warfare. Once the Second World War began, generals would be judged not on their actual combat record but on the extent to which their operations conformed to Fuller's theories, as the opening campaigns of the war seemed to provide irrefutable evidence that he was right.

Breakthrough in the Air

Anyone who dips into Fuller is treated to his scornful condescension of the British military establishment. According to Fuller the reason his ideas were not accepted was, purely and simply, the hidebound traditionalism of most armies (and especially the British) in the face of the new scientific approach to warfare he championed, in which technology, not tradition, reigned supreme.

But this is too simple. Although Fuller was the chief theorist of ground warfare after 1920, the First World War had made it clear that the war would also be fought in the air, and Fuller was not the only officer in the Great War to come up with radical ideas about how to fight the next one. In Italy his colleague, the airman Giulio Douhet, had also come up with revolutionary ideas. Douhet was a veteran of the Great War as well, and as an Italian, he had been forcibly impressed by his country's vain and costly struggles to break through Austria-Hungary's alpine defenses.

Like Fuller, Douhet was focused on the next war: "Victory smiles upon those who anticipate the changes in the character of war, not upon those who wait to adapt themselves after the changes occur. . . . Those who are ready first will not only win quickly, but will win with the fewest sacrifices and the minimum expenditure of means."[13] But where Fuller's solution was the tank, Douhet's was the strategic bomber. In fact the bomber would make armies and navies irrelevant. The way to wage war was to send over a massive fleet of bombers without even a formal declaration. These bombers would destroy the enemy's civilian population, its industrial centers, and its will to fight. They would be unstoppable, because "viewed in its true light, aerial warfare admits of no defense, only offense. We must therefore resign ourselves to the offensives the enemy inflicts upon us, while striving to put all our resources to work to inflict even heavier ones on him. This is the basic principle which must govern the development of aerial warfare."

At first glance the only thing the two men seem to have in common is a belief in the power of new technology, but further consideration suggests striking similarities. Fuller thought tanks would ensure mastery of the battlefield, Douhet felt the same about bombers. More important, both men had a shared concept of how a future war should be fought: not by an attack against the enemy's defenses and armies but by a direct blow that would strike far behind those defenses. Fuller aimed to attack the enemy far behind its lines. Douhet aimed to attack directly in his home country.

And both men posited that this successful attack would be conducted by fleets of tanks or planes, vast armadas destroying the enemy in one swift stroke. While the aim, then, remained the same as in the battle of annihilation, the means was radically different: Just as Fuller's tank force would suddenly appear in the enemy's rear, Douhet's bomber fleet would suddenly appear in the skies over its cities and factories. The one preached a breakthrough on the ground, the other in the air. Conceptually, despite their obvious differences, both men had moved to similar conclusions.

In terms of budget allocations and rival bureaucracies, however, there was an enormous difference, and nowhere more so than in Great Britain, where the air force had already been split off as an independent arm of the services and was therefore competing for resources against the army and the navy. The leaders of the RAF quickly saw the advantages of Douhet's ideas, which to a great extent paralleled their own thinking. As a recent U.S. Air Force study has it: "Douhet rejected the idea of an auxiliary air arm of the army or navy or a collection of 'knights-errant' flying fighters. Rather, he called for a fleet of massive, self-defending bombers that would dominate not only the enemy, but also the military budget."[14] While the British army stoutly resisted the idea of tanks and mechanization, the RAF saw the happy implications of the idea of command of the air for an island nation with an empire.

In their struggles they were immeasurably aided by other factors as well. Unlike tanks, airplanes had been employed throughout the war, and had proved themselves as early as 1914, when the Germans deployed them for the direction and control of indirect artillery fire. It was this that led to the first struggles for air superiority: the side that could prevent the enemy's observation and fire control had a big advantage. The war also saw the systematic use of the airplane for what would today be called tactical airpower—that is, the use of airplanes to support ground assaults.

By 1918 all the conceivable military uses of airplanes had been tried and carried out with a good degree of success (airborne drops were the only military use the war had not seen). Unlike the tank, which in 1918 was still simply a weapon of great potential, the airplane had been integrated into the military structures of all the combatants. Simple numbers tell the story: At the war's end, there were about 2,400 tanks in the British inventory, and over twenty-two thousand airplanes, so in that sense the British had been moving towards an acceptance of the importance of airpower and command of the air years before Douhet's ideas were published.[15]

The RAF was also aided by the fact that postwar, British defense planners had decided that new technologies would enable them to cut costs without risking the country's security. Planes were considerably cheaper than ships, and the RAF thus was able to make proposals designed to replace Great Britain's traditional dependence on its navy and save money at the same time. In the competition for funds—which in the immediate postwar era had been dramatically cut—the plans of the air force leaders thus fitted more neatly into the country's overall defense needs, and appeared to offer both a strategic deterrent and significant financial savings.

But the tank had no civilian counterpart. Once the pneumatic tire went into mass production, the agricultural market began to diverge: Farmers found wheeled vehicles much more practical than tracked ones. Moreover, for agricultural and industrial needs, there was no need for a tracked vehicle to be capable of any speed. However, for a tank to be successful on the battlefield, it not only had to have a speed faster than a brisk walk but it had to be able to accelerate quickly. For a tank crew to be able to survive on the battlefield, the tank had to be armored. Steel was heavy. So the tank's engine had to be powerful enough to accelerate a very large and heavy mass, and its suspension system had to be able to support this (hopefully) fast-moving mass over rough terrain.

So tank development lagged—and not necessarily for the reasons Fuller was always claiming. In Great Britain the choice was not between horses and tanks, it was between tanks and airplanes. And since Great Britain was both an island and also an empire spread all over the world, the choice was an easy one to make. All the more so since Douhet's British peers and disciples were arguing that if you had enough planes, you didn't need an army and you hardly needed a navy. Fuller never addressed the major debate: tanks or planes? In fact, one reads through his work in vain trying to find any inkling that he was aware this debate even took place.

First the Theory, Now the Reality

Both Douhet and Fuller were proponents of war as a science. Fuller's major early work was titled *The Foundations of the Science of War:* "I have stressed the scientific aspect of my subject, not because I am a trained scientist, for I am only an amateur, but because soldiers must realize what civil science means."[16]

Although Fuller was unique in Great Britain, his emphasis on quantification, on the "science of war," was a routine concept in France and in Continental countries, whose armies entered the war beset by competing theories, all of which claimed to be "scientific." In fact the whole concept of winning through attrition, and thus the importance of body counts, was simply a part of the general attempt to quantify terms in accordance with the science of war.

Where Fuller differed from his French colleagues was that his experiences during the war caused him to shift his emphasis from quantification and rules to technology. After alleging that Lord Raglan's British army of 1855 in the Crimea could easily have beaten Napoleon's army of 1815, as "Lord Raglan's men were armed with the Minie rifle," and that von Moltke's troops could easily have beaten the British army of 1855 because von Moltke's "men were armed with the needle gun," Fuller went on: "From this we may deduce the fact . . . that weapons form 99 per cent of victory."[17]

Time and time again Fuller reduced all questions to simple ones of technological superiority. He then reduced them still further. The new weapon of the future was the tank. "Fleets of tanks" would carry all before them on the new battlefield, and "the logical conclusion to be drawn from this is that . . . trenches are at best but static makeshifts, the infantryman must don armor, and, as he has not the strength to carry it, he must get into a tank."[18]

However faulty, Fuller's ideas had two strengths. On the one hand his ideas had been developed during combat and appeared to have been validated by it (not surprisingly, since Fuller played a key role in shaping accounts of the war in such a way as to prove his point). On the other he had linked his ideas to technology, and by 1920 the impact of new technologies was seen as a given. The automobile and the airplane were revolutionizing society; the idea that they would revolutionize warfare was implicitly accepted by everyone except a few diehards. Fuller's idea that machines could be substituted for men fell on fertile ground.

And therein lay the problem. The robust, heavily armed, high-speed tracked vehicles required for Fuller's plans would not begin to appear on the scene until the very late 1930s. Plan 1919 should in fact have been titled "Plan 1939," because, despite Fuller's nursing of the data, the fragile and bulky behemoths of the Royal Tank Corps in 1918 were incapable of the intensive operations the plan demanded. The tanks of 1918 had poor cross-country capabilities, they could hardly move faster than a brisk walk, and their armor could be riddled by portable infantry weapons.[19]

The type of bomber Douhet envisioned was hardly any closer at hand. It was not until 1937 that bombers capable of carrying four tons of bombs for a distance of much over fifteen hundred kilometers began to appear, and when they did, they were too slow and underarmed to be capable of successful strategic operations. Ironically, when the Second World War actually began, none of the combatants had bombers in service capable of carrying out the program of destruction Douhet envisaged.

But then neither man was much bothered by facts. Just as Fuller envisioned vast fleets of unstoppable tanks dominating some future battlefield (which would conveniently be empty of antitank defenses), so Douhet's fleets of heavy bombers would rampage freely over the enemy's cities and factories, images that are closer in reality to the Martians in H. G. Wells's 1898 science fiction thriller *War of the Worlds* than to the grim realities of combat. In other words, there is no doubt that Fuller's tanks could have won the war *if* they had been mechanically reliable, *if* they had been impervious to enemy shells, *if* the terrain had been ideal for them, and *if* they had been used properly—this last clearly being a sort of general purpose escape clause familiar to anyone who's ever used a mechanical device and complained about its imperfections. This may sound like the oversimplification of a hostile judge, but one searches Fuller and Douhet in vain for indications to the contrary. Douhet's writings couldn't be clearer about these matters.

In 1921, when Douhet published *Il dominio dell' aria,* there was some support for the belief that the bomber would always get through. German bombers had bombed both London and Paris with near impunity, losing planes to mechanical troubles but not to air defense. There was neither radar nor acoustic ranging available to ground-based forces, so the idea that bombers would always get through, would saturate the defender's abilities to anticipate where he would be struck, was not wholly unrealistic.

Not wholly unrealistic but fatally flawed. Neither Fuller nor Douhet gave any thought to the fact that technological innovation is nonrestrictive. Automobiles and airplanes developed simultaneously, as did wheels and tracks, gasoline engines and diesel engines, heavier-than-air and lighter-than-aircraft. Fuller was constantly reminding his readers of the incredible development in weaponry from the Brown Bess musket to the magazine rifle. But then, when he started talking about tanks, he arbitrarily stopped projecting future developments except in armor. He argued that in fifty years we should have airborne and submersible tanks, but he refused to acknowledge that the foot soldier of the future might have even more potent weapons, which would neutralize the power of the tank.

Antitank and antiaircraft weapons had existed during the Great War. Both were primitive and inaccurate, but the same could be said for the tank and the airplane. The Mauser antitank rifle (the *T-Gewehr*) fired an armor-piercing bullet that could go right through the thin armor of any tank of the era. Similarly, albeit in somewhat less sophisticated fashion, the basics for antiaircraft weaponry were already in use. The French had already made primitive antiaircraft guns by the simple expedient of mounting a 75-millimeter field gun on the back of a truck.

Both Fuller and Douhet envisaged their technology of choice as being deployed in a way that is strikingly reminiscent of traditional ideas about heavy cavalry, and indeed it is possible to a surprising extent to substitute the word *cavalry* for the word *bomber* or *tank* in the writings of both men without doing any violence to the sense of their argument.

Alike in their contempt for each other's ideas and for military "traditions," alike in their insistence that they had discovered the basic principles of the "science of war," the armored apostles and the airpower enthusiasts were alike in two other much more significant ways—ways that would do great damage to their nations. On the one hand, both groups endorsed the idea that the war could be won by a vast fleet of planes or tanks that would break through the enemy's positions, either two-dimensionally, on land (for tanks) or three-dimensionally, out of the air (for planes). In either case the war would be won quickly by the resulting breakthrough.

On the other hand both groups, despite their insistence on being "scientific," were almost totally impervious to the sort of experimentation and testing that denotes true science. They persisted through the war, stoutly refusing to take any notice of the actual experiences of combat unless forced to by higher authorities.

Meanwhile, in Washington, the American army's Tank Command refused to equip American tanks with a high-velocity gun, as, according to their theory, tanks were breakthrough vehicles and were not intended to fight other tanks on the battlefield, a task left up to the so-called tank destroyers.[20]

What ties these examples together is not stubbornness or incompetence. Rather, it is the belief in a theory of warfare, a theory that encompasses both ground warfare and aerial combat, and is nothing more or less than the reincarnation of the cavalry charge, which will break through the enemy's defenses and destroy its will to continue the war as surely as it will destroy its abilities.

NOTES

1. As quoted by (Col.) Bernard Serrigny, *Trente ans avec Pétain* (Paris: Plon, 1959), 56. Unless otherwise noted, the translations from French and German are my own.

2. Erich von Manstein, *Lost Victories*, trans. Anthony G. Powell (Chicago: Henry Regnery, 1958), 46.

3. A considerable body of (mainly English) opinion has attempted to depoliticize the leading German generals and disassociate them from National Socialism. A close reading of their own comments makes clear this is far too charitable an interpretation. The quotation cited above is an excellent example. Only a National Socialist or a Communist would call the legal government of Poland, a state whose existence had been ratified by the Allies at Versailles, the "Warsaw government."

4. "Hitler was to have a similar experience only a few years later—without ever learning anything from it," von Manstein opined in his discussion of the Polish war (*Lost Victories,* 40).

5. See the discussion of Montgomery's ideas about this in Nigel Hamilton, *Montgomery* (New York: McGraw-Hill, 1981), 2.811–16.

6. A. J. P. Taylor, "The Second World War," in *British Prime Ministers and Other Essays*, ed. Chris Wrigley (London: Allen Lane, 1998), 205.

7. That they were all part of one war was a conceit of Macaulay's.

8. To make this claim may seem superfluous, but in my account of the First World War I was faulted by several critics—much to my amusement—because I neglected to talk about the war at sea, the effects of the Allied blockade, or any of the political and economic factors that led to Germany's defeat, even though I thought I had made it clear in the preface that I didn't feel these were factors of any great importance. Perhaps that portion of the preface should have been printed in larger type, so I have tried to state the matter as clearly as possible here. This war, like the previous one, was decided on the ground. In Western Europe.

9. Passage taken from *Spandau: The Secret* Diaries, trans. Richard and Clara Winston (New York: Macmillan, 1976), 24. This passage apparently looks back (or rather, forward) to scenes described in *Inside the Third Reich,* trans. Richard and Clara Winston (New York: Macmillan, 1970). I am well aware of the subsequent controversies relating to the more literal question of Speer's guilt, although they strike me as excellent examples of the sort of contemporary "deconstruction" that is both contentious and problematic. Furthermore, they are irrelevant to the point being made regarding the moral culpability of senior officers in the German military.

10. The idea that men like von Manstein, Rommel, and Guderian were simply conscientious Germans whose obedience to Hitler was the result of some prototypical Ger-

manness is hardly borne out by the facts. To the contrary, these men violated a long-standing tradition in the Prussian military, as Johann Friedrich von der Marwitz's epitaph eloquently summed it up: "Fought with Frederick in all his wars; chose disgrace when obedience was incompatible with honor." It is certainly understandable why, postwar, each one would choose to minimize the more disgraceful aspects of his career—particularly since the Allies were trying and frequently executing their colleagues. The attitudes of some British historians and admirers are less so. When Eisenhower refused to shake hands with captured German generals, he was not solely motivated by what journalists or the American public would say. See note 3 above, relating to von Manstein—an excellent example of why it is well to be deeply suspicious in these matters.

11. J. F. C. Fuller, *Armament in History* (London: Charles Scribner's Sons, 1946), 139.

12. See the testimony in S. L. A. Marshall's foreword to the annotated reprinting of Fuller's *Armored Warfare* (Harrisburg, Pa.: Military Science Publishing Company, 1943), xiii.

13. Giulio Douhet, *The Command of the Air,* trans. Dino Ferrari (Washington, D.C. Office of the Air Force History, 1983), 30. This, the standard translation for American (and particularly for U.S. Air Force) readers, actually contains five separate works, the sum total of his theoretical writings. Although collectively usually referred to as *The Command of the Air*, and presented in the book as though it is one sustained text, the actual essays were published between 1921 and 1929. See "Editor's Introduction," x.

14. Lt. Col. Richard Estes, "Giulio Douhet: More on Target Than He Knew," manuscript, [USAF] Air University.

15. While it is generally held in the U.S. Air Force that Douhet's theories were the stimulus for this thinking, the British stoutly maintain that the ideas were developed independently. See, for example, the comments in Robin Higham, who is by no means uncritical of the RAF, in *Air Power, A Concise History* (New York: St. Martin's Press, 1972), 70. Complicating the issue is the fact that many of the theorists freely made use of the works of others without indicating the extent of the borrowing. See, for example, Alexander de Seversky, *Victory Through Airpower* (New York: Simon & Schuster, 1942): "We have no airpower. We have only army and naval aviation developed and used primarily as auxiliary weapons" (151). The idea of discounting "auxiliary" aviation is right out of Douhet.

16. J. F. C. Fuller, *The Foundations of the Science of War* (London: Hutchinson, 1925), 16. As he explains in the preface, the work began in 1911 and was completed in 1915 and then reworked after the First World War.

17. In the conclusion of J. F. C. Fuller, *Tanks in the Great War* (London: John Murray, 1920), 311.

18. Ibid., 318. Fuller's apologists are forced to deconstruct such utterances so as to suggest that he was talking about armored personnel carriers or similar vehicles, but the

context of the remark makes clear that his point was a rhetorical one: He foresaw no need for infantry on the future battlefield, just as Douhet foresaw no need for an army at all.

19. One reason why almost all of the 2,636 heavy tanks the BEF had in France by the end of the war were abandoned and left there. See Fritz Heigl, *Taschenbuch der Tanks* (München: J. F. Lehmanns, 1926), 78.

20. See the excellent discussion of these theories in Trevor N. Dupuy, David L. Bongard, and Richard C. Anderson, Jr., *Hitler's Last Gamble* (New York: HarperCollins, 1994), Appendix B, especially 385, 397.

2.

The Maginot Line and Hitler's Response

*Concerning defensive organization, the sense of our nation's historical continu-
ity leads to this conclusion: the fortification of her territory is, for France, a per-
manent national necessity.*
—CAPT. CHARLES DE GAULLE, 1925[1]

The "Maginot Line mentality" has come to epitomize a timid
and burrowing approach to national defense.[2] Moreover, by
putting all its resources into fortifications, France was unable
to develop the weapons it really needed, like tanks and
bombers:"There can be little doubt," Fuller noted in 1943,"that the cost
of the Maginot Line was one of the main reasons for neglect of the
mechanization of the French Army."[3] Finally, the whole project came to
nothing, as in May 1940 the Germans simply encircled it—an eventuality the French surely should have foreseen. Not that it made much difference: In the age of the tank and the dive bomber, fortifications were
of little value.

The confusion about combat in the Second World War begins with a
misunderstanding of what the Maginot Line was, why it was built, and
what actually happened to it once the fighting started. Just as von

Clausewitz had observed that the faulty disposition of one's forces is an error from which it is almost impossible to recover, faulty understanding of the important role fortifications played in the interwar years results in a similar catastrophe for the historian.

In the first instance Fuller's comment is false no matter how construed. In May 1940 France deployed more tanks than did Germany.[4] It deployed more modern tanks, and more medium and heavy tanks. Although the French organization is difficult to understand, by any fair accounting the French deployed as many armored divisions as their adversaries, and their armor was as good or better than German armor.

If the idea of extensive frontier fortifications was so indicative of a defeated, backward, and defensive mentality—if it was such a clear mistake—why did the military planners of Belgium, Czechoslovakia, Germany, and the Soviet Union all follow suit?

The German case is particularly relevant, since it is commonly believed that it was in the German army that these new doctrines of mechanized warfare, which were by and large Fuller's doctrines, first bore fruit. Actually the extensive and elaborate nature of German fortifications in the 1930s is proof in and of itself that the idea of a Maginot Line mentality is incorrect.[5] The Soviet example is hardly less relevant, since Soviet doctrine was, if anything, more oriented to the offensive than the German. Rightly or wrongly, the possession of large numbers of tanks is generally used as the indicator of the extent to which the army in question was committed to at least some of Fuller's ideas. But the Soviet Union's armored vehicles were among the most advanced in the world: The famous T-34 medium tank, arguably the best tank of the war, did not emerge from a vacuum.

The truth of the matter is that Germany had its own Maginot Line, and its leading advocate was, interestingly enough, no less than Erich von Manstein. Clearly there is more to the idea than is commonly supposed, and the matter is worth investigating. Therefore, any account of what actually happened both in the decades preceding the war and during the war itself must compare the myth of the success of the breakthrough offensive—on the ground, in the air, or both—against the reality of prepared defensive positions. An understanding of how widespread the building of fortifications was before the war suggests that we must look elsewhere than the Maginot Line (whether as a physical or mental construct) if we are to understand France's defeat.

Had the Allies understood what actually happened when the Ger-

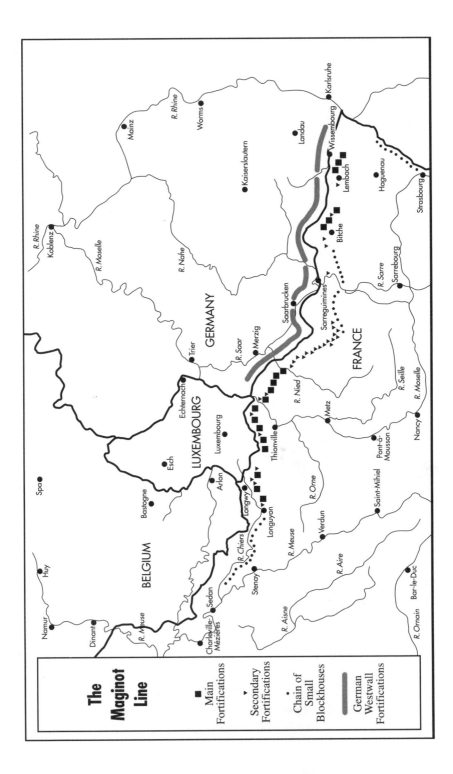

The Maginot Line

■ Main Fortifications
▼ Secondary Fortifications
••• Chain of Small Blockhouses
▬ German Westwall Fortifications

mans attacked various portions of the Maginot Line by air and land, they would have been much less sanguine about the prospects of the fall offensive through Lorraine in 1944. A good many fewer American infantry would have been killed in action. In 1944 American commanders, like everyone else, believed that fortifications were a throwback to previous wars, and that the Maginot Line was a white elephant. The result, in the autumn of 1944, was a brutal slogging match in Lorraine as Patton's exhausted infantry struggled to take Metz against a small and heterogenous group of German defenders who were, ironically, ensconced in pre-1914 fortifications. American infantry paid with their lives for the Allied failure to understand how formidable the Germans found the Maginot Line fortifications in May and June 1940.

Fortifications and Offensive Power

In planning how best to defend their country from what they assumed would be a third German invasion in the near future (1870 and 1914 being the first two), French defense planners had to grapple with questions of a basic nature about fortifications and the power of the offensive. In so doing they framed a debate that would occur in Germany as well. Because postwar, the Germans had the same problem on their eastern frontier that the French did on theirs. The big surprise the Allies faced in the opening weeks of the First World War was simply that the Germans deployed much bigger guns than anticipated, and all their weapons were much more mobile than had been thought; thus they went into action much earlier and did more extensive damage.

There were two serious problems with the prewar fortifications: their isolation and their lack of defense against gases. As the Germans had demonstrated at Liège, a combination of heavy guns and infantry armed with the right weapons could reduce any fort—if it had only its own defenses to rely on. To be a successful strongpoint, each fort had to be able to depend on suppressing fire from its immediate neighbors, so that the attacking forces would be unable to attack each successive fort in isolation.

This had been the German technique, one made all the more successful by the fact that the garrisons of the forts consisted entirely of gunners and observers. There were no infantrymen inside to emerge and beat off attacks—or indeed to conduct a defense inside the fort. As a result the garrisons, feeling themselves helpless and isolated, would eventually surrender rather than be killed. Under the impact of heavy shelling, the atmosphere in the interior of the fort began to fill up with dust, fumes, and potentially lethal gases. As these were heavier than air, they would slowly settle into the corridors and passages of the fort, which in every case were lower than the surrounding terrain. Even before the use of poison gas shells, this was a serious problem that contributed to the panic of the garrison. These serious defects were responsible for the generally quick collapse of those French and Belgian forts that were actually defended.

In 1923 the French colonel Tricaud had drawn up a plan for a new kind of fortification that would remedy them, and his sketches became the basis for what was actually built. Tricaud, however, wanted to disregard the concept of a central fort, whether sunk into the ground or no. Instead of a pentagon, hexagon, or other precise geometrical shape, his idea was like an outstretched hand—a clawed hand, which might perhaps be envisioned as like the foot of a hawk, with each claw a complex of turrets. The individual fingers, or extensions, would be linked back to a central underground block by means of tunnels. This was an extraordinarily elegant engineering solution to the problem of fortifications, which at one stroke eliminated almost all the weaknesses of earlier forts. Since the only link with each block of turrets was a tunnel, the fort could cover an enormous expanse of territory, with the forward blocks being thousands of meters from the entrance, clearly the most vulnerable part of any fort.

The complex of blocks (as each defensive grouping of turrets came to be called) could be laid out to take maximum advantage of the terrain, since no one block had to be very big. By the same token, each block could provide protective fire for its neighbors, so that the garrison in one block would be isolated. Thus the idea of infiltrating specially trained infantry like the German Pioniere to attack the fort at close range wouldn't work: The covering fire from the adjacent blocks would annihilate them. In Tricaud's scheme there was basically nothing to aim at: No gunner in the world was going to be able to hit a target three meters in diameter from a distance of six or seven thousand meters, and no aviator in the world was going to be able to hit it either.

The forts Tricaud sketched, which ultimately emerged as what is popularly known as the Maginot Line, generally withstood the actual test of combat. The defensive blocks proved to be impervious to bombs and shells. In fact, it is one of the many embarrassments of June 1940 that when the French government decided to quit the war, the high command had to send special emissaries to the commanders of the principal *ouvrages* informing them they had to surrender—much to their chagrin.

The Planning of the Forts

The Commission de la Défense du Territoire studied the problem of how best to defend France for nearly five years, and finally, on December 7, 1926, delivered its report to Paul Painlevé, minister of war, who then formed a new committee, the Commission de Défense des Frontières (CDF).[6] The CDF divided the frontier into three distinct zones, two of which, the areas forming the Franco-German and Franco-Italian frontiers, would have to be protected by fortifications. The third, the northern frontier with Belgium, would have to be treated differently. Marshal Pétain had spoken of this sector as the *ligne de passage*—that is to say, the line over which any enemy would have to advance to attack France.

Given the dense population along the frontier, and the fact that Belgium had been France's ally in the last war, there was no real possibility of fortifying this section of the front. Presumably this was what Foch had meant in his initial enthusiasms about the idea of fortifications: They would presumably force an enemy to attack through Belgium. Or, better still, they would allow the French to meet the enemy inside Belgium. It will be remembered that this had been one of Joffre's first proposals when he had assumed command of the French army well before the war: The best way to meet a German attack was to move the army into Belgium and fight them there.

This idea had been turned down for purely diplomatic reasons; in hindsight, which is sometimes useful to military planners, this was clearly a mistake. By buying into the Vauban option, France's more offensive minded generals hoped to be pushing for what might be called the Belgian option as their country's best means of an active defense. To continue the sword and shield metaphor, the frontier with Germany would be the shield, while the frontier with Belgium would allow the French to thrust with the sword.

There was one respect in which French estimates of the situation in Germany differed drastically from those abroad (and those recapitulated by later analysts). When General Fayolle had first visited Germany in December of 1918, he had written in his secret diary that "this is not a defeated country . . . there will be another war in ten years, if not sooner."[7] The French, more than anyone else in the world, were convinced that they would have to face a resurgent Germany, not in the distant future but on a scale closer to Fayolle's decade—a war fought with the weapons that would be operational in the first part of the 1930s. And thus the attractiveness of the fortification option. What the government was proposing could be constructed in a few years. This was not a long-term engineering project dependent on theory, but a short-term project making use of known materials and techniques. So, although the Chamber of Deputies pared the appropriation down to 2,900 million francs, the appropriation was approved by the lopsided vote of 270 to 22.

The Objects Themselves

A brief description of what is generally regarded as a typical fort, the Ouvrage de Fermont, makes clear what was built and how it served. Fermont is about twelve kilometers southwest of Longwy, a small town located almost squarely on the Franco-Belgian frontier.

To the north and west the ground falls off rapidly into the valley. But to the west the terrain is relatively flat for about fifteen kilometers or so, a perfect passageway into France. So the heavy firepower of Fermont, three 75-millimeter guns mounted in a casemate, was directed to the east, onto the plain.[8] These artillery casemates, invariably built into the reverse slope, and thus protected by the ground itself, completely enclosed the guns they held, and the openings were deeply recessed, so that the only effective means of destroying them was to score a direct hit on the opening with a very powerful shell.

In addition to the casemate there were six separate blocks, or clusters of turrets, armored cupolas, and casemates. Three of the blocks contained artillery: One block, the highest, comprised a disappearing turret with two 75-millimeter guns, a cupola with twin machine guns, and another with a grenade launcher. A second block had a twin 81-millimeter mortar turret and a machine-gun cupola, while a third had three small casemates containing a 47-millimeter antitank gun, a machine-gun position, and a grenade launcher. The other three blocks, devoted to automatic weapons and grenade launchers, ensured that the fixed artillery positions could not be stormed by infantry, even infantry supported by armor. The seven positions were spread out over the hill, occupying what was roughly a parallelogram about 400 meters long by 250 meters deep.

The field of fire of Fermont was enormous. The turret-mounted 75s could cover a circle more than twenty kilometers in diameter, firing into Longwy, across into Belgium, and over past Longuyon to the west. The two 81-millimeter mortars covered a circle five kilometers in diameter, which included a considerable stretch of the Chiers Valley and the roads running on both sides of the river. Like the 75s the mortars had a very high rate of fire, about twenty rounds per minute, and the weapons were permanently fixed at 45 degrees: The range was set by adjusting the charge in the round.

The machine gun cupolas consisted of two 7.5-millimeter Reibel guns using fixed magazines. The guns were fired alternately, giving a sustained rate of fire of six hundred rounds per minute out to 2,500 meters. Infantry attacks against such positions would be suicidal.[9]

There were of course tanks, but here too the French had a powerful weapon whose deployment would silence even the most ardent enthusiast. The 47-millimeter antitank gun used in the forts (and by the infantry) fired an armor-piercing round that could go through 50 millimeters of armor at 1,000 meters. In 1940 this was (still) the most powerful antitank gun in the world, easily capable of knocking out the heaviest German tank, the Mark 4, in any of its 1938–40 versions, since the bow armor was only 30 millimeters thick.

Nor was Fermont an isolated position. Facing it across the stretch of rolling plain was its twin, the Ouvrage de Latiremont, whose three casemate-mounted 75s could reach Fermont (and vice versa)—one of the planned strengths of the forts being their ability to provide covering fire for their neighbors. Stretching across the plain between them were five smaller *ouvrages*, all of which were quite heavily armed and fortified.[10]

No one at any stage of the planning of the fortifications had intended them either to be invulnerable or France's sole defense. At every step someone had clearly enunciated the idea that these forts were to serve as *couverture* for the frontier, allowing the country time to mobilize its armed forces.

Hitler's Response

Like France in 1919 Germany had a serious defensive problem and lacked the manpower to solve it in the traditional Prussian way—by raising and maintaining a large army. Germany had of course been forbidden by the Treaty of Versailles to maintain an army of more than one hundred thousand men, together with any serious offensive weapons, particularly tanks and airplanes. However, the French were complaining early in the decade that the Germans were violating these restrictions—and they were.

But the planners of the Reichswehr were faced from the first with the presence of a large and powerful state on their eastern frontier: Poland. The newly reconstituted nation, roughly the size of the state of California, was not a small country or a weak one. With a population of roughly thirty-four million, it was nearly as populous as France. Just as the German offensive against Poland in September 1939 is correctly seen as the start of the Second World War, so the state of Poland in the 1920s was responsible for Germany's immediate defensive needs. Work on the critical eastern frontier had begun in the 1920s, since the Versailles treaty did not explicitly forbid military construction there. Nonetheless the Allied Control Commission put a stop to any defensive work, and as a result not much was done until Hitler became chancellor in 1933.[11]

From a military point of view the problem with Germany's new eastern frontier was that the boundary line did not correspond to any natural feature. The some five-hundred-kilometer backward concave line that went from just west of Gdansk on the Baltic to just northeast of Kraców basically traced its way through flat and often marshy terrain offered no real natural obstacles to aid any defenders. Consequently the planners of the Reichswehr decided to use as their anchor point the Oder River, which ran roughly parallel to the new frontier, albeit about one hundred kilometers inside German territory.

The Oder is not as deep or as wide as the portion of the Rhine that formed the frontier between Germany and France, but it is no mean obstacle either, and most of the French considerations about how to defend the Rhine apply to the German positions along the Oder. Not surprisingly the solution the German engineers devised closely paralleled the French solution—a series of blockhouses, or bunkers, distributed along the high ground overlooking the river. These could be used as infantry shelters and strongpoints for machine gunners. Surviving examples are squat concrete bunkers topped by a distinctive steel cupola with four separate firing apertures: From most angles it takes a close scrutiny to differentiate the standard German bunker from its French counterpart, although, as we shall see below, there *is* one key difference.[12]

Administratively the fortifications were divided into three distinct areas, somewhat confusingly named. The central position, known as the *Oder-Wartha-Bogen* (OWB), was a fairly short (roughly eighty-kilometer) section located on the high ground running from Frankfurt-an-der-Oder up to Küstrin. It was through here that a direct thrust could reach directly to Berlin, a short drive away, and by 1938 the Germans, in order to protect Berlin from an attack from the east, had essentially built a replication of the core positions laid out by the French.

Like the French the Germans adapted the type of fortification to the position, and thus built blockhouses, or bunkers, as well as the more elaborate *ouvrages* that are seen as epitomizing the Maginot Line. This was partly out of tactical concerns and partly because the German high command had the same disagreements in the 1930s the French had gone through in the 1920s. Would the country be best served by an elaborate set of interlocking underground fortifications or by a system of infantry shelters with prepositioned machine guns and antitank weapons?

Gen. Otto Förster, who in 1934 was named head of Germany's military fortifications, clearly preferred the latter, and in October 1935 he received Hitler's authorization to begin serious fortification of the eastern frontier. As was often the case Hitler was merely ratifying by decree what had already been started. Förster's engineers had done most of the design work in 1933 or even before, and construction of the central position was well under way by 1934.

What Förster needed was not simply Hitler's approval but money, and, like everyone else in the Third Reich, he had to convince Hitler. Erich von Manstein, a young major on the staff who after 1933 seemed to have a knack for getting Hitler's attention, disagreed with Förster and thought that Germany should simply copy what France was doing.

By then (1936) the Germans had a pretty good idea of what the CORF fortifications looked like. Perhaps more important, before 1914 they had built their own fortifications (chiefly around Metz and Strasbourg), developing techniques that the French emulated and improved on in the CORF plans.[13]

But either idea—Förster's or von Manstein's—was going to be expensive. And by the time the German army engineers began serious fortification construction, they had to compete with the demands of the navy for a modern fleet, of the air force, and of the armored enthusiasts. This too was a recapitulation of the debate in France: The French had been as much aware of the theories of Fuller and Douhet as anyone else. But France was a democracy in which ideas were thrashed out rationally: After months (which turned into years) of discussion, the plans produced represented a national consensus.

In Germany matters proceeded differently. Left to their own devices, Förster's engineers made a number of decisions that impacted greatly on Germany's military capabilities, as their fortifications demanded a great deal of iron and steel. The bomb- and shellproof concrete, while theoretically better than the French process, had the great disadvantage that it required a great deal more iron (to be used as reinforcing rods which the concrete would harden around). Instead of rotating turrets the Germans protected their gun emplacements with thick metal plates—two armored shields were required, depending on the type of fortification. The larger weighed approximately thirty-eight tons and the smaller about five tons. The gross vehicle weight of a Mark 3 ausführung D tank was nineteen tons.[14] So one large plate was the equivalent of two of the greatly needed Mark 3 tanks. The scale of these fortifications in the east resulted in Germany having a good many fewer tanks in 1939–40.

By 1938 the Germans had built a formidable position in the east. Along the 230 or so kilometers of the Pomeranian position, there were about five hundred separate blockhouses, which worked out to one for every five hundred meters. To the south the Germans built 778 block-houses along the 250-odd kilometers of what was somewhat confusingly called the Oder Front.

German planners estimated that to garrison these positions would only require about twenty thousand men, less than two infantry divisions, which makes clear the attractiveness of the concept. German planners, like their French counterparts, were quite realistic about how long the garrison could hold out, but even if the line was only able to hold for a week, it would enable the mobilization and deployment of the field army. As the Germans rightly supposed the Polish army they would be facing lacked the heavy weapons of a France or a Soviet Union, the majority of the blockhouses could be constructed of lesser—and much cheaper—grades of concrete sufficient only to stop field artillery.

German engineers had been trying to construct a system of defenses in the west for some years before Hitler came to power, but apparently most of the work done had been limited to surveys, owing to the Allied Control Commission. After the militarization of the Rhineland (March 7, 1936) work was begun on a more serious level, although it is not clear exactly how much had been done, or where it had been done, before 1938. But in July 1938 Hitler intervened in the process, writing a series of specifications in his own hand to determine what would be built.[15]

What was needed was a great many small blockhouses properly protected against tanks by tank obstacles as well as antitank guns. There was no need for heavy artillery, tunnels, or any of the elaborate landship constructions that characterized the Maginot Line and the *OWB* positions. The primary objective of these blockhouses was to shelter small groups of infantry when they weren't fighting, and to enable them to defend themselves against local attacks.

Work was given a high priority, and by October 1938, five hundred blockhouses had been built. By the time war broke out, between thirteen and twenty-two thousand separate structures had been built in the west, defended by more than two hundred kilometers of antitank obstacles—this last being a new addition, and one presumably copied from the incomplete but still substantial Czech fortifications that had been constructed between Nachod and Opava in northern Bohemia.[16]

By July 1939 the Germans had put in place a considerable fortification system—at least eleven thousand blockhouses, protected by tank obstacles, and, in addition, protected by a new and terrifying weapon the Allies had not yet experienced. The French had opted to protect the approaches to their fortifications by relying on their turret-mounted field guns. As we shall see, these overlapping and interlocking fields of fire, coupled with the high rate of fire, made tank assaults impracticable. The opposing German defenses relied on a new and disturbing principle, the buried mine.

The buried landmine is a nasty weapon whose deployment came as a rude shock to the first French troops to cross the frontier in September 1939. Colonel Fuller, the U.S. Army military attaché to France, was allowed to examine what was captured, and discovered it was a 10-kilogram pressure-activated device, the explosion being triggered when a weight of 135 kilograms or more passed over it.[17] It was thus an antivehicle mine, and a particularly effective one. The most vulnerable part of the tank was the tread, followed by the lightly armored bottom of the hull. Blow the tread off and the tank was disabled.

The French were particularly disturbed by this, since their antitank obstacles consisted of ordinary railroad rails buried the ground, with only about thirty centimeters being visible. They clearly knew the weak points of tanks, and the prospect of running mechanized units over what appeared to be open terrain but was instead vast fields of mines was not an option they cared to pursue. Prior to 1939 mines had been used, but in very limited situations. It would be fairer to call them explosive booby trap devices rather than actual mines, and no army had ever encountered substantial stretches of mined terrain.

Had the Germans built fewer fortifications, they could have built many more tanks. On the other hand, had they built fewer fortifications, the few defensive troops available would not have been able to withstand a French assault. Contrary to the received wisdom, the Westwall was not a bluff. The mines were real, the thousands of bunkers operational. Although different camps inside both countries might disagree as to the scope and complexity of defensive fortifications, there was no real disagreement about their necessity.

For all his aggressive intentions and offensive mindedness, Hitler was as interested in the construction of massive fortifications as any French general or politician. He might counterfeit a rage and cry out that he would build great fleets of tanks and bombers, but at precisely the same time, from 1936 through 1938, he was writing the specifications for German's defensive fortifications.

NOTES

1. Writing in *Review militaire française,* as quoted by Roger Bruge, *Faites sauter la ligne Maginot* (Paris: Fayard, 1973), 5.

2. See, for example, studies such as Judith M. Hughes, *To the Maginot Line: The Politics of French Military Preparedness in the 1920s* (Cambridge, Mass.: Harvard University Press, 1971), whose title makes the point clear enough.

3. Fuller, *Armored Warfare,* 146.

4. Initially, of course, the Allies explained their defeat by saying that the Germans had many more tanks than they did, so, for example, Fuller believed Germany had about five thousand "modern" tanks and the Allies about four thousand, "of which the greater part was obsolete" (ibid., 6). Postwar it became obvious that the numbers were roughly equal; however, as we shall see in chapters 3 and 4, when one strips away the confusion

regarding classifications of vehicles, France alone deployed almost at least as many tanks as did Germany.

5. There are extensive descriptions of these fortifications in German, Czech, and Polish; the only English account is J. E. Kaufmann and H. W. Kaufmann, *Maginot Line Imitations* (New York: Praeger, 1998), whose title, by the way, says it all. It is an admirable study, but confusingly written.

6. Painlevé, it will be remembered, had first held that position in March 1917, just in time for the crisis of the *chemin des dames*, so he was rather familiar with the army and its troubles. He was also an able politician, having been president of the Chamber of Deputies since 1934. He was to hold the post until 1935, and to serve as minister of war from 1925 to 1929, basically a record for longevity in the constantly changing ministries of the Third Republic.

7. His exact words: "Le pays ne donne pas l'image d'un peuple vaincu. Tout respire l'ordre, la prospérité, la richesse. L'Allemagne n'est pas du tout épuisée. Si on laisse libre, elle pourra recommencer la guerre dans dix ans, et même avant." Fayolle, *Carnets secrets de la grande guerre*, ed. Henry Contamine (Paris: Plon, 1964), 322.

8. Like the vast majority of the 75-millimeter guns used in the fortifications, these guns were 1932 models, with a maximum range of twelve thousand meters, and an angle of fire of forty-five degrees. They were thus considerably more powerful than their 1897 namesake, made famous in the First World War, although the rate of fire—from twelve to twenty-four rounds per minute—was about the same.

9. There is a persistent myth that these forts were vulnerable if attacked from the rear, but this is not true. At Fermont, for example, the twin entrances (one for munitions, the other for men), twelve hundred meters back from the hilltop complex, were protected by casemate-mounted 47-millimeter antitank guns as well as light machine-gun positions. And, as they were mounted on the reverse slope, attacking troops were faced with what the French had learned through bitter experience was the unenviable task of attacking uphill against an armored and fortified position. Moreover, even if the defenders lost the entrances, they could still retreat down the tunnel and collapse a portion of it, thus sealing off the fort.

10. Another myth about these forts is that they tied up valuable manpower that could have been better used in the field. But the total garrison for all the fortifications enumerated at Fermont was basically the equivalent of a battalion of infantry. To maintain a solid defensive position with this much firepower—and so few men—is no mean feat.

11. This was precisely the sort of Allied behavior that antagonized the overwhelming majority of Germans, who perceived—correctly—that their country was to be deprived even of the most minimal means to defend itself. See the brief comment in Kaufmann and Kaufmann, *Maginot Line Imitations*, 9.

12. My discussion parallels and corrects the one provided in ibid., 9–50. Post-1945

these fortifications all became part of Poland and were left largely undisturbed, although the steel plates used to cover the firing positions were salvaged whenever possible. At that point the whole system simply disappeared into the fog that surrounded most things in Communist countries. Moreover, many of these positions, which were not designed to withstand artillery fire from heavy weapons, were completely destroyed. In the discussions that follow I am heavily indebted to unpublished Polish sources, and particularly to their photographic evidence.

13. The French have always been chary of admitting this influence. See the comments by Anthony Kemp, *Maginot Line, Myth and Reality* (London: Frederick Warne, 1981).

14. For the weights of the steel plates, see Kaufmann and Kaufmann, *Maginot Line Imitations,* 16–18. For tank weights, see Fridolin M. von Senger und Etterlin's *German Tanks of World War II*, trans. J. Lucas, ed. by Peter Chamberlain and Chris Ellis (New York: Galahad, 1967)—the numbers in parentheses refer to the page numbers in this authoritative text: Mark 1 Ausführung B: 6 tons (194); Mark 2 Ausführung D: 10 tons (194); Mark 3 Ausführung D: 19.3 tons (194); Mark 4 Ausführung C: 20 tons (196). For the eighty-kilometer-long central position, the *OWB*, Förster planned 111 *Panzerwerke* all to be connected by tunnels forty meters below the surface. After the final dissolution of Czechoslovakia, Hitler put a stop to construction, but 83 *Panzerwerke* and fourteen blockhouses armed with machine guns had already been built. No one knows exactly how much of the tunnel system had been completed, but the best estimate is about forty kilometers, so clearly this was engineering on a grand scale.

15. See the account—with references to original documents—in Dieter Bettinger and Martin Büren, *Der Westwall* (Osnabrück: Biblio Verlag, 1990), 1:92–95.

16. The Kaufmanns give a figure of 22,000 (*Maginot Line Imitations,* 42). I believe this counts all structures and is somewhat misleading. Bettinger and Büren, *Der Westwall,* the most authoritative source, gives substantially lower figures (although thirteen thousand bunkers is hardly to be sneezed at), albeit distributed in a confusing way. See, for example, *Der Westwall,* 1:341, 355. For the Czechs, see the extensive contemporaneous photographs in Emil Trojan, *Betonová Hranice: Československé Pohraniłni Opevnění 1935–1938* (Prague: Oftis, 1994). Curiously the Czechs managed to build armored vehicles in the low hundreds at the same time as they were building their fortifications: By May 1940 there were 413 Czech tanks in German service, most if not all having been built before the takeover (Senger und Etterlin, *German Tanks of World War II,* 193).

17. There is a good summary of the mines employed in Kaufmann and Kaufmann, *Maginot Line Imitations,* 66–67. As they point out, although German propaganda made much of the defenses of the Westwall and the hundreds of kilometers of "dragon's teeth," the mines were a closely guarded secret. For historians as well, apparently.

3.

The Tank Production Myths

There can be little doubt that the cost of the Maginot Line was one of the main reasons for the neglect of mechanization in the French Army.
—J. F. C. FULLER[1]

The 1920s came to an end with the French government's approval of funds sufficient to build the fortifications later known as the Maginot Line. By 1936 the forts were completed and operational. The usual analysis of this effort is twofold. First, it is argued that in response to France's reliance on obsolete defensive ideas and concrete structures, Germany opted for mobile and aggressive warfare. General Guillamat, who had argued that fortifications would sap the aggressiveness of the infantry and doom the French army to a static defense, liked to quote pronouncements by Gen. Hans von Seeckt, chief of staff of the Reichswehr, about the importance of mobile warfare in the future—this as early as 1923.[2]

Second, it is usually thought that the money spent on fortifications by France was directly responsible for its lack of tanks and planes in 1940: implicit in the argument is the idea that while the French built old-fashioned defenses, the Germans put their money into modern ones—

tanks and planes. So von Seeckt's dictum is seen as making explicit a clear choice between two kinds of warfare, the one modern and offensive, the other old-fashioned and defensive.[3]

The Tank Production Myths

The simplest point to be dispensed with is the confusion about the time line—when each country was building what. As we have seen, construction of the CORF fortifications had begun before 1929, with the bulk of the work completed by 1935. As the concrete was laid, so the money was spent. Although the vagaries of the French government's accounting system in the 1920s and 1930s made it an almost mystical entity, it is fairly clear that the funds appropriated had been spent by the end of 1934.

There are two reasons for attempting some precision about the date. The first is that the completion of the CORF fortifications occurred at roughly the same time as production began for the first operational German tank, the Mark 1.[4] German planners issued development contracts in 1933 for a five-ton light combat vehicle. The first prototype was completed by December of that year. A test production run began in February 1934, and actual production, based on a contract for 150 machines, began in July 1934. The Mark 1 entered army service in 1935, a date surprisingly close to when the CORF forts went operational, and by August 1939, 1,445 were in service.[5]

The basic problem is that this vehicle, as well as the next one in the series, the Mark 2, was, in the words of Germany's leading tank expert at the time, "unsuitable for combat," something that in the case of the Mark 1 had already been established during the Spanish civil war; moreover, "operations in Poland and France very quickly proved that neither their fire power nor their armor was sufficient for them to face enemy tanks.[6]

From a distance the Mark 1, with its low profile and turret, looks like one's conception of a tank, and this visual impression has probably contributed to the general idea of it as a competent example of early tank development. When it is seen close, and in perspective, so that its true size—and its 1930s vintage agricultural tractor suspension—becomes apparent, it is equally clear that Heinz Guderian was absolutely right. In fact the Mark 1 might more accurately be described as an overweight tankette, or a turreted machine-gun carrier: It weighed more than five tons, was armed with two machine guns, and had a two-man crew. Its 13-millimeter armor was actually less than that of the standard French tank of 1918, and could easily be penetrated by the antitank rifles of the First World War or by the equivalent of the American army's 50-caliber machine gun.

Underpowered tanks were a common feature of the First World War, when engine development was still in its infancy. Both the British and the French had consistently tried to power vehicles whose weight was far in excess of ten tons with engines developing only 100 horsepower, the result being vehicles whose cross-country speed was a slow walk (in fact, these vehicles were so slow they could be disabled by German mortar crews, and often were).

Fifteen years later, however, there was hardly any excuse for this, but the first two German tanks continued this hapless tradition. The first version of the 5.4-ton Mark 1 had a puny 57-horsepower engine, quickly corrected by using a Maybach 100-horsepower engine in the next series (series B). But as this tank weighed six tons, the improvement in power-weight ratio was less than optimal. The ratios revealed by the basic specification are troubling. The Mark 2, at ten tons, with its 140-horsepower engine, had a power-to-weight ratio—the all-important figure for tanks—only three-fifths that of the Mark 1.

The Mark 2 had a much better ground-pressure profile than the Mark 1, as well as the potential to be developed into a useful tracked reconnaissance vehicle, as indeed it was as the war progressed. However, putting a 20-millimeter gun in a ten-ton vehicle was a waste of steel, and Germany's tank authorities certainly wanted a better vehicle for their armored divisions. Nonetheless, as with the Mark 1, production continued, and by September 1939, 712 of these vehicles had been produced.

The Mark 2 was in fact a stopgap development: Officers like Guderian preferred to equip their armored divisions with real tanks, and in the 1930s two models were under development, the Mark 3 and the Mark 4. But, contrary to the image of the Third Reich as a nation single-mindedly devoted to the mass production of arms, development proceeded at a leisurely pace. In fact the Mark 3 wasn't officially accepted by the army until September 27, 1939—by which time it had been proved in combat, albeit in small numbers.

Small numbers indeed: By December 1939 Germany had produced a grand total of 228 Mark 3 and 178 Mark 4 tanks.[7] The organizational tables for an armored division as of January 1939 called for a total of 421 tanks, so basically the German army lacked the tanks it needed to constitute even one armored division. So the idea that while the French built forts the Germans built tanks is in fact the exact opposite of the truth.

Had it been built as originally proposed in 1935, the Mark 3 would have been the best tank in the world: a fifteen-ton vehicle equipped with a 250-horsepower engine and a 50-millimeter high-velocity gun. But the decision to equip the infantry with the PAK 35 (as the towed version of the 37-millimeter antitank gun was known) had already been made, so the Mark 3 went into mass production with an inferior weapon incapable of doing any damage to comparable French, British, or Russian tanks. It also gained weight: The D version, which became the main operation version of the tank, weighed in at 19.3 tons, largely because of a new and heavier engine (developing 320 horsepower) and thicker armor.

Although the D variant of the Mark 3 was still undergunned and overweight, it was the closest thing Germany had to a decent main battle tank capable of spearheading breakthrough operations. The problem may be seen easily enough by the numbers being produced: version A: 8; version B: 15; version C: 15. In all of 1939 Germany produced only 157 vehicles of this type. As late as May 1940 there were only 349 Mark 3 tanks in service.

Guderian and the other tank experts had intended there to be a second tank, this one to support the breakthrough operations. This tank would be more heavily armored and mount a gun equivalent to the standard field gun, so it would be able to destroy fixed strongpoints that the nimbler tanks had bypassed, strongpoints that conventional infantry would have great difficulty in neutralizing. The vehicle that emerged in 1936, the Mark 4, soldiered on through the war and ended up being Germany's main battle tank—largely by default, thanks to the lethargy of the German armaments industry.

Basically the Mark 4 had the same chassis as the Mark 3, initially weighed about the same, and had the same engine. The difference was that the support tank was designed to accommodate a very-low-velocity 75-millimeter gun of the sort useful for support missions. Production proceeded at a pace difficult to credit: there were 35 of the first series, 42 of the B series, and 140 of the C series. In fact, in 1939, for reasons that

Although the German Mark 4 tank was the only German vehicle with a 75-millimeter turret gun, the initial tanks had only the low-velocity weapon shown here. Although a decent infantry support weapon, the Mark 4 was actually outgunned by almost all French medium and heavy tanks. By 1941 the design was obsolete, but as Germany was unable to design and produce modern vehicles in quantity, modified Mark 4 tanks soldiered on throughout the war. (*ECP Armées Paris*)

are difficult to fathom, Mark 4 production basically stopped: 45 vehicles were produced in 1939. Production between September 1939 and May 1940 was hardly sufficient to replace the tanks lost during the Polish offensive.

Paradoxically the Mark 3, supposedly the breakthrough tank, thus ended up weighing more than the Mark 4, the support tank. As photographs of the two vehicles side by side make clear, when both vehicles were fitted (finally) with more powerful guns and thicker armor, there is little difference between them. This raises the obvious question: Why had the Germans bothered to develop two tanks with so many shared characteristics? Why not develop one tank and concentrate on producing that? And why refuse to equip the tanks with real guns?

By 1937 the Russians, the Americans, and the French had all realized that a tank had to have at least one high-velocity turret-mounted gun.

The problem was figuring out how to put such a gun in the turret. Only the Russians were able to implement the complete solution: The T34 mounted a 76-millimeter gun of respectably high velocity in a rotating turret.

In tank development the T34 is sometimes talked about as though it belongs to a much later generation of tank. But this is not true. The T34 was simply the latest evolution of a design that Soviet tank designers had been working on since 1931. At every stage, the predecessors of the T34 were better than their German counterparts, beginning with the BT5—faster, better armed, and with angled armor.[8]

In the First World War, British and French tank designers had relied on the shipbuilding techniques of the nineteenth century to join the steel plates forming the outer surface of the tank. The separate pieces of steel were riveted to frame members, the basic idea being pretty much the same as one employs in building a house. Early on it was discovered that this was not a good idea. A hit that did not actually penetrate the steel could pop the rivets loose, turning them into projectiles lethal to the crew.

French military engineers had already thought of this problem at the turn of the century: The steel turrets mounted in their extensive fortifi-

Although crudely built and finished, the Soviet T-34 embodied all the basics of modern tank design: sloped armor, a high-velocity gun (a 76-millimeter weapon in this example), and wide tracks. The low profile is notable. (*John Mosier*)

cations were all cast. Casting was an enormously more expensive process, but it resulted in a one-piece turret of extreme hardness. The turrets produced in this fashion were virtually invulnerable to direct hits, and indeed may be seen to this day, as they slowly rust away in France's abandoned fortifications.

The same technique could be applied to tanks, but there was a cheaper and equally effective system: welding. In welding, the steel plates were literally fused together, and the seams, instead of being the weakest point, were reckoned to be the strongest. The Germans and the Russians had opted for welded steel hulls virtually from the start of their tank design efforts, but the Russians went a step further.

Early tanks were box-shaped rectangular objects with vertical surfaces, a design that probably derived from existing naval practice. But the ability of a steel plate to resist being penetrated is a function not only of the thickness and hardness of the steel, but of the angle of the penetration attempt. Armor sloped at sixty degrees from the horizontal plane would be anywhere from a third to two-thirds more resistant to penetration than armor with no slope at all. A tank designed with properly angled armor could therefore weigh the same as a tank with straight-sided armor but afford its crew much greater protection.

That this was so was one of the most elementary concepts of gunnery. French, American, Russian, and even some British tanks all made use of it to one degree or another. But German tank designers ignored it. All of their prewar designs had box-shaped hulls with no angling, and this was true even of the first wartime design, the Tiger 1. Only with the Panther did German tank designers abandon the box shape and produce a vehicle with angled armor.

The failure to equip tanks with a decent gun, is, if anything, more troubling. In 1917–18 no antitank guns, properly speaking, had existed. The Germans were forced to rely on a combination of regular field artillery, mortars, and a big-bore rifle developed by Mauser, which fired a 12.98-millimeter armor-piercing bullet. At close quarters the armor of this era could also be pierced by the standard infantry heavy machine gun.

By the mid-1930s, several excellent antitank guns were in wide service. The Germans had developed a 37-millimeter towed antitank gun, the PAK 35/36, which fired a .68-kilogram shell with a muzzle velocity of 762 meters per second.[9] At 500 meters it could penetrate 50 millimeters of unsloped armor and 50 millimeters of sloped armor. Sim-

ilar 37-millimeter guns were in service in the United States, Great
Britain, and Poland.

Actually combat experience quickly established that this gun was
totally inadequate as an antitank gun. As German antitank gunners
found to their consternation in May 1940, their 37-millimeter shells
simply bounced off the thick angled armor of French tanks. The reason
for this German design failure is clear enough: No German tank in
service in 1939 had armor thicker than 30 millimeters, and the Mark 3,
the tank designed to be the breakthrough vehicle for armored divisions,
had less armor than the Renault tank of 1918.

As we have noted, the failings in quality were matched by failures in
quantity. By August 1939, there were hardly enough Mark 3 and 4
tanks—the only real tanks the Germans had—to equip one armored
division. But the German high command had organized six armored
divisions, four light divisions (each with what was initially intended to
be half the armored complement of an armored division) and several
independent tank units—far more units than the army had tanks, even
pressing all the 1,455 obsolescent Mark 1 machine-gun carriers into
service.

In fact the Germans were so desperate that they bulked out their
inadequate numbers with an obsolete tank used by the Czechoslovakian
army in 1937–38, the LTM35. As the number suggests, this was a tank
from 1935, and not a particularly good one, although it had a number of
extremely advanced features. These features mostly related to its steering
and transmission, but its 120-horsepower Skoda engine, when coupled
with the advanced transmission and steering, actually gave it better cross-
country performance than comparable German tanks with more powerful engines.[10]

By May 1940 the Mark 1 was no longer the most common German
tank, having been replaced by the Mark 2, but tank production between
the two campaigns was minimal: From October 1939 to May 1940,
Germany produced only 479 tanks, a number barely sufficient to offset
its losses in the Polish campaign.[11] Fortunately the Czechs had developed
a more modern tank, the TNHP-5, and by 1940 the Germans had 238
of these vehicles in service to make up the production shortfalls in the
Mark 3: There were actually more Czech tanks in service in the
Wehrmacht in 1940 than there were Mark 3s.[12]

Given the abysmal record of German tank production, the TNHP-5
was widely used in the German army: As late as July 1, 1943, there were

763 of these tanks in service. The suspension and drive train were extremely robust, and the TNHP-5 became the basis for one of the most successful German designs of the war, the Hetzer tank destroyer, a slab-sided turretless vehicle mounting a potent long-barreled 75-millimeter gun. But as a main battle tank, the Czech vehicle was inadequate. It had the same high-profile riveted construction as the LTM5, was thinly armored, and mounted yet another underpowered 37-millimeter gun.[13] The Germans used it because it was available and they were desperate for armor.

The story of German tank design is a muddle in which overweight, inadequately armed, and poorly armored vehicles were produced in small numbers to overlapping specifications. Whatever German generals later claimed, no matter how brilliant their theories of warfare, German production statistics give the lie to the claim that the German army was preparing for some revolutionary kind of warfare or had developed the weaponry to suit their ideas.

The Surprising Reality of French Tank Production

The quality and quantity data make it pretty obvious that German military planners had not embraced the new technology of armor at all. Germany had not devoted the time period when the Maginot Line was being built to develop a tank force. Development contracts for the four basic tanks were not even issued until most of the French defenses had been finished; the tanks only entered army service afterward, and the only vehicle produced in any quantity before September 1939 was an obsolete machine-gun carrier, the Mark 1. Moreover, during the period 1935–40, France built many more tanks than did Germany.

This feat was made possible by an ambitious French plan aimed at spending an additional fourteen billion francs on defense over the years 1936–40. This plan, approved by the Council of Ministers on September 7, 1936, allocated almost one-quarter of the funds to mechanization, and this allowed both for the production of new models and the increased production of those already in service.

The aim was to enable France to field mechanized and armored divisions. The army already had in service approximately three thousand of the Renault light tanks designed in 1917–18. The FT was the first modern tank, that is to say, the first tracked vehicle with a rotating turret and any sort of off-road performance. In contrast to the behemoths the British and French had developed to break through no-man's-land, the FT weighed only seven tons, had a two-man crew, and mounted a low-velocity 37-millimeter gun in its rotating turret.[14]

Its 39-horsepower engine would propel it at about ten kilometers an hour, and it had a range of about forty kilometers. The crew was protected in front by 22 millimeters of steel plate. Its range and speed were vastly inferior to either the German Mark 1 or Mark 2 tank (both had road ranges of about one hundred kilometers and road speeds of more than forty kilometers an hour). But the 22 millimeters of armor was substantially thicker than the armor on the Mark 1, and the 37-millimeter gun was considerably more potent than the two machine guns of the Mark 1 or the 20-millimeter weapon of the Mark 2.

The French army, however, did not see the old FT as a competitor to a new generation of light tanks; instead, the army proposed to use them as infantry support vehicles, a role for which they were well suited, as their slow speed and limited operating range was fitted to the advance of men on foot, who might under good conditions be expected to move about thirty kilometers or so a day.[15]

Having thus disposed of the problem of infantry support, the French proposed to build a strike force consisting of armored divisions. Contrary to what is usually said, the French army had begun the formation of armored and mechanized divisions as early as 1933, at about the time Hitler came to power. Like the Germans a few years later, the French toyed with two different types of structure, a "light" mechanized division and a regular armored division (as well as motorized divisions).

In the French thinking at the time, the "light" divisions would be designed for speed and mobility, the exploitation of a breakthrough, while the "heavy" divisions would compose the mailed fist capable of delivering the blow. So French and German institutional thinking on armor were almost precisely parallel. Both armies envisioned two distinct types of units, both equipped with tanks, designed to operate in complementary fashion.

The difference was that, unlike the Germans, the French had enough tanks to put these theories into practice. Perhaps more important, the French army actually had a formidable main battle tank, the B1 (and its later variant, the B1 *bis*). Development and production of the B series tanks had proceeded in leisurely fashion. In March 1925, right in the

middle of the planning for fixed fortifications, Gen. Jean-Baptiste Estienne, the father of French armor, and the man responsible for the development of the French tanks of the Great War, had laid down the
specifications for what we would call today a main battle tank.

Estienne sidestepped the problem of mounting a high-velocity gun
in a turret, and specified a hull-mounted 75-millimeter gun in addition
to a turret. Development of this vehicle was extremely slow. The B series
tanks were formidable: The B1 weighed twenty-seven tons, and had 40
millimeters of frontal armor. Its 270-horsepower engine would propel it
over a road at about twenty-five kilometers an hour. Not particularly
fast, but the BT tanks would run at that speed almost indefinitely. Particular attention had been paid to durability, and the early models of
what was known as the B1 covered 225 kilometers in twenty-three
hours in wintertime, an astonishing record for 1931.

By 1935 there were only seventeen of these vehicles, but the
increased funding changed the situation. By 1937 there were enough B
series tanks for an armored division to be organized around them, and
by the start of the war there were four hundred B1 and B1 *bis* tanks in
service. The Germans had nothing comparable. The only weapon capable of destroying the B1 was the German 88-millimeter antiaircraft
gun—which the Germans had quickly impressed into ground duty in
May 1940. In May 1940 a B series tank named "Jeanne d'Arc' received
ninety direct artillery hits in two hours and was still operating; a B
series tank named "Amiens" received two direct hits from a German
105-millimeter howitzer without any ill effects.[16]

The old FT apart, the superior armoring of the B series tanks was in
fact a characteristic of all French tanks, and reflected the concerns of the
French high command over the proliferation of the German 37-mil-
limeter antitank weapon. The French believed that by 1937 there were
roughly seven thousand of these weapons in service, and in field testing
discovered that the older standard of armor 20 to 30 millimeters thick
was inadequate against such a weapon. As a result all French tanks produced after 1934 had 40-millimeter frontal armor.

In 1935, as the CORF fortifications were nearing completion, France
issued a specification for a tank of about the same specifications as the
German Mark 2, although armed with a 37-millimeter gun. Like the
German Mark 2, the R35 was underpowered (with an 85-horsepower
engine driving a ten-ton vehicle) and consequently had similar transmission problems.[17] Although the cross-country speed of German tanks

is always stressed, the R35, despite its weaker engine and thicker armor, had the same cross-country performance as the Mark 2, while its thicker armor and heavier gun gave it a significant advantage in combat. The French were aware of the problems of the R35, and the firm of AMX, which became famous postwar for its innovative tank designs, made numerous improvements to later models.

Like the Germans, who had pursued the development of two separate light tanks (the Marks 1 and 2), the French developed an alternative model, designed to be a faster vehicle. This was developed by the firm of Hotchkiss, and its initial version, the H35, was, like the R35, too underpowered to be effective. Two years later (in 1937) Hotchkiss was able to produce a vastly superior light tank, the H39, with a 120-horsepower engine and the same 37-millimeter gun.

Actually, the situation with regard to light tanks was France's weakest link in armored development. Renault had begun building what we might call a medium tank from 1932 on. This was the D1, which was armed with a 47-millimeter gun in a revolving turret. In 1934, at the same time as the Germans were issuing specifications for their early tanks, the French firm of Somua produced a prototype for a new medium tank. Called the 35 S, it weighed thirteen tons and was armed with a high-velocity 47-millimeter gun. Its sloped 40-millimeter armor was proof against any German tank or antitank gun, and its cross-country performance and road range were better than any of the four German tanks in service.

The French 47-millimeter gun deserves special mention. This was a very-high-velocity weapon (855 meters per second) firing a 1.73-kilogram shell, so it was actually a more powerful weapon than the low-velocity L24 75-millimeter gun on the German Mark 4 tank.[18] Whether it was mounted in a tank or used as a towed antitank gun, this weapon was absolutely deadly to German armor. But then the French 25-millimeter antitank gun was actually as potent as the bigger German 37-millimeter weapon, and for the same reason: It was a much-higher-velocity weapon.

What is still not realized by most analysts is the quantity of tanks the French had on hand at the start of the fighting. The army had 1,207 R35 light tanks, 695 H35 light tanks, 200 D1 and D2 medium tanks, 285 Somua tanks, and 175 B1 and B1 *bis* tanks, or almost precisely three thousand vehicles, not counting the three thousand FT tanks, four hundred tankettes (which the French called *automitrailleuses*), and another one hundred examples of the extremely unsuccessful HCM light tank.

And these figures reflect only the totals in service as of April 1939, for—in strong contrast to Germany—in France production expanded enormously in the months leading up to the war and then up to the actual fighting in May 1940: In April there were 285 of the modern Somua tanks in service, but by May 1940 the total had risen to 410. These production increases held true for all the more French important tank designs. In April 1939 there were 140 of the newer B1 *bis* tanks in service; by November there were 190, and by the end of the war, the factory had turned out 403.[19]

A book could be written comparing French and German tank development in the 1930s, but these figures make two things fairly clear: First, France had hardly exhausted its resources in building the Maginot Line, nor did Germany take advantage of this French obsession. Second, once the fortifications had been built, France plunged into tank production with a vengeance, producing more tanks than Germany, more heavily armed and armored tanks than Germany, and in several instances, better tanks than Germany. It is simply untrue to say that the building of the Maginot Line exhausted France's military capacities, or

The French Somua S35 Tank, designed in 1935, was faster and more heavily armored than any tank in service in 1940, and its 47-millimeter gun could disable any German vehicle. By May 1940 over 400 had been produced, as opposed to only 381 of the poorly armed German Mark 3s. (*Albert J. Casciero*)

that, having built those fortifications, the French were then mentally (or militarily or financially) unable to make offensive weapons such as tanks.

Indeed, the fact that the French were experimenting in the same way the Germans were with the distribution of armor among two types of units suggests strongly that the French high command was certainly as forward-thinking as were their German adversaries. Moreover, a comparison of the French mixture of tank types with the German mix suggests that the French had a considerably more advanced understanding of what kinds of tanks would actually be successful on the battlefield.

German tanks, it is often said, were superior to French tanks in three important ways. They had a two-man turret, while French tanks did not, thus forcing the tank commander to load and fire the gun as well as direct the tank. This argument is certainly true, and no tanker would opt for a one-man turret over a two- or preferably three-man one. However, given the dramatic imbalance in firepower and armor, it is difficult to see that this advantage translated into any meaningful superiority on the battlefield in May and June 1940.

Guderian had started his career as a signals officer, and was thus unusually aware of the importance of radio communications; consequently, it is argued, German tanks were superior in action because of their ability to communicate by radio. Again, although this is true enough in theory, it is difficult to find any evidence confirming that it gave German armor any practical advantage. Significantly, on September 1, 1939, when Guderian found his forward units stalled in their advance, he did not attempt to contact them by radio—he went directly to the front and dealt with them in person.

In postwar interviews, German generals expressed a preference for speed as opposed to protection (which in turn means a heavier and less mobile vehicle). When Liddell Hart interviewed Gen. Wilhelm von Thoma, whom he justly characterizes as "the most famous of the original German tank leaders next to Guderian," von Thoma opined that "French tanks were better than ours, and as numerous—but they were too slow. It was by speed, in exploiting surprise, that we beat the French."[20]

In the same paragraph, von Thoma indicated that if he had to choose between what Liddell Hart calls "a thick skin" and "fast runner," he would choose the latter, adding, "in other words, he preferred speed to heavy armor." The problem here is the context: By the end of the war the Germans had produced some truly enormous tracked vehicles. The

G version of the Mark 4 weighed about twenty-four tons; the Panther tank weighed forty-five, and the Tiger 2 weighed almost seventy tons. Curiously, however, the actual cross-country speeds of these vehicles contradiction von Thoma's remark: The Panther was significantly faster both on roads and cross-country than the Mark 4, and the two Tiger tanks had the same speed.

The problem with these later German tanks was not their speed, it was their enormous size: the Soviet T34-85, the final version of the tank to see service in the Second World War, weighed only thirty-two tons, and it had a significantly lower profile than any of the later German vehicles.

Moreover, in the key passage from the interview, von Thoma seems to be talking not about the technical specifications of the tanks involved but about the speed with which the two sides conducted operations. There's nothing new there, and nothing that is specific to armor: The speed with which the Germans reacted both offensively and defensively was clearly evident in their operations during the First World War. But, as we shall see in the following chapters, the idea that the German offensives of the Second World War were conducted with a rapidity never before seen in warfare (and thus one that can only be accounted for by new methods of warfare) is hardly borne out by the course of the campaigns themselves.

So too for an idea which has become virtually embedded in cement, the claim that the French did not deploy their armor correctly, en masse, but distributed it in what British analysts have derisively called "penny packets." As noted earlier, part of this confusion stems from the fact that the French had so many tanks that they had the luxury of using them both in infantry support and in armored formations. But most of the contention is simply wishful thinking: It must be so because it had to be. As we shall see, the German victories of 1939 and 1940 were thoroughly conventional ones whose main causes had next to nothing to do with the use of novel tactics and new weapons.

Putting aside for a moment, then, our hindsight about May 1940, and accepting—if only provisionally—the idea that from 1934 or 1935 on, France matched Germany tank for tank, an intriguing question arises. Everyone agrees that Germany was bent on clandestine rearmament even before Hitler came to power. There is certainly no doubt that once Hitler came to power German military expenditures increased enormously. It is difficult to imagine that, even given the financial problems of the Weimar Republic, the entire German defense budget could have been consumed by the production of a few thousand lightweight armored vehicles spread out over a period of four or five years.

So what in fact was the German defense budget being spent on?

There are several possible answers to this puzzle. A great deal of money was spent on the development and production of modern artillery, on the development of an air force and a navy, and simply on the training and organization of a large standing army. This is all true. However, the curious thing is that whenever one turns to a close examination of any one of these other areas, the situation is in some measure curiously parallel to the one with tanks. Germany entered the war totally dependent on an obsolete transport plane for its air drops. It had been unable to develop a strategic bomber. In fact the general conclusion of almost every specialized study of the Luftwaffe is that it began the war without any depth to speak of, with numerous deficiencies of the most serious kind.[21]

So where did the resources go? They went on fortifications.

NOTES

1. In a note appended to the annotated edition of his *Armored Warfare,* 146.

2. See the discussion in Léon Noël, *Un chef: le général Guillaumat* (Paris: Éditions Alsatia, 1949), 126–30.

3. It may seem that by deliberately eliminating the United Kingdom from this analysis I am distorting the situation. The fact of the matter is that Great Britain had hardly any tanks in 1939–40; those that were in service were markedly inferior to French and German designs in every respect; and virtually the whole of the British tank force was abandoned in France during the evacuation.

4. Rather than employ the cumbersome German system of nomenclature, in which the Mark 1 would be called the *Panzerkampfwagen I*, I will refer to German armored vehicles 1, 2, 3, and 4 more simply as Mark 1, Mark 2, and so forth.

5. The dates for Mark 1 development are taken from Senger und Etterlin's *German Tanks of World War II,* 22–23. Because in format and convenience this text is vastly preferable to the original German one, I have used it throughout.

6. Ibid., 22.

7. Russell Stolfi advances a thesis similar to the one being advanced here, although his concern is with May 1940, and thus France and Germany. I was unaware of his dissertation until very far along in the writing of this book, but I was pleased to see the

extensive documentation his work provides for the points being made. See Russell Henry Stolfi, "Reality and Myth: French and German Preparations for War, 1933–1940," (Ph.D. diss., Stanford University, 1966), 119. Macksey, who admits that the two German light tanks weren't much good, cites a different set of figures: 98 Mark 3 and 211 Mark 4 vehicles. See Kenneth Macksey, *Guderian, Creator of the Blitzkrieg* (New York: Stein & Day, 1975), 80. The two figures aren't easily reconciled, but both support the same basic argument: The Germans didn't have enough decent tanks in 1939 to supply one armored division, much less six.

8. See the excellent monograph by Horst Scheibert, originally published as *Der Russische Kampfwagen T34* (Friedberg, Germany: Podzun-Pallas Verlag, 1989); and available in English as *The Russian T34 Battle Tank* (Altglen, Pa.: Schiffer, 1992).

9. Antitank gun data from T. J. Gander, *German Anti-tank Guns, 1939–1945* (London: Almark Publications, 1973) 63; Peter Chamberlain and Terry Gander, *Anti-tank Weapons* (New York: Arco, 1974), 36, 47.

10. There is a brief technical analysis of the tank's advanced features in Senger und Etterlin, *German Tanks*, 29. This indispensable monograph is organized by vehicle classification—that is, it begins with the Mark 1, then the Mark 2, then the Czech tanks, then the Mark 3, and so on—the point being that the Czech tanks pressed into service were rightly regarded as vehicles somewhere between the Mark 2 and the Mark 3. We have already noted that the Mark 2 was obsolete as a battle tank in 1939—the LTM35 was hardly an acceptable battle tank. The basic problem with the LTM35 was its shape: it had a high profile, and straight sided armor, which was riveted. Despite its technical sophistication, the LTM35 had an extraordinarily rough ride. It had one advantage over the German Mark 1 and Mark 2 tanks that formed the bulk of German armor in 1939: the LTM35 was armed with a 37-millimeter gun of the same sort used in Renault tanks from the First World War. In its Czech variant it was a 600-meter-per-second weapon and thus inferior even to the puny German 37-millimeter gun, which had a muzzle velocity of 745 meters per second. Given an equivalent shell weight, the higher the muzzle velocity, the more hitting power of the gun. As the two weapons fired essentially the same weight of shell, the German weapon had considerably more penetrating power against armor than the Czech gun did. Muzzle velocity—which also determines range—is an extremely important specification for a gun, and one often overlooked by military historians, who seem to believe that bigger is better, and evaluate weapons exclusively in terms of the diameter of the barrel. However, as we shall see in the chapter on France in 1940, the standard high-velocity French 47-millimeter gun was as potent as the German 75-millimeter low-velocity gun mounted by early versions of the Mark 4 tank.

11. Production figures taken from the official German data reprinted in U.S. Strategic Bombing Survey, *The Effects of Strategic Bombing on the German War Economy* (Washington, D.C.: Overall Economic Effects Division, October 1945), table 104, 278. This figure

apparently counts Czech tank production as well, and thus grossly overstates Germany's capacity. Stolfi suggests that during this period the German produced less than fifty examples of Marks 3 and 4. As we shall see in the following chapter, German tank losses in Poland were technically greater than this figure, although about a third of the tanks put out of action were repaired.

12. In May 1940 there were 381 Mark 3 and 290 Mark 4 tanks, as opposed to 143 35(t) and 238 38(t) tanks; the most numerous vehicle in the German armored divisions was the Mark 2, with its inferior 20-millimeter gun. In contrast, all the French light tanks, regardless of design, carried a 37-millimeter weapon comparable to the Czech tanks or the German Mark 3. Data taken from Senger und Etterlin, *German Tanks,* Appendix 2.

13. In German usage, the tank that in the Czech army was called the LTM35 became the PzKw 35(t), the *t* standing for Czechoslovakia (Tschechoslowakei, as it was spelled in German). The more modern tank, which in Czech nomenclature was the TNHP-5, went into the German service as the 38(t), where, in its many variants, it proved one of the outstanding designs of the war, notably as the assault gun the Germans called "*Marder III*" and the tank destroyer (*Jagdpanzer*) called "Hetzer."

14. Specifications for the Renault FT taken from André Duvignac, *Histoire de l'armée motorisée* (Paris: Imprimerie Nationale, 1947), 453; and the U.S. Army's Aberdeen Proving Ground, *Tank Data*, vol. 1, eds. E. J. Hoffschmidt and W. H. Tatum (Old Greenwich, Conn.: WE Press, 1969) [date and editors taken from vol. 2], 23.

15. See the testimony of General Velpry to the Chamber, July 10, 1937; as noted by Stolfi "Reality and Myth," 128. The army did not intend to use all three thousand of these tanks in actual combat: in 1940 ten battalions were in service, to be used as infantry support, while the other two thousand–odd were used for security and rear echelon protection (ibid., 134). Probably it was these ten battalions of infantry support tanks that encouraged the British in their idea that the French had distributed their armor to their infantry. No one at the time was able to comprehend the enormity of France's tank establishment: The French army had so many tanks that they could have both infantry support units *and* self-contained armored divisions.

16. Data taken from Col. E[mile] Ramspacher, ed., *Chars et blindés français,* (Paris: Charles Lavauzelle, 1979), 98–104; Duvignac, *Histoire de l'armée motorisée,* 453; Stolfi, "Reality and Myth," 129–30.

17. See the critical comments in Ramspacher, *Chars et blindés français,* 96.

18. The German L24 generated about 500,000 kilograms/meter of force, while the French gun generated more than 630,000 kilograms/meter. By contrast the German 37-millimeter gun generated slightly less than 200,000 kilograms/meter. The L24 was rapidly replaced in German Mark 4 tanks. The version of this tank the Allies encountered in Normandy was armed with the Kwk 40 75-millimeter gun, which had a muzzle veloc-

ity of 990 meters per second when firing the model 40 armor-piercing shell. At 457 meters this shell would penetrate 89 millimeters of angled armor. As the thickest armor on the British Cromwell tank was 76 millimeters, and only 62 millimeters on the American Sherman, both were basically defenseless against a Mark 4 series G tank. As it was these more potent versions of the Mark 4 that the Allies encountered in combat in North Africa and later, there was a natural tendency to assume that the Mark 4 had always been like the G version. Not so, and all the models in combat in 1940 were armed with the low-velocity gun, and thus were basically outgunned by the French.

19. Stolfi has the figures as of April 1939 ("Reality and Myth," 134) displayed in tabular form. Ramspacher gives the later figures in the course of the discussion; for the tanks mentioned, see *Chars et blindés français,* 102–4.

20. As reported by Basil Henry Liddell Hart, *The German Generals Talk* (New York: William Morrow, 1953), 93–94.

21. See, for example, the concluding sentences in Hanfried Schliepahke, *The Birth of the Luftwaffe* (Chicago: Regnery, 1972), 58; Edward L. Homze, *Arming the Luftwaffe* (Lincoln: University of Nebraska Press, 1976), 269.

4.

Lessons Mislearned: Poland and the Winter Wars

The Second World War, comprising two successive and contradictory periods, provides a window on the ambiguities of Communism and anti-Fascism. From September 1939 to June 1941, Stalin was Hitler's principal ally; from June 1941 to May 1945, his most determined enemy. It is the second period, authenticated by victory, that has been retained in the selective memory of nations; the first period, however, must also have its historical due if we are to avoid solely a winner's version of the past.
—FRANÇOIS FURET

Supposedly Poland's collapse was the result of National Socialist Germany's quantitative and qualitative military superiority, a qualitative superiority that introduced the world to such terms as *Panzer, Stuka,* and *Blitzkrieg.* These terms imply a radically new form of warfare the Poles were helpless to resist. The Germans were victorious because they understood this new warfare. The Allies were defeated because they did not. The key was the deployment of tanks to punch deep holes through the enemy's defenses and the use of close air support to demolish its strongpoints. The Allies, whether Poles, Belgians, or French, were accustomed to the older, foot-and-horse rhythms of warfare, and were unable to match the rapid moves of Germany's highly mechanized forces.

The Fall of Poland: Politics Not Tactics

Actually Poland's military was much better equipped, and gave a much better account of itself, than Western sources admit. In the war that broke out on September 1, 1939, Poland was certainly doomed, but more for political reasons than purely military ones. The major reasons for Poland's defeat had little to do with either the new warfare or Germany's technological superiority—and everything to do with the political situation at the end of August 1939. It is doubtful that any country, no matter how well equipped, could have held out given these circumstances; conversely, given Poland's situation in September 1939, any competent European army could have defeated it. If ever a war was lost before a shot was fired, this was it.

Clearly it was impossible for Great Britain to raise an army and send it to Poland in time to be of any use. The Poles therefore counted on strategic air and naval support. An intensive bombing campaign would cripple Germany's ability to supply its troops in the field, and demoralize the civilian population, which, it was felt, was increasingly restive: If Hitler's successes were checked, if he sustained even the slightest of setbacks, his regime would collapse.[2]

The French promised to begin a major offensive in the west within two weeks of mobilization.[3] The Poles, not unreasonably, assumed that in the event of a German attack, the French would mobilize. Thus, if they could hold out for two weeks, they could plan on the French offensive forcing the Germans to shut down their offensive operations against Poland and move westward. In the actual event the Allied response to the German attack was feeble. The net effect of the impotent Allied responses was that Poland was left to its own devices. Instead of having to contain a German advance for two weeks, the Poles had to fight Germany entirely on their own—and with a traditional enemy, the Soviet Union, as Germany's ally.

The Hitler-Stalin pact was for Poland the veritable shot in the head: Stalin knew that Hitler intended to occupy those parts of Poland that the Germans considered to be historically German. The moment he saw that happening, and realized that the Allies were unable to stop it, he sent his own troops into Poland (on September 17). For propaganda purposes it was claimed that the country had already collapsed, and the Allies, no less than Hitler, were delighted to support this claim. Unlike the Allies, Hitler's reasons for claiming that he had smashed Poland over the weekend were obvious. If he could persuade the world that the Germans had smashed Poland in a few days, the rest of the world would be even more terrorized by German arms, and particularly by German airpower.

Militarily, however, some possibility exists that Poland might have been able to fight Germany into a protracted and costly stalemate, had the war been confided to those two powers alone. The chance is small, but it does exist, as the Finnish case reminds us. But with the entry into the war of the Soviet Union, there was absolutely no chance at all that Poland would survive for more than a few weeks.

Thus the whole question of tactics and technology really becomes a moot point: As the Allies left Poland unaided, and as it was inconceivable that it could fight off both invaders, the country was doomed. The surprising thing is how long Poland held out. The last major Polish forces inside Poland didn't surrender until Friday, October 6, 1939, and despite early German claims that the city had been occupied on Friday, September 8, Warsaw did not actually surrender until Wednesday the twenty-seventh. As German troops were being transferred to the Western Front by Monday, October 2, it seems fair to say that Poland held out—technically at least—for thirty-two days.

The Two Sides

As a result of early wars, nationalist aspirations, and a realistic awareness of the nation's precarious geographical position, Poland maintained a sizable army of thirty divisions, and relied on a system of training and mobilization derived from French practice, which by 1939 meant that the 280,000-man active army could be supplemented by 1.5 million reservists, with another 500,000 men available for static defenses. On mobilization this would mean an army of more than 2 million men, divided (very roughly) into forty-three infantry divisions, three mountain brigades, eleven cavalry brigades, two mechanized brigades, and fourteen national guard brigades.[4]

A postcampaign German inventory of captured artillery listed 3,214 field pieces, so the Polish army was reasonably well-equipped with artillery (in August 1914 the French army had only 4,300 guns in service). Although the fact is little mentioned in most accounts, Poland had acquired reasonable stocks of the Swedish 37-millimeter antitank gun, which by the standards of the 1930s was a potent weapon, as it fired a .74-kilogram shell at 850 meters per second, and was thus capable of penetrating the armor of any German tank in service in September 1939.[5]

The only way Germany could come close to matching this in manpower was to pare the western defenses down to the bone, and in August 1939 that was precisely the situation: Germany deployed five armies (the Third and Fourth in Army Group North and the Eighth, Tenth, and Fourteenth in Army Group South), totaling 1,240,000, men. With another 276,000 allocated to the high command's reserves, this came to 1,516,000 men, somewhat less than the number of troops Poland could put into the field.[6]

Of course Germany was a much larger country than Poland. It could put 1.5 million men in the field in the east and still have a considerable army in the west, and Army Group C, charged with the defense of Germany's western frontier, comprised thirty-three divisions plus the Second and Third Air Forces, almost half a million men. The size of Army Group C is a not unimportant detail, and one often overlooked by analysts. These troops—and this is also contrary to the received wisdom— would be moving into fortifications that were largely completed, and particularly so in the key areas where the French would likely mount an offensive.[7]

The fact that Poland could deploy as many men against a German offensive as the Germans could is usually dismissed as irrelevant, given the German strength in weaponry. There is certainly no doubt that the Germans had more and better weapons than their opponents, but the German advantage was not nearly so overwhelming as claimed. In August 1939 Germany lacked either the doctrines, the command commitment, or the equipment to engage in breakthrough warfare.

Most German tanks, for example, were obsolete Mark 1 and Mark 2 vehicles, which, as we have seen, were little more than tracked machine-gun carriers. There was in fact a sizable Polish armored force, consisting of some 700 light tanks, essentially modified versions of the British Mark 6 tank, and a mixed force of between 150 and 200 French R35, Vickers Export, and Polish 7TP tanks, all mounting 37- or 47-millimeter guns.[8] The Poles were outnumbered by about two to one (at least), but being outnumbered is not the same as having none at all.

In his postwar interrogation by the American air force, Gen. Paul Deichmann estimated Germany's strength (committed to an attack against Poland) as 1,588 "first-line" aircraft, to Poland's 400.[9] Knowing they faced an attack that would come as a tactical surprise, the Polish air command moved its planes off the main airfields, saving them for a future counterstroke. In their attempt to save their air force, to keep it intact, they failed to make the all-out commitment in the first days of the war necessary to blunt the German attack. Attempting to keep their air force, they ended up losing it one plane at a time—and the country as well. In hindsight, an obvious mistake. But Poland was the first country whose air commanders had to face this decision. When it was the turn of Great Britain and France in 1940, the mistake was repeated—and with even more disastrous results.

Poland's Defense

Poland is a surprisingly large country whose terrain is divided into clear sections by its major rivers. A fighting retreat slowly south and east, destroying the bridges across the rivers, would have a powerful effect on the speed of any advance. An important consideration, as the Poles really believed that if they could stall the German advance for two to three weeks, Allied pressure would bring an end to offensive operations in Poland. And Poland's military strength, as we have noted earlier, was hardly negligible.

The three most significant aspects of the German plan of attack had nothing whatsoever to do with mechanization. First was the decision to attack without warning. Presumably this was both to deprive the defenders of the opportunity to mobilize and to allow the execution of an air campaign in conformance with Douhet's ideas that the only successful way to wage one was by a surprise attack that would destroy the enemy before it had the chance to get its bombers into the air and destroy you. This last leads to one of the few truly novel aspects of the

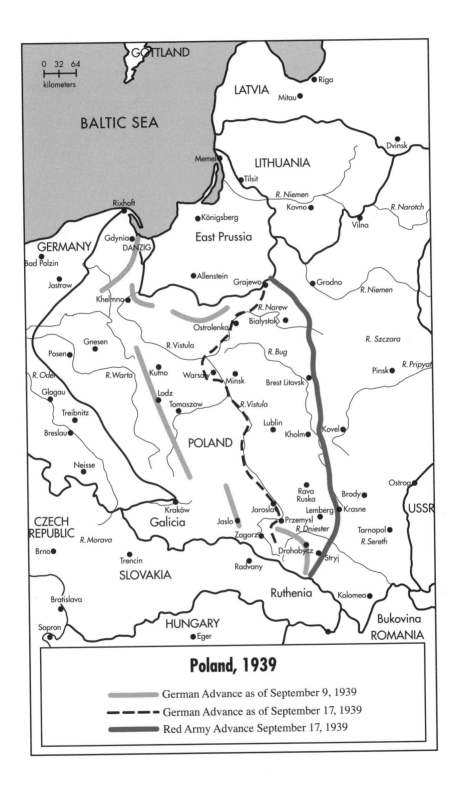

Poland, 1939

━━━ German Advance as of September 9, 1939
╍╍╍ German Advance as of September 17, 1939
━━━ Red Army Advance September 17, 1939

Map labels:

GOTTLAND

BALTIC SEA

0 32 64 kilometers

LATVIA
Riga
Mitau

Dvinsk

Memel
Tilsit
LITHUANIA
R. Niemen
Kovno
Vilna
R. Narotch

Rixhoft
Königsberg
East Prussia

GERMANY
Gdynia
DANZIG
Bad Polzin
Jastrow
Khelmno
Allenstein
Grajewo
Grodno
R. Niemen

R. Narew
Ostrolenka
Bialystok
R. Szczara

Gnesen
Posen
R. Vistula
R. Bug
Pinsk
R. Pripyat

R. Oder
R. Warta
Kutno
Warsaw
Minsk
Brest Litovsk
Glogau
Lodz
Treibnitz
Tomaszow
R. Vistula
Breslau
Lublin
Kholm
Kovel
Neisse
POLAND

Rava Ruska
Brody
Ostroa
Kraków
Galicia
Jaslo
Jarosla
Lemberg
Krasne
USSR
CZECH REPUBLIC
Zagorz
Przemysl
R. Dniester
Tarnapol
R. Morava
R. Sereth
Brno
Drohobycz
Trencin
Radvany
Stryj
SLOVAKIA
Ruthenia
Kolomea
Bratislava
Bukovina
Sopron
HUNGARY
Eger
ROMANIA

German attack: It would be the first time when one country attacked another from the air without warning. The mission of the Luftwaffe was to destroy the Polish air force (particularly its bases), interdict communications, and prevent the movement of troops and equipment. Contrary to Douhet's ideas, prevalent beliefs about how airpower would be used, and subsequent propaganda, strategic bombing was not a part of the plan. Air attacks on Warsaw as a city began only after its refusal to surrender.

This seems to contradict much that has been said, and so much eyewitness testimony, that it deserves a brief note of explanation. A chapter that follows examines the issue of accuracy in aerial bombardment in some detail, but the short answer is simple enough: There wasn't any. This was why the Luftwaffe had become so interested in what was being done by the American navy to develop what was called the dive-bomber.[10]

In the event, however, the Luftwaffe entered the war with just over 350 JU 87 dive-bombers, airplanes that subsequently became known as the infamous Stukas. But the bulk of the bombing force, about 1,100 planes in 1939, consisted of level-flight bombers, and the 1,200-odd fighter planes on hand were also capable of limited ground attack missions. So essentially the JU 87, the only reasonably accurate delivery system the Luftwaffe possessed, constituted only a fraction of the ground attack force.[11]

The use of the air force to deliver an attack coordinated with the ground assault was thus quite new. In general it was successful, although the Luftwaffe losses for this campaign (more than a third of its aircraft out of action or destroyed) suggest that the German air force did not achieve its primary mission of establishing mastery of the air over Poland. What it by all accounts did was destroy the ability of the Polish high command to conduct a coordinated defense, thus enabling the German army to defeat the Polish forces in detail in a series of confused engagements that lasted most of September.

A third novel feature of the German offensive gets hardly any attention at all, and yet in some measure was the most significant. This was the use of airborne troops to seize the bridges the advancing ground forces would need if they were to move rapidly into the country.

The problem in using airborne troops quickly revealed itself. The presence of the planes betrayed any surprise, and there was no way to ensure that parachutists would land in a group near their objective. In fact the history of airborne operations in the Second World War is a sad record of dispersed drops that landed the hapless airborne troops everywhere but near their objectives. The men then paid for this failure with their lives. Airborne troops were too lightly armed and too immobile to be capable of fighting their way to a defended target.

Since these first airborne operations were failures, it is easy to see why they were ignored. But in the German army, as in any competent organization, men studied failure and made their plans accordingly. On May 10, 1940, the Allies would find out the cost of ignoring the lessons of Poland: German airborne units were landed all over Belgium, Holland, and Luxembourg. And this time, by and large, they were successful.

Seizing bridges ahead of your advance and destroying your enemy from the air in a surprise attack were key elements in achieving a quick

In the early years of the war, the Junkers 87D Dive-Bomber, often known simply as the Stuka (an abbreviation of the German word for dive-bomber), enabled a level of accuracy in air-to-ground operations unattainable with ordinary level-flight tactical bombers. Although successive modifications enabled the 87 to carry up to 1,500 kilograms of bombs, the plane was far too slow—it remained in service after 1941 only because of the failure of the aircraft industry to produce a modern replacement. (*National Archives*)

victory. As the Germans figured on an Allied response within fourteen days of the attack, the emphasis was on speed.[12] The Poles had prudently moved their planes out of range of the first attacks, which largely destroyed abandoned airfields. The problem the Poles faced was one that would become familiar in later wars: The disruption of the air force command and control facilities by the Germans in the first few days of the war reduced the Polish air force to independent units blindly attacking the enemy. It was in precisely such circumstances that the superiority of German aircraft, notably the ME109, became decisive.

Although little noted as such, Poland is the first instance of what has by now become a familiar dilemma in aerial warfare: Does one throw up all of one's planes in an attempt to inflict crippling losses on the enemy, even though this will result in the loss of one's own air force? Or does one hold back and wait for the right moment? Close study of the Polish case suggests that the only option is to throw everything in the air—the air force commander who waits will end up with no planes to commit and no way to direct them. Like all the lessons of the Polish campaign, this one was lost on the rest of the world.

Paradoxically it was the Third Army, the least mechanized of all the German armies, which made the most rapid progress in the first seventy-two hours of the war, crossing the Vistula above Bydgoszcz (in German, Bromberg) and linking up with elements of the Fourth Army by Tuesday, September 3. Thus the whole Polish corridor was cut off and occupied almost immediately, with the Polish parts of Danzig (Gdansk) surrendering on the first day of fighting. This was of considerable importance, as it meant that the Germans had an uninterrupted ground supply route connecting East Prussia—the base of the Third Army—with the rest of Germany, once they had repaired or replaced the bridges.

Virtually every student of the war is familiar with the famous account of how a then unknown German general, Heinz Guderian, commander of the Fourth Army's Nineteenth Armored Corps, began his own personal war. The passage, however, is worth study:

> There was a thick ground mist which prevented the air force from giving us any support. I accompanied the 3rd Panzer Brigade. . . . Unfortunately, the heavy artillery of the 3rd Panzer Division felt itself compelled to fire into the mist, despite having received precise orders not to do so. The first shell landed fifty yards ahead of my command vehicle, the second 50 yards behind it. I reckoned the next one was

bound to be a direct hit and ordered my driver to turn about and drive off. The unaccustomed noise had made him nervous, however, and he drove into the ditch at full speed. . . . This marked the end of my drive. I made my way to my corps command post, procured myself a fresh vehicle, and had a word with the over-eager artillery-men. [13]

This inauspicious start was followed by an even more vexatious incident:

After successfully changing vehicles, I rejoined the 3rd Panzer Division whose most forward troops had now reached the Brahe [river, about 25 kilometers from the start line]. The bulk of the division was between Prisczcz and Klein-Kolonia and was about to settle down for a rest.

That is, having advanced approximately fifteen kilometers and broken through the first line of Polish defenses, the troops commanded by Germany's greatest exponent of the Blitzkrieg now proposed to "settle down for a rest." Nor should they be blamed. As Guderian recounts, their lead vehicles had encountered Polish antitank gunners, who "had scored many direct hits," killing ten men, including two officers.

As is well known, Guderian took charge personally and followed the advice of a young officer who was of the opinion that the Brahe could be forded. And so it was, after Guderian put a stop to "the idiotic firing" of his tankers and infantry, who were happily blazing away at the entrenched enemy on the opposite bank.

A litany of errors and hesitancy is not surprising with an army composed mostly of new recruits, but the sequence of events Guderian relates makes pretty clear that the Germans had no preconceived doctrine that required them to make deep armored thrusts as they broke through. Like any army they advanced, and when they reached what they perceived as a major obstacle, they stopped. The other two components of Guderian's army corps fared little better. By dawn the next day, the twentieth Motorized Division was camped out in the town of Konitz, about a kilometer across the border, and the Second Motorized Division had hardly cleared the border.

None of this is to denigrate Guderian's leadership, and by the morning of the fourth, Guderian's troops had advanced about fifty kilometers and crossed the Vistula. The point, rather, is this: The fighting described is highly conventional, revealing an advance on a broad front with the aim of defeating the enemy in detail as its troops appear or attempt to counterattack.

Moreover, although Guderian glosses over this in his memoir, in reality his armor ran out of fuel and ammunition on the second day of the advance, forcing infantry and supply units to fight their way through to them. It was this engagement which gave rise to the quasi-legend of Polish cavalry attacking tanks. In actuality, the cavalry were overrunning the infantry who were trying to link up with Guderian's stalled armored columns.

The Polish army was simply overpowered by the force of the German offensive, in which airpower and infantry were closely integrated. Unlike the Poles, the Germans were willing to lose planes in order to maintain the rhythm of their attacks, and did so. Analysts are quite correct to note that the real key to German success lay in the integration of the two forces, particularly given the Luftwaffe's superiority over the battlefield.[14] But the reality of the powerful armored thrusts achieved much less than was claimed. Guderian's fuel problem illustrated two problems no theorist had foreseen. The armored enthusiasts of the 1920s and 1930s had postulated their operations as though the tank were a perpetual-motion machine impervious to mechanical failure. In reading Fuller's breathless descriptions of how future wars would be won by great armored thrusts, anyone with any vehicular experience must surely be muttering under his or her breath, but what happens when they run out of fuel? All four of the early models of German tanks had a fuel consumption of more than one liter per kilometer, and their maximum range, motoring along on a hard-surfaced road, was barely 150 kilometers; cross-country it was usually two-thirds of that.[15]

There was thus a practical limit to an armored thrust: It had to be within refueling distance of its fuel trucks. As there is hardly anything quite so volatile as a tanker truck on a battlefield, this put an extremely effective cap on the speed of any advance. The predicament in which Guderian's tankers found themselves suggests a second problem. Armored columns have their own unique vulnerabilities. When immobilized they become easy targets for a determined infantry. This was particularly true for the thin-skinned armored vehicles of the German armored divisions in 1939: Stalled and drawn up in a column, they were so many targets. The ferocity of the Polish counterattacks suggests that this was not lost on the Poles. On September 5 Polish tankers managed to knock out thirty German vehicles with the loss of only two of their own, and as the campaign progressed, Polish infantry and cavalry (which, contrary to legend, mostly fought dismounted) had begun to develop tactics for attacking tanks, when, operating in columns, they became stalled.[16]

On Friday the eighth German newspapers announced that their troops had reached Warsaw. Broadcasting from Berlin, William Shirer didn't detect much rejoicing in the capital over the news of this great victory—whose announcement turned out to be premature, as Warsaw actually held out for weeks. But the propaganda moves were shrewdly timed. They encouraged the Allies to believe that Poland had already collapsed, and although Stalin doubtless had his own intelligence sources, the German news strengthened his hand, giving greater plausibility to his bland announcement on the seventeenth that his armies were advancing into a Poland that no longer existed.

In his nightly broadcast that Friday, Shirer spoke of the campaign as though it was finished, beginning:

> It was just two weeks ago this Friday morning that the Germans began what they call their great counter-attack against Poland. In fourteen days the mechanized German military machine has rolled back the Polish army some 200 miles, captured 100,000 prisoners, including entire divisions with their staffs and guns, surrounded the capital and—so it is believed here—practically liquidated Poland in a military sense."

Clearly the Germans had every reason to make the claim, and, as we have seen, the Allies every reason to accept the claim, as it absolved them of doing anything significant to come to Poland's aid. In fact, at almost precisely the time the Germans announced the fall of Warsaw, on the eighth, the Polish Poznan and Pomorze Armies counterattacked, fighting what the Poles call the Battle of Bzura, which lasted until the twenty-first. A similar effort was involved around the city and fortress of Lvov, which the Germans attacked on the twelfth.

That these cities (and others) were still holding out after the fifteenth suggests that the new German method of warfare had failed to solve a fundamental problem: how to capture a city. Other than Danzig (which was largely German anyway) and Kraców (a historic city the Poles didn't try to defend), the Germans had basically been unable to seize any of the country's major urban centers in the first two weeks.

In August, Stalin and Hitler had agreed on how to divide up Central Europe. Now that he was sure that the Allies would not open much of a war on the Western Front, Stalin acted. On Sunday, September 17, the Polish ambassador was told that as his country no longer existed, the Red Army would have to move in to "protect" non–Polish nationals living in the eastern part of the country.[17]

Now Poland fought on alone, conscious that there would be no aid. On the seventeenth, the Germans destroyed one of the last intact Polish armies, at Kutno, and captured Brzeg. On the nineteenth the Polish government fled into Romania. On the twenty-first, Lvov surrendered, followed by Warsaw (on the twenty-eighth). Still the Poles continued their struggle. The last major force wasn't defeated until October 6, at Kock.

Conclusions, True and False

Everyone agreed that Poland had been crushed—and quickly—by the speed of the mechanized German army. When Shirer calculated it for his audience on September 8, 1939, he calculated it, with reasonable accuracy, as being "about twenty-five miles a day."[18] Impressive, but this— roughly what a German infantryman could cover on his own two legs—was almost precisely the average covered in August 1914.[19] And in fact the infantry of the thirty-eight German divisions (including the three mountain divisions) comprising the first wave of Army Groups North and South marched through Poland at about the same speed as their fathers had marched through Belgium, France—and Russian Poland—in 1914.

Poland in 1939 was no exception. Most German soldiers were in infantry divisions, and they advanced—and fought—on foot, one reason why on several occasions Polish cavalry attacks were quite successful. And indeed the Germans themselves used cavalry units throughout the war, beginning with September 1939, when a cavalry brigade was deployed out of East Prussia. It is often said that although most German soldiers were footbound infantry, the real successes around which victory was built were scored by the mechanized troops, particularly the armored divisions. But an examination of the German high command's own situation maps reveals this to be quite untrue. Although the armored divisions were, particularly in the south, clearly in the first wave of attacking divisions, they were mixed in with the other units: Thus on September 3, 1939, at what the high command saw as the close of the first phase of Army Group South operations, the two divisions shown as having the greatest penetration were the forty-sixth Infantry Division (advancing on Końskie), and the twenty-forth Infantry Division, which had crossed the Bzura north of Lodz.[20]

Fuller had opined that in a future war, the infantry would have to be in an armored vehicle: The Wehrmacht went through the entire war heavily dependent on footbound infantry and horse-drawn artillery. In 1940 all its opponents were more heavily mechanized than were the Germans themselves, and as late as 1944 it was still the least mechanized (or motorized) army in combat.

Polish casualties were heavy, German casualties were light; but this obscures the situation. Germany attacked Poland with a force of about 1.5 million men and suffered roughly forty thousand casualties over the course of the six weeks of fighting.[21] Polish killed and wounded came to about two hundred thousand, not counting prisoners of war—most of whom died in prison as the result of harsh treatment.[22] One speaks of the "destruction" of the Polish army, but this was hardly the case. By May 1940 there were 84,500 Polish soldiers fighting with the Allies in France, Norway, and Syria. Even though most of these men were trapped inside France and had to surrender, by 1944 Poland was contributing an airborne brigade and an armored division to the fighting in France, and an army corps (two infantry divisions and an armored brigade) in Italy. Polish aviators formed a significant component of the RAF in the Battle of Britain, and the post-1939 Polish naval flotilla was surprising: two cruisers, ten destroyers, and eight submarines. If Hitler and Stalin had intended to destroy Poland completely, they hardly succeeded.

During the course of the fighting, the Poles put 674 tanks out of commission, along with 319 armored cars, 6,046 trucks, and 5,538 motorcycles. Given the woeful inadequacy of German tank production, these losses were hardly trivial: Given the revised tables of strengths, Poland cost Germany an entire armored division.[23] More troubling was the high proportion of the "main" battle tanks totally destroyed in combat: 45 Mark 3 and 4 vehicles, which were supposedly the backbone of the armored spearhead. German aircraft losses too were surprisingly high: 564 aircraft out of commission, of which 285 were totally destroyed.[24] Based on the generally accepted figures for the numbers of aircraft deployed, this suggests that the Germans lost close to 40 percent of their air strength. Germany was militarily much weaker in October 1939 than it had been in August.

The Poles had been promised military assistance by both Great Britain and France. When the war broke out, the British retaliated with a series of strategic bombing raids, and the French mounted an armored thrust into Germany. Both offensives were conducted in accordance with the theories of how airpower and armor should be used, and both immediately failed.

Douhet had postulated that the bomber would always get through, and that ground-to-air defenses were useless.[25] But the RAF attacks of September 1939 were costly failures.[26] The raids were a failure of such dimensions that the RAF's whole approach to strategic bombing had to be reconsidered: By the spring of 1940 the RAF had stopped daylight bombing operations entirely, and flew only at night, when the Luftwaffe's air defenses were minimally effective. Had the fall 1939 bomber raids continued with the same rate of loss, Great Britain's strategic bomber force would have been wiped out in a few months.

When the Poles had asked the French for concrete plans of assistance, they had been told that there would be a ground offensive within fourteen days of mobilization. In reality, Gen. Maurice Gamelin, the French commander, had begun an offensive across the Franco-German frontier much earlier than that. Like the British, the French attacked; and like their ally, they promptly discovered that the theories of the prewar period didn't work. In the French case the theory was that armor could break through defensive positions and thus avoid the slaughter of the infantry that had been such a horrific part of the Allied offensives of the First World War.

The French felt that the most vulnerable part of their common border was the Saar, and that was where they planned their attack, spearheaded by the 504th Groupe de Battalions de Chars, consisting of 180 R-35 tanks, backed up by the infantry of the Fourth North African Division. On the left of the Fourth North African Division were two additional North African divisions (the Second and Third), and over on the far right were the Fifteenth Mechanized Division and the Fourth

Colonial Division—all powerful units, mechanized and well armed.[27]

As the R-35s of the Twentieth BC went to the attack on the morning of Saturday, September 9, they promptly ran into a minefield. They had already negotiated their way around one such obstacle, but the second one caught them by surprise: Four tanks of the Third Company were blown up, and three others were lost as they tried to work around the mines.[28] When the tankers tried to extricate themselves, they discovered the area was sown with antipersonnel mines as well. Sublieutenant Rousseau was killed by one of them, thus becoming the first Allied tanker killed in the Second World War. In effect, by Monday the armored spearhead was stopped, entangled in a maze of minefields and tank traps and unable to engage. When the twenty-sixth Infantry Regiment called for help, the tankers were unable to come to the infantry's assistance, owing to the mines.

Airpower theorists had scoffed at antiaircraft guns; armored theorists hadn't even considered the impact of the land mine. An armored attack deployed into a minefield was an invitation to slaughter. French tankers, like British bomber pilots, may be forgiven their hesitation in the face of an unforeseen and potent threat. The mine and the tank trap rendered most ideas of armored warfare moot. In Poland the Germans had discovered that the practical limit of an armored advance was determined by the speed with which secure fuel supplies could follow. In practice this meant a rate of advance little faster than that of a decently trained infantry division. And now French armored commanders were learning the practical limitations posed by a prepared defense.

Hitler, flushed with success after Poland, immediately ordered an attack in the west.[29] Gamelin, the French commander, alerted by his intelligence services, did what any prudent commander would do: He began to dispose his forces to fend off the attack he had been told was in the offing.

Finland

During the 1930s Hitler's propagandists had conducted an extremely skillful campaign in which they bamboozled almost all foreign observers into the belief that their army and air force were enormously larger and more potent than they really were. Consequently the Allies believed that

Germany was considerably more efficient at building armaments than it in fact was. As we have seen, German tank production was leisurely to the point of inactivity: Less than fifty tanks were produced in the fall of 1939. No attempt had been made to put the economy on a wartime footing, and certainly nothing remotely approaching what had been done in 1914–18.[30]

While the Allies tried to devise a working strategy against Hitler, Stalin struck again. His pact with Hitler was not, as is often believed even today, simply a nonaggression pact. What Hitler and Stalin had done was to roll back the national frontiers to July 1914. Hitler was given the territory of the two German emperors, and Stalin the territory of the Romanovs.

All the historic Romanov territory that had been lost postwar now consisted of separate states established by populations who were emphatically against a Russian, much less a Soviet, occupation. But Stalin manufactured a series of provocations, and over the course of the next eighteen months, the Soviet Union absorbed Estonia, Latvia, Lithuania, and Moldova.[31] And in November 1939 Stalin attempted to complete his territorial acquisitions by occupying Finland, which made clear just how openly and ruthlessly he was proceeding.

Little is known about the Russo-Finnish conflict, and, perhaps as a consequence, it is usually thought to have no real bearing on the course of the Second World War. A discussion of the political and strategic relevance of this war to the larger flow of history lies outside the subject of this book.[32] But the war itself is important: It demonstrates that the two foundations of the Blitzkrieg, armor and airpower, were not nearly the mystical combination everyone had assumed after the fall of Poland.

The Winter War (1): The Failure of Airpower

Having determined to attack Finland, the Soviet Union proved itself an enthusiastic supporter of Douhet. It began the war by conducting a massive aerial bombardment of the Finnish capital, Helsinki. As had been the case in Poland, the attack was a de facto declaration of war, and thus achieved what Douhet had argued was the vital element: surprise. This was in fact precisely the kind of indiscriminant bombing of civilians that President Roosevelt had asked the combatants to avoid. But since it was

Scandinavia, 1939–1940

▬▬▬ Red Army Offensives Against Finland, 1939–1940
▬▬▬ German Landings, Norway, April 8, 1940
IIIIIIIII Anglo-French Landings, Norway, April 10–May 27, 1940

North Cape

North Sea

Hammerfest
Vagso
Vardo
Petsamo
Murmansk
SOVIET UNION

Narvik
Saila
Kandelaksha
Kiruna
Keraijarvi
Gallivare
Rovaniemi
Bodo
IRON ORE MINES

Lulea
Gulf of Bothnia
Oula
FINLAND

Namos
Vindel An

Molde
Alesund
Trondheim
Dombas

Lillehammer
SWEDEN
Turku
Vupuri
Hamar
Helsinki
Gulf of Finland
Leningrad
Bergen
NORWAY
Hanka
Narva
Oslo
Talinn
Haugesand
Larvik
Stockholm
ESTONIA
Stavanger
Kristiansand
Baltic Sea
Pskov
Cape Lindesnes
Skagerrak
Göteborg
Gottland
Riga
Libau
LATVIA
Kattegat

Arhus
Memel
DENMARK
Copenhagen
Kovno
Odense
Malmö
LITHUANIA
Königsberg
R. Niemen
Danzig
EAST PRUSSIA (Germany)
Hamburg
Stettin
R. Elbe
GERMANY
POLAND
R. Weser
R. Oder

0   150   300
kilometers

by now an article of faith that the Germans had done this in Poland, the point was moot.

What was not was the almost comical inaccuracy of the raids. The first Soviet planes had appeared over Helsinki at 9:20 A.M. on Thursday, November 30. A second wave appeared an hour later. The first attack had been directed at the airport, the second at the port and the railroad station. Having released their bombs, the planes then flew over the city, machine-gunning whatever they saw.[33]

Helsinki had no air defenses. Indeed Finland hardly had an air force, and so the bombers weren't attacked. Visibility on this Tuesday was apparently perfect. The Soviet bombing attack was thus conducted under ideal conditions, and conformed perfectly to Douhet's recipe for a surprise attack from the air. Scores of civilians were killed, most of them when bombs were dropped on the square in front of the train station. The station itself, like the port and every other militarily important target, went unscathed. At the airport the bombers hit one hangar. Downtown they bombed the Soviet legation to Finland, although one presumes this was by accident. The most noteworthy fact was that this surprise bombing raid failed even to hit such highly visible and completely undefended structures, despite making low-level bombing attacks. Remarkable too was the behavior of the civilian population, which, as Tanner remarked, seemed to ignore the falling bombs.

Soviet bombing raids continued throughout the war, but foreign aid was received until the end of the war; the only bottleneck in receiving it was on the other end. The Allies were reluctant to make the commitment in equipment needed. They assumed, based on their appreciation of the Polish experience, that Finland would fall in a few weeks at most, and that any equipment sent would thus be lost. The Soviet high command planned for a twelve-day campaign. Given Finland's lack of tanks, aircraft, and artillery, as well as its size, the question arises as to how the Finns managed to hold out as long as they did—until the middle of March 1940.

Part of the key lay in the incredible ineffectiveness of strategic airpower. Although Douhet had not considered this in detail, it is clear from what he wrote that in his view the best attack was a surprise attack: It was those early raids that would destroy the enemy's means of waging war and will to fight.

Over the course of the war, the Soviet air force claimed to have flown more than forty thousand sorties, and the Finns recorded 2,075 separate strategic bombing attacks. Finnish civilian losses were about 2,600 killed and wounded.[34] Somewhere between three and four hundred Soviet planes were shot down by Finnish antiaircraft defenses, and Finland's handful of pilots claim to have shot down another two hundred. Such figures suggest a low level of military effectiveness on the part of the Soviet air force.

The Winter War (2): The Failure of Armor

Like the Germans in Poland, the Soviet plan for the invasion of Finland consisted of a broad-front attack: Technically there were ten separate offensive operations, all timed to launch simultaneously. The most significant of these thrusts was the one in southeastern Finland, known as Karelia. The logic of the thrust was simple: Karelia was the gateway to the southern Finnish coast. Once it was taken—along with Helsinki—the rest of the country, given how far north Finland is, would be entirely cut off.

To that end the Russian deployed nearly as many tanks in their Karelian offensive as the Germans had for the entire Polish offensive. Meretskov, the hapless Soviet general who had been given the task of breaking through Karelia, had more than one thousand tanks for his 120,000-man force. Surely this was the armor to infantry ratio that any tanker had dreamed of during the interwar years.

Moreover, the Soviet Union had not made the mistake that the Germans (and the French, British, and Americans) had made in tank development. Although none of the later famous T34 tanks were committed to this campaign, the Soviet Union had already built fast, powerful tanks with potent guns. In fact the very excellence of the T34 has obscured the accomplishments of Soviet tank designers in the 1930s.

As is well known, early Soviet tank designs derived from the experimental vehicles developed by the American inventor Walter Christie, the first man to build a truly fast tank. The story of American tank design is a sorry one, and nothing illustrates just how appalling it was than the rejection of Christie's designs. It was true that in his obsession with speed, Christie built tanks with numerous problems. But his basic suspension design, easily identified by the four to six large wheels on each track, was the basis for all successful postwar tank suspension systems.

As in France, Soviet designers constructed numerous tanks, all of which were in service in 1939. The most threatening of these was the KV-1, the best heavy tank in the world in 1939. It mounted the same 76.2-millimeter gun later made famous by the first production runs of the T-34, and, despite its 43,000-kilogram weight, it had good cross-country performance and a surprisingly high top speed of thirty-five kilometers an hour. The reason for the great weight was the armor: the KV-1 had 30 millimeters of frontal armor, which meant that it was impervious to other tanks, and to all antitank guns then in service.[35] So the Soviets had developed excellent tanks and then produced them in quantity. There was basically no comparison between the overweight, underpowered, underarmored, and undergunned German tank force of 1939 and its Soviet equivalent.

The usual caveat is that the Red Army had no idea what to do with its tanks, but this is hardly borne out by either the various service regulations distributed by the Red Army in the 1930s or the accounts of foreign military observers. Great Britain's Colonel Martell, who saw Soviet maneuvers in September 1936, described the tank deployments as "brilliant," an opinion apparently shared by the French observer, General Loizeau.[36]

In actual fact Soviet doctrine seems to have adhered almost completely to Fuller's idea of the use of armor in great masses to effect breakthroughs, and Soviet regulations of the period spoke of the need to penetrate the enemy positions in depth. Where the Soviets differed from Fuller was in their adherence to the importance of the role of infantry. Like the French and the Germans, the Red Army saw a successful offensive as requiring the coordination of all arms of service: "The isolated use of different arms would give the advantage to the enemy: it would give him the opportunity to strike our troops piecemeal, cause futile losses, and in due course bring defeat during a given stage of battle."[37]

There was hardly any difference between how the Germans and the French used tanks in September 1939 and how the Russians used them in December. The French and Russian deployments, in which tanks were to break through the defensive positions, probably corresponded more closely to the theories of men like Fuller than the German practice in Poland. And the Soviet Union was the only country capable of deploying a massed armored force of the sort that armored enthusiasts had advocated: fast, powerful vehicles with powerful guns and adequate armor.

But the Red Army ran into some of the same problems the French had encountered in their advance into the Saar. The Finns hadn't been able to devote the enormous sums of money to constructing fortifications that the French and the Germans had, nor did they possess the engineering skills French army engineers could bring to bear on matters military. But they had built a rough and rugged defensive line across most of the Karelian isthmus, and although Field Marshal Carl Gustaf Mannerheim, the Finnish commander, would later remark in some exasperation that the line that bore his name was nothing but the Finnish soldier in the snow, this is simply untrue. There were 109 reinforced concrete structures for the 130-kilometer stretch of the line.[38]

Perhaps more significant, the Finns had constructed a belt of antitank obstacles across the entire width of the isthmus. These obstacles, of the now familiar "dragon's teeth" variety, five to seven rows deep, appear to have been the same type of obstacle first deployed by the Czechs and then used by the Germans in the west with good effect.

Although it appears that no one in the west was watching, the performance of the Soviet-adapted Christie suspension more than vindicated Christie's principles: Russian tanks could often cross over the teeth, provided each tooth was short enough, while French (and later American) tanks were stopped cold. But such crossings were hazardous: The most vulnerable part of the tank, other than its tread, was its relatively unarmored underbelly. A tank that raised its underbelly up as it attempted to surmount an obstacle was vulnerable even to machine-gun fire, and unless the teeth were hit at precisely the right angle, they would snare a tread, leaving the vehicle a helpless target.

The problem for the Finns was that they had nothing like the required heavy weaponry for destroying armor even if it was immobilized. Desperate to stop the armored thrusts, they began to improvise. Finnish engineers developed two distinct types of mines, the first a steel pipe stuck in the ground, the second an almost undetectable (as it was antimagnetic) wooden box buried in the ground.

Mines, as the French had already discovered, either stopped tank advances outright or forced them to proceed behind a screen of infantry who looked for mines. In the west this involved magnetic detectors and sharp eyes. The Soviets used penal units who found the mines by trial and error. But in either case mines were formidable antitank devices whose impact on the battlefield armored theorists had totally failed to appreciate. The problem posed was so serious that as the war progressed, the British would develop an entire family of armored minesweepers designed to clear paths through minefields.

But such paths in themselves presented problems. In theory tanks didn't need roads: They could traverse fields, cross ditches, and lumber through forests. True enough, but their cross-country speed was much less than their speed on a road, even if it was no more than a deeply rutted track. The apparently open fields of Europe—including Poland and Finland—were in reality cut up by streams, ditches, stone walls, and small forests. The shortest, fastest, and safest way to get from one point to another was invariably by road, and tankers thus preferred roads right from the start.

Each geographical area had its own unique way of separating a road (whether paved or unpaved) from the terrain on either side: stone walls, ditches, streams, lines of densely planted trees (or even hedges). In 1939 very few roads in Europe simply cut across open terrain, absent any sort of barrier or natural barricade on either side. In Finland there was an added problem: Deep snowdrifts on either side that, during the winter, helped to keep the roads relatively clear of snow.

What the Allies would find out to their horror in Normandy in 1944, the Russians now found out to their consternation in Finland in 1939: An armored column moving down a road presented the same sort of hapless target as a barge moving down a canal. What was worse was that if the lead vehicle was immobilized, it was often impossible for the other vehicles to extricate themselves. Most roads were too narrow to allow a medium tank to turn around, and oftentimes the tank that used the roadside for this maneuver would tip over as the weight of the vehicle collapsed the side of the embankment or ditch running alongside.

Thus one mine, properly laid, could immobilize an armored column. The problem for the Finns was how to destroy the rest of it. In this respect the Finns were surprisingly well equipped. The Russians, like the French and the Germans, had quickly appreciated that armored columns without any supporting infantry were almost useless. There were too many situations in which tanks were held up by the sort of block just described. As the infantry depended on armored firepower to clear the way for them, so did the armor depend on the infantry.

Fuller had opined that the infantry would hardly be required on the future battlefield, and a generation of theorists had dutifully agreed. But when it came to actual deployment, everyone used the same formula of tanks plus infantry. Already the Red Army had realized that tanks made reasonably successful improvised personnel carriers: the infantry rode on the hull and dismounted once the shooting started. This was hardly as elegant as the German idea of designing special armored personnel carriers from which the troops could fight without even dismounting, but the Red Army was never much concerned about losses, and this method had the merit of being readily at hand: As the war progressed, scores of photographs would show Russian, German, and American troops clustered on tanks as they moved toward combat.

The weapon of the infantryman, however, remained the bolt-action rifle first perfected in the decades before the First World War. But the Finns, although lacking artillery and heavy machine guns, led the world in infantry weapons. Although Finnish soldiers were mostly equipped with Finnish-built and -modified versions of the old Russian Moisin-Nagant bolt-action rifle, they had two extremely potent weapons that in 1939 had no equal in any other army in the world.

The first of these was the ponderously named *Automaatikvaari Lahti-Saloranta Malli 26* machine gun. The M26, like the considerably more famous Browning automatic rifle (BAR) and the Bren gun, could be rested on a bipod or fired like a rifle. As it weighed 8.5 kilograms and had a barrel only 566 millimeters long, it was a handier weapon in this latter role. Unusual for the time, and like the contemporary assault rifles used by modern armies, the M26 allowed the user to select between firing one round and automatic firing. With a muzzle velocity of eight hundred meters per second and a cyclical rate of fire of five hundred rounds a minute, this was a formidable weapon that could be fired by one man.[39]

As the references to the Bren and the BAR suggest, other countries (although not the USSR) had similar weapons; but in such armies, as was the case with the British and the Bren, the weapon was used in more or less the same way as ordinary tripod-mounted machine guns: Significantly, the British army's light-tracked tankette was known as the "Bren gun carrier." Lacking such luxuries, the Finns were reduced to using the M26 as Browning had originally intended the BAR to be used—as a sort of handheld automatic shotgun, and to telling effect.

The other, perhaps more famous, weapon was the *koompistolet*, generally known outside Finland as the Suomi. *More famous* is a relative term: Outside the world of small arms experts, the gun is virtually unknown, but it was one of the most influential weapons of its time. As the authors of the standard encyclopedia of automatic weapons put it: "The skillful use of the Suomi submachine gun by the Finnish Army demonstrated to the world that this weapon was vital in small-unit operations."[40]

It so impressed the survivors of the Red Army's disastrous winter campaign that the Russians began to introduce a version of it into their own ranks, where it became famous: judging from wartime photographs, the PPSh submachine gun was almost the standard weapon of the Soviet infantry.

The Suomi was in fact a sort of super–Tommy gun of the sort first popularized by gangsters in the United States. Unlike the American weapon, which had the relatively low muzzle velocity of under three hundred meters per second, the Suomi fired 9-millimeter shells at the respectable velocity of four hundred meters, and, like the much heavier M26, could be fired one shot at a time, as well as on automatic.

John T. Thompson, the inventor of the first "submachine" gun, had intended it for trench warfare, where, he realized, combat was all at relatively close range. There was no need to give a soldier a rifle accurate out to a range of one thousand meters if all his practical fighting would be at ranges of a tenth of that. Moreover, bolt-action rifles were inherently awkward and clumsy. The awkwardness came from the great length required to give them the range and penetrating power thought necessary, as well as providing a suitable holder for the bayonet. The clumsiness came from the length, but also from the necessity of pulling the bolt back after each shot in order to insert a new round into the chamber.

In retrospect weapons like the two Finnish guns were the only sensible solution to the changing realities of infantry combat. But the generals of the various armies all knew better. Hitler essentially forbade the deployment of the early versions of the assault rifle developed by the Germans, and the British army was still resisting the use of automatic fire weapons into the 1970s, the fear being that the inexperienced soldier would shoot off all his ammunition. Apparently no one had told the Finns about these problems, and so Finnish soldiers armed with automatic infantry weapons simply annihilated the supporting Russian infantry. As one of the senior Russian officers who survived this campaign would later recall, the Red Army had turned down rapid-fire weapons using the same argument used by other armies: They were only good for police work. But "now, having encountered the widespread use of submachine guns in the Finnish Army, we bitterly regretted these miscalculations," General Voronov remembered.[41]

The Winter War marked the first time a reasonably well-trained army had deployed automatic infantry weapons en masse, and the result was a slaughter.[42] So much for the infantry, but clearly machine guns were useless against tanks, and here the Finns adopted a rather suicidal weapon, later made famous as the Molotov cocktail. This was, quite literally, the creation of the country's state alcoholic beverages commission: An ordinary vodka bottle filled with a mixture of tar, gasoline, and low-grade fuel oil. At first these were ignited by the appallingly primitive technique of setting fire to a gasoline-impregnated rag that had been wrapped around the bottle, but in short order a more sophisticated model was produced in which the ignition was provided by an ampule of sulfuric acid. Over the course of the 108 days of fighting, the Finns used seventy thousand of these.[43]

British analysts had always claimed that the introduction of the tank on the battlefield in the First World War had caused widespread panic in the German army. Based on the tank losses suffered, this seems something of a stretch, but it was repeated so many times that it became accepted as axiomatic, and theorists like Fuller had basically posited that infantry confronted by armor was helpless and could easily be scattered.

The idea of giving the infantry the weapons to destroy tanks on their own was still in the future. But in their desperation, the Finns hit on this first as well. Taking on a tank, even with a portable rocket launcher such as the American Bazooka or British PIAT, requires a great deal of courage: a missed shot and the tank is quite capable of obliterating the gunner. Running up to a tank and tossing a Molotov cocktail at it takes both desperation and an almost suicidal approach to life. But it soon transpired that in a good many situations on the battlefield, the tank was vulnerable to just this sort of response. Over the course of the fighting the Soviets appear to have lost about half of their tank force.[44]

The Balance

Of course no one seriously believed that Finland could hold out. In this case it was like Poland, although with the advantage of being attacked only on one side, and having its supply routes to the west intact. What no one had anticipated, and certainly not the Red Army, was the appalling cost of the war to an attacker armed with the best and most modern weapons available to any army.

Finland lost 24,923 killed with another 43,557 wounded. As most

Finns would be quick to point out, in a country with a population of about four million, this was staggering. But Finland, although it lost territory and lives, remained a free country. Given what happened to the other countries Stalin devoured, this was no small achievement.

Initially the Soviets claimed to have lost "only" 48,745 dead and 149,000 wounded, but, like all other data released during Stalinist times, this figure is widely—and correctly—thought to be a fiction. The current estimate accepted by most Finnish historians is for a death toll in excess of a quarter of a million men, with another quarter of a million wounded. Khrushchev, in a famous passage in his memoirs, claimed that Soviet losses came to a staggering total: "I'd say we lost as many as a million lives."[45] It is fashionable to dismiss this figure as an exaggeration, but Khrushchev had access to data that ordinary historians did not have.[46]

Khrushchev's figures in other areas have proven if anything conservative. In 1956, for example, in a letter to the Swedish prime minister, he claimed that Russian losses in the Second World War were more than twenty million—this at a time when the official figure was about eight million and the internal accounting given to the Politbureau came to "only" fifteen million. But as Gen. Dimitrii Volkogonov remarks, "The only thing certain about his statement is the 'more than.'" The general's own accounting runs the total up as high as twenty-seven million.[47]

But either figure suggests an almost unparalleled slaughter several orders of magnitude beyond the defeat inflicted on Poland in 1939, or on the Allies in 1940. When mentioned at all in connection with the Second World War, the whole affair of Finland is dismissed with some disparaging remark about the ineptitude of the Red Army. But in January 1942, only twenty-two months after the end of the Winter War, this same army had fought the Germans to a standstill outside Moscow—with appalling losses, it is true, but massive institutions do not abruptly change course in the space of a dozen or so months.

The Finnish war is largely ignored in discussions of the Second World War because it disproves the cherished ideas of military theorists of the era. The reality was bad enough: Soviet airpower was ineffective, its armor deployment a failure. But this was not necessarily because of some inherent deficiency in the Red Army, caused by Stalin's purges or the failures of communism. Soviet equipment, by the standards of the period, was excellent, their doctrine pristine, and they applied the conventional wisdom as well as anyone could be expected to apply it in combat. The problem was quite simply this: The theories didn't work.

NOTES

1. François Furet, *The Passing of an Illusion: The Idea of Communism in the Twentieth Century,* trans. Deborah Furet (Chicago: University of Chicago Press, 1999), 315. Furet's *La passé d'une illusion*, published in France in 1995 by Robert Laffont, is the definitive essay on the subject, written by the man who was (he died in 1997) France's great authority on the French Revolution.

2. The most persuasive and comprehensive account of the precarious state of the Third Reich in summer 1939 is to be found in Donald Cameron Watt, *How War Came: The Immediate Origins of the Second World War* (New York: Pantheon, 1989), particularly 479–529. Frankly this is so much wishful thinking. But it was a belief widely held by people who should have known better; the Poles were as entitled to the belief as anyone.

3. "In 1940 our troops captured a letter, dated 10 September 1939, from General Gamelin [the French commander in chief] to the Polish military attaché in Paris. . . . It follows from this that Poland did in fact have a guarantee from the French. . . . Poland's defeat was the inevitable outcome of the Warsaw government's illusions about the actions its allies would take" (von Manstein, *Lost Victories*, 46). Von Manstein adds that it was also a function of the Polish army's "over-estimation" of its ability to offer lengthy resistance, but this is highly doubtful.

4. The exact figures are uncertain. Robert M. Kennedy, in *The German Campaign in Poland (1939)* (Washington, D.C.: Department of the Army, 1956), 51–52 gives a peacetime strength of 30 divisions, of which two were mountain, eleven "active" horse cavalry brigades and one motorized cavalry brigade. On mobilization fifteen reserve divisions would be created. Andrzej Suchcitz, in a monograph written for the Polish Ex-Combatants Association in Great Britain in 1995 to mark the fiftieth anniversary of the end of the Second World War, says that "Poland mobilized 39 infantry divisions, 3 mountain brigades, 2 motorized armored brigades, 10 cavalry brigades, artillery, engineers and other specialized formations" (2). The differences are probably a function of how much of its reserve Poland was able to mobilize and get into action, given the speed and tactical surprise of the German attack.

5. In the Polish service, this gun was called the wz.36. The 37-millimeter Bofors gun was such an excellent weapon that it was used by German mountain divisions, and, as the QF37-millimeter Mark I, by the British army. See the invaluable monograph by Chamberlain and Gander, *Anti-tank Weapons,* 36.

6. German figures in this and the following paragraph taken from Kennedy, *German Campaign in Poland,* 76–77.

7. Half of these divisions were third- and fourth-line units, but not much can be

drawn from that. During the First World War, German units of this same type, fighting from fortified entrenchments, routinely stopped Allied offensives with great loss to the attackers. The breakdown suggests that the Germans intended the same sort of defense: The inferior troops would man the static defenses, and the first-line units would mount countering attacks to destroy the attackers if they succeeded in a penetration.

8. The original Carden-Lloyd design was a true tankette, that is, a tracked vehicle without a revolving turret, and armed only with machine guns. Although the TK weighed half as much as the German Mark 1, it was faster, its armor protection was somewhat better, and it had a lower profile—all significant characteristics. In fact the TK series tanks were good enough for the Germans to refurbish and put into service. See the photographic essay in Werner Regenberg, *Captured Tanks in German Service: Small Tanks and Armored Tractors* (Altglen, Pa.: Schiffer Publishing Company, 1998), 5–11. A comprehensive albeit somewhat inaccurate table of comparative Polish and German armored strength is displayed in J. W. Kaufmann and H. W. Kaufmann, *Hitler's Blitzkrieg Campaigns* (Conschocken, Pa.: Combined Books, 1993), 68. The Kaufmanns are quite correct, however to assume that not all the tanks produced were actually involved.

9. Gen. Paul Deichmann (of the Luftwaffe), *German Air Force Operations in Support of the Army,* ed. Littleton B. Atkinson, USAF Historical Studies: Number 163 (New York: Arno Press, 1962), 154. Poland had nearly one thousand aircraft, organized into ten reconnaissance, seven fighter, seven fighter-bomber, and six liaison groups. Poland deployed abut four hundred fighter planes and about three hundred bombers. Many of these planes were obsolete. But the Luftwaffe began Polish operations with its own share of truly obsolete aircraft, the He–45 and He–46. The more modern of the two, the He–46, had been developed in 1930. As Deichmann points out, "The speed, operating range, and operating maximum altitude of this plane were inadequate for tactical reconnaissance missions," so the plane was obsolete in both of the first two senses as well (20). Clearly the Luftwaffe deployed planes that were inferior, obsolete, or unsuitable for their task.

10. The idea, which was borne out in countless tests, was that a plane diving almost vertically at a target, and then releasing its bombs just before it pulled up, had an enormously greater chance of actually hitting the target than did a plane in level flight. A dive-bomber could hit its target about 25 percent of the time. A level-flight bombing run basically had an accuracy of zero. See the analysis of dive-bombing in ibid., 34–38.

11. Accuracy is an elastic concept. In September 1939, in the dust-saturated landscape of Poland, German pilots couldn't tell friend from foe, or military from civilian. Columns of vehicles looked like columns of vehicles, regardless of what actually composed them. At the same time, in accordance with what the German air force had discovered in its dive bombing tests, the actual targets generally escaped without damage, thus fueling the feelings of those on the ground that they were being deliberately attacked. Problems with the Luftwaffe attacking German ground forces are mentioned

by Kennedy, *German Campaign in Poland,* 125, in his summary of what the Germans learned from their Polish offensive. This valuable study, the only analysis of the campaign prepared specifically for military use, is routinely neglected by British authors.

12. As Ernest R. May points out in *Strange Victory* (New York: Hill & Wang, 2000), hardly anything the French did was a secret to the Germans for very long. See his brief summary on 457.

13. Heinz Guderian, *Panzer Leader,* trans. Constantine Fitzgibbon (New York: Da Capo Press, 1996), 68.

14. The Swiss military historian Maj. Eddy Bauer provides the most succinct summary of this superiority: *La guerre des blindés* (Paris: Payot, 1962), 1:54.

15. Specifically: the Mark 1 ausführung B carried 145 liters of fuel, and had a highway range of 140 kilometers and a cross country range of 115 kilometers. The Mark 2 ausführung D carried 200 liters of fuel and had ranges of 200 and 130 kilometers. The Mark 3 ausführung D carried 300 liters of fuel had had ranges of 165 and 95 kilometers. The Mark 4 ausführung C carried 470 liters of fuel and had ranges of 200 and 130 kilometers (figures from Senger und Etterlin, *German Tanks of World War II,* 194–96).

16. See the brief account in Kaufmann and Kaufmann, *Hitler's Blitzkrieg Campaigns,* 90–91. The accounts of Polish cavalry attacking armored columns has its origins in German propaganda accounts; see the report of this in William L. Shirer, *This Is Berlin: Radio Broadcasts from Nazi Germany* (New York: Overlook Press, 1999), 77.

17. The pretext concerned the fate of the (mostly) Ukrainian peoples inside eastern Poland. In Soviet Ukraine, of course, about six million of them had already been deliberately starved to death under Stalin's rule. The figures are so high that no one really knows the details, but in a 1993 conference given by the Ukrainian Institute of History to commemorate the sixtieth anniversary of the famine, the estimates ranged from a low of four million to a high of seven million (AP Wire Service, May 12, 1993, 21:27 EDY V0037). Volkogonov says simply that the "collectivization of agriculture" between 1930 and 1935 killed 9.5 million people, but clearly this count includes the entire Soviet Union: Dmitrii Antonovich Volkogonov, *Autopsy for an Empire,* trans. Harold Shukman (New York: Free Press, 1998), 104.

18. William L. Shirer, *"This Is Berlin,"* 80. Shirer's censored broadcasts are an excellent source, as they give a measured day-by-day account of what seemed to be happening at the time—as opposed to what people said in retrospect was happening.

19. Comparisons with the earlier war produce some interesting conclusions. As we shall see in the chapter on May 1940, on several occasions German troops were in the same place they had been in August and September 1914, and after almost the same period of time had passed from their starting date.

20. This map is reproduced in Kennedy, *German Campaign in Poland,* as map 9. The First and Fourth Armored Divisions, and the Second and Third Light Divisions were also

in advanced positions, but it is not clear that they were any deeper into Poland than the infantry divisions.

21. There were 8,028 killed, 5,029 missing, and 27,278 wounded, according to Kennedy, *German Campaign* (120). Suchcitz (the monograph cited in note 3 above) has a slightly higher figure: 16,000 killed (he lumps the killed and the missing together) and 32,000 wounded (3). The difference is a function of the fact that the army figures only include army personnel, and exclude German air force losses. Although he makes some good points, the figures in Lt. Gen. Mieczyslaw Norwid Neugebauer, *The Defence of Poland*, trans. Peter Jordan (London: M. I. Kolin, 1942), 199–200, are clearly nothing more than propaganda, as are his conclusions. In *Hitler 1936–1945: Nemesis* (New York: W.W. Norton, 2000), 236 and notes 18–20, Ian Kershaw, who seems entirely ignorant of the Polish and American analysis of the casualties, reprints partial figures gleaned from German accounts: These are much lower, as they exclude the missing and the Luftwaffe personnel.

22. U.S. Army Signal Corps photographers documented some of this. See photographs in the National Archives 111-SC (World War 2) Box 61A: 203356S and 203360, for example.

23. In the last four months of 1939, Germany produced 247 tanks, and in the first four months of 1940, 304, including fifteen assault guns. Given the number of vehicles either destroyed outright or damaged beyond repair, German tank production between the two campaigns was barely sufficient to make up the losses. Data on tank production taken from U.S. Strategic Bombing Survey, *Strategic Bombing,* table 104, 278.

24. Loss figures from Kennedy, *German Campaign in Poland,* 120, Suchcitz's unpublished monograph cited in n 3 above (3), and Kaufmann and Kaufmann, *Hitler's Blitzkrieg Campaigns,* 92, are all in broad agreement. Matthew Cooper, *The German Air Force* (London: Jane's, 1981), 100, gives losses of about 500 aircraft out of 1,939 engaged, while Higham, in *Air Power,* 100, gives figures that come to 1,581 aircraft engaged, 285 lost, and another 279 damaged. The *Strategic Bombing* study does not break down German aircraft production figures by months prior to 1941, but as 8,295 aircraft were produced in 1939, and another 10,826 in 1940, it would seem that the Luftwaffe was easily capable of making up its equipment losses (table 101, 277). Trained aircrews were another matter, and this shortage was severe even before the start of the campaign. See the conclusion by Schliepahke, *The Birth of the Luftwaffe,* 57–58.

25. "For my part I maintain—and war experience has already confirmed me in my opinion—that the use of antiaircraft guns is a mere waste of energy and resources." Douhet, *Command of the Air,* 55. No clearer testimony to the remarkable power exerted by Douhet over air force planning than the note attached to this comment by Douhet's U.S. Air Force editors: "Since this was written, in 1921, antiaircraft fire has been greatly improved in both range and accuracy and has become immeasurably more effective.

Still, this does not alter the essential validity of the author's premise and argument" (55, note 3).

26. As were the raids later that fall. On December 18, 1939, for example, 9th Squadron lost five Wellingtons, 37th Squadron lost five Wellingtons, and 149th Squadron lost two Wellingtons, and the note to the loss of one of these planes, note 2962, says that "it was the first Wellington to be shot down during *this* operation" (26, emphasis added). This make a total of twelve planes lost. In *Famous Bombers of the Second World War* (Garden City, N.Y.: Hanover House, 1950), the usually authoritative William Green says that "ten aircraft were lost and three severely damaged" (65). See the loss data in W. R. Chorley, *Royal Air Force Bomber Command Losses of the Second World War* (Leicester, England: Midland Counties Publications, 1992), 1:14.

27. Confusingly, instead of calling their armored brigades by their logical name (armored brigades), the French used the idiosyncratic designation GBC, the idea being that a "group" could be expanded or contracted to suit the mission. The 504th GBC, which consisted of the ninth, tenth, twentieth, and twenty-second Battalions de Char (BC), each composed of forty-five R-35 tanks.

28. Data taken from the semiofficial account in Ramspacher, *Chars et blindés français*, 136.

29. The quote is from Liddell Hart's interview with Siewert, *The German Generals Talk,* 109. Liddell Hart links all this to the alleged "plots" to depose Hitler, but this is highly questionable.

30. Speer, *Inside the Third Reich,* 213; "Even at the heights of the military successes in 1940 and 1941 the level of armaments production of the First World War was not reached. During the first year of the war in Russia, production figures were only a fourth of what they had been in the fall of 1918. Three years later, in the spring of 1944, when we were nearing our production maximum, ammunition still lagged behind that of the First World War—considering the total production of Germany together with Austria and Czechoslovakia." See also ibid., note 19.

31. Soviet annexations were in two areas: (1) The Baltic. In September 1939, the Soviet Union forces Latvia and Estonia to sign "mutual assistance" treaties and let the Red Army occupy important areas. On June 17, 1940, Estonia was occupied by the Red Army, and in August the country was incorporated into the Soviet Union: Over the next year some fifty thousand Estonians were deported to labor camps. Latvia suffered the same fate at the same time, with about thirty thousand Latvians being sent to labor camps (where most of them died). After the occupation of Poland, Lithuania was forced to cede land, but in return received those parts of Poland that had been recognized as Lithuanian by the USSR in 1920. The usual "treaties" were signed, and on June 15, 1940, the country was annexed, being formerly incorporated into the Soviet Union in August. Lithuania was the least affected by deportations. (2) The Balkans. The land

between the Prut and the Dniester Rivers, now the country of Moldova, had historically been Russian, although the Romanians felt they had a claim to it, and in 1919, the Romanian army seized the area, which was incorporated into Greater Romania, although the Allies had not authorized this—it was a fait accompli. In the spring of 1940, therefore, Stalin took it back.

Although Romania was by now virtually a German satellite, Hitler forced the country to cede back the historically Hungarian Ardeal (Erdely) to Hungary, and the Dobruja to Bulgaria. At the same time the Hungarians negotiated a new frontier between Hungary and Slovakia. The net result of all these moves, triggered by the Hitler-Stalin pact, was to effect a return to the boundaries of 1914.

32. Two points that seem to me quite persuasive: (1) the capture of Soviet code-books by the Finns led directly and unambiguously to massive decrypting exercises that enabled the United States and Great Britain to understand the extent of Soviet penetration of their governments (these efforts are generally referred to under their code name, *Venona*); (2) that Finland was, as a result of the war, led to become an ally of Hitler's is disturbing confirmation of the starkness of the choices facing the smaller nations.

33. The most thorough account of the Russo-Finnish war is William R. Trotter's excellent and detailed *A Frozen Hell* (Chapel Hill, N.C.: Algonquin Books, 1991); information on the bombing raid comes from 48. As Trotter points out, there is excellent and hitherto undisclosed information in the appendixes to Eloise Engle and Lauri Paananen, *The Winter War* (New York: Charles Scribner's Sons, 1973). See also the general account of Finnish military history in Tomas Ries, *Cold Will: The Defence of Finland* (London: Brassey's, 1988).

34. Casualty data taken from Trotter, *Frozen Hell,* 188–91.

35. A limited number of these tanks saw service in the Winter War; the heavy tank available in the greatest numbers was the multiturreted T-35. See John Milsom, *Russian Tanks 1900–1970* (Harrisburg, Pa.: Stackpole Books, 1971), 117–19.

36. Milsom reprints their comments, ibid., 44–46. Of course the Soviets were masters at staging carefully choreographed events that dazzled Western observers, whether show trials or military exercises. But Martell in particular appears to have been a careful observer, and his internal reports to his superiors emphasized such practical factors as the high degree of Soviet mechanical reliability: that the Soviets could run 1,200 tanks for four days with "practically no mechanical trouble," as he recorded, suggests a high degree of competence.

37. As quoted at length by Milsom, *Russian Tanks,* 47, this article in the *Soviet Tank Journal* went on to conclude that the real value of infantry lay in maintaining a "tactical defense" during battle. Post-1945, Soviet tank experts postulated that this emphasis on cooperation was valid, as was, perhaps confusingly, the idea of the breakthrough. See the analysis by Colonel Begishev, as quoted by Milsom, *Russian Tanks,* 47.

38. See the analysis by Trotter in *Frozen Hell,* who inspected them himself: "[I]

crawled around inside one that looked as though it had been beaten into the earth with a giant ball-peen hammer—but enough was left to draw some conclusions. First of all, these were not anything as big or elaborate as the multilayered dinosaurs of the Maginot Line. They were, however, massive, thick, multichambered blockhouses; if manned by stubborn defenders they would have been very tough to take" (63). Trotter evaluates Mannerheim's contentions about the age and insufficiency of these fortifications and, rather diplomatically, suggests that they are highly misleading. The figure of 109 positions is Trotter's, citing an unnamed Finnish historian whom he alleges counted them all. Mannerheim's comment has a certain irony about it, as the good field marshal didn't speak Finnish.

39. Trotter, *Frozen Hell*, 44–46, calls attention to the importance of this weapon, which is so little known in the West that Peter Chamberlain and Terry Gander's authoritative *Machine Guns* (New York: Arco, 1974) doesn't even have a picture of it. Basic data taken from this text (9).

40. Thomas B. Nelson and Daniel D. Musgrave, *The World's Machine Pistols and Submachine Guns* (Alexandria, Va.: TBN Enterprises, 1980), 2A: 548–49.

41. As recorded by Trotter, *Frozen Hell*, 46. Basic data on Finnish small arms taken from ibid., 44–46.

42. Technically the Chaco War between Bolivia and Paraguay in the 1930s was the first occasion for this, but neither side was particularly well trained.

43. Production data taken from Engle and Paaranen, *Winter War*, 39.

44. No overall accounting has been made, but in *Frozen Hell*, Trotter enumerates five specific engagements and gives tank losses for each: 412 tanks captured or destroyed (121, 137, 140, 169, 221). Using the same ratios as prevailed in Finland (for every vehicle totally lost, two other were disabled on the battlefield but repairable), a reasonable total of slightly over 1,200 tank kills can be computed. In the conditions of the Winter War, the ratio may be erroneous, but, on the other hand, Trotter clearly does not give figures for every engagement fought, either.

45. Notice the qualifying "almost as." This passage is taken from *Khrushchev Remembers*, trans. Strobe Talbott (Boston: Little, Brown, and Company, 1970), 155.

46. For instance, I have an account from a woman whose father was an officer in the Red Army during the war. A friend of his managed to save him from deportation and certain death, but he never regained his former position. It is clear from her account that her father felt himself extraordinarily lucky to have escaped with his life, from which I infer that there were many other cases where this did not happen. The tendency of observers to overestimate losses has led historians to an almost reflexive compensation, often without performing the most elementary checks. Ries, in *Cold Will*, 125, apparently thinks the Soviet leader's figure is correct.

47. Volkogonov, *Stalin*, 505.

5.

The Germans and the Allies Prepare for War

I am just as puzzled as the French . . . at our [air] arrangements.
—HENRY POWNALL, BEF CHIEF OF STAFF[1]

In the spring of 1940 a series of events caused the German high command to change its plans for the constantly aborted offensive against France. Like the quasi-mythical Schlieffen Plan of August 1914, the new plan has exercised a peculiar fascination on military analysts. The story goes like this: Prior to January 1940 the German plan was entirely conventional, involving a broad thrust right through Belgium. The Allied armies would be defeated either inside that country or on the Franco-Belgian frontier. But on January 10, 1940, a German officer carrying a copy of the current offensive plan went down near Mechelen-sur-Meuse in Belgium. The officer attempted to destroy the documents, but an alert Belgian officer managed to retrieve most of them. Consequently the German high command believed that the Allies now knew the details of their offensive (whose latest starting date was, by coincidence, January 17, 1940).

This provided the impetus for a young staff officer, Erich von

Manstein, to develop a new and revolutionary plan in which a massive German armored force would traverse the Belgian Ardennes Forest, cross into France above Sedan, and cut off the advanced French and British forces like the sweep of a scythe—hence the name *Sichelschnitt* (scythe cut). This plan, which Hitler adopted over the objections of his generals, resulted in the brilliant German success of 1940.

Several stories ride along in the wake of this. The main one: In their various guises these emphasize the defensive mentality of the French, the foolish neutrality of the Belgians, the failure to appreciate the power of armor and the loss of air supremacy to the Germans. The only part of the story that redounds to the credit of the Allies is the successful evacuation of the bulk of the British army at Dunkirk.

Not surprisingly, given this last, the authors of these tales are British apologists. A more objective account of the events of 1940 makes clear that these stories are designed to justify a series of British blunders that led to the virtual abandonment of the continent to Hitler and Stalin, and the end of Great Britain as a major military power. Led by a great commander, Montgomery, British troops would return to Europe and participate in the victory over Hitler. But those soldiers would be mostly armed with American weapons, they would be operating under overall American command, and they would be vastly outnumbered by American soldiers.

The Scandinavian Obsession

Any discussion of May 1940 is complicated by the ineptitude of the leadership on both sides. On the Allied side the ineptitude may be explained quite simply: up until the moment of the actual attack, the Allies were focused on Scandinavia, an obsession culminating in their amateurish excursion against Norway. As Brian Bond remarks, "In the knowledge of the outcome of the German onslaught on the Low Countries and France in May 1940 it now seems almost incredible that in the period from January to April inclusive the Allies were more concerned, one might fairly say obsessed, with extending the war to Scandinavia."[2]

A study of the actual engagements in the Norwegian fiasco is far outside the thrust of this book. Other than demonstrating the almost total incompetence of the Allied military commands, it holds no particular military lessons for the course of the war, and its military importance to the war is peripheral.[3] But while a minor and insignificant operation in itself, it had enormous negative repercussions for both France and Great Britain. Thus a few words about the campaign are in order.

In the winter of 1939–40 the Allied leadership was pressed on two separate but related issues: to do something, anything, to combat Hitler, and to intervene on the Finnish side in the Russo-Finnish war. Public opinion was particularly restive in France (where, on March 20, 1940, the government finally fell as a consequence of Allied lethargy), but in retrospect it is difficult to say which country was the most intent on seeing action.

Initially the French had two separate schemes to propose. One was to reequip the sizable Polish army that had been re-formed in the fall of 1939 (there were nearly one hundred thousand Poles in uniform by May 1940), transport it to Finland, and let it thrash the Russians. The other was to mount a strategic bombing strike against Soviet oil fields in the Caucasus. British analysts have traditionally hooted down these suggestions, particularly the second, as preposterous, but they were hardly less so than the actual scheme the British government adopted. Basically this was an attempt to solve both problems with one operation: the Allies, taking advantage of a League of Nations resolution condemning the Soviet Union, would land an expeditionary force at Narvik in Norway and move it by rail across northern Sweden to Finland.

As a byproduct this expedition would traverse the Swedish iron ore fields. Just as the French believed that the USSR and Germany were dependent on Soviet oil fields, the British believed that Germany was dependent on shipments of Swedish iron ore. Without iron ore the German armaments industry would grind to a halt. In an attempt to remain in power post–September 1939, Chamberlain had taken Winston Churchill into the cabinet as First Lord of the Admiralty, and Churchill was hearing reports from the Admiralty about the desirability of cutting off the ore shipments as early as September 18.[4] The Admiralty believed that Germany was importing over four-fifths of its iron ore, some 9 million tons, from northern Sweden, and it was on this fact that Allied military policy—right up until May 10, 1940—all hinged.[5]

So Churchill had proposed a scheme to interdict the iron ore traffic, which in the winter mostly went down the Norwegian coast. He and the Admiralty wanted to mine the coastal waters, thus forcing the ships out to sea, where the Royal Navy could (it was thought) promptly dispose of them. The obvious problem with this scheme was that it involved an act (planting mines in the territorial waters of a neutral country) that was about the most flagrant violation of international law imaginable. So much so that even the Allied leadership had doubts, and this in turn led to the idea of an expeditionary force. Sir Edmond Ironside, the author of the scheme, thought it was a chance to "get a big return for very little expenditure," and proposed a force of some thirty thousand men.[6]

Modern readers of military history are accustomed to the term *mission creep*—that is, the tendency of small contained operations with definite goals to escalate into major affairs with no set objectives. Norway is the first modern case. By January 29, 1940, Ironside's 30,000-man force had become a 150,000-man expeditionary force that would depart on March 12, 1940, and land in Scandinavia on March 20. Helping Finland receded into the background: "We are quite cynical about everything except stopping the iron ore," Ironside noted gloomily in his diary.[7]

In their planning the Allies neglected two basic factors. The pretext for crossing Norway and Sweden was to help Finland. But by the end of January it was pretty clear that Finland couldn't hold out for more than a month or so at most. Would there even be any fighting going on by March 12? Probably not, and in fact there wasn't. And then no one had thought to ask the Norwegians and the Swedes how they felt about an Allied force of 150,000 men camping out on their national territory.

By a grim coincidence the original date for the sailing of the Allied expedition, March 12, 1940, was the date on which the Finns capitulated, with the "peace" being signed the next day. So the British, after a suitable delay, simply issued an ultimatum to the Norwegians, in which they asserted their "right to take such measures as they may think necessary to hinder or prevent Germany from obtaining in these countries resources or facilities which, for the purposes of the war, would be to her advantage or to the disadvantage of the Allies."[8] The reaction in Scandinavia was violent and bitter.[9]

On December 12, 1939, Adm. Erich Raeder, commander in chief of the German navy, had brought up the problems inherent in a British occupation of Norway. On March 12, 1940, Jodl, Hitler's military chief, recorded the hopelessly ingenuous remark that "now that peace has been concluded between Finland and Russia, England has no political reason to go into Norway—but neither have we."[10] Hitler, however, agreed with Raeder.

So both sides planned to invade Norway. The Germans not only had a more comprehensive scheme of invasion, they were able to execute it more effectively. Despite the Royal Navy's command of the seas, the Germans managed to land an entire invasion force in Norway by sea without being intercepted; in the ensuing naval battles, both sides lost heavily. The British claim that German naval losses were worse, and technically this is true. But the Royal Navy lost what was essentially a carrier battle group: the *Glorious*, two cruisers, seven destroyers, and four submarines sunk, with another three cruisers and six destroyers out of commission through damage. Given the supreme importance of carrier-based aviation in the war—and Great Britain's desperate need for destroyers—the loss of a significant part of the German surface fleet was poor consolation indeed.[11]

It is at this point that the Norway campaign begins to impact the Allied war effort in two important ways. On the one hand, incredibly, during the spring of 1940, the Allies began to transfer men and equipment from France to Norway. As General Pownall recorded bitterly in his diary: "We are losing driblets away, not very much they may seem individually, but collectively the sum mounts and mounts."[12] The driblets did indeed mount up.

Nor was the drain restricted to the British. By May 10, 1940, France had sent its crack alpine warfare specialist (General Béthouart) to Norway, along with four battalions of French alpine troops, two battalions of the Legion, and the Polish Podhalanska Brigade (four battalions). Now, these were precisely the sort of elite troops whose presence on the battlefield had always had an enormous impact in French military history. In the First World War, French alpine troops had frequently been the margin between a retreat and a route during the disasters of August and September 1914. Like the soldiers of the Legion, these units had an impact on the battlefield completely disproportionate to their numbers. The veterans of the Podhalanska Brigade had the inestimable advantage of having fought the Germans before. As Pownall said, the driblets added up.

Then there is the final blow. His troops having seized Norway and Denmark, Hitler gave little thought to their fate. For the next few weeks, his energies were turned to the next offensive, France, while the

Allied leadership was if anything increasingly turned toward Norway, and in more ways than one. The British and French publics—as opposed to their leaders—were growing increasingly aggravated by the lack of action. Although minorities in both countries—and particularly in France, where the Communist Party was strong politically—would continue to attack the whole idea of a war, the general population had long since turned the corner. They wanted Hitler stopped. Their countries were at war, and they wanted action.

On March 20, 1940, the Daladier government had fallen, and on precisely this point: France's failure to do anything military that anyone could point to. And in fact the collapse of the French government was one of the reasons the Allies had embarked their troops for Norway: They realized they had to be seen to do something, anything, and this was the only plan they had on the table.

The problem of course was that the Norway campaign was a fiasco. Anyone could look at a map and see that the only way the Germans could get to Norway was by water. Everyone realized it: The combined navies of Great Britain and France were the largest and most powerful fleets in the world. Yet they had failed to stop the invasion and now couldn't eject the Germans from the country.

In Great Britain, and particularly in Parliament, criticism of the Norway campaign was mounting, and although Chamberlain's main concern was to remain in office as prime minister, the leaders of the House would have no more of him. But who would replace him? The Chamberlain government collapsed at precisely that moment when the Germans began the run up to their offensive in the west. While the British tried to come up with a new prime minister, Germany attacked. Quite literally: On the evening of May 9, after the usual round-the-clock party conferences and negotiations, Winston Churchill became prime minister. While in London members of the House of Commons trooped home, doubtless with a certain feeling of contentment at having solved the problem, German soldiers were trooping off to their airplanes and gliders, waiting anxiously for the dawn of the tenth.

In the First World War, Great Britain had the great misfortune to have as its military commander Sir Douglas Haig, a man with many of the characteristics of Chamberlain, and certainly with the same determination to keep himself in power. And now the pattern repeated itself.

German Plans

Lloyd George, the British prime minister from November 1916, had noted with some irritation in his memoirs how the British high command had turned defeats into victories, magnifying their successes and minimizing those of the enemy.[13] Accounts of May 1940 followed the same predictable trail. The British were surprised by a new and daring German plan, overwhelmed by new tactics and weapons. Above all they were badly let down by the French, the Belgians, and the Dutch; had no choice but to retreat; and, by their skill and tenacity, turned the defeat into a victory at Dunkirk, evacuating their army almost intact and going on to fight another day. Other than the fact that the BEF did retreat and was mostly evacuated at Dunkirk, little in this account actually holds up to inquiry.

As noted earlier, Hitler was insisting on an immediate attack against France in early October 1939. Although the German high command resisted the directive as best they could, throwing up countless excuses to account for the delay, the staff had, in obedience to Hitler's directives, drawn up a plan of attack. In three key particulars this plan was simply the repetition of the plan used against Poland. It would begin with a surprise aerial attack aimed at destroying the enemy's air forces and giving Germany command of the air. Simultaneously airborne troops would be used to seize all the key bridges into the Netherlands and Belgium.

A ground attack on a broad front would begin right behind the air drops, with the aim of overrunning the Belgian defenses and forcing a passage through that country into France. As in Poland, the ground attack would be on a broad front. The plan envisioned three separate army groups, each mounting a separate offensive: Group B would attack through the Netherlands and Belgium, Group A through Luxembourg, and Group C directly against France. The planners hoped, rather nervously, that this attack would be synchronized with an Italian offensive in the south. Such an offensive, or at least the threat of it, would force the French to disperse their forces.

In the October order of battle, Group B was the largest of the three groups, comprising twenty-nine infantry divisions and eight of Germany's armored units, divided into three armies, the Second, Fourth, and Sixth. Group A, with a much smaller front, consisted of the Twelfth and Sixteenth Armies, twenty-six infantry divisions and one armored division. Group C, charged with an offensive against French territory, consisted of twenty-five infantry divisions.

By March 1940 both the composition of the army groups and their areas of responsibility had been shifted.[14] In the initial plan both army groups were to move east-west in an almost straight line, simply cutting across Belgium. By March the axis of advance had been shifted: They would move in a southwesterly direction, pivoting on the French frontier, and then head northwesterly toward the French coast. It was this last—a change in the direction of maneuver rather than in any other aspect—that gave the plan its name, as the trajectory of the two armies resembled nothing so much as the sweep of a scythe.

That being said, it is clear enough that the German high command made very few real changes to their offensive plans from October to March. Two main features of the plan—the airborne drops and the aim of achieving tactical surprise in the air—were clearly referred to in the remnants of the captured documents and remained unchanged.[15] Nor was there any shifting of forces from north to south. All that had changed was the direction of maneuver. Two of the three elements that were indispensable to the German success in 1940—the surprise airborne seizures of bridges and crossings and the equally surprising air onslaught—were thus firmly in place long before von Manstein's fabled visit to Hitler on February 17, 1940, when—in the popular retelling of the story—he was able to convince Hitler to make great changes to the plan.

Nor was there anything particularly revolutionary about the shift. Since Frederick the Great, German commanders had always preferred oblique maneuvers that would trap and surround the enemy, and it had been this same sort of maneuver, albeit on a grander scale, which von Moltke the Younger (and Ludendorff, his operations chief) had planned for August 1914. Even Hitler could understand this, and even von Manstein's immediate superior had grasped it, as had the senior German planners: It was one of those obvious ideas simply waiting to be discovered.

The chief objection to it, which was made by German generals at the time, had nothing much to do with the idea that an armored thrust through the Belgian Ardennes would be difficult if not impossible, owing to the terrain. The objection was that the new plan required a German advance in which the entire left flank would be liable to interception by French forces moving up into the Ardennes and Luxembourg. Nor could these forces easily be stopped, as they would be shielded by the Maginot Line.

Then there was the question of airpower. Mechanized columns, when stretched out along a two-lane road, of necessity went on for tens of kilometers. There were excellent roads running through the Ardennes into France, but those roads had far too many places where armored columns would be exposed and unable to find any cover. It was easy to prophesy a true disaster in which the armored units were decimated from the air, trapped on roads with no easy escape, and then attacked piecemeal by French and Belgian troops well supplied with antitank guns and backed by heavy artillery.

Then too, the outcome of this gamble depended on speed: The Germans had to cross the Meuse and start moving up toward the English Channel before the French, attacking from three sides, could cut them off and annihilate them. Because, as the German command was gloomily aware, the French were hardly going to camp out along the frontier and wait to be attacked.

The Allied Plan

The French had always known that the only effective military strategy in a Franco-German conflict was an advance through Belgium. Joffre had proposed this before 1914, and had been overruled on political grounds: The government was concerned that news of such a plan might in fact force Belgium into the German camp. The construction of the CORF defenses considerably reduced the chances of a successful German attack anywhere to the east of Sedan (technically, east of Carignan, a small town about forty kilometers east of Sedan).

As the expected German attacks failed to materialize, Gamelin, the French commander, began to consider more seriously the idea of an advance into Belgium, so that the Allies could meet the advancing Germans head-on. Accordingly, on March 20, 1940, he gave a supplementary set of orders that envisioned a broad-based Allied thrust into Belgium. Subsequently known as the Dyle Plan, since it contemplated an advance to the river Dyle in Belgium, Gamelin's strategy was subsequently ridiculed by analysts, but this was to create scapegoats with the benefit of hindsight.

All Gamelin was proposing was the sensible idea that the Allies could travel the one hundred kilometers or so they needed to cover to get to the Dyle faster than the Germans could fight their way across the same distance. In September observers had spoken with admiration of the rapid German advance in Poland, but it had taken them four or five days to make a serious penetration, and the Poles, as we have seen, had nothing to compare with the Allies in terms of frontier fortifications, airpower, armor, and antitank weapons.

There were other considerations as well. The Belgian army—and the defenses it manned—was a powerful force. In 1914 Belgium, trusting that its neutrality would protect it, had had a small army (and its defenses consisted almost exclusively of fortifications around Namur, Liège, and Antwerp). It was, as Belgian experts admitted after the war, extremely small for a country of Belgium's size, and poorly equipped. In the 1930s the Belgians had realized the folly of this approach, and had raised and trained a surprisingly large military. Its purpose was purely defensive, but in 1940 Belgian troops were well armed with modern weapons, and heavily mechanized. Although Belgium had only about three hundred armored vehicles, light tanks derived from British or French models, its army was highly mechanized, and the towed 47-millimeter antitank gun, a Belgian derivation of the high-velocity French gun, was a formidable weapon.[16]

Finland had shown what a determined citizen army could do, even without much support, so the idea that Belgium's six-hundred-thousand-man army could, if supported promptly by the Allies, give a good account of itself was quite sound. Moreover, at the same time, the Belgians had built what may fairly be regarded as the largest fort in the world. Called Eben Emael, it dominated the Meuse River crossings in the northeast tip of the country, where, in a sort of geopolitical anomaly, a strip of the Netherlands hung down between Germany and Belgium (the Maastricht Appendage).

In August 1914 the Germans, respecting the neutrality of the Netherlands, had eschewed trying to cross this section of Dutch territory, and instead had attacked the fortifications around Liège. Although the heroic defenses of the Liège forts soon passed into the mythology of the First World War, in reality advancing German troops had gone around the neutralized fortifications on both sides of the city and crossed the Meuse River at Sedan on August 23, 1914.

The Belgians had learned from those experiences, and Eben Emael was built in a place where it not only blocked the way for troops violating the Maastricht Appendage but dominated the newly renovated and expanded circle of Liège forts. Gamelin's belief that he could get to the Dyle before the Germans crossed it was hardly a delusion.

So Gamelin's plan envisioned a front along the Dyle held by a mixture of forces. The French Seventh Army would advance toward Antwerp, their left flank on the Channel, in an attempt to link up with the Dutch defenders. Gamelin realized that prompt support of the invaded neutrals was a political necessity. The Allied pattern of making promises and then standing by impotently had to be broken.

He had another reason as well. In the fall of 1914 the Allies had failed to block the German advance along the coast: The Germans had laid siege to Antwerp and taken it (in early October) along with the main Channel ports, which promptly became a thorn in the side of the Allies, as German submarines based there began to attack Allied shipping. The Allied command had recognized—too late—the importance of this strip of territory, and Gamelin, quite sensibly, wanted to make sure it wasn't abandoned as it had been in the previous war.

The boundary of the Seventh Army stopped south of Antwerp. Between Antwerp and Louvain the front would be held by the Belgians themselves. The BEF would hold the section from Louvain to Wavre, and from Wavre to Namur the front would be held by the French First Army. From Namur on down it would be held by the Second and Ninth Armies. This scheme gave the BEF only about twenty kilometers of the projected front, but that would make it easier for the BEF to expand northward and take up sections of the Belgian-held front.

All this was of course hypothetical. Gamelin was laboring under a double disadvantage. On the one hand no one really knew when the Germans would attack, or if they really would (recall the number of postponements since October 1939). On the other Belgium and the Netherlands had become increasingly neutral after 1938. Both countries distrusted Allied intentions and were doubtful of the value of any Allied commitment. To the failure to save Poland or Finland was now added the clear intention of violating Norwegian neutrality. And the Belgians, in particular, were understandably testy. The country had been ravaged in the First World War; the Belgians, with a good deal of justice, spoke of theirs as the country most affected by the horrors of that war. And to what end? By the 1930s a good many Belgians looked back on August 1914 and wondered if their country had not perhaps made a mistake.[17]

Would not its suffering have been less had it simply let Germany have the passage through that it demanded?

Clearly this was not a question to which there was an easy answer. But regardless of how it was answered, the fact of it being raised meant that Belgium was not simply going to be backed into a corner where it was forced to cooperate with the Allies. Nor was the Netherlands, which had been neutral in the previous war.

Both the British and the French subsequently used this to blame the two countries: Had they allied themselves with Great Britain and France, May 1940 would have turned out differently, the claim goes. Their neutrality was a foolish safeguarding of privilege, an act of denial in the face of a common enemy.

But this is nonsense. The Belgians and the Dutch managed to let the Allies know what their defensive plans were, and made no secret of the fact that if they were attacked, they would call on the Allies for aid and welcome their troops. Nor was Belgium on a different planet. It was right next door, and Allied officers had months to visit it, study the terrain, familiarize themselves with it, and plan their dispositions accordingly. As we shall see, they did nothing of the sort. Nor is there any evidence of local commanders trying to make contact with their opposite numbers in the Belgian army to establish an informal understanding.

The clearest evidence of this systemic failure on the Allied side would come in the opening days of the war, and it is a devastating indictment. In August 1914 German infantry had marched down the Meuse Valley and through the Belgian Ardennes, breaking into France along a broad front running roughly from Montmedy past Charleville-Mézières. Their advance had been successful because they had defeated the French forces sent into Belgium to counter this advance, notably at a battle outside the small Belgian town of Rossignol, where the Colonial Infantry, some of the best troops France possessed in 1914, had been virtually annihilated by their opponents.

Anyone studying that portion of southern Belgium to the north of this section of the French frontier quickly discovers that there is a marvelous natural defensive position defined by the Semois River. The French section of the Meuse, as it meanders in a northwesterly direction south of the Franco-Belgian frontier, is in the center of an extremely broad riverine valley. At Sedan, for instance, it is a good six or seven kilometers wide, and the high ground on the northern side slopes gently down into the valley.

But the Semois Valley is a different affair entirely. On the south side the ground rises abruptly, in some cases forming almost vertical bluffs. Both sides are thickly forested, and in the late spring the riverbanks form a sort of moat in many places. It was this that had led Pétain to conclude that military operations out of the Ardennes were impossible for the Germans: All the French had to do was move across the frontier and establish a defensive line on the southern side of the river. And it was probably this basic geographical knowledge that led several senior German officers in the spring of 1940 to opine that the German attack would never even get to the Meuse. Once the handful of bridges across the river were destroyed, it was in most cases unfordable with the bridging equipment German Pioniere, or combat engineers, possessed. But the French officers stayed resolutely in France. When the offensive began they would opt to man their defensive positions on the Meuse, thus giving the German forces the invaluable opportunity to navigate the crossings of the Semois undisturbed.

Nevertheless Gamelin planned to send his troops into Belgium, meet the attacking Germans there, and defeat them, either by holding a line along the river Dyle or by defeating them in the field. Once Germany attacked, the Belgians and the Dutch would want Allied help. Gamelin had great faith in the defensive positions along his right flank, all the way down to the Swiss frontier, and equally great faith in the offensive power of his heavily mechanized and armored forces.

This faith was hardly irrational. In 1940 everyone (still) thought of the British army as a formidable war machine, and in contrast to 1914, the BEF of 1940 was a significant force, four or five times the size of its ancestor, and in the spring, with an armored division as well. Sadly this machine existed only in the mind and on paper. To list its deficiencies in detail is to beat a dead horse, but they were numerous.

It is customary to blame Neville Chamberlain for Great Britain's policies of appeasement, which, everyone agrees, simply empowered and emboldened Hitler. This claim is to a certain extent exaggerated: in 1938 appeasement was a sensible policy and had hardly been discredited; indeed, the fact that it continued as a tendency in the West for a half century or more after the end of the war suggests that it resonated with many intelligent people.

When Chamberlain was chancellor of the exchequer at key periods in the interwar years, the British, in a frenzy of penury, slashed their defense expenditures to the bone, and what money was allocated went mostly to the RAF. To say that tank development suffered is a gross understatement. Although the British had produced dozens of different models, none of the tanks were any good, and hardly any of them were actually in service.[18]

By May 1940 the French, as we have seen, had twelve armored divisions, comprising literally thousands of tanks, together with twenty-eight independent battalions of R35 and H35 tanks.[19] By that same point the British had managed to assemble one armored division, the First, comprising 156 Cruiser tanks and 174 Mark 6 vehicles, 100 Matilda tanks in two independent tank regiments, and another 200 or so Mark 6 tanks distributed among the "cavalry" regiments.[20]

Like the Germans and the French, the British were still thinking about how to deploy armor, so in addition to separate cavalry regiments equipped with light tanks, there were two independent tank regiments equipped with "infantry" tanks, which in 1940 meant a vehicle known as the Matilda, owing to its ungainly waddling movement. The Matilda 2 was a massive vehicle weighing about 27,000 kilograms and armed with a two pounder gun. It was decently armored, and certainly the best tank the British had. The problem was that production was late starting (in September 1939 there were only two of them) and plagued by mechanical problems. In France the BEF had far too few of them to make much of a difference on the battlefield, although the combination of thick armor and a hard-hitting gun gave the Germans some nasty shocks in late May.

Although in retrospect the British tank industry was foundering (post-Dunkirk the British army relied almost totally on American tanks), in 1940 the British tank force was not really any worse than the German, and in several respects the BEF was much better equipped: Its artillery was all mechanized, and its infantry traveled by truck and personnel carrier.

Curiously, given its subsequent reputation, the German army of 1940 was the least mechanized army in the field. Outside of the handfuls of mechanized and armored divisions, the Germans were still heavily dependent on horses. Gamelin's belief that his motorized armies could cross Belgium faster than their horsedrawn and foot-powered adversaries was hardly irrational. And, as we shall see, he was right: the Allied defeat didn't have much to do with mechanization or armor, or even combat.

Another Failure of Airpower

In one area, however, Great Britain was formidably equipped. During the 1930s the Royal Air Force had been the only branch of the military funded to anything like the proper level, and, as we have noted, in 1937 it was widely regarded as the largest of the world's air forces. Its core consisted of two separate divisions, Bomber Command and Fighter Command. The travails of Bomber Command in the fall of 1939 have already been noted. But, as our discussion made quite clear, the general failure of the RAF's strategic-bombing campaigns was a systemic failure inherent in the ideas of the airpower strategists. It was not a uniquely British failure.

Besides, the projected battlefield (the Netherlands, Belgium, and northeastern France) was well within operating range of Bomber Command's long-range bombers. Moreover Great Britain possessed a large force of what in 1940 were called light bombers, planes that, properly speaking, we would now term tactical ground-attack aircraft, that is, planes whose primary mission would be the destruction of enemy ground forces as they moved up onto the battlefield. In anticipation of this, the RAF had moved a sizable advance force into France, where they would be operating out of airfields close to the actual combat zone.

Although Douhet had insisted that such planes were a waste of effort, the airpower strategists and planners of the 1920s and 1930s had, sensibly enough, ignored this part of his theories. Like the Germans, the French and the British both had a fleet of ground attack aircraft and the fighter planes to give them support. The situation the Luftwaffe would face in Western Europe would be nothing like the situation in Poland. The French air force was deficient in strategic bombers, but then so was the Luftwaffe. But France had a large and modern force of fighters and ground-attack aircraft.

This last may come as a surprise to the reader, since it is virtually an article of faith that in 1940 France went to war with a collection of antiques. As the one air force specialist who has investigated the matter seriously has concluded, the French air force was made the scapegoat for the political and military failures the country suffered. Briefly, the French had "produced enough modern combat aircraft (4,360) by May 1940 to defeat the Luftwaffe, which fielded a force of 3,270."[21] And this does not count the British air forces stationed in France, comprising a formidable group of modern fighter planes and light bombers.

There was however one clear area where the Allied air forces were greatly inferior to the German. In German doctrine the air mission was totally subordinated to the ground campaign. Air fleets were attached to the army commands, their mission to support the ground offensives, and to that end the Germans had a well-articulated and -defined system of liaison with the ground troops, with air force personnel operating in conjunction with their army counterparts at very low unit levels.

This was a radically new idea, and a complicated one to execute. In Poland there had been more than a few problems: The leading complaint of the army was that its forward units had been attacked by their own planes far too often. But experience, in the German army at least, was a good teacher, and by May 1940 there had been numerous improvements to the coordination efforts.

Last but hardly least the Germans had achieved a remarkable integration of tactical air defense systems. They had done so by the simple expedient of letting air defense be handled by Luftwaffe personnel who operated alongside the ground units. This of course was a total denial of one of Douhet's basic ideas—that the bomber would always get through—and a total rejection of another even more fashionable belief, which was that a nation's air force was a separate branch of the military operating independently of the army.

This was, then, the one clear area where the two sides were asymmetrical. The RAF and its French equivalent were left to devise their own plan of action, and as the plaintive cry of General Pownall makes clear, they did so without paying much attention to what the ground forces were planning to do. When the fighting started, the air forces would conduct their own war in their own way.

This was the real recipe for disaster, and it had nothing to do with armor or a defensive mentality, or even the poor state of the BEF or the independence of the neutrals. Put simply, the British and French air forces had no understanding of the most important aspect of the German plan: the surprise attack from the air, aimed at giving the Germans mastery over the battlefield.

As we now know, in campaigns such as these, the air war is basically lost or won in the initial hours of battle. The attacker who obtains air superiority in those first forty-eight hours (or so) is likely to keep it, even if the other side possesses more planes. This had happened in

Poland. As we have seen, the Germans did not, as was claimed at the time, destroy the Polish air force on the ground in its initial attacks. But by not putting up their entire air force immediately to counter the Luft-waffe, the Poles lost the war in the air, and their air force was then destroyed piecemeal.

Neither the French nor the British had absorbed this lesson. Instead they envisioned a more leisurely conflict in which great fleets of planes would clash in the air, and the bombers would always get through. Consequently, although the Luftwaffe's losses were so heavy that by June 1940 the French actually had more planes than the Germans, the Allies were never able to recover from the effects of the initial twenty-four hours of air attack. In a famous dictum, Von Clausewitz had observed that mistakes in the initial disposition of forces were difficult if not impossible to overcome. Nowhere was this more true than in the air, and at no place was it more true than France and Belgium in 1940.

NOTES

1. As quoted by Martin S. Alexander in "Fighting to the Last Frenchman," in Joel Blatt, ed., *The French Defeat of 1940: Reassessments* (Oxford, England: Berghan, 1998), 300.

2. Brian Bond, *Britain, France, and Belgium* (London: Brassey's, 1990), 48.

3. Initially Chamberlain claimed that the expedition had inflicted severe losses on the Germans: "If we had losses, the Germans had far heavier losses," Chamberlain told the House on May 7, 1940; but not even Derry, the official British historian for this campaign, can swallow this claim, and recites army casualties as 3,734 (1,869 British, 530 French and Polish, and 1,335 Norwegian), while German casualties are given as 5,296. Data and Chamberlain quote taken from Thomas Kingston Derry, *The Campaign in Norway* (London: Her Majesty's Stationery Office, 1952), 229–30.

4. To the extent that in his excellent discussion of the Norway disaster, François Kersaudy entitles his chapter on the early discussions "Churchill's Solitary Crusade": *Norway 1940* (Lincoln: University of Nebraska Press, 1998), 13–37.

5. Kersaudy cites the relevant documents (ibid., 15). In all the discussions it appears that no one has ever bothered to find out what the actual situation was, even though the figures have been available since 1945. In the three years preceding the start of the war, German iron ore imports averaged 20,339 metric tons, contrasted with the British estimate of 11 million tons. During that same period 8,774 metric tons were imported from Sweden. So although the British were roughly correct in their estimation of the tonnage

exported from Sweden, the conclusion they drew was completely wrong: only 43 percent of Germany's iron ore needs were met by the Swedish imports. Data taken from U.S. Strategic Bombing Survey, *Strategic Bombing,* table 67, 247, which in turn references the relevant German documents obtained by Allied investigators.

6. The quote is from Trotter, *Frozen Hell,* 237, who has the best brief summary of what was going on. The most comprehensive account is in Kersaudy, *Norway,* 89. There are drastically different accounts from the British side—for example, Bond, *Britain, France, and Belgium,* 48–50; and Roy Douglas, *The Advent of War, 1939–40* (New York: St. Martin's Press, 1978), 59–91. Despite its title, Donald Cameron Watt, *How War Came: The Immediate Origins of the Second World War* (New York: Pantheon, 1989), devotes only 4 or 5 pages to Finland (out of 624 pages of text) and Norway isn't even listed in the index—but then these are not the happiest incidents in British affairs. Watt's main purpose is to whitewash the British government's actions during this period, and, given the facts, suppression is the best defense.

7. *The Ironside Diaries,* eds. Roderick Macleod and Dennis Kelly (New York: David McKay, 1963), 215. Trotter, *Frozen Hell,* 239, uses this same quote.

8. "Disdainful," the Norwegian foreign minister was quoted as saying: "the language of a sovereign to a vassal." As quoted by, among many others (this is a memorable quote), Kersaudy, *Norway,* 61.

9. As quoted by Douglas, *Advent of War,* 103. An earlier reaction from the Swedish Foreign Ministry, also in Douglas, is notable: "I should have thought that the British Government had the fate of a sufficient number of smaller states on their conscience as it was" (86).

10. As quoted by Walter Warlimont, *Inside Hitler's Headquarters,* trans. R. H. Barry (Novato, Calif.: Presidio, 1964), 68. Warlimont's account, although curiously organized, is clear enough on the essentials, and is greatly to be preferred to more recent narratives, for example, Ian Kershaw, *Hitler 1936–1945: Nemesis* (New York: Norton, 2000), 287–89, 293.

11. See the analysis in Derry, *The Norway Campaign,* 231–32, who has to fall back on the argument that these losses deprived the Germans of forces they would otherwise have used in the invasion of Great Britain. True, but as there is little evidence to suggest Hitler ever seriously planned such an invasion, the point is moot. Kersaudy demolishes the various arguments neatly enough, concluding by pointing out that the British most emphatically did not learn from their mistakes in Norway (ibid., 225–27).

12. As recorded by Bond, *Britain, France, and Belgium,* 50. Earlier, in March, Pownall had deplored the fact that his projected ten-division BEF in France would be reduced by three divisions: The Fifth Division was being withdrawn and the Forty-second and Forty-fourth divisions wouldn't even arrive. And now, in April, he listed key areas—particularly antiaircraft—he was being stripped of or not sent.

13. "The reports passed on to the ministers were, as we all realized much later, grossly misleading. Victories were much overstated. Virtual defeats were represented as victories, however limited their scope. Our casualties were understated. Enemy losses became pyramidal. That was the way the military authorities presented the situation to Ministers—that was their active propaganda in the Press. All disconcerting and discouraging facts were suppressed in the reports received from the front by the War Cabinet—every bright feather of success was waved and flourished in our faces." David Lloyd George (in autumn 1917) as revealed in his *War Memoirs* (London: Odhams, 1938), 2: 1313.

14. This shift is sometimes seen as the reaction to the Belgian capture of detailed Luftwaffe plans for the offensive when a German airplane blundered into Belgian airspace and was captured. However, this does not seem to be the case: the captured plans related to air deployments, and apparently said nothing about the disposition of the ground forces.

15. So far as I am aware, this claim was first made by Eddy Bauer, a Swiss military historian whose account of the war remains one of the best to date. See Bauer, *La guerre des blindés,* 1: 86. Bond, one of the few British analysts to acknowledge Bauer's work, attempts to dismiss it, but his argument is essentially a misdirection (Bond, *Britain, France, and Belgium,* 45–46).

16. Belgian data taken from J. Wullus-Rudiger, *La défense de la Belgique en 1940* (Villeneuve-sur-Lot: Alfred Bador, 1940), 181–86. The Belgian army had tanks: See the discussion—together with pictures of them—in Jean Paul Pallud, *Blitzkrieg in the West* (London: Battle of Britain Prints, 1991), 63–64.

17. See a similar passage by Douglas, the only British historian to show much sympathy for the Belgians: "A patriotic Belgian could reasonably ask whether his country would have fared better if King Albert had been less heroic, and if the Germans had been permitted to enter with no more than a formal protest" (*Advent of War,* 139).

18. The few tanks actually in service were not very good designs. The Mark 6 was a 5,300-kilogram machine-gun carrier; like the German Mark 2, it was basically unsuited for modern warfare (its 4-millimeter hull armor was one-fourth the thickness of the old Renault R17 tank from 1918), and its most distinguishing characteristic was its great height: At 2.28 meters, it had almost the same profile as the German Mark 3 (2.5 meters), and was actually higher than the corresponding French light tanks—although these of course had actual guns mounted in their turrets. According to the British tank expert Steve Crawford, "the Mark VI was actually no more than a reconnaissance vehicle," *Tanks of World War II* (Kent, England: Grange Books, 2000), 56. See, among others, David Fletcher, *The Great Tank Scandal* (London: Her Majesty's Stationery Office, 1999), especially 7–13. His is a more objective account than that of Peter Beale, *Death by Design: The Fate of British Tank Crews in the Second World War* (Phoenix Mill, England: Sutton,

1998), but Beale makes some excellent points, and we shall have occasion to refer to him later on, citing his discussions of British armor in 1944.

19. Technically there were three armored divisions (a fourth was in action by May 21). The core of each division was a *demi-brigade* of the formidable B1 *bis* heavy tank (seventy tanks), together with a *demi-brigade* of ninety H39 tanks. But, as we noted earlier, the French army had two other kinds of armored divisions, and in 1940 in addition to the four heavy divisions, there were eight divisions (called, confusingly, *Division Légère Mechanique* and *Division Légère de Cavalerie*). To simplify, these eight divisions had the same armored firepower as most panzer divisions. For example, the Ninth Panzer had ninety-seven machine-gun-equipped Mark 1 and 2 vehicles and fifty-six Mark 3 and 4 tanks (with another nineteen tracked combat vehicles and fifty armored cars). The Third DLM had eighty H39 tanks, eighty S35s, sixty H35s, and forty Panhard P178 armored cars—and all these vehicles were equipped with guns, as opposed to the machine-gun carriers that still, in 1940, formed the core of the German tank force. See the comparative data in Pallud, *Blitzkrieg in the West*, 62.

20. The Cruiser 4s the BEF was using in 1940 were ungainly 14,000-kilogram vehicles with less hull armor (6 millimeters) than French tanks from the First World War. The only good thing about this tank was that it was equipped with a decent gun, the two-pounder (40-millimeter), which was about half again as potent a weapon as the corresponding German 37-millimeter weapon. The two-pounder's 853-meters-per-second gun (as opposed to the German 37-millimeter gun's 763 meters per second) meant that its force was about 400,000 kilograms per meter, almost exactly twice that of the German gun—which in turn meant that its range and armor-piercing abilities were correspondingly greater.

21. Information and quote taken from Lt. Col. Faris R. Kirkland's U.S. Air Force study, "The French Air Force." Although unpublished, this study has been disseminated by the Air University of the United States Air Force. It appears that Colonel Kirkland, who served in Korea and Vietnam and then went on to get his doctorate, died before he could develop his intensely researched thesis on this subject any further. Kirkland's evidence about French aircraft production seems compelling, and is supported by much anecdotal evidence, for example, the testimony of French fliers, of whom the most famous is Antoine de Saint-Exupéry, a combat veteran and an eyewitness, whose book *Flight to Arras* (Toronto: W. Heinemann, 1943) is one of the classics of aviation literature.

6.

The German Assault and the Fall of France: May–June 1940

It is a favorite illusion that historical events would not have happened but for such a disclosure, or might have been prevented by some skillful démarche here or pronunciamento there. . . . Journalists and diplomats, even historians, thrive on such fantasies; I have, in the exercise of my profession, aired many, not one of which had the slightest validity.
—MALCOLM MUGGERIDGE[1]

Each month since October 1939, the Allies had anticipated an attack in the west. And now, at the end of April, they received another notice, this one from the British Embassy in Rome, which was followed by—if we are to believe Lord Halifax—information from the Vatican that seemingly confirmed the threat. Churchill, still First Lord of the Admiralty but increasingly the man in charge of Great Britain's defense effort, issued an order for the British to be on twelve-hour notice instead of twenty-four; in other words they would be prepared to react to an attack within twelve hours.[2]

These early warnings contained some false information—Halifax apparently had been told that an attack was contemplated through

Switzerland, for example—and the Allies had received such warnings before. But Churchill's actions suggest that they were taken more seriously, and the Dutch, generally the best informed of the military establishments in the West, took them seriously indeed.

Since the Mechelin incident on January 10, 1940, the Allies, and certainly the Belgians, had at least some idea of the key elements of the German plan. Moreover they had recent history as a guide. In both Poland and Finland, the real declaration of war was delivered from the air, and consisted of a furious assault, accompanied by a ground attack, and, certainly in the case of Poland, the use of airborne troops to seize objectives important for a successful advance.

Although, as a narrative of the actual events of May 1940 makes fairly clear, there was absolutely nothing strange about the Allied defeat (or the German victory), the almost absolute and total failure of the French, the Belgians, and the British to anticipate the opening moves of the war is peculiar, and the strangest part of it is the lack of any plan on the part of the air forces involved to counter the German air assault.

Apparently everyone was surprised, and yet, as Churchill's directive makes clear, they shouldn't have been. A corollary to this idea of surprise is the idea that the attack was unprecedented and novel; it could not be prepared for, the proof being that no one was prepared for it. But this isn't true. One country was prepared, fought bitterly, and exacted an enormous toll on the attackers: the Netherlands, whose military had last seen action at Waterloo.

Soldiers of Orange

Although the Dutch were aware of Hitler's invasion plans, and expected to be attacked, they were very much aware as well that in the event of such an attack they would be in the same position as the Finns and the Poles. The most revolutionary aspect of the German plan had been from the very first the attempt to seize the Netherlands from the air. Concurrent with the bombing attack, airborne troops would be dropped onto the major airfields, thus allowing the landing of transport planes bringing in still more troops. Simultaneously special operations forces would attempt to seize all the key bridges, thus clearing the way for the arrival of ground forces.

Seizing the bridges intact was a vital part of the plan. From Liège north into the Netherlands, the Meuse (or the Maas), is a formidable barrier separating Germany from the core of the Netherlands. Nor is the Meuse the only water barrier. Indeed, the basic Dutch plan of national defense called for defending a sort of bastion defined inside the national territory by a series of water barriers.

Were the Germans to cross these successfully, in theory their armies could attack Belgium from the north. Before the First World War, von Schlieffen had needed the Maastricht Appendage in his plans because he couldn't figure out how to get enough troops into Belgium from Germany otherwise. His successor, von Moltke the Younger, utilizing the services of Ludendorff, who was responsible for most of the planning for the German offensive, calculated this wasn't needed. The Germans had left the Netherlands alone. Serious fighting had begun on August 7, 1914; German troops had broken through the Belgian defensive line on the Meuse a week or so later; and by August 23 they were in France and fighting for the hills overlooking the Meuse south of Sedan (the engagement took its name from the woods overlooking the city, the Bois de la Marfée).

In May 1940, as was the case with Scandinavia, the German strike was a preemptive defense. The Germans knew in 1939, as they had known in 1914, that in the event of an actual conflict, the neutrality of important strategic countries would be rapidly discarded, as the Allies had already done with Norway. The problem was that the Netherlands was an excellent staging ground for an attack into the most vulnerable part of Germany, the industrial center of the Ruhr. Without it, and with the Belgians holding a defensive position somewhere to the east of the river Dyle, Germany could find the tables turned very quickly. So there was a sound military reason for attacking the Netherlands.

All this made seizing the bridges intact a high priority, and in 1939 the German army assembled what was basically the first special operations group, the Bau Lehr Bataillon zur Besonderen Verwendung 800. The lengthy name was ambiguous, suggesting a demonstration or instructional engineering unit, but the special purpose hinted at in the name was simply the use of covert means to seize important objectives such as bridges.

As the battalion was based in the town of Brandenburg, its men became known as the Brandenburgs, and in the opening hours of the war Brandenburg teams tried to seize all the key bridges along the

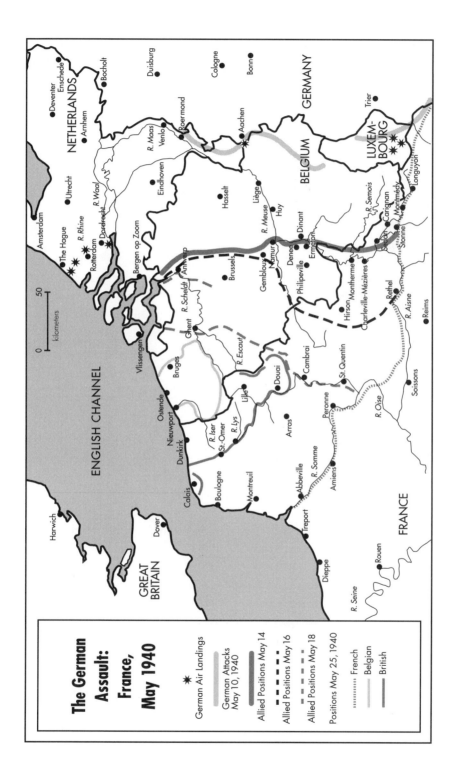

The German Assault: France, May 1940

German Air Landings

German Attacks May 10, 1940

Allied Positions May 14

Allied Positions May 16

Allied Positions May 18

Positions May 25, 1940

French
Belgian
British

ENGLISH CHANNEL

GREAT BRITAIN

Harwich
Dover

NETHERLANDS

Deventer
Enschede
Bocholt
Duisburg
Cologne
Bonn

Amsterdam
The Hague
Rotterdam
Utrecht
Arnhem
Roermond
Venlo
Aachen

R. Maas
R. Waal
R. Rhine
Dordrecht

Vlissengen
Bergen op Zoom
Antwerp
Ghent
Bruges
Ostende
Nieuwpoort
Dunkirk

GERMANY

Trier
LUXEM-BOURG
Longuyon
Montmédy
Carignan
Sedan
Stonne

BELGIUM

Eindhoven
Hasselt
Liège
Huy
Namur
Dinant
Denee
Philippeville
Ermeton
Gembloux
Brussels
Charleville-Mézières
Hirson
Montherme
Rethel
Reims

R. Meuse
R. Semois
R. Aisne

R. Scheldt
R. Escaut
R. Lys
R. Iser
St.-Omer
Lille
Douai
Arras
Cambrai
St. Quentin
Soissons
Peronne
R. Oise

Calais
Boulogne
Montreuil
Abbeville
Treport
Amiens
R. Somme
Dieppe
Rouen
R. Seine

FRANCE

0   50
kilometers

Dutch frontier, while another specially organized assault team, consisting of Pioniere, or combat engineers, attacked the Belgian crossings dominated by the great fort of Eben Emael.

Typical of the way the Brandenburg teams operated was the attempt to seize the railroad bridge at Gennep, south of Nijmegen. The idea was that a six-man team would seize the bridge, and the Germans would then run two trains over it containing lead elements of the 256th Infantry Division, as the German high command realized that the Brandenburg teams could not possibly survive for very long in the face of armed resistance. In order to fool the Dutch guards, the team had with them members of the Dutch National Socialist Party, dressed in Dutch uniforms. After a good deal of confusion, the Brandenburgs were able to capture the Dutch demolition post, and the troop trains sped into the Netherlands.[3]

Elsewhere, however, the Brandenburgs were less successful. The Dutch destroyed both the Nijmegen bridges, as well as over half of the bridges between that town and the Belgium-Netherlands frontier on the Meuse. Insofar as the Germans were simply using the southern part of the Netherlands as a route into northern Belgium, the successes of the Brandenburgs, together with the achievements of the Pioniere at Eben Emael, ensured the rapid deployment of German troops.

Both the Dutch and the French had planned for this, albeit separately. The Dutch, realizing that the southernmost part of the country would be indefensible in the event of a German attack, had based their defensive plan on the concept of *Vesting Holland* (Fortress Holland), taking advantage of the fact that the provinces at the core of the country were essentially an island—at least potentially. In the event of an attack, the Dutch would flood portions of the country and defend only the central core, which also contained the bulk of the population and all the major cities.

The French had therefore planned to move their Seventh Army into northern Belgium and thence into the southern part of the Netherlands as soon as practical, to counter a German advance that would otherwise be uncontested.[4] As time passed, however, the Dutch expanded their ideas, and by May 1940 were committed to defending the entire country.

So the Germans, faced with an interminable series of bridges, together with the possibility of widespread flooding, had decided to conquer the Netherlands through an airborne assault. One division (the

Seventh Airborne) would be dropped directly into the center of the country, seizing the major airfields, so that a large infantry force (the Twenty-second Air Landing Division) could be air landed in support. As with the Brandenburgs, the Luftwaffe commanders appreciated that a few thousand lightly armed paratroopers would be quickly overwhelmed by the Dutch army unless there were immediate reinforcements. But even those troops would be defeated unless substantial land-based forces could reach them, so the whole plan of attack depended on perfect timing.

The Dutch had watched the previous German offensives carefully, noting the use of surprise aerial assaults, and although the scale of the offensive surprised them, neither the tactics nor the timing did. In fact the Dutch had two nasty surprises in store. The Dutch army was small and in general badly equipped, and it had no tanks, but it did have twenty-six armored cars equipped with machine guns and 37-millimeter cannons. These vehicles, stationed near the main airports, proved a devastating weapon, since the paratroopers had no antitank guns.

The armored car is perhaps the forgotten vehicle of this war. When armor enthusiasts spoke of armored fighting vehicles, they meant tanks and tanks alone. Guderian, for instance, was such a purist that he was even opposed to the construction of tracked and armored turretless vehicles. Armor, in other words, meant tanks—vehicles with tracks and rotating turrets. So armored cars were beneath contempt.

This was the perfect example of how theory blinded experts to the realities of combat. Most of Europe had all-weather roads, and much of the rest of the road network was navigable by a wheeled vehicle, provided it had the right combination of tires and propulsion. There was also a considerable rail network, and the Germans had decided early on that not only would Germany build armored cars, but they would be built so they could run on the rail tracks. Their French equivalent had taken a different route, and produced vehicles capable of what in modern parlance we would call serious off-road travel.

Relatively light vehicles with their weight distributed onto four or six large pneumatic tires, with all axles driven, were in fact capable of running without roads, and were a practical way of delivering highly mobile firepower onto the battlefield. The Germans used armored cars primarily in the reconnaissance units attached to the armored divisions. The French used them the same way but also saw them as capable of carrying out the traditional screening activities of the cavalry.

Now the Dutch added a new and hitherto unsuspected use. As the

German paratroopers landed, Dutch armored cars raced to the scene and engaged them. In the German order, paratroopers dropped without any weapons whatsoever, and had to retrieve them from supply canisters that hopefully dropped where the men did, so they were basically unarmed.

After Poland the Germans were aware of the major difficulty in using airborne troops: Transport planes were no better at hitting drop zones with men than bombers were in hitting targets with bombs. Dispersed, lightly armed, and dropped thousands of meters away from where they should have been, paratroopers were more calculated to spread confusion than accomplish anything of more direct importance.

So the Germans had sensibly decided to rely on actual air drops as little as possible. In the assault on the Netherlands, roughly three thousand paratroopers were dropped, but the bulk of the invasion force—over 20,000 men—would be landed in transport planes on the airfields the paratroopers had hopefully seized.

The transport force consisted of some 430 JU 52 transport planes, venerable aircraft totally unsuited for either role: they had practically no armor and a light payload. As a result, in addition to the three thousand paratroopers, the air assault would have only about four thousand men on the ground during the first day. It was there that the Germans received the second unpleasant surprise—actually, a series of nasty surprises in rapid sequence.

Unlike the Belgians and the Allies, the Dutch air defense system was on full alert on the morning of May 10, 1940. Perhaps one should say that, unlike the Allies, the Dutch actually possessed an air defense system: about 275 modern antiaircraft guns, including 150 20-millimeter Oerlikons, 81 75-millimeter Vickers Skoda weapons, and 42 40-millimeter Bofors guns.[5]

During the short but violent air war that followed, the Dutch air force was basically wiped out, with eighty-eight of its 123 aircraft destroyed.[6] But the Luftwaffe suffered heavily as well, losing 328 aircraft out of the 930 engaged, most of them in the first day of fighting. The JU 52s were annihilated. Those that were not shot down by the Dutch defenders, landing successfully on the airfields, discovered that for various reasons it was difficult if not impossible to take off again, as the planners had envisaged. So of the 430 transports, 280 were destroyed, which basically meant the end of Germany's airborne offensive capabilities in the near future. "From the German point of view the major disaster of the attack on Holland was that it consumed 310 of the 430 transports employed; and as these were mostly flown by instructors from bomber training units the chain reaction effect on German operations was out of proportion to the value derived," is how one analyst put it.[7] Given how thin the Luftwaffe was in terms of trained flight crews, the personnel losses were horrific and would have a major impact on the Battle of Britain.

On the ground the fighting was a confused series of engagements that sprang up wherever a group of paratroopers had landed successfully. Given the problems with the JU 52s, only 10,500 Germans actually made it into the Netherlands during the first few days, although these were soon reinforced as conventional forces fought their way through. But the toll was heavy: There were four thousand German casualties out of the ten-thousand-odd actually engaged in those first few days. And the Dutch fought bitterly on: In the five-day battle they had 2,032 men killed, which probably makes the fight for Fortress Holland one of the bloodier battles of the Second World War.

The fighting was at its most intense around Rotterdam, where German units had broken through and were trying to relieve the paratroopers who had been surrounded by the Dutch army and marines and were on the verge of being wiped out. By the fourteenth the German plan was to attack at 3:30 in the afternoon, the attack to be preceded by a combined air and artillery assault. That morning the arrangements having been made, the German commander, Lt. Gen. Rudolf Schmidt, had an ultimatum sent to his Dutch counterpart in the city, and negotiations began.

Given their situation the Dutch were not at first inclined to surrender; however, the German emissaries were convinced that they would, and duly dispatched an order to call off the artillery bombardment and the bombing attack. In the resulting confusion (which was hardly helped by conflicting time zones being employed by the two sides: when it was 3:30 P.M. for the Germans it was 1:50 P.M. for the Dutch), the Luftwaffe ended up bombing the city even though the German ground commanders had indicated they wanted the assault delayed.

The Allies were quick to inflate the resulting conflagration, which was certainly bad enough, with much of the central city burned to the ground and more than nine hundred civilians killed. On the heels of the "destruction" of Warsaw, the bombing of Rotterdam quickly became a potent symbol both of the wickedness of Hitler and the terrifying power of the bomber.[8] The wickedness was real, but the bombing was accidental.

The devastation visited on Rotterdam, whether accidental or not, had a major effect. That evening, General Winkelman, commander of the Dutch forces inside Fortress Holland, decided to surrender, and on the next day, the fifteenth, he did so. Queen Wilhelmina, who like any responsible monarch was concerned most with the safety and well-being of her subjects, had quickly been persuaded to let the government capitulate, and, perhaps unwisely, let herself be hustled out of the country to Great Britain.[9]

In the mythology of the successive capitulations of 1940, the Netherlands was at this point totally destroyed militarily. But this was rather far from the case. As Pallud points out, most Dutch soldiers had not yet seen action, and those who had "did not regard themselves as beaten."[10]

Proportionally the Dutch took more casualties and inflicted more losses on the attackers than did any of the other armies. They basically destroyed the Luftwaffe's transport fleet and rendered its elite troops *hors de combat*. Dutch soldiers gave their lives for their country, often—as in the case of Maj. Willem Pieter Landzaat, refusing to surrender and dying in battle, even when surrounded and outnumbered.[11]

For a military that had last seen combat in the age of the musket, this was not a bad record, and it suggests what could have happened had the Dutch devoted any serious attention to self-defense before the war. As the well-known Dutch historian Louis de Jong observed, "A people which neglects its defense puts its freedom at risk."[12] A failed policy of national defense is its own punishment, Bismarck had observed. Sadly he was correct. The Netherlands would suffer more than any country in the West under the German occupation.

Belgium

In the immediate aftermath of the collapse of 1940, the British and the French made Belgium and its unfortunate monarch the scapegoats: It was the hapless Belgians who had brought about the defeat in the West. In the first instance they persisted in remaining neutral long after the foolishness of this approach was obvious. In the second instance the Belgian army didn't fight, and in the third instance, the country promptly surrendered, leaving the Allied armies, and principally the British, in the lurch.

None of this was true, but it was not for want of trying. Only the prompt intervention in Great Britain of Sir Roger Keyes, a distinguished British naval officer who in the course of the previous war had become friendly with the Belgian royal family, scotched the smears the British government initially released. In addition to being a distinguished sailor, Keyes was also a member of Parliament. In the First World War his French equivalents had caused no end of difficulty for the French government, and now Keyes (and other Britons who had a dual capacity) were doing the same thing, keeping the government from fictionalizing the war to its own advantage. Like the French in the previous war, the British government, if it couldn't win, could certainly manage a marvelous public relations campaign to justify its own behavior and blame everyone else for its failures.

The Belgians hadn't been neutral in the First World War, but a combination of events had given them the determination to stay firmly and definitively outside the Allied camp in 1940, particularly after the events of September 1939. And the impotence of the Western democracies in the face of the Soviet invasion of Finland had hardly been the sort of event that would change that.

So the Belgians, like the Scandinavians, felt that neutrality was a meaningful option. Moreover, as was the case also in the Netherlands, there was a sizable and vocal minority who were infatuated with both Hitler and with fascism, just as there was an equally large minority who felt the same way about Stalin and communism. So the Belgians, sensibly enough, built up their army and insisted on their neutrality. In the event of an invasion, they could mobilize six hundred thousand men, and by some measures the Belgian army of 1939–40 was a formidable defensive force.

There was also—contrary to popular belief—a Belgian air force of around three hundred planes.[13] Belgium, like the Netherlands, had developed its own fighter plane, beginning in 1936, and in 1939 had gotten a license to build British-designed Hurricane fighters. Gloomily aware that the country could be overwhelmed from the air, the Belgians had also devoted considerable resources to antiaircraft defenses, and the eleven air defense groups were armed with the Swedish Bofors 40-millimeter antiaircraft gun, as well as British- and Belgian-designed weapons of even greater power.

The country's defensive system rested in the first instance on the fortifications dominating the Meuse River, but the Belgian command had a fallback position along the river Dyle as well. As in France the need was for a defensive line to hold off an invasion long enough for the army to mobilize, which was why the Belgians had rebuilt and reorganized the Liège forts in the 1930s.

This had been the chief entry point for German armies in 1914. Indeed, when Moltke the Younger had set out the plans for the invasion, he had noted that the key was the neutralization of the Liège forts, and the centerpiece of the German plan in August 1914 was what he called a coup de main against the forts. Contrary to Allied propaganda at the time, von Moltke's coup was successful. The forts were attacked on August 7, 1914, and within a few days German troops were streaming around the neutralized forts and marching through Belgium. In less than two weeks they were in France, despite fierce French resistance.

As in 1914, so in 1939: The Germans had been giving some thought to this problem, and had developed a solution. The thing to do was to seize all the bridges crossing the Meuse in northern Belgium before the Belgians could destroy them. In the Netherlands this task was largely the responsibility of the Brandenburg detachment, but the Meuse was not the border between Belgium and Germany, so the troops would have to be delivered by air.

In the Netherlands the Germans had no real choice but to use air drops, but here, where precision was essential, they would use gliders. The glider was an inherently more accurate way of delivering small, self-contained groups of infantry. A trained glider pilot could set his craft down with remarkable precision, and the men inside were already armed, indeed could carry machine guns or, in the case of the German troops landing in Belgium, explosive charges.

Given the mechanism for delivery, in which the glider was released far from the target and steered into it, the glider had another advantage over the soldier dropped from an airplane: There was none of the telltale engine drone overhead to signal his approach. Lacking a motor, the glider was silent.

Moreover, in May 1940, the glider had another great advantage: No one had ever used it in combat before, and this compensated almost completely for what would prove to be its overwhelming defect. If spotted, a glider was an easy target even for ordinary infantry armed only with rifles.

Besides precision there was the advantage of carrying capacity. Because there was no way the operation could succeed unless the guns of the great Belgian fort, Eben Emael, could be silenced. If they weren't, seizing the bridges intact was beside the point. German armored columns would be destroyed on the roads, because the guns of Eben Emael controlled the river crossings and the roads leading to them.

In fact, the failure to build a fort at this position in the years before the First World War had been one of the chief reasons the German offensive was so successful: Brialmont, the great Belgian military engineer who had designed the forts, had wanted one there, but, mainly for reasons of economy, it hadn't been built. But in the 1930s the Belgians had rectified this problem with a vengeance.

What we think of as Eben Emael is actually an enormous hill about eleven hundred meters long and eight hundred meters wide, rising up out of the relatively flat terrain on the western bank of the Meuse above Liège. It sticks up out of the terrain like Gibraltar, a massive rock the Belgians had honeycombed with artillery positions. Indeed, the liability of the fortress, its weakness, was its very size. The French had constructed their artificial fortifications so that the forward gun emplacements were all capable of supporting fire, and so that the majority of the guns were in rotating turrets with 360 degree fields of fire.

The size of Eben Emael largely precluded that. The various gun emplacements and turrets were therefore completely independent. But of course it was difficult to see how infantry, assuming they got close to a turret or casemate, could disable it. Only a direct hit from a heavy artillery piece could do that, and there was absolutely no way that such a gun could be brought in close enough range to fire.

Anyone who crossed the Meuse could look up and see Eben Emael. The Germans knew, therefore, that it was a major problem, and they had devised a solution. The glider-borne assault troops would land on the fort itself by surprise, and they would carry with them a most potent new weapon, one that had never been used in combat before, the hollow charge.[14]

The hollow charge was not a new principle. The traditional approach to piercing a steel plate was to fire an extremely dense piece of metal at the highest possible velocity, so the resulting force expended on the plate would pierce it. Given the armor used in 1939–40, the standard French antitank gun would do this at most ranges. But the steel embrasures and cupolas used in Belgian, French, and German forts were impervious to such weapons. The German 88-millimeter antiaircraft gun could pierce most cupolas if it was fired at a range of less than 500 meters, but the prospect of moving a gun the size of a tank—but without any armor protection—within that range while under fire made this a most unlikely eventuality. So, given the inherent inaccuracy of bombing, it was widely assumed that thick steel plates were basically invulnerable.

Back in 1888 a scientist named Munro had discovered that if you clamped a charge onto a steel plate, and shaped the charge so the part of it in contact with the plate was actually hollow—that is, a cavity, with the explosive on the other side—when the charge was ignited, it would form a sort of high-temperature molten jet that would cut through the steel plate completely. The penetrating effect of a hollow charge was phenomenal. But to Munro it was simply a curiosity, as no one had any idea how the principle could actually be used.

The Germans, however, had seen the application: The hollow charge could be equipped with powerful magnets that would clamp it to the surface to be penetrated, and this suggested the method of neutralizing Eben Emael. Pioniere would land on top of the enormous fort by glider, so that when they landed, they could deploy what the Germans called a *Hohlladung*, or hollow charge, magnetic packs of 25 and 50 kilograms that they would attach to the metal plates of the Belgian turrets on the fort.

The plan was sound enough, given the great size of Eben Emael, which meant that its gunners were largely isolated and couldn't provide covering fire. Moreover the Belgians hadn't attempted to protect the top of the great hill, or the areas around it, with any sort of passive antipersonnel protection. In this regard the French were far ahead of everyone else and had provided their clusters of exposed turrets with barbed-wire fencing and antitank devices that would have ripped the bottom out of any glider and probably caused serious injury to anyone who landed on one. Then too, the French fortifications were lavishly provided with fixed machine-gun positions covering every approach to a casemate or turret. But the Belgians had conceived of their forts, even the newer ones like Eben Emael, strictly as artillery positions.

Along with the Brandenburg operations, the glider landings were the first actions of the new war. Seventy-seven Pioniere landed on the fort, while much larger forces landed by the three key bridges nearby, all told, eleven officers and 427 men. It took the seventy-seven combat engineers who landed on Eben Emael approximately twenty-eight hours to neutralize the fort, while their comrades seized the all-important bridges.[15]

Along the German border with Luxembourg, the Brandenburgs were also active, supported by one of the more curious and innovative operations of the war. By now the German high command had run out of conventional means to mount airborne assaults. One airborne unit was stranded in Norway, the rest were committed to action in the Netherlands, along with all the transport planes, and the remainder— together with all the gliders—had been sent against Eben Emael. But the German high command decided that two additional diversionary operations were needed. One of these would block the deployment of the two crack Belgian units, the Chasseurs Ardennaise, into the Belgian Ardennes by cutting down trees across roads and similarly destroying communications. The other would attempt to facilitate the advance of the German units into Luxembourg by mounting a holding operation along the frontier with France, thus impeding the advance of French units moving into Luxembourg.

Lacking conventional air delivery systems at this point, the planners tasked each group differently. For the Ardennes, they decided to take infantry from Germany's elite unit, Gross Deutschland, put most of them into Fiesler 156 planes, and land them at key places in the intensely forested Belgian Ardennes. For operations along the French frontier with Luxembourg, they selected 125 men from the Thirty-fourth Infantry Division, gave them special training, and aimed to put them in Fieseler Storch aircraft. Both groups would simply land behind enemy lines.

The problem was that the Fi 156 was a small reconnaissance plane that could hold at most two men and the pilot. To get four hundred equipped soldiers into action would take—literally—two hundred Fi 156 aircraft two trips, and that was assuming all went well. Similarly, it would take twenty-five Storch aircraft working in a sort of shuttle operation to land the 125 infantry along the frontier.

As it turned out, the Ardennes operation was totally unnecessary: The Belgian plan was to withdraw through the area, not to try to defend it. There was an additional complication: the senior Luftwaffe officer for the mission got lost and landed in the wrong place. As his was one of the lead aircraft, other planes followed him. Despite their theoretical advantage over parachutists, basic navigational incompetence dispersed the four hundred men all over the Ardennes. To add insult to injury, their demolition work, expertly done, had only one effect: It blocked the roads for the advancing German forces.

Meanwhile, their comrades along the border promptly found themselves engaged in a firefight with the advancing French, who, contrary to
the received wisdom, had crossed the Luxembourg frontier almost at the
time the German troops had landed and begun to organize.[16] By the
time the combat had ended, roughly a quarter of the German detachment, known as the Hedderich Air Commando (after its senior officer),
had been killed.[17]

The Fighting Begins in Earnest

If one were to look at a map of the disposition of the opposing forces,
together with their location, a snapshot of the situation on the evening
of Saturday, May 11, the Allied line would resemble nothing so much as
a backward letter S. The line curved up along the Meuse to Namur, then
curved in the opposite direction, the apex of the curve being to the east
of Eben Emael. The line then slowly curved back as it rose up into the
Netherlands.

Below Eben Emael, the line had already collapsed slightly, but the
BEF and the French First Army were already in position along the Dyle.
Although the German Twelfth Army was advancing through the
Ardennes, and the Sixteenth Army through Luxembourg, other German
armies—the Sixth and the Fourth—were moving against the center. The
picture so frequently drawn, then, of the Allies advancing to meet a
phantom enemy whose real strength was engaged to the south of them,
is simply not true.[18]

By the next day, Sunday, advance units of the German Twelfth Army
were crossing the Franco-Belgian frontier above Sedan, and the Sixth
Army was forcing the core of the Belgian army back to the Dyle, where
the BEF and the French First Army were. The German Fourth Army at
this point was in fact attacking to the northeast below the town of Huy.
In fact the German advance through central Belgium resulted in the
first—and only—major tank battle of 1940.

The reason was simple. Contrary to general belief, French ground
forces had started moving promptly enough. By midmorning on the
tenth the French were advancing into Belgium (and Luxembourg) from
the west and the south. Although the Germans were moving much
more quickly than had been anticipated, there was still no reason why

the Allies couldn't reach the Dyle before them, and in fact they did.

Proponents of the entrapment theory, in which the Germans let the Allies pour into Belgium in order to cut them off with a sweep through the Ardennes, overlook the fact that the French were advancing south-north as well as west-east. Nor were the Germans in Army Group B strong enough to defeat the Allies on their own. This of course was what the Germans themselves had feared: The advancing forces of Army Group A would be caught between the Maginot Line forts and the Allied armies in north and central Belgium, and attacked on both flanks.

And now this fear seemed to be realized. Because at the same moment that the bulk of the German armored forces were beginning to penetrate the frontier above Sedan, the advancing French mechanized units engaged the advancing armor of the German Sixteenth Army Corps in central Belgium. The two German tank divisions of the Sixteenth Corps were shielding the main armored advance to their south. Clearly, if the French broke through their screen, the whole idea of the German offensive would promptly implode.

And now the Germans found a serious adversary, the French Cavalry Corps. Despite its name, the Cavalry Corps was a formidable armored and mechanized force, and in the ensuing fight gave a good account of itself. The French H39 tank, for example, was capable of destroying a German Mark 4. The problem was that the French were vastly outnumbered and had no air support. On the other hand their artillery was vastly better than anything the Germans had. The fire was so accurate that at one point the staffs of the tank brigades of the Fourth Armored Division were "chased out of their command posts and two battalion commanders killed," according to the divisional diary.[19]

The result was the only large scale tank engagement of 1940, and, in point of fact, the most intense large-scale battle of 1940. Fighting began on the morning of the fourteenth, and by the end of the day the Germans had been repulsed. The next day they returned to the offensive, but the French artillery and tanks did heavy damage, gravely wounding the senior officers of the Fourth Armored Division, who had to be evacuated.

Over the course of the battle, the French had more than one hundred tanks destroyed outright, but they gave somewhat better than they received—the German Third and Fourth Armored Divisions between them lost more than 150 vehicles, with as many more being severely damaged. By the evening of the fifteenth, the Germans had abandoned the battlefield. Given the size of the armored forces involved on the German side, two divisions with slightly more than 250 tanks apiece, and given the usual ratio of completely destroyed to unserviceable tanks, the Germans had basically lost one entire armored division in this engagement.

The Battle of the Gembloux Gap thus epitomizes the paradoxical nature of May 1940. In the first (and only) serious battle, the only large-scale tank-versus-tank engagement, the French had prevailed and forced the Germans to retreat. Postwar German analyses of the battle opine that if Prioux had been reinforced—instead of told to withdraw—the "whole German front in Belgium might have crumpled."[20]

So much for the idea that the French had no notion of how to deploy armor. But General Prioux, the architect of this victory, was promptly ordered to withdraw. While he was beating the Germans around Gembloux, the French line had been pierced at Sedan. This event, or rather the interpretations of this event, have so overshadowed everything else that occurred during this first fatal week of the May fighting that in hindsight almost every other engagement has been shoved into the background. Even when noted as happening, the Battle of the Gembloux Gap is relegated to obscurity.

Why is the battle ignored? Partly because it happened at almost the same moment as Sedan. There were two reasons for this. On the one hand it was a given that the French either had no tanks or had no idea of how to use them. So a major tank battle in which the French prevailed was impossible. On the other hand it was also a given that the whole move into Belgium, the Dyle Plan, was a clever German trap. While the Allies obligingly rushed into the center and the north, the Germans cleverly deployed in the south. The hundreds of tanks destroyed at Gembloux testify to the fact that it happened. And since it did, the whole basis for interpreting May 1940 begins to collapse. As we shall see, the great tank battle at Gembloux is not the only evidence that the received wisdom is erroneous.

The War in the Air

In accounts of the German victory of 1940, the power of the Luftwaffe, together with the impotence of the Allied air forces, is given as one of the main reasons for the collapse. Neither of the other reasons has any factual basis. As the Battle of the Gembloux Gap illustrates, there was serious fighting in central Belgium, and the French clearly understood how to use armor, since the Cavalry Corps was temporarily victorious over no less than two German armored divisions.

But it has always been clear that German airpower was the key to their success. The Germans had a large and modern air force, while the Allies, a few British planes excepted, had a small and obsolete one. However, this idea has to be seriously qualified. The observation that the British and French air forces were not nearly as small or as old as was often claimed only compounds the mystery. Why was it that in May 1940 there was an almost universal cry by the Allied ground forces that the "skies were empty" of our aircraft?[21]

In the account of the defense of the Netherlands, we noted the havoc wrought by the Dutch on the German transport fleet, pointing out that in large measure this was because the Dutch, alone of the countries attacked, had their air force and their air defense system on alert, so their few fighter planes were actually taking off at the moment of the German attack.

While German troops poured into Belgium across the intact bridges, the Luftwaffe attacked the bases of the Belgian air force. Unlike the Dutch, who had been on alert, the Belgians had counted on having some sort of notice, so the Germans caught many of their planes on the ground. Of the 160 planes operational and ready for combat on May 10, it appears that more than seventy were destroyed on the ground in the initial attack. But enough planes survived to enable the Belgian air force to mount 210 sorties over the next eighteen days of the battle. At the end of those eighteen days, seventeen planes had been shot down in aerial combat, and twenty-two were shot down by ground fire. The Belgians counted eighteen German planes shot down, and lost thirty-four men from their flight crews.[22] That the Dutch and the Belgians were defeated does not mean that they simply gave up a fight against overwhelming odds.

Nor were the British and French idle. On May 10 the RAF lost thirty-four aircraft, only three of them destroyed on the ground by German bombers. The rest were shot down as they made bombing attacks on the advancing Germans, and an inspection of the locations and recorded causes—insofar as they are known—makes clear that many of these planes were in fact shot down trying to stop the advance through

Luxembourg and the Belgian Ardennes, and that a surprising number of the losses came not from air-to-air attacks but from ground fire.[23] On the next day, Saturday, the RAF lost twenty-three bombers—and this time, an appreciable number (eight) were lost to enemy bombing attacks—but the same pattern continued. On Sunday the RAF lost another thirty-four bombers, most of them again to ground fire as they tried to stop the German advance.

Given the number of tactical bombers available in France to the Allies, losses at this level—thirty aircraft a day—were intolerable. At this rate the Allied tactical bomber force would be wiped out in a few days, which is essentially what happened (the initial RAF deployment in France only amounted to some 400 aircraft, most of which were fighter planes). Nor did this happen because the Luftwaffe enjoyed command of the skies. British and French fighters were inflicting considerable damage on the Luftwaffe.

The problem was that neither the French nor the British air command had given any serious attention to the basic problems of tactical bombing. They both subscribed to the idea that level-flight bombing could destroy targets on the ground, and had neglected the impact of antiaircraft fire on such attacks, when, by definition, the bombers flying at low altitudes would be most vulnerable.

The Germans, for whom airpower was tactical, had taken care to provide their ground troops with the means of air defense. Göring, Hitler's designated successor and commander of the Luftwaffe, had assumed control over everything military that was remotely connected with the air: Thus in the German system the air force had control both over airborne units and the air defense system. So the antiaircraft weapons mentioned earlier that accompanied German units into battle were manned by Luftwaffe personnel.

The German military, like most militaries, prepared for a war against the force it knew best—its own. As we have seen, the German air force was primarily tactical, and thus centered around ground attack. That was why the Germans had developed the dive-bomber—it was the only reasonably accurate system of bomb delivery. Tactical bombers were terribly vulnerable to enemy fighter planes, whether they were dive-bombers or level-flight bombers. To be successful in any shape or form, they needed to operate in skies cleared of enemy aircraft, which demanded air supremacy. Not unreasonably, therefore, when the Luftwaffe assumed the role of providing air defense for the army, it thought in terms of its own airpower doctrines.

Since these were tactical, it therefore developed a first-class ground to air system, built around a simple principle: The best way to shoot down tactical bombers was to saturate the air space they had to fly through to drop their bombs. Unlike the German army, which went to war rather badly equipped when it came to artillery and antitank guns, the flak units that accompanied them had three excellent weapons capable of a high volume of fire, and these weapons existed in huge numbers: about 6,700 rapid-firing special-purpose guns, one of 20 millimeters and the other of 37 millimeters, supplemented by 2,600 heavier weapons, mostly the famous 88-millimeter gun.[24]

The Dutch and the Belgians were nearly as well equipped with anti-aircraft guns, proportionally speaking, as the Germans. But the British and the French were sadly deficient in ground-to-air systems. The only truly automatic weapon available in quantity was the Hotchkiss 8-millimeter machine gun used by the French, a weapon totally inadequate for the purpose. Allied bombers were massacred when they tried to attack the advancing German ground forces, while the Luftwaffe was able to attack Allied ground forces almost at will.

The Allies had no real equivalent to the German Stuka, the JU 87 dive-bomber: Allied level-flight bombers were rarely able to hit anything they aimed at, while the JU 87 was a reasonably accurate delivery system. The Allied failure, then, was deeply entwined with airpower doctrines, and these had led the RAF, which in reality was the largest and most powerful air force in the world, down a series of blind alleys.

Thus the basic military reason for the Allied disaster had nothing to do with tanks or tank tactics; it was a function of the 586 Allied planes the two German flak units claimed to have shot down in the fighting.[25] To leap ahead forty-eight hours in our narrative, and bring this matter to its logical conclusion: when, on Tuesday, May 14, the Allied high command saw the dangers of the German breakthrough above Sedan, they mounted intensive bombing raids. Bomber Command lost no less than forty-seven of its medium bombers on that one day in a futile attempt to stop the German advance. As one sympathetic and knowledgeable British aviation authority has noted, "It was one of the blackest days in RAF bomber operations."[26] In that one engagement Bomber Command lost more than half of the aircraft deployed.

When, in the succeeding days, the RAF bombing raids ceased, the reason was simple: The aircrews to mount those raids were either dead or were prisoners. Like the BEF of 1914, the Advanced Air Component of the RAF had simply been annihilated, losing 70 percent of its strength, with the French figures being almost precisely the same.[27]

Most accounts of the air war in 1940 have focused on the fighter-to-fighter conflicts. In general both the French air force and the RAF Fighter Command gave a good accounting of themselves in these battles. Frequently the only Allied fighter planes mentioned are the British Spitfire and Hurricane, which formed the core of Fighter Command. Less well known are the exploits of their French counterparts. French squadrons equipped with the Curtiss 75A fighter shot down 33 German fighters and lost only three of their own; units equipped with the Morane-Saulnier 406 fighter plane shot down 31 German planes and suffered only six losses—this despite the fact that the MS 406 was thought to be obsolescent. Units equipped with the Bloch 152 shot down 156 German planes and lost 59. French pilots flying Dewoitine 520 fighter planes lost forty-four of their own and accounted for 175 Germans.[28]

The surprisingly competent performance of the French and British (and Dutch and Belgian) fighter pilots has to a large extent obscured the massacre of their ground-attack craft, which has in turn led to a series of misconceptions, first about the air war itself, and second about the extent to which the Allies were "tricked" or "surprised" by "new" German tactics and technology. The one major cause of the defeat was clearly the Allied airpower failure—specifically the failure to have the right kinds of airplanes for tactical bombing, as well as a doctrine requiring the coordination with the ground forces. As with tanks, the Allies had plenty of planes, and in air-to-air combat, they clearly knew how to use them. Where they signally failed was in a fundamental misunderstanding of tactical airpower and the defenses against it.

There was one other weakness on the Allied side, which is usually passed over and goes a long way toward explaining why the ground forces felt so overwhelmed by German aircraft. German airfields were only half an hour's flying time from their initial targets. The short distances allowed the Luftwaffe to take advantage of a unique feature of the air war. It was customary, for obvious reasons, to register the strengths of opposing armies by counting men, guns, and vehicles. One armored division deployed into battle had the strength of one armored division. It could only be deployed once. But aircraft could fly over the target, drop their bombs, return to base, refuel and re-arm, and launch another mission, which is why nowadays one speaks not of aircraft but of sorties, one aircraft flying one mission.

In strategic bombing this distinction hardly came into play. It would take a bomber hours (and, given the speed of the bombers of 1939 and the distances to targets, many hours) to get to its target and hours to return. The result, given the maintenance needs of both aircraft and flight crew, was a leisurely tempo of operations. But if the aircraft were immediately adjacent to the battlefield, one plane could fly three, four, five sorties a day, and particularly in May, when it was light nearly fifteen hours or more.

Since the Germans flew many more sorties per day than their opponents did, this had the practical effect of multiplying the size of their air force. If one air force deploys five hundred planes and each plane flies two sorties a day, and the other air force deploys the same number of planes, but each plane flies four sorties a day, then to all intents and purposes, the first air force is outnumbered two to one in the air.[29]

In the case of May 1940, the imbalance was much worse than that. The RAF, although it was averaging about two sorties per plane per day, was still thinking strategically, not tactically. Airfields in France were located far behind the frontier, so the planes were protected from enemy attack. But that meant it took the planes longer to get over the battle-field, so the logistics of the situation virtually guaranteed that the RAF would operate less efficiently in the air than its opponents.

To say that no one had pondered this is an understatement. Once the fighting started, the RAF actually deployed more of its airpower than did the French, twelve of its forty operational fighter squadrons, while the French air force only committed 580 of its 2,200 fighter aircraft to the battle—so the British commitment was proportionally greater than the French (a fact that would lead to a certain justifiable bitterness on the part of the RAF and the British).

But in order to compensate for the greater number of sorties being flown by the Luftwaffe, the RAF would have been forced to commit all of its fighter strength, and the French would have had to have at least doubled their commitment, simply because the Germans were able to mount more combat missions with fewer aircraft than their opponents. And since they deployed as many aircraft as the Allies, the net effect was

one of overwhelming superiority in the air. This accounts for the perceived initial advantage of the Germans over the Allies. By mounting
more sorties per plane initially, the Germans had a great advantage, but
had the war continued, the advantage would have turned to the Allies;
first because the wear and tear on their planes was substantially less (as
they flew less), and second because the Allies had committed a significantly smaller portion of their aircraft to the fight.

The Panic

In almost all accounts of the war the German advance into Sedan is
characterized both as the demonstration of the superiority of German
armor and as the beginning of the end. Here it was less than five days
after the start of hostilities, and the Allies had already been beaten, their
plans in disarray, the disaster so total that the Belgian army quit and the
British had to withdraw. Whether the failure was one of ground-attack
aircraft, a faulty deployment of forces, the element of surprise—or all
three—there was total panic on the French side when the first German
tanks appeared at Sedan.

None of this is precisely true, however. Let us deal first with the idea
that the German movement through the Ardennes was a total surprise,
and that the crossing of the Meuse at Sedan produced total panic. Fortunately we have a witness who was present at French headquarters during this time period, Gen. Beaufré:

> Very early on the morning of the 13th I put up on General
> Doumenc's map board the information which had come in during
> the night. The air reconnaissance reports were the clearest: it was evi-
> dent that the main German thrust was not coming in Belgium but
> on the Luxembourg-[Charleville-]Mézières axis. . . . The direction of
> the German effort corresponded with one of the possible eventuali-
> ties which had been foreseen.[30]

The next morning, about 3 A.M. Beaufré was wakened by a phone
call for General Doumenc: General Georges needed him urgently at
headquarters. The account is worth quoting in full.

Georges got up quickly and came to Doumenc. He was terribly pale. "Our front has been broken at Sedan! There has been a collapse. . . ." He flung himself into a chair and burst into tears. . . . Doumenc, taken aback by this greeting, reacted immediately. "General, this is war and in war things like this are bound to happen!" Then Georges, still pale, explained: following a terrible bombardment from the air, two inferior divisions had taken to their heels. Tenth Corps signaled that the position was penetrated and tanks had arrived at Bulson [south of Sedan] at about midnight. Here there was another flood of tears. Everyone else remained silent, shattered by what had happened.

So far Beaufré's narrative seems to confirm the standard account: tears, panic, everyone shattered. But the account continues in a way that reveals the situation in a much different light.

"Well, General," said Doumenc. "All wars have their routs. Let us look at the map and see what can be done." . . . We had at our disposal three armored divisions. . . . Broadly speaking, the situation could be considered as restored.

One of those three, the First Armored, was about to head to the Dyle. It was hastily rerouted and diverted south. This led to the second great armored battle of the war, as the heavy B1 tanks of the French First Armored Division tried to stop the southward movement of Gen. Hermann Hoth's XV Armored Corps, which consisted of the Fifth and Seventh Armored Divisions (the latter being commanded by Erwin Rommel). These two units were moving slowly down toward the French frontier, having left the vicinity of Dinant, astride the main road from Dinant to Philippeville, where the highway then drops due south into France, about twenty kilometers to the northwest of Charleville-Mézières.

The French had about seventy B1 *bis* tanks and another ninety-odd H39s, while the two German armored divisions had about five hundred, but as most of these were Mark 1s and Mark 2s, the actual tank component of the two German divisions was closer to two hundred.[31] Still, the French were outnumbered and had no air support. Worse, the French tanks were running low on fuel.

What followed was the first of the great armored clashes of the war. Gembloux had been a larger battle, but it had involved infantry and artillery as well as tanks, and several survivors described the scene of the conflict as being like some battlefield of the First World War. But Flavion-Denée—to use the names of the two villages close to the fighting—was a straight tank-versus-tank and antitank-versus-tank fight, a bloody melee in which the French B1 tanks destroyed one Mark 4 after another, only in their turn to be destroyed by direct hits from 88-millimeter flak guns and infantry howitzers hastily brought forward in an attempt to stop the slaughter.

And slaughter it was. All the main French officers were killed in action, and several of their opposite numbers were seriously wounded. Eventually the French lost forty-five B1s and fifteen H39s. The Germans lost somewhere between thirty and forty tanks, mostly Mark 4s they could ill afford to lose. Earlier the Germans had discovered that the H39 was a formidable adversary: There is an extant picture of a Mark 4 with its turret blown off as a result of an H39 direct hit.[32] Now another pair of German tank divisions had discovered that there was an even more potent French tank, the B1. Unfortunately the surviving French tanks were running out of fuel, and there were no other French units able to stop the German advance.

But the French still had powerful forces to the southeast of Sedan. For the Germans to drive south, they would have to fight their way across the hilly and wooded terrain that dominated the riverine plain of the Meuse from Sedan eastward. Although the deployment of the newly formed Third Armored Division was haphazard (and justly criticized, by, among others, Beaufré), this should not obscure the fact that the improvised French defensive plan successfully held the Germans along the heights. Indeed, the Battle of Stonne (so named for the chief peak of the region) was one of the bloodiest battles of the war for the Germans: 10 percent of all German war dead from May–June 1940 came as the Germans tried to break through the French positions there. Although during June the French were slowly being pushed back, technically the line was never broken.[33]

So, while the German crossing of the Meuse at Sedan was a major setback for the French, Doumenc was quite right in his observation all wars have routs. And of all the world's armies, the French in 1940 should have been the most institutionally resilient: the Fall of 1914 was one long series of unmitigated disasters, in which the French were fighting desperately right outside of their capital, after a series of routs far worse than Sedan.

The tactical danger of the German move was simple. It enabled them to throw the bulk of their armored divisions into a major northwesterly sweep, which threatened to cut the Allied defensive line in two, with the Belgians, the BEF, and the French Seventh Army on one side and the remaining French armies on the other. This was the basic German plan, or rather we should say their intent.

After the failure of the Allied air attacks on the fifteenth, the German advance intensified. By the evening of the sixteenth the German Twelfth Army had created an enormous bulge in the Allied line, between Charleroi and Rethel. This bulge, or rapidly expanding salient, was as hazardous in execution to the Germans as it was potentially disastrous to the French, since it exposed them to the threat of an offensive by the BEF as well as by the French Seventh Army, which was rapidly moving southwesterly in an attempt to sew up the rupture. And on the southern side the Germans were simply unable to break through.

So although the potential for disaster was there for the defense, it was equally present for the offense, whose lines of communication and supply were becoming ever more tenuous with each passing hour. Moreover, although the Belgians and some French units had seen hard fighting, a substantial proportion of the Allied army had hardly seen any combat at all, including the BEF.

Collapse at the Top

Here is where the panic came in, and with a vengeance. Not where the fighting was, but at the rear. Gamelin, the overall French commander, was, like General Georges, simply overcome. It was France's tragedy that at the crucial hour instead of the phlegmatic and unblinking Joffre, the French army had Gamelin. Moreover the country still had the same sort of excitable civilian government it had endured in August 1914, when the civilians had packed up and abandoned Paris.

The same thing, unfortunately, was true in the BEF, whose commander panicked as well. Like Sir John French in August 1914, the only thought of the senior British commanders, both civilian and military, was to save their army. Instead of attacking into the salient, they began a retreat. In this respect, General Lord Gort, the BEF commander, was a most unfortunate choice. Although he is usually spared any serious blame for the debacle that followed, it would seem that he was pessimistic from the very first moment he arrived in France, and by May 1940 his only instinct was to cut and run.[34]

This was the real disaster of May 1940. In the weeks that followed, the French army proved itself much more resilient than its commander (who was sacked, and replaced by General Weygand). The fact that the French were still fighting desperately, trying to stabilize a defensive line well into June 1940, clearly undercuts the idea that the hysteria that Gamelin communicated to the government, and thence to the British, had any real basis.

That it was, as General Doumenc had observed, a rout, is clear enough. But no more so than the initial battles of 1914. On the contrary, the situation then had been much worse, because not only had the French lost most of the northeastern section of France, but they had lost most of their best infantry as well. After less than a week of fighting, the French Army was in surprisingly good shape. If it hadn't been, the war would have been over on May 16, 1940. As it was, it went on for five more weeks.

The point is important, because the entire justification for the precipitous withdrawal of the BEF rests on the idea that the French army had lost the war and was ready to quit it at any moment. There is no question that at the crucial moment, the morning of May 15, the French prime minister, Paul Reynaud, told Churchill by phone that his country had been defeated; it had lost the war. So one can hardly blame Churchill and the British high command for deciding the time had come to save themselves. Reynaud was, after all, the leader of the government.

The problem was that the German aim in this campaign had always been to "separate the British from the French armies, and occupy Belgium together with Northern France," so the British, when they decided to pull back toward Dunkirk, effectively accomplished the key German aim.[35]

So at this vital juncture, Churchill made a catastrophic misjudgment, all the more glaring because he should have been the most aware of the historical precedents of the French government being inclined to panic, and in the contrary precedent, of a country that historically had been willing to fight on regardless of what happened to that same government. In 1870 the French had fought on after seeing their ruler captured on the field of battle, together with almost their entire army. In 1914, when the government had fled Paris, the hysteria had only made the general population more willing to fight. And Churchill was by temperament a historian, a man who had trained himself to think in terms of precedents and the past. Indeed, his first response to Reynaud's babbling was to remind him of one of Marshal Foch's maxims (to the effect that the only solution to a military crisis was an offensive), so clearly his mind was fixed on the past.

But for some reason, at this critical juncture, perhaps because he had been prime minister for such a short time, Churchill took the French at face value and decided that the BEF should think seriously about the possibility of evacuation. Given the nervousness of the senior British commanders, the mere hint of the possibility was enough. Ostensibly the order given on the sixteenth was simply to retreat, but this simply precipitated the collapse.

There were two reasons, the first and most obvious being that a retreating army finds it extremely difficult to turn to the attack. So the order to retreat essentially foreclosed the option that would have been the most advantageous for the Allies: a British attack down into the salient. Instead the whole focus of the British effort was on extricating the BEF together with its equipment. Thus Reynaud's statement became a self-fulfilling prophecy: Without the British and the Belgians, the French could not possibly hope to prevail against the Germans.

This led to the next step in the collapse. The BEF was in position on the right of the Belgian army, not its left. So a British withdrawal would not only force the Belgians back into a position along the seacoast, it would make it impossible for them to maintain a base inside their country sufficient to defend it. Of all the leaders, military and civilian, it was the king of the Belgians, Leopold III, who saw this the most clearly: if the British retreated, the Belgian army would be cut off and forced to surrender. Without those two armies, the French could not hope to defeat the Germans. So the British decision to withdraw guaranteed that the Germans would win.

In the received wisdom the British had no choice. Not only had the French thrown in the towel, but the Germans had the Allies completely outclassed, and, in the earlier accounts, outnumbered as well. Moreover, not only had the French been beaten and were on the verge of quitting, but the BEF itself was poorly equipped and trained, its officers with no idea how to deploy armor; while, on the other side, German tanks motored majestically along French roads like herds of rampaging cattle.

As by now should be fairly obvious, the great German advantage in armor, whether in equipment or tactics, was mythical, and the French and Belgians had already made a serious dent in the German tank force. On May 31, 1940, only half of the surviving German armored strength was operational. At the end of June 1940, the German gun-tank inventory was still only 87 percent of what it had been on May 1, 1940, despite the addition of nearly three hundred new tanks produced in May and June.[36]

Losses in aircraft were more critical: as we have seen, in the Netherlands assault the Luftwaffe lost three quarters of its transport capacity. Over the course of the offensive about 40 percent of its bombers were destroyed or put out of action owing to damage, and the same held true for fighters.[37]

Clearly the Allies had losses. However, owing to the peculiar nature of the struggle, with major Allied units almost untouched by combat, and with the bulk of the French and British air forces not yet deployed against the Luftwaffe, the idea that the Allies were at the end of their rope on May 16, 1940 is preposterous. The conventional wisdom was that the French Air Force was ineffectual and nearly destroyed, whereas in truth it was the German Air Force that was the most severely damaged and, in a prolonged war, would have entirely lost its air superiority.

But after the sixteenth no Allied leader (save for King Leopold) was thinking rationally. The Germans won, then, not because they beat the Allies on the field of battle, but because the Allied leadership quit. There was no mystery about the collapse. It did not come about because the armies involved stopped fighting. Indeed, once Weygand replaced Gamelin as French commander, the French Army fought on, alone and without allies, for a month. In some instances, notably along the fortifications of the Maginot Line, the garrisons never did surrender: After the armistice the government had to send emissaries instructing them to turn over the forts to the Germans.

Great events often have simple causes. In this case the cause was Churchill's acquiescence to Reynaud's panic, a decision that brought the curtain down on one of the most discreditable periods of the European democracies and was the culmination of two years of betrayals and capitulations. Here were two leaders who could, if they had stayed the course, have fought Hitler to a bloody stalemate. Instead they panicked, Churchill no less than Reynaud.[38]

Since the justification for Churchill's panic was in the first case the panic of the French, and in the second case the desire to save the British army so that it could fight on, the fact that he was fundamentally wrong is invariably glossed over. After all, the implicit reasoning goes, the decision *did* allow the British to save their army, that somewhere between May 16 and May 20 the Allies had completely lost the battle for France, and the only option open to the British was either total defeat or a unilateral withdrawal. The argument rests on a fallacy. The potential loss of three hundred thousand men may well have been a calamity, but it pales to insignificance beside the British casualties in North Africa, Italy, and northern Europe.

Of course the British might have lost those men in combat and still failed to defeat Hitler, but this is to beg the question. The British never seriously tried to test this option to see what its chances were. They simply turned around and headed for the coast. The Admiralty had begun assembling the shipping necessary for the task almost instantly on Churchill's announcement that evacuation might be a possibility.[39] A prudent move, clearly, but in the context, it was fatal, as it suggested that the real option was withdrawal. Churchill's first response to Reynaud had been to remind him of Foch, a commander whose response to any setback was an attack. His instinctive response was right; it was the more reasoned one that was wrong.[40]

The Final Phase

The battle now entered its final phase. The BEF, which had hardly been in action at all, now began its famous retreat. The fact of this retreat doomed the Belgian army, which consequently surrendered. In the many British accounts of the war, this sequence of events was reversed: The British retreated because the Belgians had quit. But in reality it was the other way round.

In retreat, as they held the bridgehead, the British fought magnificently— a gloomy reminder of the true capabilities of the BEF in combat.[41] As though to undercut their competence, the successful evacuation is charged off against some eccentricity of Hitler's, who, it was initially alleged, wanted to let the BEF escape so as to enhance his chances of a negotiated peace with Great Britain. The actual case is simple enough. As the Germans reached the perimeter of the evacuation area, they were not enthusiastic about engaging the British army in battle. On the one hand their forces were exhausted. On the other they were much more aware than Reynaud of the fighting capacity of the French army.

So was Hitler. He had already given orders for an advanced head-quarters to be constructed so he could be close to where he assumed the fighting would be. A small village in southern Belgium was selected, Brûly-de-Pesche, and in early June, Hitler actually moved there so he could direct the rest of the war.[42] The village was close to Rocroi, right on the French frontier; clearly Hitler felt the war would continue for some time, and wanted to be close at hand to direct his armies.

He was in fact already nervous about the next stage of the war. Unlike Reynaud, who thought France defeated, the Germans, looking back on 1870 and 1914, assumed that the war might well go on for months, and were busily preparing a plan, Case Red, for an all-out offensive against the largely intact French army and air force.

So all factors militated against a direct ground assault on Dunkirk. Moreover, Hitler, like most dictators (and many other leaders in all walks of life), believed his own propaganda. Germany's victories came from its command of the air, and this was to be expected: The Luftwaffe was the most National Socialist of the three branches of the military, and its commander, Göring, was the only senior German military officer whose allegiance to Hitler was unquestionable.

So the decision to use airpower was a foregone conclusion, the result of a series of independent decisions made both by the commanders on the ground and Hitler himself. Given the heavy losses sustained by the German air force, it was also a foregone conclusion that the attack on Dunkirk would not succeed. The Royal Air Force's Fighter Command lost 106 aircraft, and the Luftwaffe lost 156—of which a good many were lost to fire from naval vessels. In an attempt to turn Dunkirk into a major victory, the British and French turned what was at best parity into victory, and claimed that the RAF had dominated the skies over the beaches, thus allowing the evacuation to proceed.[43]

The main reason the evacuation succeeded was because of a tough and well-organized defense of the port by the French navy, the tenacity of the British infantry in combat, and their maintenance of discipline under fire. The numbers were impressive: The Allies evacuated 338,226 men, including 139,911 French. But it was hardly a victory. Only twenty-two armored vehicles came back to Great Britain. Other figures were equally awful: Of the 2,794 guns the BEF had brought to France,

2,472 were left there, along with 63,879 motor vehicles out of 66,618. The Allies lost 228 ships, including destroyers that would be badly needed in the months ahead.[44]

The enumeration of these figures suggests the unintended consequences of the catastrophe. As we have seen, German armaments production was dilatory. But now, given the captured vehicles, Hitler would be able to paper over the problem almost indefinitely. It would be another two years before the realities of German industrial inefficiency would be realized.

By all accounts the war in France was now well and truly lost. The British knew it; Reynaud and the hapless politicians of the Third Republic knew it; the world knew it. Everyone in fact but the French army. On May 23 the Germans, who had still not pierced the French lines on the heights of the Meuse below Sedan, mounted an all out assault. But in this, the Battle of Tannay–Mont Dieu, the gains were reminiscent of an earlier war. The French still were hanging on to key pieces of ground, and the German advance had been measured not in kilometers but in meters. Finally, on June 11, the French, threatened with encirclement, had to withdraw. Not surrender, but withdrawal, and the best measure of how well they fought is a German evaluation made after the battle: "These woods and hills were defended by an adversary who, although almost completely surrounded, fought on with an extraordinary bravery, a competency and a tenacity quite incredible."[45]

While tens of thousands of French soldiers fought and died, the mythology of the defeat was already taking wing. In their attempt to justify their panic, the French leaders blamed their army for collapsing, Belgium for quitting the war, and the British for not committing their entire air force to the defense of France. The British in turn blamed the Belgians, but mostly the French, whose defeatism and ineptitude was seen as the root cause of the disaster. For the British to blame the Belgians was particularly unjust. Not only had the BEF's unilateral withdrawal destroyed any chance for the Belgian army to defend their country, but the Belgians actually had more men killed in action than did the British.[46]

The followers of Charles de Gaulle picked up this last charge and gave it a peculiarly eloquent twist, blaming the politicians of the Third Republic. Vichy France came to symbolize all that was rotten and degenerate in French life, the logical successor to the corruption of the Third Republic. For their part the rulers of Vichy France had their own explanation. As Jean Dutourd explains it: "After the collapse of 1940, the Vichy regime organized a press campaign to tell France that the real authors of defeat were Marcel Proust and André Gide," so the blame was clearly laid—one way or the other—on the inherent wickedness and degeneracy of the French, for whom the aging Pétain was either the savior from or the symbol.[47]

Or, as Dutourd would put it, paraphrasing Vichy propaganda: "Pétain, the Père Goriot of France, the Christ of patriotism, had made us a gift of himself. France was the daughter of this blameless old patriarch—a prodigal, shameful, daughter. She threw herself into his arms and begged forgiveness with great sobs for having read too many novels. They were the explanation of why a big brute had beaten her black and blue, poor thing."[48]

Between May 10 and June 22, 1940, at least one hundred thousand French military personnel were killed in action or died of wounds.

NOTES

1. Malcolm Muggeridge, *Chronicles of Wasted Time 1: The Green Stick* (New York: Morrow, 1973), 384.

2. See the précis in Douglas, *The Advent of War*, 119–20.

3. There is an extensive and detailed account of both the Brandenburg operations and the fighting in the Netherlands in Pallud, *Blitzkrieg in the West*. For the Brandenburgs, see 76–77; for the Dutch campaign, see 107–53. Pallud's narrative is unexcelled. There are errors, but his book remains the single best account of May and June 1940, despite the recent publication of Ernest R. May's *Strange Victory* (New York: Hill & Wang, 2001). Although May's book is a much-needed corrective to the traditional simplistic view of May 1940 found in authors like Alistaire Horne, *To Lose a Battle: France, 1940* (Boston: Little, Brown, 1969), and Colonel [Adolphe] Goutard, *The Battle of France, 1940* (New York: Ives Washburn, 1959).

4. These complementary plans are a good example of why the subsequent British complaint about the neutrals refusing to cooperate is completely unfounded. In point of fact it was the British who refused to become involved. When, in 1935, the Belgians had attempted to initiate planning discussions with the British, they were rebuffed, and it wasn't until 1939 that the British even entered into talks with their nominal ally, France. Not surprisingly there is no mention of this in any of the standard British accounts, and those written after the publication of Roger Keyes, *Outrageous Fortune: The Tragedy of*

Leopold III of the Belgians (London: Secker & Warburg, 1984), simply ignore the facts Keyes uncovered (see especially 48–50).

5. See the accounting in Franz S. A. Beekman and Franz Kurowski, *Der Kampf um die Festung Holland* (Herford, Germany: Verlag E. S. Mittler und Sohn, 1981), 30; also Pallud, *Blitzkrieg*, which has pictures of some of these modern weapons (for example, p. 109). "Modern" with respect to antiaircraft weapons mostly means a high rate of fire.

6. See the accounting in Beekman and Kurowski, *Kampf um die Festung Holland*, 212–13. There is a competent narrative of the fighting in Brian Cull, Bruce Lander, and Heinrich Weiss, *Twelve Days in May* (London: Grub Street, 1995), although their enumeration of the strengths of the various combatants should be disregarded: 9, 15–18.

7. Higham, *Air Power*, 104.

8. Thus whether the bombing was a genuine mistake or not, it was turned into a horrific symbol that in turn justified the Allied bombing raids that destroyed German cities—testimony to the potency of wartime propaganda. In my judgment the attack was an error, whose root cause was a genuine confusion about what time it was, since the Dutch followed an absurd time system. Robin Neillands, who is not shy of apportioning blame to the Germans whenever possible, believes it was simply an error: *The Bomber War* (New York: Overlook, 2001), 41–42.

9. Perhaps unwisely, because it would appear that those countries occupied by Hitler whose monarchs stayed on appear to have suffered less. An arguable point, clearly. In *Outrageous Fortune* Keyes discusses this at length. It is a serious issue; Leopold's decision to stay with his country rather than flee is by no means a decision to be despised, and, in the context of the war, may well have been more courageous than Wilhelmina's decision to leave and form a government-in-exile. Perhaps both decisions are equally admirable as far as courage goes, but, as Keyes suggests, the all-important question is this: Would the Dutch have fared better had she stayed? A troubling question.

10. Pallud, *Blitzkrieg*, 150. The same point is made by the Dutch director Paul Verhoeven in his 1977 film version of the famous Dutch wartime memoir by Erik Hazelhoff Roelfzema, *Soldier of Orange*.

11. Landzaat and his men were killed in the fighting in the Ouwehands Dierenpark. There is a picture of his memorial in Pallud, *Blitzkrieg*, 136.

12. De Jong had this inscription added to the tablet put up to mark the spot where General Winkelman surrendered to the Germans. Pallud has a photograph and identifies the inscription: *Blitzkrieg*, 150.

13. British historians are scathing in their denunciations of the Belgians, and their air force, for example, Cull, Lander, and Weiss, *Twelve Days in May*, 8, 19. But see below for a more accurate summary.

14. In contemporary NATO usage there is a distinction between the shaped charge

and the hollow charge, but both depend on the same basic principle in physics. There is an excellent discussion of the hollow-charge principle, together with illustrations, in Col. James E. Mrazek, *The Fall of Eben Emael* (Washington, D.C.: 1971) 55–57.

15. Even today the exact details of these operations are confused, with many authors still speaking of parachute drops. There is an excellent account of this action by Mrazek, *Fall of Eben Emael*. The key German eyewitness account is by Gerard Schacht, who commanded one of the assault teams. According to Mrazek, 203, Schacht's account was originally published in the *Wehrwissenschaftliche Rundschau* (May 1954), 217–33. I am indebted to the U.S. Army Military History Institute for the typescript of their translation of this article.

16. Again, the only systematic account of this operation is in Pallud, *Blitzkrieg,* 88–93. I think it fair to say that one of May's chief points in *Strange Victory* is the overwhelming superiority of German military intelligence; see especially 456–58. But the German misreading of Belgium's defense plans, taken together with the unexpectedly fierce Dutch resistance, suggests that, on the contrary, German intelligence was not particularly knowledgeable.

17. Pallud, who has a summary of this (*Blitzkrieg,* 91–93) seems to think that the actions of Luftkommando Hedderich ensured that the Germans "had easily beaten the French to it in the Grand Duchy," but given that a quarter of them got killed almost immediately, this conclusion is hard to fathom—a perfect example of the way hindsight shapes perceptions: Since the Germans won, their actions are always seen to be successful.

18. Such maps exist. They were prepared by the Belgian government and can be found in *La campagne de mai 1940* (Bruxelles: Les Presses de l'Institut Cartographique Militaire [May 1945]).

19. As reported by Michel de Lombarès, *Histoire de L'Artillerie Française* (Paris: Charles-Lavauzelle, 1957), 308. There is a brief account of this battle in May, *Strange Victory,* 402–3.

20. To use May's words in *Strange Victory,* 402. See his note 6 for the German accounts.

21. The title to a book on the fall of France: [François Pierre Raoul] D'Astier de la Vigerie, *Le ciel n'était pas vide* (Paris: Juilliard, 1952). I have paraphrased it slightly to bring into alignment with the more usual English expression.

22. This accounting is taken from a manuscript by Paul Ameye, written in 1961 at the Belgian École Royale Militaire, "Les Belges dans la Royal Air Force," 7.

23. Unfortunately, there are no similar statistics available for the French Air Force, but the anecdotal evidence suggests a similar pattern. See the brief references to equivalent engagements in Vice-Admiral R. Vercken, *Histoire succincte de l'aéronautique naval* (Paris: ARDHAN, 1993), 54–55. For the British bomber losses, see Chorley, *Royal Air*

Force Bomber Command Losses: The losses for May 10, 1940, are tabulated on 46–48.

24. Numbers taken from Patrick de Gmeline's eccentric but well researched *La "Flak" 1935–1945: La DCA Allemande* (Tours, France: Editions Heimdale, 1986), 4. Judging from its appearance in numerous photographs (some of the best of which are in Pallud, *Blitzkrieg* 187, 223), the 20-millimeter Flak 30 was ubiquitous in May 1940.

25. These figures from Gmeline, *Flak* 6. Unlike the Luftwaffe claims, which later research has revealed to be invariably inflated, usually by a factor of 3x (RAF estimates seem to be off by about 2x), the flak unit totals are reasonably accurate. If we accept the figure of 1,151 fighters and 1,043 bombers and ground-attack aircraft as the total operational strength of the four air forces deployed against the Germans in May, then the two flak units alone accounted for 838 of the 2,194 planes deployed, or nearly 40 percent. Air strength estimates from Matthew Cooper, *The German Air Force* (London: Jane's, 1981), 119–21. For research on the inflation factor, see Richard Hough and Denis Richards, *The Battle of Britain* (New York: W. W. Norton, 1989) 310–11.

26. Owen Thetford, speaking of the massacre of the Fairey battles, in *Aircraft of the Royal Air Force Since 1918* (New York: Funk & Wagnalls, 1968), 233.

27. This data taken from the summary of French sources in Kirkland's essay, "The French Air Force."

28. After the fall of Poland, the French had two squadrons of Polish pilots, who flew aging Caudron 714s. These squadrons didn't become operational until June 2, but shot down seventeen German planes and lost five of their own. This data taken from the summary of French sources in ibid.

29. This is not a theoretical example. When Colonel Kirkland analyzed the sorties of the air forces involved, he found that the French averaged less than one sortie per aircraft per day, while the Germans averaged almost four (ibid., 8).

30. André Beaufré, *The Fall of France,* trans. Desmond Flower (New York: Alfred A. Knopf, 1968), 181–82. Interestingly, other historians have relied on this passage but omitted the concluding remarks. See, for example, Keyes, *Outrageous Fortune,* 225–26.

31. According to French sources, the number was closer to 700, but this may be counting armored cars and self-propelled guns as well as tanks. See the account in Ramspacher, *Chars et blindés français,* 150–51. The only account of this battle in English is Pallud, *Blitzkrieg,* 241–54, as almost all English historians seem unaware of this engagement. The pictures accompanying Pallud's account are horrifying.

32. The tank belonged to the Fifth German Armored Division, and was hit near Marche by an H39. It appears that this hit set off the ammunition supply, and the consequent internal explosion blew pieces of the tank along the road. One of the many remarkable photographs in Pallud, *Blitzkrieg,* 194.

33. The Battle of Stonne has been virtually ignored in English accounts; there is a brief mention in May, *Strange Victory,* 433, who seems not to understand exactly where

the fighting was. There is an excellent and detailed account of the fighting in the French Ardennes by Gérald Dardart, *Ardennes 1940* (Charleville-Mézières: Editions Ardennes 1940, 2000), 91–143.

34. A harsh although not overly harsh judgment. See the comments in Hamilton, *Monty,* 328–30.

35. The quote is from General Röhricht, who was responsible for the German analysis of the campaign. See the discussion in Liddell Hart, *The German Generals Talk,* 109. The quotation is from 114–15.

36. Figures from Senger und Etterlin, *German Tanks of World War II*, appendix 1. Gun tanks were the two Czech vehicles, the Mark 3 and the Mark 4. I have excluded other categories of tracked vehicles from the count. The production estimate comes from Kaufmann and Kaufmann, *Hitler's Blitzkrieg,* 263.

37. Losses are estimated from several sources, the most detailed being Kaufmann and Kaufmann, *Hitler's Blitzkrieg,* 263. See also Cooper, *The German Air Force,* 119, who apparently only counts planes written off. In "The French Air Force," Colonel Kirkland comes to the conclusion that by June 1940 the French air force was actually stronger than the Luftwaffe, since the French had initially deployed only about a quarter of their total air strength in the northeast.

38. Churchill's panic took a different form. Instead of hysterical pronouncements about how the war was lost, he embarked on a series of mad enterprises, the most foolish being a projected political union of France and Great Britain. But poor decisions are as revelatory of panic as hysteria, and perhaps more so. See the sympathetic discussion of this insane enterprise in John Lukacs, *The Duel* (New York: Ticknor & Fields, 1990), 129–34.

39. In point of fact, they had started soliciting for shipping before that. See Arthur Durham Divine, *The Nine Days of Dunkirk* (New York: W. W. Norton, 1959), 17.

40. This may seem unfair to Churchill vis-à-vis Reynaud, but the difference is easily explained. Although flawed, Churchill was a great leader. Probably no one else could have done the job he did as prime minister during the war. Reynaud was simply a politician, and of the worst type, the sort of man who, having wrecked his country in a nervous fit, then craftily arranged events so that the onus of the actual surrender would fall on someone else's shoulders. In one of those mysterious twists of fate, in the English and American mind, he is generally seen as a leader who wanted to fight on regardless, and was flummoxed by a defeatist military and cabinet; see, for example, the entry on Paul Reynaud in the *Encyclopaedia Britannica.*

41. One of the many anomalies in the existing accounts of the war. Allegedly the BEF was grossly undertrained and underequipped—an army that had no chance whatsoever against the Germans. But when the fighting actually started, not only did the BEF

give an excellent account of itself, but it conducted an orderly withdrawal under fire—an operation which is the true test of a trained army.

42. Although the village is cited as one of Hitler's headquarters, the timing and the significance of the move are generally unremarked. Given Hitler's obsessions at the time with being near the battle lines, the move is highly suggestive: he clearly thought the war would be prolonged for months, or else he wouldn't have moved there. See the extensive account by René Mathot, *Au ravin du loup: Hitler en Belgique et en France* (Bruxelles: Editions Racine, 2000).

43. Divine thoroughly debunks these ideas in *Nine Days,* 270–71.

44. Official figures for equipment taken from L. F. Ellis, *War in France and Flanders* (London: Her Majesty's Stationery Office, 1953), 327.

45. See the complete account of this fighting in Robert Leclercq's *Les combats de Stonne-Tannay-Oches-Sammauthe* (Vouziers, France: Imprimerie Félix, 1997). The quotation is taken from an article in the German army magazine *Feldzeitung* (July 11, 1940), 32.

46. About 7,500 Belgian soldiers and airmen were killed during the campaign, as against a British total of 3,457. Most of the British casualties came during the defense of the beach—up to that point British casualties, including wounded, were about five hundred or so. The BEF hardly saw action until Dunkirk. There is general agreement as to the casualty figures. See, for example, Pallud, *Blitzkrieg,* 609; Kaufmann and Kaufmann, *Hitler's Blitzkrieg,* 308. The traditional figure for French losses has been 92,000 for many years, but there is increasing agreement in France that this figure is too low, and that the actual total is slightly over 100,000.

47. Jean Dutourd, *The Taxis of the Marne,* trans. Harold King (New York: Simon & Schuster, 1957), 108–9.

48. Ibid.

7.

The Uses and Misuses of Armor: North Africa, Italy, the Eastern Front

In modern mobile warfare, tactics are not the main thing.
The decisive factor is the organization of one's resources.
—GENERAL VON THOMA

As noted earlier, the Second World War was a peculiar conflict in that for many years it was a series of separate conflicts, conflicts that for Europeans were seemingly on the periphery of the Continent. The military action of the First World War had begun with the chief adversaries fighting one another directly: Germany had invaded Belgium and France; France had invaded Alsace; Russia had invaded Germany and Austria-Hungary; and Austria-Hungary had invaded Serbia. Within a month the major powers were desperately locked in conflict.

But the Second World War began with a series of campaigns that left the central core of Europe untouched: Germany invaded Poland; the Soviet Union invaded Finland; Germany and the Allies both invaded Norway; and Germany invaded Denmark (largely in order to get to Norway). It was nearly nine months before the Allies and the Germans engaged in actual ground combat, although there had of course been fighting in the air and at sea.

And then, when warfare started in earnest in Western Europe, it was over almost before the Allies had started to fight. On the evening of May 9, 1940, Great Britain and France felt reasonably certain of victory against Germany. By the evening of June 9, 1940, the British had withdrawn almost completely from the Continent, and it was only a matter of time before the French asked for terms.

Although the British had done a marvelous job in turning Dunkirk into a sort of victory, the four-hundred-thousand-man army they had ferried home was smaller than the Belgian army that had gone into action on May 10, and it had fewer tanks. Its allies consisted of a handful of governments-in-exile camped out in London. These might claim to be the legitimate governments of their countries, but they had no armies to speak of. Ironically the only large and organized military ally Great Britain now possessed was Poland, and the 145 Polish aviators who now fought in the RAF represented, practically speaking, the largest foreign contingent still left to fight the Germans.

In terms of ground warfare the pattern of conflicts on the periphery continued, as did the pattern of conflicts between countries only marginally involved in the original issues. Although Italy was allied to Hitler, its participation in the war against France had been tardy and inconsequential—and also embarrassing. Mussolini aimed to occupy those parts of southeastern France that had traditionally been Italian. His armies attacked the massive fortifications built as part of the Maginot Line, and were unable to effect any progress at all.

This was further proof of the importance of fortifications in modern warfare, but by then no one was listening. The idea of lightning thrusts, of great aerial armadas raining down death and destruction from above—of the breakthrough—had become the order of the day.

Hitler and the Breakthrough Myth

After June 1940 Hitler reverted to his early preoccupation with a move eastward. He had toyed with the idea of invading Great Britain but was apparently of two minds as to how to accomplish it. Technically—and perhaps in his mind as well—the air attacks were simply the first phase of an invasion. But in the summer of 1940 Hitler also seemed to have the idea that a peace was possible, hence his reluctance either to escalate the air war with Great Britain or to insist on a cross-Channel invasion.[2] This belief was not entirely misguided. After March 1938 the British public had largely abandoned the idea of appeasement to prevent war, and after Dunkirk they were grimly prepared to fight on regardless of the cost.

This was not necessarily the case with the men in the government itself. In this sense the term *appeasement* is highly misleading. For appeasement is, or was in the 1930s, a rational approach to conflict resolution created out of the gloomy realization that the behavior of the victorious Allies in 1919 was largely responsible for the series of hatreds and aggressions that followed.

So much of Churchill's energy in his first two months of power was devoted to trying to ensure that the political leadership of the country was actually willing to continue fighting.[3] As a result, in those first weeks of June, Hitler actually had a window of opportunity, and one that was considerably more accessible than is often claimed.

But Hitler now had his eyes on the Soviet Union; by the fall of 1940 he had already directed that plans for an invasion be developed. There were ideological and personal reasons for this: Early in his political career Hitler had spoken both of the need for Germany to expand to the east, and of the need to fight communism. But the response was also, on a grand strategic level, extremely rational. The raw materials the Germans could obtain by occupying the southwestern part of the Soviet Union would enable them to flout the traditional British naval blockade with impunity.[4] Those early ideas of his called for a series of bold thrusts that would strike deep into the country and destroy its military capacity. The basic ideas could have been dictated by Fuller himself, and are the perfect embodiment of the concept of the breakthrough.

Reality, or Mussolini, intervened. Unlike Hitler, Mussolini wanted to make Italy powerful, but not at the risk of destroying the country. To him power meant territorial possessions. He aimed to revenge his country for its colonial setbacks, and to gain for it what he—along with many Italians—felt had been denied them at the end of the First World War.

So while Hitler fantasized about eastward expansion, Mussolini sent his army into the Balkans and then tried to construct an empire in North Africa. The unhappy history of the Italian army need not detain us here. The end result was a series of German interventions, first in the Balkans and then in North Africa itself. The resulting conflict was justified by the Allies on the grounds of grand strategy. If the Germans could seize North Africa, and particularly the Suez Canal, they could strangle the British Empire.

Whether or not there was any real merit to this idea, the North African campaigns became an important part of the war. Combat there finally produced an Allied general who understood how to defeat the Germans, and it gave the Allies—now including the Americans—a place to fight that they could get to and occupy with some reasonable chance of success. North Africa may well be important only insofar as it gave the Allies the confidence they had lost in May 1940; given the unbroken string of calamities after September 1939, this was no mean accomplishment.

Seen from the other side those same achievements had certainly brought about a great change in Hitler: In October 1939 he was content merely to issue general directives and let the army command both plan and execute. By May he had inserted himself directly into the command chain, and after June 1940 he was sporadically micromanaging the German military. By December 1941 he was exercising, or attempting to exercise, the sort of direct control over the battlefield not seen since Wellington and Napoleon had fought at Waterloo.

That the unbroken string of German triumphs went to Hitler's head is to understate the obvious. From June 1940 on, his military ideas were dominated by the concept of vast, sweeping offensive actions. Although initially he jibed sarcastically at the idea of the blitzkrieg and the notion that the Germans had employed some novel form of warfare, as he increasingly seized control of the German military command system, what emerges is a very definite idea of great offensive strikes. In both Russia and North Africa Hitler insisted on what were clearly breakthrough operations, even when the basic conditions for the success of such offensives were lacking.

North Africa and the Failure of Armor

Superficially the desert war seems to confirm the idea that armor, or at least mechanization, had transformed warfare. In September 1940 the Italians, who had occupied what we now call Libya at the turn of the century and turned it into an Italian colony, attacked the British forces in Egypt. As the Italian high command well knew, this was a gamble; its success depended on how badly the British had been demoralized by May 1940.

The answer soon became clear: Commonwealth troops under the British general Sir Archibald Wavell defeated the Italians and drove them back into Libya. The enormous distances covered by the British in their advance seems proof that mechanization had transformed warfare, and the lesson was to all appearances repeated in June 1941, when the Germans drove the Red Army all the way back to the outskirts of Moscow.

But underlying these dramatic movements was a more sobering reality: the real contribution of mechanization to modern warfare was not that it enabled the offense to make some great breakthrough, strike deep into the enemy's rear and destroy his armies; but that same mechanization enabled the defender to retreat in organized fashion. The Italian army, as weak as it was in tanks and vehicles, was mostly able to retreat across the desert faster than the victorious British could advance. As in all retreating armies, there was disorder and confusion; the British captured enormous numbers of prisoners and believed they had won the war in the desert.[5]

This was an illusion. At the end of 1940 Hitler was forced to send a small army to North Africa to help the Italians. This force, which would become famous as the Afrika Korps, was entrusted to one of the few German generals in whom Hitler had confidence, Erwin Rommel, who had been in charge of his military bodyguard in September 1939, and had then gone on to command an armored division in May 1940. The former guaranteed that whatever his achievements were in the latter, they would be greatly magnified. As noted in an earlier chapter, to read through Rommel's papers is to read the account of a man who believed he had won the campaign in the west almost single-handed.[6] Hitler was simply the first of many admirers, and now he chose him to save Mussolini. Rommel was a competent enough soldier: He had been a distinguished infantry commander in the First World War, where, ironically, he had fought against the Italians—and his experiences there did not inspire him with a very high opinion of his new allies and their commanders.

Like all professional German officers, Rommel had been trained to pay close attention to logistics, and in the desert this was all important. His opponents, like almost all professional British officers, had not been, and the difference was quickly demonstrated. In the spring of 1941 Rommel and his combined force of Germans and Italians drove the British back out of Libya. Churchill promptly sacked Wavell and replaced him with Claude Auchinleck.

Perhaps more important, the British began to receive aid from a new source, the United States, aid which gave the Germans a nasty shock. In May 1940 the British had left all their tanks in France, and their tank industry was unable to make up their deficit, either in numbers or in advanced designs. As the fighting in Africa intensified, they turned to the United States for help, and began receiving substantial shipments of American vehicles.

The Americans, like the Germans, had been designing and building tanks with a certain disdain for their competition, and the results were poor. The first tank the British received in numbers was the M3, which the U.S. Army had begun building in 1940. In theory the M3 wasn't a bad light tank. At six tons, it weighed about the same as the German Mark 2, but, unlike that vehicle, it was armed with a 37-millimeter gun, so it had the same firepower as the German main battle tanks of 1939–40, and roughly the same profile. Early versions were of riveted construction, like the Czech tanks of this period, but this was soon rectified: The M3A1, which began production in the fall of 1941, had a cast and welded turret, and the M3A3 had welded armor. By the middle of

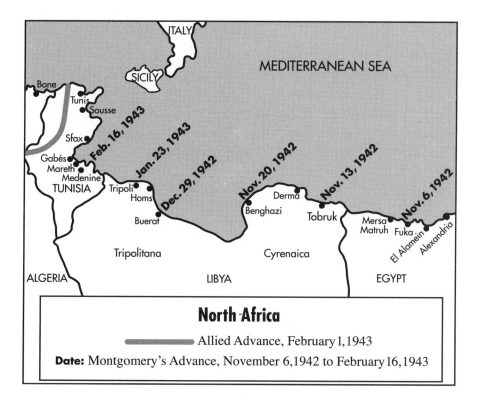

North Africa

▬▬▬▬▬ Allied Advance, February 1, 1943

Date: Montgomery's Advance, November 6, 1942 to February 16, 1943

1943, when the M3A3 went into production, the army had decided that the tank was obsolete, but as there was no other light tank available, production went on, and by the end of the war the United States had produced more than three thousand.

By the middle of 1941, 84 vehicles had been sent to the British Eighth Army in Africa, and by November of that year, there were 163 in service. Given the wretchedness of the basic British light tank (the Mark 7), the M3 was welcomed by British tankers, who paid it the honor of giving it a nickname, the "Honey" (officially American M3s in British service were called Stuarts, after the Confederate cavalry general).

Rommel's tank problem basically was that he wasn't getting any. After June 1941 the main priority was the Eastern Front. Nor were the Germans and Italians able to send in reinforcements at the same pace as the British. By the end of 1941 the British Eighth Army, under Gen. Sir Neil Ritchie, had driven Rommel back into Libya. The pattern had repeated itself: first the Italians had advanced deep into Egypt, then the British had driven them back deep into Libya, then Rommel had repeated the early Italian success, and now Ritchie had replicated the British one.

The war in the desert was simply a great mobile racetrack. Neither army was able to defeat the other completely. Once the initial engagements had been lost, the loser simply scooted back toward his bases. Rommel was a better general, the evidence being that he was able to do more with less. But he didn't have enough to enable him to defeat his opponents decisively.[7] And, like his British adversaries, he was firmly committed to the idea of great sweeps of armor that would give him the sort of victories that Hitler wanted, Fuller had envisioned, and the world believed the Germans had accomplished in May 1940.

In January 1942 the pattern repeated itself for a third time. Rommel drove the British back to the Libyan port of Tobruk. Earlier the British had managed to use Tobruk as a blocking point to stop the Axis advance, which suggests the great inherent weakness of theories of armored warfare. So long as there were enormous areas in which to maneuver, there was the illusion of momentum. But wherever the advance came to a fortified point, the advance slowed.

The Germans had discovered the same thing in the Soviet Union. They could chase the Russians back across hundreds of kilometers of open ground, surrounding whole armies and capturing them. But when they came to defended urban areas, a more conventional form of warfare asserted itself. German armored columns could advance to Leningrad, but the city was too big to get around and too urbanized to fight through. As with Leningrad in the north, so with Stalingrad in the south.[8]

The French, the Dutch, and the Belgians had been so horrified at the thought that their cities might become battle grounds they had abandoned them. Stalin, who didn't care how many Russians died or how much of historic Petrograd (as the city had originally been called) was turned to rubble, had no such qualms.

Tobruk was hardly a city on the order of even a small European one, but it was a decent defensive position nonetheless. The defenses, which had originally been prepared by Italian engineers, were in the main held by Australian troops. Their artillery was excellently handled, and they were determined to stop the German advance.

Rommel paid little attention to the defensive situation: On April 14, he mounted his first attempt on the city: a coordinated tank and infantry thrust that the Australians stopped in short order. Irritated, Rommel blamed both the Italians and his own commanders, notably Gen. Johannes Streich, who had taken over command of the newly arrived Fifth Armored Division on April 10 when its original commander, Gen. Heinrich von Prittwitz, had blundered into a defensive position and been killed.

Streich knew Rommel from France, and despised him. While Rommel slowly tightened the hold on Tobruk and prepared for a second attack, Gen. Fredrich von Paulus, who was then chief of operations for the German high command, arrived to look over the situation. The Italians, who were nominally Rommel's superiors, were not keen on another attack, but von Paulus was convinced by Rommel's enthusiasm, and a second attack was launched on April 30.

Although Rommel put a good face on the results, this attack was essentially a failure. Von Paulus returned to Germany with great misgivings both about Rommel personally and about the North African campaign in general, which, he rightly feared, would drain off resources urgently needed for the offensive against the Soviet Union.[9] Unable to take the city, Rommel bypassed it, leaving the besieged garrison to hold out until June 1942.

Undeterred either by Paulus or his own failures, Rommel advanced eastward to the Egyptian frontier. The British were desperate to relieve Tobruk. They realized correctly that its fall would be a catastrophe of the first order—yet another defeat in what now seemed to be an unbroken string of defeats at the hands of the Germans. So in June, Wavell mounted a powerful offensive operation across the frontier with the aim of securing the vital Halfaya Pass and breaking through to Tobruk, a distance of some 150 kilometers.

The resulting battle, which began on June 15, was probably the high point of Rommel's career. Although the British managed to seize Capuzzo, Rommel's intelligently placed antitank guns simply destroyed the British tank forces. Only one British tank survived the attack on the pass, and this level of loss was unfortunately typical. Although Battleaxe (as the British called their offensive) was the first serious clash of British and German armor, and the mobility of the Germans seemed to confirm the ideas about how armor should be deployed, Rommel's defeat of the British, like his earlier check at the hands of the Australians, reveals battles demonstrating the power of the defense. What the fighting of May and June revealed was the power of emplaced guns, particularly antitank guns.

But defeats are defeats. For the British, and for Churchill in particular, Battleaxe was a disaster. He was busily trying to persuade the Americans to invade North Africa, a move that ran deeply against the grain of the senior American commanders, who perceived, rightly, that Hitler was going to be defeated in France, not in Libya or Tunisia or Algeria.

It is easy to sympathize with Churchill's frustrations. From the intelligence intercepts, he was keenly aware that Rommel was mentally and physically exhausted, that he was outnumbered, and that he wasn't getting anything close to the supplies he required.[10] After two years of fighting, the British needed a convincing victory. Instead they had gotten an inconclusive seesaw back and forth across the desert and then a major defeat. Churchill also needed to be able to convince the Americans that they had a competent ally, because by the spring of 1942, the United States had made a heavy investment in supplying the Eighth Army.

The American M3 light tank was soon followed by a considerably more potent weapon, generally although inaccurately known as the Grant.[11] The Grant was not a very good tank. The main model, the M3, weighed nearly fourteen metric tons, had a riveted hull, and mounted a low-velocity (567 meters per second) 75-millimeter gun in its hull. This weapon would penetrate 60 millimeters of 30-degree sloped armor at 500 meters.[12]

But even as late as 1942 the German tanks sent to Africa were the same obsolescent vehicles that had fought in France: the Mark 2 tankettes with their 20-millimeter guns, the Mark 3, still armed with a 37-millimeter weapon, a handful of Mark 4s with the low-velocity 75-millimeter gun, and a few Mark 3s with a 50-millimeter weapon.[13] So, as far as tanks went, the British were considerably better equipped than the Germans.

However, in late 1940 the British were desperate for vehicles, and the Grant was already in production. The British contracted directly with manufacturers and had modifications made. Two hundred of these vehicles were shipped in late 1941, and by May 1942 there were enough on hand to equip an entire armored brigade (167 tanks in the Fourth armored). After March 1941 American-specification vehicles were shipped to the British. As a result, despite its losses, the Eighth Army had some 250 Grant tanks by June 1942.

For Churchill the knowledge that Rommel was, both literally and metaphorically, out of gas, that Auchinleck was doing a good job of rebuilding the Eighth Army, was cold comfort indeed. Nor was he pleased to find that the British general, despite his growing superiority in men and equipment, was unwilling to go over to the offensive any time soon. Churchill was considerably more rational than Hitler when it came to military matters—he at least paid attention to the relative strengths of the forces involved—but both leaders shared an impatience with their military commanders. The fall of Poland and France had apparently produced in both the idea that great victories were possible on the cheap. What Hitler had done in Europe, Churchill wanted in Africa—a great and decisive victory.

From Auchinleck's point of view the problem was simple. Rommel, having exhausted his offensive opportunities, now resorted to the traditional German tactic of establishing a first-rate defensive position around El Alamein. If Auchinleck was to defeat him, he would have to mount a direct assault. Despite their stout belief in how they won the First World War by defeating the German army in the field in the fall of 1918, British senior commanders were almost traumatized by the thought of ordering their men into another one of those slaughterhouse frontal advances. Auchinleck could advance all the cold rational reasons in the world justifying a delay, but in his heart, Churchill—like everyone else—knew what was really being said.

There was no real way to go around El Alamein. The British would have to go straight through it and over it, and that would mean casualties. Churchill, like Lincoln (and Joffre), was determined to find men who would succeed in combat. He sacked Auchinleck, brought in Gen. Sir Harold Alexander to become overall commander in the Middle East, and picked an obscure general named William Gott to command Eighth Army.

On the face of the evidence, Gott seems in retrospect a remarkably poor choice. However, no one will know if he was or not, as he was killed before he could assume command. An even more obscure British general, Bernard Montgomery, was sent to take his place. Hitherto, his only achievements had been as a trainer, if one discounts incurring life-long enmity among his superiors and his peers. Quite possibly Bernard Montgomery was, in August 1942, the most disliked general officer in the British army. He then proceeded to compound the offense by becoming its best-known general.

Success breeds jealousy and hatred. Rommel, whom Montgomery overcame on the battlefield and then proceeded to drive back across North Africa, is scathing in his assessments of his adversary. In fact the appearance of Montgomery and Patton on the field would, postwar, constitute a sort of turning point in military history, which would become as much a digest of gossip and personal anecdote as tactics and technology.[14]

By all accounts Montgomery was an exasperating fellow and in many respects a most unpleasant one: a supremely irritating subordinate, a treacherous friend, an ungrateful child, and a psychologically abusive parent. But what is the relevance of any of this to political and military success? The briefest and most cursory list of the behaviors of the leading figures in this war makes the idea preposterous. For example, Churchill smoked cigars at breakfast and often appeared to be drunk. Hitler was extremely well liked by his secretaries, and fond of animals. He was in addition a teetotaler and a vegetarian, and Stalin took time out from murdering his fellow communists to write long letters to his mother. So much for biography. The only important thing about Montgomery is that he was the first British general since Wellington to be consistently successful in the field.

Part of the attack on Montgomery stems from his refusal to fight according to the ideas of the theorists. Auchinleck had been afraid to attack the defensive positions Rommel had prepared, and worried that, after the loss of Tobruk, he couldn't defend his own at Alam Haifa. In fact, the main British defensive plan was simple: retreat.[15]

In the meantime, Hitler was pushing Rommel just as Churchill was pushing his commanders. Both leaders were determined to attack and win. Montgomery understood that Rommel would be forced to attack, and he welcomed the event. In this Montgomery had a major advantage. As an officer in the First World War, he had seen firsthand how successful defenses could simply destroy an attacking army. He intended Alam Haifa to be exactly that sort of battle.

And so it was. Rommel launched his attack on August 31, 1942, an attack that conformed perfectly to Fuller's theories—his armor would sweep around the main defensive positions and penetrate to the undefended rear. This was the execution of the classic breakthrough offense: a mass of armor penetrating deep into the enemy's position. As Fuller had been explaining for decades, such an operation could not be stopped.

The sweep of attacking armor ran straight into a series of deep minefields such as had never before been seen by German armored commanders, two of whom were promptly put out of action (Gen. Walther Nehring, the overall German commander, and Gen. Georg von Bismarck, commander of the Twenty-first Armored Division). As daylight came the Germans encountered something else they had not yet experienced. Montgomery had managed a unique achievement: He had persuaded the RAF to coordinate its air war with what was happening on the ground, or, in other words, to function as a tactical air force deployed in the German fashion. But Rommel had no real air force by August 1942, so the RAF was as effective in destroying his ground forces as the Luftwaffe had been in May and June 1940.

Montgomery now committed a third sin (the first two had been his unwillingness to mount offensive operations and his second to win a great defensive battle at Alam Haifa). Instead of chasing after the retreating enemy in the way the British had done twice before, he aimed at a slow and steady coordinated advance that would finally force Rommel to stand and fight, would fix him in place so that he could be destroyed.

Churchill, ever the amateur general, saw the danger quickly enough. The delay, he felt, would "result in Rommel fortifying a belt twenty miles deep by forty miles broad . . . we should never get through owing to a series of Maginot defenses."[16] At one level this was preposterous. Rommel was hardly going to be able to construct a new Westwall, or even a Mannerheim Line, out in the sand in a couple of months. But in one sense it was perceptive: The prime minister realized that, despite all the emphasis on armored thrusts and sweeps, the war in North Africa was going to be won—or lost—in a very conventional way. And the man who had written his own history of the war, a history in which he had incurred universal ostracism for his claim that the German successes were a function of their superior defensive skills, was deeply pessimistic about the ability of any one British general to change that rule.

Montgomery was the first general in the Second World War to apply what is now recognized as a fundamental principle: not to move until you have an overwhelming advantage at the decisive point. At El Alamein he had an enormous advantage in manpower: Rommel had less than 50,000 men in the Afrika Korps, and possibly as many Italians, while Montgomery had well over 150,000 troops. He had about thirteen hundred tanks. He had equally strong advantages in artillery and airpower. His advantage in armor was even more overwhelming than the numbers indicate. By the summer of 1942 the Americans had begun shipping their newest and most modern tanks to the British, and most of these went to the Eighth Army.

Although the M4, universally known by its British appellation, the "Sherman," was a mediocre design, it was a marked improvement over the Grant. Its profile was almost half a meter lower, and its turret-mounted 75-millimeter gun was considerably more potent than what was still the standard gun on the German Mark 4 tank, as it had a muzzle velocity of 700 meters per second compared to the German weapon's 570 meters per second. It was, in addition, reasonably fast and reliable. Problems soon emerged, but there is no question that the Sherman gave Montgomery an enormous advantage. In addition to the Grants and Stuarts, he had 319 Shermans, of which a good 250 were combat ready.[17]

The Germans had hardly any comparable tanks to put into action, and these advantages have led many armchair strategists to conclude, with a certain contempt, that almost any general could have beaten Rommel at El Alamein, given the superiority, while Rommel's admirers (a group that seems to encompass all the major British historians) have no shortage of reasons to explain their hero's defeat.[18] But, hidden behind all this, like the proverbial skeleton in the closet, was the knowledge that, despite decades of fictionalizing their experiences in the Great War, the British had never actually beaten the Germans in a major battle. Churchill knew it. His generals knew it. So El Alamein was important, and not just as a temporary boost to Churchill's schemes or to the morale of his hard-pressed countrymen. El Alamein was important because it was the first clear-cut British victory since Waterloo.

Nor was it an easy victory. Rommel now knew as much about minefields as his opponents. He also knew of the tendency of British armored commanders to engage in wild cavalry charges of the sort that a hasty misreading of Fuller would appear to mandate. He knew that the British were proverbially slow to react, that their officers were no match for his, and that their contempt for the Italians facing them was undeserved. His men were used to being outnumbered, and they were by now accustomed to waging war with obsolete equipment. And he had a final advantage: El Alamein was a reasonably fortified position. Not so great as Churchill had feared, but all in all, difficult to break through.

And he was right. In a week of hard fighting, the British still had not cracked the position. The offensive began on the evening of October 23, 1942, and by the twenty-ninth, the British high command was close to panic. They had visions of the Somme, Third Ypres, and the murderous autumn of 1918, when their troops had actually suffered heavier casualties than on the Somme. Montgomery was well on his way to having more than thirteen thousand men killed, and nearly half of his armor was out of commission. But both he and Rommel were convinced a British victory was inevitable. It was only Hitler's stubborn refusal to countenance a withdrawal that kept the Germans fighting. If Rommel had been left to fight the battle independently, he would already have withdrawn his shattered forces. The battle went on simply because Hitler was unwilling to let Rommel retreat.

With each passing day the likelihood of a successful disengagement diminished. Paradoxically, then, the closer the Germans and the Italians were to an outright defeat, the more bitterly they fought on. Finally, on November 4, Rommel, who had already given up any hope of holding the position, persuaded Hitler to let him withdraw. The British had won. Although the Red Army had fought the Germans tenaciously in 1942, and although, as we have seen, there had been isolated engagements in which the French had beaten the Germans in 1940, this was the first significant Allied victory.

Just as Hitler's propagandists had created a Rommel myth, so the British now created one for Montgomery. There was a difference. Montgomery's reputation was based exclusively on victory in the field, Rommel's on the need for a proper National Socialist military hero. Based on Rommel's record in May 1940, he was no better or worse than a dozen or more other German generals. Given the high level of military competence in the German army's commanders, this is hardly to damn with faint praise. On the contrary, it is a commendation of the first order. Montgomery excepted, neither Great Britain nor the United States had any senior commanders to match men like Guderian, von Manstein, or von Rundstedt—to cite only a few of the more familiar names.

The Rommel myth—the idea that he and he alone understood the proper deployment of armor—is hardly sustained by his battlefield record. But there is also a Rommel reality: He was a shrewd master of small unit combat and the logistics of warfare, and a superb motivator of men. The same could be said of Montgomery. Although the two men are usually seen as quite different, in reality they were men with similar abilities. That this is largely ignored is because the inflated views of Rommel established early in the war by Hitler's propagandists was largely accepted as sober fact by British analysts, while Montgomery's popularity—and his equally inflated reputation—were viciously attacked by those same analysts. In the new theories of warfare, it was not enough to win; one had to win using the correct principles as they were understood by the theorists.

One of the reasons Montgomery was a great commander was that he had a very precise understanding of the strengths and weaknesses of the British army. He perceived one of the great paradoxes of the war: that although the Germans had many fewer tanks and trucks than the Allies, they were still much quicker to react, could switch from retreat to attack with a speed the Allies were never able to match. In this he was a general very much like Pétain had been in the First World War: he realized that the only way to compensate for the superior training and mobility of the German army was to overwhelm it—that if it could be pinned down, Allied superiority in men and equipment would prevail. Criticisms of Montgomery's slow and methodical approach at bottom rest on an appreciation of the British army totally at odds with its actual capabilities.

In the curious postwar accounting, the fact that Montgomery was successful is set off against the fact that he was not successful in the way he originally claimed he would be. This too reveals a fundamental misunderstanding about combat. Like all great generals, Montgomery wrote down very clear and concise orders, and he did his commanders the courtesy of telling them what he expected them to do and how the battle would unfold. He did not bewilder them with a dozen different contingencies. But clearly he had these in his head, which is why he was able to make changes so promptly during battle—something Rommel clearly did not anticipate.[19]

Montgomery's ultimate sin was that he won the battle the wrong way—that is to say, not by adhering to how Fuller had insisted battles should be fought and how armor should be deployed, but by the same application of combined-arms tactics that had been the hallmark of German success in World War I. When on the defensive, the British relied on minefields, artillery barrages, and tactical air strikes to enable their infantry to mount successful defensive operations from behind prepared positions. On the offensive, Montgomery patiently built up his forces so he had an overwhelming advantage at the point where his offensive would impact the enemy. He proceeded slowly and surely, and moved from success to success—precisely the same tactics that Pétain had insisted the French Army use in the summer of 1917.[20] But these were the tactics of the First World War. In the new dispensation it was not enough simply to win; the battle had to be conducted with a due appreciation of military theory.

Given Rommel's disadvantages in men, equipment, air support, and supplies, it is certainly no surprise that he was overpowered. Churchill was able to read his communications. He had to coordinate his efforts with the Italians. He had to deal with Hitler. Given all these problems, he did very well, and it is not surprising that he was promptly elevated to cult status, while the man who beat him was criticized from every possible point of view. The Rommel myth would persist, although interestingly, not for Hitler. Rommel ended up in what was regarded in Berlin as a backwater, trying to organize the defense of France, where he tried to apply what he had learned in the desert about the potency of airpower and the effectiveness of old-fashioned ideas about what Pétain had called the prepared battlefield, in which concrete strongpoints and preregistered artillery enabled the defenders to massacre the attacking infantry.

By and large, however, his words fell on deaf ears. Montgomery would have the same experience: Whenever he tried to apply the lessons of North Africa to Europe, he was promptly greeted with the response that conditions there were so unique that no transference of skills was possible. Similarly Rommel was unable to convince other German commanders of the realities of ground combat against an enemy who had mastery of the air. North Africa was different. Nothing learned there applied.

The proof that Rommel was brilliant at handling armor and Montgomery was not came from the observation that the British had lost twice as many tanks as their opponents (at least) even though their armor was technically superior. That the British were still losing more tanks in combat against the Germans was due to Rommel's astute handling of antitank weapons. The most potent weapon in the African desert was not a tank. It was the German 88-millimeter antiaircraft gun. The Germans had already realized the value of this weapon against armor and fixed targets in France. They had no choice: German designers had given the infantry a 37-millimeter antitank gun that hardly justified the cost of towing it into combat. German infantry divisions had an excellent fieldpiece, a 105-millimeter howitzer. But howitzers were designed for high-angle supporting fire and not designed to fire over a flat trajectory; their low-velocity shells were hardly more effective than those of the 37-millimeter antitank gun.

So the 88 was the only gun with the range and penetrating power to destroy one of the strongly armored French tanks, and in North Africa the Germans relied on it heavily. British doctrine had always seen the tank as a weapon to be used against other tanks, and in the initial months British vehicles (still equipped with the two-pounder) and the new American tanks were certainly capable of taking on the lightly armored and poorly gunned German tank force.

The heavy losses came when the British tried to use their tanks as Fuller had claimed they should be used, in armored thrusts designed to break through the German positions. Rommel preferred to break those charges not with his undergunned tanks but with defensive deployments of 88s. Rommel might sneer at Montgomery for not using his armor correctly, but this is to undercut his own very real achievements.

Montgomery defined a new maxim of modern warfare: Attack only with overwhelming force—and then use that force to win. Rommel, for his part, saw the power of antitank weapons on the new battlefield. Had Montgomery not waited until he had a great superiority in armor, he would have lost El Alamein. Rommel was invalided home in disgrace: Hitler now hardly shared the high opinion of him that subsequent British historians would have.[21] Exiled to command in France, Rommel attempted to inject a note of realism into what he saw as the new order of battle for Germany. The loss of air superiority in the face of a resolute enemy who had more men and more and better equipment meant that great sweeping armored thrusts were no longer possible.

At precisely the moment when the idea of the Blitzkrieg became the order of the day for the high commands on both sides, Rommel perceived that it was no longer even a possibility for the German army, just as Montgomery had realized that the idea would never work against them. They were simply too quick to react, their lower-level commanders too well trained. Moreover, when the Germans were on the defensive, their weapons were, at least temporarily, superior.

But the power of failed ideas is remarkable. The North African campaign had demonstrated—should have demonstrated—that the new theory of ground warfare was incorrect. The only real advantage it conferred was that it enabled the losing side to retreat faster than the victorious side could advance. This was hardly the desired result. But both Hitler and the Allied high command ignored what had actually happened in favor of what could be made to look like happened. In this, curiously enough, both Rommel and Montgomery had similar experi-

The high profile of the Flak 36 88-millimeter, coupled with its success as an antitank gun, led the Germans to subsequent low-profile versions intended solely for antitank use. The PAK 43 was the last and most successful of the low-profile mounts: The weapon could be fired from its four-wheeled carriage or from its base when the wheels were removed. (*Albert J. Casciero*)

ences: When they attempted to inculcate what they had learned in the desert into the great armies that were forming for the European struggle, they were simply ignored.

Whatever the strategic importance of the North African campaign, it had a direct impact on the subsequent fighting in Europe, as it involved the same generals, the same equipment, and many of the same units. Both Rommel and Montgomery saw the relevance of what had happened there, although neither one had any success in transmitting what they had learned as they prepared for the invasion of France.

As is well known, the end for the Germans in North Africa came when the Allies mounted their invasion of western North Africa. This invasion initiated two more: the conquest of Sicily, and a series of landings in Italy itself. Neither Marshall back in Washington, nor Eisenhower, now overall commander of the Allied forces in Europe, favored the idea. In general the Americans saw clearly enough that the only way to defeat Hitler was to land in France and drive directly through into Germany, just as Stalin was trying to do in the east.

Breakthrough on a Grand Scale

To many American planners the British insistence on North Africa and then Italy appeared to be simply another instance of putting imperial interests over the needs of the alliance itself, but this is unfair. Churchill was simply following the precedents established during the First World War, when, frustrated by the Western Front, the Allies had tried to start major offensives elsewhere, notably in Italy and the Balkans. In 1916 this had meant bribing Italy to come into the war on the Allied side; in 1943 it meant attacking Italy itself. But in both cases the idea had been based on a fundamental geographical ingenuousness. Churchill liked to speak of the "soft underbelly of Europe," an idea only possible to a man whose knowledge of it came from looking at political maps and old-fashioned globes: anyone looking at a relief map of Europe would see quickly enough that the "soft" underbelly was in reality a series of alpine extensions.[22]

Given the inherent inaccuracy of air-to-ground attacks, the Allied superiority in the air was of only marginal help. Given the terrain, the superiority of German armor had an equally marginal impact. Despite his professed—and genuine—horror of becoming bogged down in infantry struggles reminiscent of the First World War, Churchill's plan, when considered tactically, involved precisely that.

The realities of ground warfare in Italy and Sicily have to a certain extent blinded analysts to the original idea. However, if one were to grant the flat-map view of Europe that had traditionally prevailed in the British government, then Churchill's idea was perfectly feasible. It represented, in other words, the melding of the grand strategic thinking of the past with the post-1918 ideas of how new technologies made such grandiose schemes possible. It was the breakthrough idea on a grand scale, now made possible by the Allies' immense technological advantage, and made with the same dismissal of the facts of the case that was the hallmark of the ideas of the theorists. Churchill's blithe assumption that Europe had a soft underbelly was no more foolish than Douhet's belief that antiaircraft guns were worthless or Fuller's that tanks were invulnerable perpetual-motion machines, an observation that goes a good way to explaining why the decision has always been treated so charitably by historians.

Allied air force planners supported the decision because "the occupation of mainland Italy up to a line north of Naples-Foggia would give two valuable constellations of military airfields from which they could launch offensives at a favorable range against southern and eastern Germany and also her main supplier of oil, Rumania."[23] A perfect example of how the chimera of strategic bombing was now a factor in propelling ground operations, and, as a consequence, the Italian campaign represents the fusion of the two ideas—Churchill's historic preoccupation with a breakthrough in southern Europe and the obsession of the two bomber commands with similar theories as applied to the air.

Seen up close, none of the main reasons for the Italian offensive hold water, particularly given the nature of the combat that the terrain guaranteed. That the resulting campaign was a series of failures of one sort or another is usually charged against the main Allied ground commanders (Clark, Montgomery, and Patton). But the American idea of using airborne units in the Sicily invasion stands out as a testimony to the failure of the planners involved to study the result of similar tactics when they were used elsewhere by another army.[24]

Predictably the Sicilian airdrop (the invasion began on July 10, 1943) was a debacle, with paratroopers scattered all over the southern part of the island. The twin landings succeeded largely because of the weather, which was so awful that no one expected a landing to be made. But although the Allies, once ashore, slowly occupied the island in the face of determined German resistance, it is difficult to see Sicily as much of an Allied triumph.

The numbers tell the tale. The Germans, with about 65,000 men, fought off half a million Allied troops for nearly five weeks, and then, adding insult to injury, managed to escape to the Italian mainland. Roughly four-fifths of the 50,000 German soldiers remaining in Sicily by early July were successfully evacuated to the Italian mainland between July 10 and August 16.[25]

In the week of September 3 the Allies landed in Italy proper. A brief chronology of what followed makes the problem clear enough. By the end of September 1943, the Allies had secured what the bomber commands regarded as the important parts of the peninsula, the Foggia airfields. By October 4, 1943, the Allies controlled both Corsica and Sardinia. Insofar as the Italian campaign had a rational objective—to secure bases for strategic bombing missions—those objectives had been secured. The Corsican airfields put all of southern France within striking distance, while Foggia made raids on Austria, southeastern Germany, and Romania practicable. Moreover, as Mussolini had been ejected from power at the end of July, the Italian army was hardly going to be a factor in any fighting. The sensible thing to do was to wind down the offensive.

Instead the Allies were determined to seize Italy. And eventually they did. On June 4, 1944, Allied troops entered Rome. They had tried to get there much earlier. Balked by the German defenses, the Allies planned what was hoped would be a true breakthrough offensive: They would leapfrog up the peninsula, taking advantage of their by now total command of the Mediterranean, put ashore forces at Anzio, which was about fifty kilometers southwest of Rome.[26] The resulting threat to seize Rome and cut off the German defenders to the south, would, it was thought, force the Germans to abandon their defensive positions and retreat to the north.

Anzio was a poorly conceived and badly executed idea. Although the initial landing, on January 22, 1944, was successful, the troops landed couldn't get out of the beachhead. Kesselring, a first-rate defensive commander, promptly put together a counterattack, and the Allies spent the next months of 1944 penned up exactly where they had disembarked.

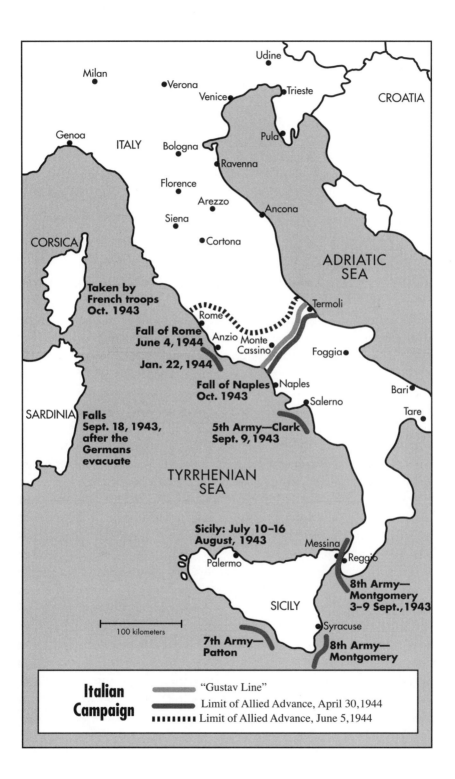

Udine

Milan

Verona

Venice

Trieste

CROATIA

Genoa

ITALY

Bologna

Pula

Ravenna

Florence

Arezzo

Ancona

Siena

Cortona

CORSICA

ADRIATIC
SEA

Taken by
French troops
Oct. 1943

Rome

Termoli

Fall of Rome
June 4, 1944

Anzio Monte
Cassino

Foggia

Jan. 22, 1944

Fall of Naples
Oct. 1943

Naples

Bari

Salerno

Tare

SARDINIA Falls
Sept. 18, 1943,
after the
Germans
evacuate

5th Army—Clark
Sept. 9, 1943

TYRRHENIAN
SEA

Sicily: July 10–16
August, 1943

Messina

Reggio

Palermo

8th Army—
Montgomery
3–9 Sept., 1943

100 kilometers

SICILY

Syracuse

7th Army—
Patton

8th Army—
Montgomery

**Italian
Campaign**

"Gustav Line"

Limit of Allied Advance, April 30, 1944

Limit of Allied Advance, June 5, 1944

The decision made in the fall of 1943 to fight up the Italian Peninsula would have a dire effect on operations in the fall of 1944, when the Allies desperately needed more infantry in northern Europe.[27] The usual claim is made that the fighting forced the Germans to divert precious resources to Italy that would otherwise have been used in France or the Eastern Front, but this argument collapses on even the most cursory examination: Italy sucked in more than three Allied soldiers for every German one.[28] Factoring out the air force personnel included in this total, what it all comes down to is that some four hundred thousand Germans tied up one million Allies for the duration of the war.[29]

The Eastern Front and the Development of Armor

A consideration of the Eastern Front lies far outside of the purpose of this book. With a few exceptions, it was mostly fought with units that did not see service in France, and to a surprising extent, may be considered as an entirely different war, one almost as distant from the European theater as the Solomons.[30] Insofar as tactics went, the war was curiously parallel to North Africa: enormous advances that, no matter how successful and dramatic, failed to destroy the retreating armies; the decisive battles being conventional struggles for fortified positions. Although at first blush the conflict seemed to sustain the idea of breakthrough operations, by the time of Stalingrad it had become clear enough that these had failed, and the Red Army offensives that followed were by and large a repetition of the same tactics that General Brusilov had used to good effect in the First World War: broad-front attacks systematically forced the enemy into continuous retreat.

But in one important way, the fighting there had an enormous impact on what happened in the west. Already, toward the end of 1942, the British in Libya (and then the Americans in Tunisia) began to encounter German armor far more powerful than anything they had seen, and this was a direct result of what had taken place during the Russian campaign.

By the summer of 1941, the Germans had made an appalling discovery: the T34. As noted in the discussion of the Winter War with Finland, Soviet tank design was considerably more advanced than in the West. But the T34 was a major step forward even for the Russians. In 1941 (and in 1942) no one had anything even remotely comparable. The T34 was a fast tank with a high-velocity 76-millimeter gun mounted in a rotating turret. Its high-output aluminum engine and wide treads gave it excellent cross-country performance, its low profile (2.44 meters as opposed to 2.69 for the Mark 4) made it hard to target, and its sloped armor made it difficult to destroy.[31]

So the dismay occasioned by the T34 in the German army was real. In June 1941 the Germans had no tank capable of defeating the T34, or even surviving an engagement with it, as one hit from its 76-millimeter gun would destroy any German tank outright, while its own angled armor rendered it well nigh invulnerable to the low-velocity German tank guns—most of which were still 50 millimeters or worse. Only the 88 could stop a T34, and only at ranges in which gunners were loathe to operate. All the more so as the crews were composed of Luftwaffe personnel who had been trained to shoot at airplanes. Belatedly, and with a sense of panic virtually unique in the history of the German army, a whole series of crash programs were begun.

Now, finally, the tank bureaucracy realized that a tank without a high-velocity gun was useless. A program to equip the Mark 3 with a

Armed with a high-velocity 75-millimeter gun, by 1943 the obsolete German Mark 4 tank was still a formidable weapon: Its wide tracks gave it better performance on rough terrain than the Sherman, and hardly any Allied tracked vehicle could withstand a hit from the high-velocity gun. (*John Mosier*)

50-millimeter gun had already begun, and 470 vehicles had been produced in 1940. But in the face of the T34, the idea was already obsolete.
For want of anything else Germany continued to produce Mark 3s
armed with this gun; it was not until 1942 that vehicles armed with a
75-millimeter weapon went into production. But the Mark 3 was
already at the end of its life, and only 660 of the upgunned versions were
produced.

Work on a new and improved Mark 4, with a more potent weapon,
was surprisingly slow: Only 837 were produced in 1942 despite the
obvious need. Toward the end of the North African campaign, Rommel
had a few dozen of these new Mark 4-F2 vehicles. Their powerful 75-
millimeter guns enabled them to destroy any Sherman before it could
get within range. It was an ominous portent, but a few dozen tanks were
nothing against the hundreds of Shermans and Grants.

And the new Mark 4-F2 and G were barely at parity with the T34.
The Germans were gloomily aware of this, and new tanks were being
designed, but in the summer of 1941, they were months—even years—
away. Desperate to save their infantry, the Germans began to deploy several new generations of towed antitank weaponry.

The problem with the 88-millimeter gun was that its profile was virtually the same as a tank's. As an antiaircraft weapon, this was hardly a
problem, but it was certainly a liability in ground combat. If the gun
crews were to survive, they needed a lower-profile weapon. Better still,
they needed some sort of armored protection, and in order to fight tanks
they needed mobility. So one development was to provide the 88 with a
low-profile mount, or, mount it in an armored vehicle.

Both options were pursued, but the development of a new gun carriage robust enough to support the 88, and low enough to give the gunners some chance of survival, was a complex task, and designing an
entirely new tank was even more so. So in the interim the Germans
improvised a series of interim solutions, most of which depended on the
use of captured Soviet equipment. In point of fact, in the summer of
1941, the Soviet 76.2-millimeter gun was the only reasonably portable
weapon the Germans had that was capable of successful antitank actions.
So German designers fitted it to the standard light howitzer carriage as a
towed antitank gun, where it gave excellent service throughout the war.

What was really needed, however, was a mobile antitank weapon
capable of going where tanks went. Both the Germans and the French
had been slowly moving toward the development of tracked artillery

well before 1940. The idea was sensible enough. Mount a field gun on a tank hull, and the result was an artillery piece that could not only keep up with the tanks and the infantry but could relocate itself rapidly and thus escape counter-battery fire.

The course of events forced the issue. The Germans took Mark 2 tanks, removed the turret, put a gun platform and a shield on in its place, and fitted the Soviet 76.2-millimeter gun. They did the same thing with the Czech 38(t) tank designs. Dubbed "Marder 2" and "Marder 3," these vehicles provided the infantry with much needed antitank protection, and remained in service throughout the war, together with a host of lesser known adaptations.

It was soon realized that if the turret was not installed, the vehicle had much better performance and could mount a much more powerful gun—so long as the weapon was fixed—because turrets were enormously large and heavy objects. Not only could the hull and chassis be produced more quickly than the turret, but vehicles now seen to be obsolescent could be converted relatively easily. Alternatively, the assembly line could simply keep turning out the basic components and a new superstructure would be mounted.

The outstanding German armored design of the war was the Hetzer, a tank destroyer mounting a high-velocity 75-millimeter gun. At sixteen tons, it was a fast and maneuverable vehicle. The Hetzer was essentially a Czech design: the chassis was that of the prewar TNHP-S tank, which entered German service as the 38(t), and Hetzers were all built by Czech firms. (*John Mosier*)

The most outstanding example of this process was the "Hetzer," which was essentially the Czech 38(t) chassis with a sloped hull and a fixed gun, initially the 76.2-millimeter Russian weapon, but as the Germans began to produce more potent guns themselves, Hetzers were fitted with high-velocity 75-millimeter weapons of German manufacture. With its low profile and great mobility, the Hetzer was the best antitank vehicle of the war—and was so good that the Swiss used them for decades afterward. The Hetzer was termed a *Jagdpanzer*, or "tank hunter," and by the end of the war, the Germans had produced a veritable family of tank hunters of various sizes, all based on the chassis of an existing tank.

Germany's problem, however, was twofold. On the one hand it had failed to develop the powerful new tanks—and tank guns—it needed, and on the other it had failed to develop the industrial base required to produce weapons in mass quantities. Great Britain and the United States alone were producing twice as many tanks as Germany was.[32] So turretless armored vehicles with powerful guns represented an attractive option, as these vehicles could be produced more quickly; by the summer of 1943 Germany was producing slightly more of these vehicles than it was tanks.[33]

Impervious to its past experiences, the industry now replicated the same process. Germany built what was basically a very large version of the Mark 4, the difference, other than size and weight, being that the new tank mounted an 88-millimeter gun. This tank, technically the Mark 6, but generally known as Tiger 1, reflected all the prewar German design failures. It was overweight, underpowered, mechanically unreliable, and resolutely ignored all the latest innovations in design. With a range of barely 60 kilometers cross-country, it signaled a decisive end to any idea of enormous advances of armor, and at 55 metric tons, it was too heavy to operate effectively in such operations in any event. Moreover, the tank industry couldn't build it in quantity: Only 78 were produced in 1942, and only 1,348 during the entire war. So the only positive feature of the Mark 6 was its gun.

The other side of German development was the Panther, which was, on paper anyway, the ideal. Its high-velocity 75-millimeter gun was more powerful than almost any other tank gun, and, for the first time, the design employed sloped armor. For its bulk the Panther was a surprisingly fast vehicle, with good cross-country performance. But the Panther was enormous. At 45 metric tons, it weighed nearly twice what a late-model Mark 4 or T34 weighed. Although it weighed less than the Tiger, they were both so huge that the difference was largely academic, and in fact, with its three-meter profile, the Panther was higher than the Tiger—a conspicuous target. The Panther, in other words, continued the German tradition of overweight and overengineered vehicles begun with the Mark 1.

It is often said that the production of these tanks marked a shift in the German army from an offensive to a defensive mentality. Panther and Tiger were simply unsuccessful designs. German tankers were unanimous in what they wanted: the T34. But the Germans couldn't build a replica. And, in their defense, as Hitler increasingly began to micromanage armaments production as well as the battlefield, the emphasis shifted to bigger and bigger tanks: Tiger 2, the last German tank to see combat, weighed 69 metric tons.[34]

Nor is this surprising. As we have seen, the entire German tank force was an overlapping series of failed designs. The truth is the only competent tank design to see any real use in the war was the Soviet T34. The qualifier is necessary because, although by the very end of the war, both the British and the Americans had actually designed and produced some good tanks, the problem was these tanks arrived on the battlefield too late to have any impact on the fighting. The British Centurion was an excellent tank, the first six of which reached British tankers in May 1945, when the war was basically over. So too with the American Pershing, which corrected the worst faults of the Sherman but arrived only in early 1945. But as the Germans never got to that point, it must be said that in this area—tank design—as in many others, the Allies actually outperformed the Germans.[35]

When the Allies began combat in Europe in earnest, Allied tanks faced an array of vehicles all of which were more heavily armed and armored. Even the oldest of the German designs, the Mark 4, now had a 75-millimeter high-velocity gun which, if firing armor-piercing shells, had a muzzle velocity of 990 meters per second, a gun that could disable any Allied tank before it could get in range. And the Germans had an array of extremely potent wheeled and tracked antitank guns of even more power. In the crucial months of 1944, the more heavily armed Germans would wreak havoc on the Allies.

Unlike the German failure, which was based on the inability of its tank production plants and designers, the American failure was a failure of doctrine—that is, theory. American armored theorists, who had all apparently read Fuller attentively, had developed the curious idea that the tank was a breakthrough vehicle. Its job was not to fight other tanks, but to break through the enemy's defenses and strike through to its unprotected rear. The Sherman, a fast and maneuverable tank with a decent gun, was ideal for this task, and theorists saw no need for a tank with a more potent gun or heavier armor.

How did the theorists plan to stop enemy tanks? The U.S. Army's planners had developed their own bizarre approach, which paralleled what the Germans were doing out of desperation: the tank destroyer. The idea was to make a more agile vehicle and equip it with a more potent gun, enabling it to destroy enemy tanks before they could get into range.

But there was a crucial difference, revealed, interestingly enough, by the two differing names. The Germans called their vehicles tank hunters, the idea being that the *Jagdpanzer* was like a hunter stalking deer, or a sniper stalking enemy soldiers. In their insularity the American theorists imagined that a lightly armored vehicle with a powerful gun would always prevail, and hence the name, "destroyer." The problem was that by the time the serious fighting started in Europe, the actual vehicles themselves no longer had the great advantage the theorists assumed would accrue to them owing to their firepower. Nor was the distinction feasible in actual combat. The Germans were aware of this problem, one reason their tank hunters were heavily armored. It had to be, if it was to withstand enemy tank fire, as the tank hunters would not always have the luxury of outgunning their adversaries.

The Americans had simply ignored this crucial distinction, assuming that the more powerful gun would enable the tank destroyer to stand back and hit its adversaries without them being able to return fire. Part of this belief rested on the rather eccentric belief that American ingenuity had produced a gun mount that enabled the tank to fire accurately while on the move.

Everyone else in the world of armor had realized that this was simply beyond the limits of what was technically feasible in design—as indeed it was until very recently. The only hope of a tank gun hitting anything it aimed at was if it was standing still so its gunner could aim his weapon. But the U.S. Army was so committed to the idea of the rapid advance that the Sherman had a complex stabilizing system designed to enable gunners to fire while on the move.[36] In theory this gave the American gunners a remarkable advantage—and so it did, forty-odd years later when a much different system was actually made to work. In practice in 1944, however, the idea was unworkable, as was the idea of the tank destroyer, a lightly armored tank with an open-topped turret and the gun that should have been put in the Sherman in the first place.

This was an appalling error, and it was compounded by the refusal of the experts in the United States to pay any attention to the feedback from the men in the field. It was obvious almost from the moment that Americans went into combat in Tunisia that the Sherman had problems, and that the most glaring problem was its gun.[37] But the fitting of a new gun of any potency was stoutly resisted until December 1944, and then it took what was virtually a direct order from General Eisenhower's headquarters to force the fitting of a decent gun.

American (and Allied) troops, then, went into combat dependent on three highly unsatisfactory pieces of equipment: the M3 light tank, which had already been declared obsolete in August 1943; the weakly armored and poorly armed Sherman; and the thin-skinned M10 tank destroyer. By the spring of 1944, any one of these vehicles was a sitting duck for any German tank, *Jagdpanzer,* or *Sturmgeschütz* they would be likely to meet, not because of some failure in manufacturing capacity but because of an obstinate belief that the tank was a breakthrough vehicle and only that.

NOTES

1. As quoted by Liddell Hart, *The German Generals Talk,* 165. Von Thoma concludes this quote by saying that the purpose of organization is to allow one "to maintain one's momentum."

2. "Hence" does not mean that there were not other reasons as well; historians have consistently underestimated the extent to which Hitler deferred to Göring, who had assured him that the war could be won from the air. Nor was this idea as strange as it is sometimes made to sound; as we have seen in earlier chapters, the conventional wisdom in the 1930s was that cities would be quickly destroyed by bombers.

3. Understandably, this is a sore point in the history of Great Britain. See the analysis by John Lukacs, *The Duel: 10 May–31 July 1940: The Eighty-Day Struggle Between Churchill and Hitler* (New York: Ticknor & Fields, 1991), which records the various components, from an active dislike of Churchill by many cabinet members and politicians (60–61), to the home-grown fascists (77–79) to what we might call in retrospect the capitulators (139–40); not neglecting the pernicious and quite possibly treasonous role played by the American ambassador, Joseph Kennedy (138). These pages enable a sampling only; for an appreciation of the point Lukacs makes, the entire book must be read.

4. There was also the fear that Stalin might be likewise tempted to attack, an idea first advanced by a defecting Soviet intelligence agent in the 1980s. See Viktor Suvarov, *Ice-breaker: Who Started the Second World War?*, trans. Thomas B. Beattie (London: Hamish Hamilton, 1990). Western analysts have been universally skeptical of this claim—in most cases apparently without reading the book itself. The snide dismissal in Rolf-Dieter Müller and Gerd R. Uberschär's *Hitler's War in the East, 1941–1945: A Critical Assessment* (Oxford, England: Berghan, 1997) is typical (30–31)—but note that this volume is simply a combing over of the material written about the war, a bibliographical essay, not an evaluation. The best brief summary of the situation with regard to Hitler and the East is in John Lukacs's *The Hitler of History* (New York: Random House, 1997), 148–59. One problem here is that Lukacs—like Müller and Uberschär and a good many other analysts—simply can't bring himself to the critical state of mind necessary to discuss Stalin and communism; "Anticommunism" is for them fundamentally a pejorative expression, and anyone who is deemed to be such is automatically disqualified.

In Russia itself, however, the idea does not seem nearly so far fetched. Moreover, the derisory treatment given Suvarov's ideas by Western analysts ignores the obvious point that it makes little difference what Stalin's true intentions were; the only thing of importance is what Hitler believed those intentions to be. A man given to preemptive attacks on neutrals for purely strategic reasons (as was the case with the Scandinavian campaign) may reasonably be supposed to see this as a successful tool against his enemies.

5. There is no shortage of accounts about the North African fighting. For what happened before Rommel arrived in 1942, the most penetrating account is Barrie Pitt, *The Crucible of War: Western Desert 1941* (London: Jonathan Cape, 1980). The best short account of the entire campaign is Samuel W. Mitcham Jr.'s somewhat misnamed *Rommel's Desert War* (New York: Stein & Day, 1982).

6. Liddell Hart remains one of the few British historians to judge Rommel objectively, and notes that his military reputation was deliberately fostered by Hitler. See his discussion, "Soldier in the Sun," in *The German Generals Talk*, 45–54.

7. Rommel and the Italians also suffered from a formidable disadvantage: the British had decrypted the German code used to transmit messages to the ground commanders in North Africa. As a result, they knew not only what Rommel's orders were, but the exact timing of the supplies he desperately needed in order to fight successfully. See the succinct summaries of this in Martin Gilbert's condensed biography, *Churchill, A Life* (New York: Holt, 1991), esp. 731–32.

8. Ex-Soviet officers I have talked to about the Blitzkrieg were apparently taught that the great failure of the tactic was the impossibility of adaptation to what properly speaking is urban warfare. For reasons I think rather obvious, I am unable to provide precise documentation on this point, but it seems sensible enough.

9. This account may seem unduly critical of Rommel; however, as his best biogra-

pher observes: "the 1941 attacks on Tobruk undoubtedly show Rommel at his worst—leading troops into battle hastily and without preparation or coordination, sacrificing method to speed in a way which the situation condemned." David Fraser, *Knight's Cross* (London: HarperCollins, 1993), 146.

10. Rommel's illness seems to have been mostly psychosomatic. See the comments made by Captain Alfred Berndt in a letter to Rommel's wife: "At the beginning of February [1943] the physical and mental condition of your husband had reached such a state that Professor Horster considered an immediate course of at least eight weeks' treatment to be indispensable. . . . An aggravating factor contributing to your husband's condition was the unresolved command situation." As quoted in Erwin Rommel, *The Rommel Papers*, ed. B. H. Liddell Hart, trans. Paul Findlay (New York: Harcourt, Brace, 1953), 410. See also Rommel's letter to his wife of January 21, 1943: "I'm so depressed I can hardly do my work" (391); this last also noted by Nigel Hamilton in *Master of the Battlefield* (New York: McGraw-Hill, 1983), 136. Hamilton's is still the best account of the North African fighting.

11. In the U.S. Army, a confusing system was employed whereby the first production model of any weapon was called M1, the next model the M2, and so forth. As a result there was an M3 light tank and an M3 medium tank. Successive variants were called M3A1, M3A2, and so on. The system was even more confusing than the ponderous German one. For the sake of clarity, we will call the M3 light tank in its various iterations the Stuart, the M3 medium tank the Grant, and the M4 tank the Sherman. These are British names, but they cut down on confusion. Technically the initial M3 medium tank existed in two versions: the tank built to British specifications was called the Grant. Any M3 medium built for U.S. Army use but sent to the British army was called the Lee, after the Confederate general. For the sake of simplicity, however, we will refer to this tank by its more popular name—the Grant.

12. Peter Chamberlain and Chris Ellis: *British and American Tanks of World War II* (New York: Arco, 1969), 108–10, 206). Although most of these vehicles were M3s with a riveted hull, about four hundred were built with welded hulls (M3A2/A3/A4).

13. The retrofitting of the German Mark 3 tank has caused a certain confusion among those writing about the conflict in North Africa. Beginning with the E series, Mark 3 tanks were equipped with the 42-caliber 50-millimeter gun as of August 1940. By December of that year there were 434 tanks so equipped in the inventory, as opposed to 484 vehicles with the 37-millimeter gun. By January 1942, shortly before Rommel departed for North Africa, there were 2,229 vehicles armed with the larger gun and only 174 equipped with the 37-millimeter weapon. But the German tank expert Walter J. Spielberger gives Rommel's tank strength as of May 26, 1942, as 60 Mark 3 tanks, 261 Mark 3 vehicles with the 37-millimeter gun, 38 Mark 3s with the 50-millimeter gun, 40 Mark 4s with the short-barreled 75-millimeter gun, and 9 of the newer Mark 4 tanks armed with the new high-velocity 75. By October 1942 Rommel had only 88 of the

newer Mark 3 tanks and 30 of the newer Mark 4 vehicles. See the first three (unnumbered) pages of Walter J. Spielberger and Uwe Feist, *Armor in the Western Desert* (Falbrook,
Calif.: Aero Publishers, 1968). In an attempt at simplicity Spielberger and Feist unfortunately complicate the issue by referring to the Mark 3-E and the Mark 4-F2 as "Specials."

14. As we have seen, there was no shortage of Rommel criticism on the German
side, from von Paulus and Streich to von Rundstedt, who openly mocked Rommel's
competence. Curiously, then, much of Rommel's reputation derives from the admiring
accounts of his (mostly British) adversaries. Even Fraser, who scrupulously records these
criticisms, distances himself from their cumulative force. See especially *Knight's Cross,* 146.

15. Montgomery's many detractors have glossed over the British plan for respond-
ing to future German attacks; but Auchinleck aimed at yet another retreat—there was no
thought of defending the position. The analysis of this by Hamilton seems to me
irrefutable. See *Monty: The Making of a General,* 592–93, and especially 608–9. As is often
the case in military history when the facts conflict with national interests or personality cults, the response by Montgomery's critics has simply been to ignore the evidence
presented—the main reason why so much historical controversy is specious.

16. As quoted by Norman Gelb, *Ike and Monty, Generals at War* (New York: William
Morrow, 1994), 154. Gelb's study is a useful compendium of the common mistakes made
by military historians—often deliberately—as they pursue some personal agenda: in this
case yet another attack on Montgomery. See notes 11 and 15 to this chapter.

17. The first shipment of Grants, it will be recalled, had been produced to British
specifications; subsequent shipments were of American specification vehicles, so when
they arrived in North Africa the British had to fit them with British specification radios
as well as sand shields and the external storage containers so beloved of British tankers,
so the usual figure of "300 Shermans" is slightly exaggerated. Data in Roger Ford, *The
Sherman Tank* (Osceola, Wis.: MBI Publishing Company, 1994), 49–50; 49,234 M4
through M4A3E2 tanks were produced between July 1942 and July 1945.

18. Thus Gelb: "Unless it committed absurd blunders, it could not possibly be
defeated" (*Ike and Monty,* 157). Compare with Liddell Hart's summary of General
Thoma's remarks made after the war: "He said the Eighth Army's immense superiority of
strength in all the decisive weapons made its victory almost a certainty before the battle
opened" (*The German Generals Talk,* 164). This is the sort of illogical thinking that dis-
figures military history. As our analysis of fighting strengths has made clear—and this fact
is really not an issue in dispute—Rommel had been grossly outnumbered throughout
the entire campaign. Nor is the claim tenable as a more general proposition: The substi-
tution of "Red Army" for "Eighth Army" makes clear the ludicrousness of the claim.
Even amateurs like Hitler recognized the speciousness of this argument: "It would not be
the first time that a strong will has triumphed over bigger battalions," Hitler wrote Rommel on November 3, 1942 (as recorded by Mitcham, *Rommel's Desert War,* 166).

19. John Keegan has made this point—tellingly—with respect to the American Civil War, citing Grant's orders as the paradigm of clarity, while at the other end of the spectrum Walter Warlimont makes the same point with regard to the confusing orders emanating from Hitler's creatures after he assumed total control of the command. See John Keegan, *The Mask of Command* (New York: Viking, 1987), 200–201; Warlimont, *Inside Hitler's Headquarters*, 30–31 (confirmed at length by Keegan, *The Mask of Command*, 293–97).

20. The only discussion of these tactics in English is in my study *The Myth of the Great War* (New York: HarperCollins, 2001), 278–280. That these were the tactics used is not however open to dispute: See the extensive treatment by Louis Gillet, *La bataille de Verdun* (Paris: G. Van Ouest et Cie., 1921), especially 253–74.

21. Given Rommel's reputation, the reality of his fall is mostly unremarked, but no less real. In his own words in March 1943: "The Führer won't let me go back to Africa again.... [I've] fallen into disgrace and could expect no important job for the present." As recorded by his son, Manfred Rommel, in *Rommel Papers*, 425. In *Hitler 1936–1945* Ian Kershaw sporadically records Rommel's fall from Hitler's favor: "Encouraged by Göring, Hitler was now [early 1943?] convinced Rommel had lost his nerve" (546; see also 595).

22. The key Churchill quote actually only uses the term "underbelly," but the sense is the same—to a certain extent the term "soft underbelly" is a redundancy. Montgomery, like Marshall, was opposed to the whole idea. Richard M. Leighton has a detailed and somewhat muddled discussion of these conflicts in *Command Decisions*, ed. Kent Roberts Greenfield (Washington, D.C.: Office of the Chief of Military History, 1960), 255–86.

23. This quote is taken from Dominick Graham and Shelford Bidwell's *Tug of War: The Battle for Italy, 1943–1945* (New York: St. Martin's Press, 1986), 22–24, which makes the case for the invasion. Typically these British analysts give short shrift to the American objections, reducing the whole thing to a system of personality disorders: Marshall, for example is described as "rigid and fundamentalist" (22), so his strategic concern is simply a sort of obsessive compulsive personality disorder (23).

24. Eisenhower's staff had worked up nine separate operations (not all of which involved airborne landings), of which five were aimed at the "boot" and four aimed at the middle of the peninsula. See the informative chart and table in ibid., 28–29.

25. This does not of course count Italian troops—about sixty thousand Italian soldiers were evacuated as well—but as Mussolini had been deposed on July 25, 1943, the king instructing Marshal Pietro Badoglio to negotiate an end to the war, so far as Italy was concerned, their situation was largely irrelevant.

26. They had abandoned an earlier and totally bizarre plan to drop airborne troops into Rome so as to prod the Italian government into action on the Allied side and keep the city out of German hands. In *War in Italy*, Lamb asserts that this plan was not nearly as crazy as everyone else has made it out to be (2), but never discusses it in any detail. See the brief discussion in Gelb, *Ike and Monty*, 236–37.

27. In *Circus of Hell: The War in Italy 1943–1945* (New York: Crown, 1993), Eric Morris details the gradual collapse of the Allied offensives in October (see especially 394). See also the brief remarks by Graham and Bidwell, *Tug of War,* 409.

28. By July 1944 Kesselring's command, Army Group C, had a little over 400,000 men. The Allied Fifth and Eighth Armies opposing Kesselring had a strength of almost 550,000, which suggests that the whole notion was ludicrous, and in reality the imbalance was far greater: The total Allied strength in Italy was actually 1,677,000 men. The whole issue of numbers is treated with great coyness by historians—for obvious reasons. In *Tug of War,* Graham and Bidwell try to massage the numbers so they end up being equivalent, by factoring out the support troops on both sides (400–402). But this is preposterous: The Allies deployed their men in divisions, as did the Germans, if the German army was more efficient, i.e., a greater percentage of the strength of each division consisted of combat troops, it is true enough that this gave the Germans a substantial manpower advantage: They could deploy fewer divisions and have more troops fighting. But the Allies couldn't magically reorganize their armies: in order to put 350,000 men into combat they had to have 550,000 troops deployed (if we accept the basic calculations). Although the figure of 1,677,000 men is not in dispute, it is explained away—it is alleged that this higher number reflects air force personnel. True enough, but the British and American air forces hardly had 1.1 million men in Italy—about half that number was engaged in what Graham and Bidwell correctly specify as "headquarters and line of communication staffs" and "the logistical infrastructure required to support a force overseas" (401). Exactly.

29. There is a meticulous accounting of the units involved in the index to Graham and Bidwell, *Tug of War,* 433–38. Although Kesselring had some first-class units (including most of what was left of Germany's airborne troops), the bulk of his army consisted of divisions formed from such unlikely sources as Luftwaffe ground crews with nothing to do and ethnic minorities taken prisoner on the Russian front. On the Allied side, some of the best combat troops available were being deployed: the British Eighth Army, veterans of North Africa; a powerful French "Army," the Corps Expéditionnaire Français, built around four North African divisions; and an almost equally powerful Polish force, the Second Army Corps, leaving aside the various American units involved, some of which, like the First Armored, the Third Infantry, and the Eighty-second Airborne, would clearly have served the Allied cause better elsewhere.

30. There were of course exceptions in both instances, but far more similarities. For example, both Germany and the United States kept the core of their elite combat troops out of Western Europe entirely. The German Gross Deutschland Division, the premiere unit in the German army, was on the Eastern Front for the whole war, just the U.S. Marines spent the war in the Pacific. In any event a study of the fighting on the Eastern Front makes clear that although the size and scale was greater, combat reduced itself to the same struggle as in North Africa, for example, Stalingrad and Leningrad. Indeed

Soviet officers postwar were apparently taught (correctly, in my view) that the great weakness of the Blitzkrieg was its failure to handle cities which sat astride major invasion routes and thus couldn't be bypassed.

31. In his memoirs Heinz Guderian professes total astonishment at the new Soviet tank: Guderian, *Panzer Leader*, 147. But his comments are extremely disingenuous—as a result of the Finnish war Guderian should have been familiar with Russian armor, and the idea that the Mark 3 with its new 50-millimeter gun was a better tank than the BT-7 is ludicrous.

32. See the discussion in Strategic Bombing Survey, *The Effects of Strategic Bombing U.S.*, 168.

33. The so-called *Sturmgeschütz*, or "assault gun," which in some forms—for example—the 75-millimeter gun mounted on a Mark 3 tank chassis, looks like a *Jagdpanzer*, while in others it looks like a standard fieldpiece mounted on a tracked vehicle. Compounding the difficulty of untangling these overlapping categories is the fact that the Allies themselves frequently had them confused. See, for example, table 104 in ibid.

34. As is well known, Hitler wanted even larger designs, for example, the Porsche-designed Maus, which weighed 188 tons. But even heavier tracked vehicles than Tiger 2 saw combat: the Jagdtiger tank hunter, which mounted a 128-millimeter gun and weighed 71.7 metric tons, and the Elefant, which weighed 68 tons.

35. See the discussions on both the Centurion and the Pershing in Chamberlain and Ellis, *British and American Tanks*, 52–60.

36. American armored enthusiasts are far too charitable in their assessment of this mechanism. In *The Sherman Tank*, Ford, for example, lists the "accuracy of their gun control systems (as well as the stabilization system fitted to the gun mount . . .)" as one of its strengths, a statement that, when read to every American tanker I have encountered, has produced a good deal of sarcastic laughter (quote from 53).

37. Most survivors would disagree, and say that the lack of sufficient armor protection was the worst fault. But in combat, this could be—and often was—overcome by various jury-rigged expedients, such as sandbags, while the gun was an insurmountable difficulty. Compounding the problem was the widespread belief among tankers that the gun chosen to replace the original 75-millimeter weapon, the 76-millimeter, fired shells that were inferior to those fired by the older gun. Analysts who have noted the resistance of tank commanders themselves to the new gun apparently don't realize that the resistance was based not on size but on performance. The solution, which the British saw quickly enough, was a gun comparable to the now (late 1943) standard 75-millimeter gun used by the Germans. When the British figured out how to stuff the seventeen-pounder into the standard Sherman turret, they produced the only Allied tank capable of meeting German tanks at anything close to parity.

8.

The Failure of
Strategic Airpower: 1940–1944

You have not dropped 200 tons of bombs . . . you have exported *200 tons of bombs, and you must hope that some of them went near the target.*
—SIR ROBERT SAUNDBY[1]

All through the 1930s, the leaders of the West constantly pro-claimed to their frightened citizens that warfare had changed: In a future war their cities would be destroyed in a matter of hours or anyway, days, as the bombers would always get through. Future prime minister Stanley Baldwin, then Lord President of the Council, had put it perfectly in a speech made to Parliament: "The bomber will always get through . . . the only defense is in offense, which means that you have to kill more women and children more quickly than the enemy if you want to save yourselves."[2] Douhet had seen this surprise attack on the centers of industry and population as the crucial act in a future war, and the antifascist propagandists of the 1930s had seized on the bombing of Guernica during the Spanish civil war as a horrific example of these ideas. When the war broke out in earnest, the destruction visited on Warsaw and Rotterdam seemed conclusive. As

Alexander McKee would recall:

> I was interested in the books of the air power theorists, which I still
> have on my shelves; but I was naïve. Re-reading them now is like
> browsing through a British *Mein Kampf.* The horror to come is all
> there between the lines. What they are really advocating is an all-out
> attack on non-combatants, men, women, and children, as a deliberate
> policy of terror.[3]

People, most of them civilians, died in either case. And there is no
doubt about the horrific nature of what followed. More Germans were
killed by Allied strategic bombing raids in Europe using conventional
bombs than died at Hiroshima and Nagasaki combined. For that matter
more Japanese civilians were killed in the firestorm raids on Tokyo than
were killed by the two atomic bombs. Taken in the aggregate, the death
toll was so awful that it produced—justifiably—a revulsion against the
whole idea. And, as we have seen, the degree to which the bomber
barons of the Second World War concealed the gross inaccuracy of their
main weapon hardly allows the defense that this was simply unavoidable
collateral damage.[4]

Surprisingly, however, a more sober inquiry into the two great strategic bombing campaigns, one German and one Allied, leads to a somewhat disturbing conclusion. Neither campaign was particularly effective.
Other than destroying cultural landmarks, killing large numbers of civilians, and leaving enormous numbers of people without shelter or basic
services, neither campaign contributed much to ending the war.[5]

German Losses: The Battle of Britain

Hitler, like most dictators, not only believed in propaganda but was
highly susceptible to his own. He apparently believed that his air force
was all powerful. He had an additional, political reason for so believing,
as in the new order the Luftwaffe had been the most National Socialist
of the three branches of the military. Significantly, although Hitler had
approved, or ordered, or let come into being, an armed branch of the
party, the Waffen SS, this was restricted to ground troops. The Waffen SS
had no air force equivalent. It had no naval equivalent either, but then

Hitler was a typical Central European: he had no particular interest in things naval or in naval strategy.

Unlike his British and French adversaries, Hitler discounted almost entirely the idea of a naval blockade as having any significant impact on his new empire. He could get everything he needed from inside Europe: iron ore from France and Scandinavia, oil from Romania and the Soviet Union, agricultural products from his new allies, satellites, and conquests. In this one area he was a shrewder analyst of the First World War than his adversaries: He knew that a great Continental power could not be brought to its knees by a naval campaign. The navy in Hitler's view had performed its one great function: It had enabled the conquest of Scandinavia and humiliated the Royal Navy in a way that Adm. Alfred von Tirpitz had been unable to do in the previous war. Now he simply ignored it, leaving its leaders to their own devices.

In the summer of 1940 then, Hitler, believing in the power of his air force, left it to them to destroy Great Britain. The destruction of Warsaw and Rotterdam had aroused horror in the West, and now Hitler, in one of those confusions typical of dictatorships, conflated the destruction inflicted as part of a tactical air campaign with the apocalyptic prewar visions in which it was widely believed that bombers would destroy all the great European cities in a matter of hours, or anyway days.

Who would tell him otherwise? He was now at the zenith of his powers. Whatever qualms Germany's generals had possessed in April 1940 had by June entirely vanished—which suggests their postwar apologiae were less than sincere: So long as Hitler was victorious they were content to bask in the reflected glory. Although as the war progressed, Göring's power and authority declined, in June 1940 he was the second most important member of the German government, and he was very much in command of the German Air Force. But, after Goebbels, he was also the man most in thrall to Hitler's power. He was the last field marshal on the planet to tell Hitler anything that contradicted whatever his beliefs of the moment were.

As we have seen, the Luftwaffe only existed as a tactical air force. It had no strategic bomber force. There were three reasons for this. First, as we have noted, German military doctrine saw the air force as subordinate to the ground forces: it worked in conjunction with them to achieve objectives. The idea that it would carry on a separate war, or be the main combat force, was explicitly rejected. And indeed, this doctrine was a crucial factor in the early German successes.

While the Allied ground commanders tried to ascertain what their respective air forces were doing, the German attacks were highly coordinated. Rotterdam was destroyed not because the Luftwaffe subscribed to Douhet's ideas about airpower but because the troops on the ground were faced with fighting their way into the city and needed air support.

But Germany's decision was not purely theoretical. It was also personal and economic. In the 1930s the Luftwaffe, like every other air force, had been interested in building long-range bombers. The chief exponent of the need for a strategic air force was General Wever. An ardent Nazi, he apparently had read *Mein Kampf* (a feat that made him virtually unique among the senior military and civilian leadership), and thus took Hitler's claims about a *Drang nach Osten* (drive toward the East) seriously.

His reasoning was logical: In a war with the Soviet Union, Germany would need long-range bombers to destroy Soviet industry, since it was highly improbable that the ground forces could occupy the entire country in any reasonable amount of time, if at all. So Wever pushed for a strategic bomber, and, under the personal fiefdoms Hitler encouraged in the new Germany, the air force began work on a long-range bomber. Fortunately for the Allies, Wever was killed in an accident, and the exponents of a strategic bomber force lost an important voice, since in the Third Reich there was no such thing as integrated planning, or the development of a policy based on consensus. Those who had Hitler's ear, or could arrange to have it for a few moments, were able to push their own projects. Those who did not were shoved to the background.

Which is not to say that the situation was totally capricious.[6] The great body of career officers and civil servants went about their work unchallenged, while Hitler delivered orations to his secretaries and pondered his architectural designs. But as the air force planners considered the needs of the service, they came to the conclusion that Germany simply lacked the resources to build both a strategic bomber force and a tactical air force at the same time. There was only so much refined metal available, and only so much money.

Seen from the outside the Luftwaffe was frightening: thousands of advanced aircraft, an industry far in advance of anything in Great Britain or the United States. Seen from the inside it was frightening as well: not enough planes, not enough new planes on the drawing boards, far too few trained crews, and those with far too little time in the air. When

Germany entered the war Hitler had the nucleus of a good tactical air force: an excellent fighter plane (the famous ME 109), a competent dive bomber (the JU 87), and two decent level-flight medium bombers (the HE 111 and the JU 88), and a versatile multipurpose plane, the Dornier 17. But all of these planes were tactical aircraft developed almost exclusively for ground-support missions. They lacked the range for strategic operations, nor had there been any thought of designing a range of aircraft for that purpose. Moreover Germany was never able to develop successful replacements for these airplanes, which were nearing the end of their operational life as advanced first-line aircraft in 1940.[7]

The failure at Dunkirk was therefore an important sign, although in retrospect it seems it was lost in a propagandistic haze of claims about the qualitative superiority of the Royal Air Force's Spitfire fighter over its German adversaries, the result being that most people assume that the failure of the German attack was mainly a function of British fighter planes. An analysis of the loss data suggests that, on the contrary, the RAF sustained heavy losses without forcing the Luftwaffe to pay an equivalent price.[8]

The German aerial assault was a failure. The British lost more aircraft than their opponents, but the Germans were unable to massacre the infantry. Why? Because Germany's bomber force was too slow and vulnerable. The JU 87 dive-bomber was only successful when there were no enemy aircraft about, and it could select its targets and dive onto them unmolested. But the plane was far too slow and unwieldy to defend itself against even an obsolete fighter plane.

This speaks to the repeated failures of the air forces opposing the Luftwaffe. Except for the Dutch, they were more concerned with conserving their striking power than with destroying the air-ground assault. All that Dunkirk revealed was the effect of a determined effort in which control of the skies was contested. And if the Luftwaffe was unable to score a tactical success over the Channel beaches, where its planes were operating entirely over land and flying for short distances, what chance would it have over Great Britain?

The answer was basically none at all, although Great Britain had its share of handicaps in the contest. It had lost far too many fighter pilots in May. It also suffered from being the first country to experience a strategic bombing campaign. No one knew precisely how to combat the bombers, mostly because, as we have seen, the conventional wisdom throughout the 1930s had been that there was no defense. Surprisingly, given the prevailing ideas about the bombing offensives, British fighter pilots and antiaircraft gunners managed to shoot down 1,733 German aircraft, while losing 915 of their own, so the German air offensive was a total failure no matter how it was considered.[9]

In retrospect this struggle revealed the formidable power of a mobilized industrially competent democracy. Judging from the sarcastic comments made in *The Times*, in the 1930s Great Britain essentially had no air defense system.[10] Such hopes as it had of protecting itself from strategic bombing were invested entirely in the RAF's fighter component, and in most accounts of the Battle of Britain it is to this handful of superbly trained Spitfire and Hurricane pilots that Great Britain owed its ultimate defeat of the German aerial offensive.

But in actuality the British success was a function of an integrated system in which an array of sophisticated tracking systems (radar being only the most famous) as well as ground-to-air weaponry, was deployed. Given that Great Britain essentially constructed this air defense system from scratch, it was a stunning achievement considering the views of all the prewar experts. Moreover the British had a considerable handicap: Soviet agents inside the country were relaying the country's technology secrets to Stalin, who then passed them on to Hitler.[11]

Whatever hopes the Germans had of some sort of precision bombing campaign when they began, their raids rapidly degenerated into nothing but collateral damage. Over the course of the war the Germans were never able to inflict decisive damage on Britain's production of war matériel: the only real achievement was the deaths of 60,595 civilians.[12] Nor was this surprising. The Germans were, if anything, worse at level-flight bombing than the British.

But this too revealed a fatal weakness in the concept of strategic airpower. The idea had always been that the effects of bombing, even if the cities were not obliterated overnight, would be so devastating that the country being bombed would quit the war. The conventional interpretation of the events leading to the surrender of the Netherlands confirmed this, as, in a more convoluted way, did the bombing of Guernica and Warsaw.

Instead the civilian population of Great Britain went about its business with if anything a renewed determination. Instead of going into a mass panic, contemplating surrender, or becoming depressed and incapable, the British people promptly set a new standard for the conduct of civilians in wartime. The principal effect of strategic bombing, then, was to produce a deep sense of angry resolve on the part of the people being bombed. And in a democracy, such resolve is crucial.

An Allied Failure: The Strategic Bombing Campaign

There is no evidence to show that the Blitz reduced the determination of the British to fight and win. To be fair it must be said that the immeasurably greater Allied bombing campaign had only a marginal effect on the population of Germany, and even there the evidence seems susceptible to other interpretations.[13] But the courage and resolution of the British people doomed Hitler's concept of airpower to total failure.

The lesson was plainly there, but the RAF refused to see it and embarked on their own costly and largely ineffective strategic bombing campaign, convinced that they could cripple German industry. As we have seen almost from the start of the war, Bomber Command had found that the losses in daylight bombing raids were prohibitive. The RAF would have lost its entire bomber force in five or six weeks, given the initial loss rates.

Initially Bomber Command had to depend on the Vickers Wellington, a two-engine bomber developed before the war. Although the Wellington had a decent bomb payload and operating range, like all the prewar strategic bombers it was far too slow (the final versions only had a delivery speed of about 260 kilometers an hour) to escape fighters once detected. Since Douhet had assured students of airpower that it was impossible to detect and intercept strategic bombers, not much attention was given to the matter. But, as noted, the early massacres of Wellingtons on bombing raids in 1939 brought an abrupt halt to their deployment in the daytime, and a shift to night bombing, a tactic that greatly reduced the chances of successful interceptions and ground-to-air defense.

How accurate was the bombing? Bomber Command operated on the assumption (as would the Americans later on) that bombers flew over the target and hit it. Churchill wasn't so sure. So in August 1941 Lord Cherwell (Frederick Lindemann), Churchill's science adviser, had one D. M. B. Butt make a study of aerial photographs taken of selected targets. Butt examined "over 700 photos taken on 100 raids on some 28 different targets and came up with some disturbing conclusions."[14] Disturbing indeed. Butt found that only one out of three bombers dropped its bomb load within eight kilometers of the target, which sounds bad enough, but this was actually a gross understatement, as the "target" was defined as a circle with a diameter of sixteen kilometers.

So, for example, if Bomber Command tried to hit the Dresden train station, bombs that leveled the nearby resort town of Pirna or flattened the porcelain works at Meissen would be called "accurate." If a bomber was trying to bomb Le Bourget, which was then the main airport of Paris, and hit Sacré Coeur, by the standards Butt was using, it would have been right on target. The other two bombers would presumably have dropped their bombs outside this rather large circle—assuming that they dropped them at all. And if visibility was poor or the air-defense system was active, accuracy went down even more. At night there was no accuracy at all. So Bomber Command, in an understandable effort to preserve the lives of its air crews, had adopted a tactic that guaranteed wild inaccuracy. They were simply exporting high explosives.

The Butt report forced Bomber Command to change its methods, and to a certain extent they did. The RAF solution was more and better bombers. They had always realized that the Wellington was not a true strategic bomber, as it lacked the range and payload required. For the proper combination of speed, range, reliability, and payload, what was required was a four-engine bomber, but like the Germans, the British continued trying to develop a heavy bomber with only two engines, and work had begun on one well before the war. The initial plane was known as the Manchester, which was in production at the start of the war, and made its first bombing run on February 24, 1941.[15] The Manchester was a dud. It was slower than the Wellington, and its two Rolls-Royce engines, known as Vultures, were grossly unreliable. It was then realized that the two Vulture engines could be replaced by four Merlin engines mounted on the same airframe. The resulting plane, initially called a Manchester 3, flew on January 9, 1941, and was christened "Lancaster 1."

Despite its peculiar development history, the Lancaster was the best British bomber of the war, able to carry increasingly heavy bomb loads into the center of Germany, and by the end of the conflict, more than two-thirds of the bomb tonnage dropped by the RAF had been carried in Lancasters in 156,000 sorties.[16]

The heavy bomb loads were important, because the British had figured out early on that, given the accuracy problem, a bigger bomb was the only way there was any real chance of hitting the target: The more explosives in the bomb (hence the heavier), the greater the blast radius and the less accuracy required. Conversely, if a heavier bomb actually was to hit its target, the consequences would be devastating. By September 1943 the British had managed to fit a bomb of more than five thousand kilograms (twelve thousand pounds) into the Lancaster, a considerable feat. In its more normal configuration the Lancaster was a good 15 percent faster than the Wellington, had a much greater range, and could carry a heavier payload.

The problem was that this was simply not good enough. Although during the course of the war Lancasters had some spectacular successes dropping special types of bombs, the fact was that the planes were too slow to escape fighters, and as they began their bombing runs—whether in daylight or at night—they had to fly at low altitudes where they were vulnerable to antiaircraft fire. In general, then, level-flight bombing was as inaccurate in 1943 as it had been in 1940.

The B-17, designed in 1934, was the world's first successful long-range bomber. Early versions were insufficiently armored and woefully undergunned, but in the E series aircraft, shown here, these deficiencies had mostly been remedied. (*National Archives*)

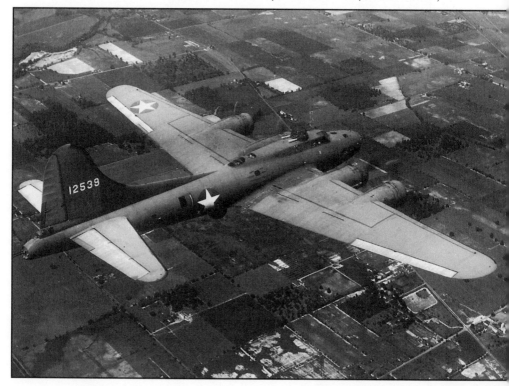

When the American air force entered the campaign in 1942, it did so with a certain complacency, believing it had better planes, better bomb-sights (the famous Norden bombsight), and a better doctrine.[17] Whether or not the bomber the U.S. Air Force brought to Great Britain was actually better than the Lancaster is problematic. It was a significantly faster plane: The B-17 was capable of sustained speeds roughly 25 percent greater than the Lancaster, top speeds about half again as great, and the short-range bomb load was prodigious, nearly eight thousand kilograms.

But regardless of how good the B-17 was, its losses in daylight raids followed the same gloomily predictable trajectory as the Wellington's. Unlike Bomber Command, whose raids were principally directed against widespread targets, the American Eighth Air Force planners aimed at the destruction of a key industry, the prime example being antifriction bear-ings, as it had been discovered that half of Germany's entire antifriction-bearing production was located in one city, Schweinfurt.

On October 14, 1943, the Eighth Air Force launched 291 bombers against industrial targets at Schweinfurt. The city was not the only target hit, but it was singled out for attention owing to the heavy concentration, and two-thirds of the bomb tonnage dropped on antifriction-bearing plants was dropped on Schweinfurt. The October raid did enormous damage: In this one raid 10 percent of the machinery used to make antifriction bearings—together with a fifth of the finished materials—was destroyed.

Postwar the Germans, notably Albert Speer, confessed that further raids against Schweinfurt, mounted in rapid succession, might well have brought German armaments production to a halt, as almost every piece of machinery required by the military used antifriction bearings in one form or the other.

But the phrase "had the raids continued" flies in the face of what both strategic bomber forces had already discovered. Further raids might or might not have destroyed Germany's antifriction-bearing production, but they would certainly have destroyed the Eighth Air Force. Of the 291 aircraft sent out on that October raid, 228 arrived over the target. Sixty-two bombers were shot down, and 138 of the survivors were seri-ously damaged, seventeen of them beyond repair.[18] Less than a third of the original strike force was capable of a second raid. Assuming the ratio of losses continued—and it seems remarkably constant over the period—three or four raids later there would have been no bombers left to deploy elsewhere.

So long as the bombers continued to fly into Germany unescorted by fighters, losses would be prohibitive. Eventually—although not before the two bomber commands had lost thousands of airmen and scattered high explosives all over Europe to no real effect—the Allies managed to solve one part of the problem. This was to have fighter escorts accompany the bombers and intercept the German fighters, and when this was realized, losses went down markedly.

In justifying their losses the strategic bomber apostles insisted that they were doing the best that could be done with the existing technology, that they began using fighter escorts as soon as they confronted the problem, and that only after the proper long-range fighters were developed was it possible to deploy them. But the bomber barons believed that massed bomber formations could defend themselves in enemy airspace.

On the face of it this defied logic, but the commanders of both air forces justified their own losses the same way Allied generals had done during the First World War: Our losses were heavy, but their losses are much worse. This was nonsense. During two major bombing campaigns that stretched from March to November 1943, one against the Ruhr and the other against Hamburg, RAF Bomber Command made more than 35,000 sorties, losing 1,567 bombers outright and another 3,249 seriously damaged.

Civilian loss of life in Germany was catastrophic. Bomber Command attacks on Hamburg destroyed a third of the city's housing and killed nearly forty-eight thousand people, almost all of them civilians.[19] But within five months Hamburg was operating at 80 percent of its former industrial capacity, and in 1943 Germany's ability to manufacture equipment and sustain its war effort actually increased. Tank and airplane production actually doubled: In 1942 Germany had produced 5,573 armored vehicles, and in 1943 output rose to 11,897; 12,950 aircraft had been built in 1942, and this increased to 22,050 the following year.[20] In no area did German production go down as a result of the 1943 bombing campaign.

Clearly the prewar theory that said that massed bombers could defend themselves was entirely fallacious. Part of the solution therefore was to produce a long-range fighter that could accompany the bombers on their sixteen-hundred-kilometer roundtrip from Great Britain into the heart of Germany. The American air force commander, Gen. Henry H. "Hap" Arnold, had seen the problem clearly enough, and in fact had

directed that such a plane be put into service by January 1944 at the latest. As the first American bomber raid with long-range fighter escort
(the famous P51 Mustang) took place on January 11, 1944, the usual
conclusion is that this was a triumph of American ingenuity.

But the reality is more distressing. The RAF had originally ordered the
plane for British use; the first model flew in 1940, and it was in service by
November 1941.[21] The Mustang had all sorts of advanced features, the
most notable being a streamlined airframe that made the plane capable
of extremely high speeds. But its engine, a liquid-cooled Allison power
plant, was inadequate; in particular it couldn't produce enough power at
high altitudes. As it stood then, the plane was simply another one of the
numerous partially successful aircraft that designers on both sides kept
developing.

The British at first used it for photographic reconnaissance and
ground attack, and the Americans toyed with using it as a dive-bomber.
The first RAF missions were in May 1942, and eventually the RAF realized that the same thing could be done to the Mustang that had been
done to the Manchester: Take out the Allison engine and install a Merlin. The result was an extremely fast plane with so much power to spare
that it could carry enough fuel to enable it to accompany the bombers
all the way into Germany.

Although the idea was British, the Americans then proceeded to
build modified P51s in vast numbers, and everyone credits the fighters—
correctly—with enabling the bomber force to operate successfully without the crippling losses that had marked its deployment since September
1939.

But the dates suggest the problem. The potential of the Merlin
engine was well known to the RAF. The engine was already there. So
was the airframe. So was the pressing need for fighter escorts. Why did it
take basically three years for the problem to be sorted out and solved?

The theory of strategic bombing said that the bombers would always
get through, so there was no need to consider alternatives. During the
European war the Allied air forces lost the staggering total of 21,914
bombers. In fact the Allies lost substantially more bombers than any
other type of plane. Consequently the vast majority of the 158,546 airmen lost in action were lost flying bombers.[22] There was no Mustang
long-range fighter until December 1943 because Bomber Command
(and its American equivalent) persisted in their adherence to the basic
tenets of strategic bombing.

The P51 was originally designed for the Royal Air Force and went into service in 1940; initially the plane was inferior to most other fighter designs, but its remarkable range and endurance at high speeds made it the only fighter capable of providing an escort for long-range bombers, and it was the Mustang that enabled Allied bombers to operate over Germany without suffering crippling losses. Unfortunately, this didn't happen until January 1944. (*National Archives*)

Anatomy of Failure

Despite the horrific losses incurred by Allied airmen, the Allies made the claim that, by the fall of 1944, the air campaign had an appreciable effect on Germany's ability to fight. "The index of total armament production, which had risen until the third quarter of 1944, fell by 10 percent in the fourth quarter," is how the United States Strategic Bombing Survey puts it, going on to observe that the actual damage done to the German economy in 1944 was considerably more serious than this figure suggests.[23]

Postwar the contention has been that the bombing campaign suffered from two faults. On the one hand not nearly enough bombs were dropped. More then four-fifths of the bombs dropped on Germany were dropped after January 1944, and nearly three-quarters of the total tonnage was dropped after July 1, 1944. So the main reason that the economic indicators didn't begin to turn down until the last part of 1944 was that was when the bombing became really intensive. At the same time it was argued—largely by the Americans—that the bombing campaign was too dispersed. About a fourth of the tonnage, for example, was simply dropped over German cities, and only about a third was aimed at specifically military targets. Strategic bombing, then, would have been more successful had there been more of it, and more of it concentrated on selected industries vital to the war effort, such as the antifriction-bearings factories.

After the war the United States sent in survey teams to attempt to estimate the extent to which the strategic bombing campaign had crippled the German war effort. The result supported the contention that strategic bombing had a substantial impact, beginning in the last half of 1944, when all the main economic indicators went into decline. The survey teams argued that this was proof the campaign had been a success. But they failed to consider other reasons why the index had dropped so sharply. For example, by September 1944, Germany had lost both its major source of iron ore (France) and oil (Romania), and these losses would clearly have a major impact on the production of anything dependent on oil or iron ore.[24]

The survey teams also attempted to measure the extent to which civilian morale had suffered as a result of the bombing, as that had been one of the chief ideas behind the attacks on civilian targets. Again, although the teams attempted to use their data to support the idea that the bombing campaign had been successful at destroying civilian morale, the conclusion seems questionable.[25]

There is another issue the survey teams left largely untouched. The RAF's bombing command, unlike the American one, frankly aimed to destroy the morale of the civilian population by inflicting heavy damage on Germany's major cities. Certainly by the end of the war, the combination of deliberate British policy and American collateral damage had inflicted enormous harm. The Germans estimated that by January 1945 more than a quarter of a million lives had been lost. German police records, which seem reasonably authentic, estimate the death toll for the Dresden raid (which occurred after January 1945) in excess of 200,000 lives.[26] The U.S. Strategic Bombing Survey summary dodges the Dresden issue but still comes up with a total in excess of three hundred thousand deaths.[27] No one pretends that these were to any significant degree military casualties, and the survey teams were surprisingly candid in admitting that killing some hundreds of thousands of people had no particular impact on the German war effort.

So Douhet was wrong about that, just like all those in power who read him, and seriously misjudged the impact of strategic bombing. Even by the admissions of the survey teams, the air campaign killed 305,000 and wounded another 780,000 (mostly) civilians living in Germany. It deprived another twenty million of essential services and rendered another five million homeless. If its purpose was to turn postwar Germany into a pile of rubble, it was a great success. If its aim was military, it was a near complete failure, a failure that, not coincidentally, also cost the lives of well over one hundred thousand Allied airmen. What those airmen could have accomplished had their efforts been devoted to a different sort of air war will be seen clearly enough in the following chapters.

NOTES

1. As quoted by David Irving, *The Destruction of Dresden* (London: Futura, 1980), 24.

2. As reported—without comment—by Denis Richards in the first volume of the official RAF history: *The Fight at Odds* (London: Her Majesty's Stationery Office, 1953), 2–3. As one historian remarks, "The argument that the bomber would always get through was in large measure true only because little work was being done in defensive measures by offensively-minded air marshals who refused to take into account the lessons of the 1914-1918 battle of London." Higham, *Air Power,* 71.

3. Alexander McKee, *Dresden 1945: The Devil's Tinderbox* (New York: E. P. Dutton, 1982), 13.

4. Which is not to say that the raids were morally unjustified, a matter to which there is no easy answer. Given that the received wisdom of the power of aerial bombardment was common knowledge in the 1930s, the country whose leaders began such a campaign certainly invited retaliation in kind. Was this retaliation moral? In a purely objective sense, perhaps not, but I believe that subjectively, it was—that is, the men who ordered these attacks really believed that this was a strategy that would destroy a wicked enemy that in their view had attacked them without provocation. This I take it is the point made by Neillands in *The Bomber War,* 382–406.

Unfortunately Neillands, like most airpower enthusiasts, keeps switching arguments. On the one hand he believes the raids were justified as a means of punishing the German population for its support of Hitler, while at the same time he wants us to believe that the targets were justifiable on military grounds. This leads him into absurdities. Dresden, for example, was a justifiable military target because—among other things, "the city manufactured most of Germany's cigarettes—a vital product for maintaining wartime morale" (352). This sentence is slightly taken out of context, but Neillands's justification of the bombing on military grounds really does rest on a sleight of hand: In order to destroy strategically important factories in the suburbs, it was necessary to incinerate the downtown. But these suburbs were dozens of kilometers away—as anyone who takes the trouble to visit Dresden today can clearly see. Nor were they particularly damaged.

5. The best the authors of the most recent study can come up with is that the strategic bombing campaign deprived the Germans of some ten thousand antiaircraft weapons, which, they observe, "would have had a significant impact on the ground war in the east or west in 1943 or 1944." Fair enough, but the Allied planes—and air crews—deployed would have had an equally great impact elsewhere, so the argument does not hold up. See the conclusions in Williamson Murray and Allan R. Millett, *A War to Be Won* (Cambridge, Mass.: Harvard University Press, 2000), 332–34 (the quotation is on 332). Their otherwise excellent summary blurs the distinction between tactical and strategic bombing, which allows them to be reasonably positive about the bombing campaign.

6. Although Wever's death was a blow, there were other reasons as well. See the discussion in Schliepahke, *The Birth of the Luftwaffe,* 38–39, which is much the same as that of Homze, *Arming the Luftwaffe,* especially 265–66.

7. German fighter development illustrates the point perfectly. The first of the famous Messerschmitt 109 fighters flew at the 1936 Olympic Games, was delivered to the Luftwaffe in spring 1937, and flown in combat in Spain that same year. The Germans knew that a new fighter was needed for the 1940s, and the existing policy was for there to be a standard fighter. Heinkel already had two designs in the prototype stage for the replacement, but instead, in 1937 Focke-Wulf was charged with developing the new fighter, even though the design existed only on paper. As a result, their model, the FW-190, did not make its first test flight until 1939, and it took another two years to get the plane sorted out so its performance was satisfactory: early models featured inadequate armaments and an underpowered BMW engine prone to overheat. As a result, the FW190 didn't see action until summer 1941, and Focke-Wulf records show a bewildering series of desperate modifications, mostly aimed at fixing the blunders in the original design. As a result the Messerschmitt 109 soldiered on until the end of the war. See the brief discussion in Heinz J. Nowarra, *The Messerschmitt 109* (Fallbrook, Calif.: Aero Publishers, 1963), 62. FW-190 data taken from Eberhard Weber and Uwe Feist, *Focke-Wulf 190* (Fallbrook, Calif.: Aero Publishers, 1968), especially the unnumbered final pages of the text.

8. Basically RAF Fighter Command lost 123 fighter planes in Dunkirk operations, of which 65 were Spitfire 1s. During this same time period the Luftwaffe lost 137 aircraft over Dunkirk, which suggests a rough parity. But clearly many of these planes were downed by ground fire—the Royal Navy alone has thirty-five confirmed downings of

German aircraft, and there were also French naval vessels and French and British ground-based antiaircraft defenses. As only 3 RAF fighters are listed as having been hit by ground fire, the presumption is that the others were downed by German aircraft. In *The Nine Days of Dunkirk,* 271, Arthur Durham Divine lists as one of the four "legends" of Dunkirk the idea that the RAF inflicted enormous damage on the Germans. After analyzing the figures, he concludes, "It is difficult to read into these figures any justification for the widely repeated declaration that Fighter Command established qualitative superiority over Dunkirk."

9. At the time, aircraft losses were wildly wide of the mark: the RAF claimed 2,698 aircraft destroyed, and the Luftwaffe claimed it had shot down 3,058 British planes. Data from Hough and Richards, *The Battle of Britain,* 310, who point out that according to these figures, British estimates were off by a factor of 2, German by 3. But since the inflated scores were the ones used to determine a pilot's personal scores, clearly a good bit of revisionism is in order. As Hough and Richards observe, this "is a subject which, understandably, few chroniclers of the Battle [of Britain] have chosen to explore in depth" (311). Or at all, one might add. Another casualty of the inflated totals: the day chosen in Great Britain to commemorate the battle (September 15) is not actually the day on which the Luftwaffe suffered its heaviest losses.

Chroniclers of the RAF have been silent about the percentage of the German losses caused by Great Britain's formidable antiaircraft system. See, for instance, Richard Overy's *The Battle of Britain* (New York: W. W. Norton, 2000), 128, which implies that all the losses are attributable to the RAF. Clearly this is impossible. In the summer of 1940 the British deployed 1,317 heavy guns (over 75 millimeters), 700 light weapons (30–40 millimeters), and about 3,000 20-millimeter weapons and machine guns (appendix 9, Hough and Richards, *Battle of Britain*). Clearly a good many of the German losses were caused by this arsenal.

While it is understandable that an exact breakdown would be impossible, the silence on the subject is suggestive. See, for example, Richard Townshend Bickers's elaborate *Battle of Britain* (London: Salamander, 1997) which discounts their utility entirely. Bickers claims that on the night of October 15, 1940, London's antiaircraft weapons fired 8,326 shells and managed to shoot down only two German bombers and damage two others, implying that ground fire was "ineffectual" (90). Fair enough, but according to Bickers's own figures later on (184), the British lost 12 planes and the Germans 13 that night, which suggests that (*1*) antiaircraft fire accounted for 15 percent of the German losses even in the night raids, and (*2*) the RAF did not fare nearly so well in the exchange as its apologists claim. Of course this is simply one example—but since it is his example supporting the claim that antiaircraft guns were largely ineffectual, my point seems well taken.

10. See, for example, the account of air raid drills in *The Times* of April 28, 1925, 14,

15. There was a curious inconsistency in the RAF about this. On the one hand it explicitly endorsed the effectiveness of its strategic bombers, while at the same time lobbying for money for advanced fighters, the logic apparently being that RAF fighters could stop enemy bombers, but enemy fighters couldn't stop RAF bombers. At no point were ground-based systems taken seriously.

11. A complex and still little known matter. There is an excellent albeit somewhat technical discussion of the situation with respect to German and British countermeasures during the Battle of Britain in Nigel West, *Venona* (London: HarperCollins, 1999), 62–65.

12. Death toll from McKee, *Dresden 1945,* 12; up through the end of September 1940, about thirteen thousand people had been killed, according to Hough and Richards, *The Battle of Britain,* 304.

13. The results of the surveys conducted in Germany after the war are reported in U.S. Strategic Bombing Survey, *Overall Report (European War)* (Washington, D.C.: Overall Economics Effects Division, September 1945,) 95–100. I have yet to encounter a study of the strategic bombing campaign that actually examines the USSBS data closely, or even pays it lip service.

14. The quote is from Neillands, *The Bomber War,* 58, who has the most complete explanation of the Butt report. This is the basis for Higham's scathing remarks in *Air Power,* 132. The problem is that British and American analysts of the air war simply fail to comprehend the density of German cities, which virtually guaranteed that a sustained bomber attack on a "military" target of any sort would result in the mass destruction of large parts of the city itself. The account in Dudley Saward, *Victory Denied* (New York: Franklin Watts, 1987), attempts to present the report in a light slightly more sympathetic to the RAF (see especially 234–36).

15. Green, *Famous Bombers,* 126.

16. This estimate is from ibid., 134. During the war, Bomber Command dropped 1,235,609 tons and the United States dropped 1,461,864 tons, according to table 1 of the USSBS *Overall Report* (these tons are American tons of 2,000 pounds, as opposed to metric tons of 1,000 kilograms).

17. At this point the American Air Force was still a branch of the U.S. Army, and technically known as the USAAF, unlike the RAF, which was a distinct branch of the military like the navy and the army. For the sake of simplicity, however, the term "air force" will be used, and indeed the USAAF in 1942 was already acting like the USAF of the postwar decades.

18. There are minor variances in these numbers; the ones used here are from the USSBS *Overall Report,* 26. Similarly, although the popular term is "ball bearings," I have used the report's term, "anti-friction bearings."

19. This figure from McKee, *Dresden 1945,* 12, who gives a figure for the entire war for Hamburg as 55,000.

20. Chester Wilmot, quoting German figures derived independently of those compiled by the USSBS; but he notes, correctly, that the differences are trivial: *The Struggle for Europe* (New York: Harper & Brothers, 1952), 147.

21. See the thorough discussion of what happened when and why in Robert W. Gruenhagen's *Mustang* (New York: Arco, 1969), especially 56–81.

22. The USSBS makes clear that fighter bombers were counted in with fighters and reconnaissance aircraft. Basically the Allies lost 40,379 aircraft, of which 21,914 were bombers, and yet bombers flew less than a third of the sorties mounted during the war (4,129,079 sorties, of which 1,442,280 were by bombers). Data taken from table 1, summary, page x.

23. USSBS, *Overall Report, 37.*

24. USSBS, tables 66 and 67. It is typical of the advocates of strategic bombing to ignore the meat of the USSBS data and only cite its more general conclusions. See, for example, the brief discussion in Neillands, *The Bomber War,* 383–84. Although the dozens of tables prepared by the survey team are impressive, to a certain extent they constitute a set of dependent variables, not independent measurements. In other words, as the amount of iron ore available declined, the amount of steel produced would automatically decline also. And as the amount of steel available declined, the production of tanks, guns, and other items heavily dependent on manufactured metals would obviously drop as well. The vast majority of the tables produced by the survey team in justification of the bombing effort measured forms of production whose output was totally a function of certain other materials.

Consider a simple case, the production of tanks. If the tank factory was bombed, production would go down. But as the survey teams discovered, it would soon be restored to normal. But tanks could not be built without steel. Nor could they run without gasoline, and these two requirements were a function of Germany's ability to import oil and iron ore. Once the iron ore production centers were lost, it made no real difference whether the plants were bombed or not. There would be a time delay between cause and effect, given the inventories on hand at each step of the process, but while this complicates the issue, it does not change the fundamentals. Measuring the drop in production in this industry or that and then attributing the decline to the strategic bombing campaign is a further logical confusion. Even in the most controlled situations, it is a questionable exercise.

25. In this regard, it should be said the survey teams showed a commendable candor in admitting that while "Allied bombing widely and seriously depressed German civilian morale, but depressed and discouraged workers were not necessarily unproductive workers" (USSBS, *Overall Report,* 37). This conclusion is a perfect example of the carefully qualified general conclusion that researchers like Neillands ignore (*The Bomber War,* 383–84).

The actual data, however, hardly supports the warrant of this sentence. In heavily bombed cities, 64 percent of those surveyed were tabulated as "willing to surrender," while in unbombed cities, the percentage was 57 percent—the difference hardly supports the conclusion. The civilian morale assessments are in US, *Overall Report,* 95–98.

26. The report of the police president of Dresden, dated March 22, 1945, gives the following information: "Up until the evening of 20th March 1945, 202,040 bodies, primarily of women and children, were recovered. It is to be assumed that the death toll will climb to 250,000. . . . 68,650 of the bodies were incinerated. . . . As the rumours far exceed reality, open use can be made of the actual figures." As the last sentence quoted suggests, this report was intended to be circulated to other police jurisdictions to calm the fears of the general populace, so it is hardly an exaggeration. The question arises of course as to the accuracy of a count taken so soon after the disaster. If we weight this figure accordingly, we get a death toll of 125,000 people. As the document quoted was uncovered by David Irving, it is generally ignored, although the facts of the case suggest it is true enough. See Irving, *The Destruction of Dresden,* 225–26, 260–61.

McKee, who claims to admire Irving's work, ignores the figures, but notes the widespread belief in Germany that the death toll was in excess of a quarter of a million, a figure I have heard as well. Officially the German Democratic Republic admitted only that the toll was 35,000, but this figure was always qualified: 35,000 was the *minimum.* McKee, who discusses these figures, feels that the total is higher: "The [GDR] figure of 35,000 for one night's massacre alone might easily be doubled to 70,000 without fear of exaggeration, I feel. No one will know for sure" (McKee, *Dresden 1945,* 321–22).

27. "The basic *direct* effects on civilian life were as follows (these figures are higher than the German Air Ministry figures; they are based on statistical estimates made by the Survey): killed, 305,000 . . ." USSBS, *Overall Report,* 95.

9.

Normandy and the Breakout
at Saint-Lô: Summer 1944

Twelve days after the last shot had been fired in the Falaise Pocket, Mont-
gomery entered Antwerp. Twenty days after this same last shot,
Bradley crossed the Siegfried Line before Trier. Overlord had not anticipated
such speed. For D-Day + 120, i.e., October 6th, the plans
had envisaged an anchorage on the Somme estuary.
—EDDY FLORENTIN[1]

Both the background to the Normandy offensive and the campaign itself are well known, so much so that any comment
about them runs the risk of being simply a repetition of previous accounts.[2] However, in the light of the competing theories of airpower and armor we have been exploring thus far, a modestly
different view of the key events emerges that may perhaps explain some
of the controversies. At the very least, seeing events from this slightly different perspective has the advantage of freeing the discussions of the final
phases of the war in Europe from the thrall of biography and national
chauvinism, in which key decisions are seen through the prism either of
Anglo-American rivalries or of personality conflicts among the military
leaders of the Allies (and, to a lesser extent, among the Germans as well).

The Plans

As is well known, the Allies, and particularly the Americans, had been militating for an invasion of France virtually since the United States entered the European war. This had led to what may fairly be regarded as the first great operational split between Great Britain and the United States, with the former, or anyway its prime minister, urging that the first step had to be a strike at the "underbelly" of Europe (after North Africa was secured) and the United States, or anyway its most prestigious military leader, General Marshall, arguing that the main blow should be delivered in France.

As noted in a previous chapter, Churchill's idea conformed to ideas developed during the last war, to the grand strategic thinking that had dominated Lloyd George's post-1916 cabinet, and, perhaps more importantly, to the idea of the breakthrough. All three ideas converged (with many lesser ones) in Churchill's mind, and, as a result, the Allies invested their energies during 1943 in a long and costly ground offensive in Italy, an offensive from which, as we pointed out, they were unable to extricate themselves no matter how many imaginative breakthrough operations they planned or executed.

The Normandy offensive had an awkward birth. Planning had been going on since 1942, when the British command had directed Gen. Sir Bernard Paget, commander of the Home Forces, and Lord Louis Mountbatten, head of Combined Operations, to begin planning an invasion of France. This plan was formally known as Roundup, and it was Mountbatten's staff who hit on the idea of Normandy as the invasion site.

By early 1943 Roundup was merged into a new proposal, called Overlord, developed by a group of British staff officers headed by Lt. Gen. Frederick Morgan, chief of staff to the supreme Allied commander. As the acronym for his title was COSSAC, the first version of Overlord was known as the COSSAC plan. Morgan had three problems. The Allied high command had decided to appoint him before they appointed the actual commander (General Eisenhower). Administratively he was chief of staff without a chief, and hence a planner without a supervisor: Militarily Morgan had no real combat experience, had never commanded anything more than an artillery battery, and had never directed the planning of a major offensive. This may well explain why he was unable to resolve the most serious problem: Morgan was essentially told what resources would likely be available for the invasion and told to plan accordingly.

The best way to proceed would have been for the actual supreme commander to have laid down a set of goals for the invasion—for a plan to have been developed with the specific objectives allowing the Allies to achieve those goals, with those objectives in turn establishing the forces needed. Montgomery's comment that "there was no one . . . who knew what was necessary, or how to build up an operation, or the operational repercussions of decisions given" thus seems fair enough, but the COSSAC plan reveals the two fundamental flaws of the plan, flaws that reveal what had become a sort of institutional mindset in both armies.[3]

First, as is well known, the original plan envisioned an amphibious landing on a narrow front. Second, the plan called for the successive forces being deployed ashore to move through those forces already there. Both assumptions were flawed, but it is useful to study the flaws to reveal how the Allied staffs now thought and planned.

To begin with, they had failed to understand the enormous logistical problems caused by mechanized warfare. Armored and mechanized columns required vast amounts of fuel to keep them operating, and the fuel, together with everything else, had to be close behind. An armored division, no matter how mobile and powerful its tanks, was in this respect just like a prisoner with an enormous steel ball chained to his leg or a bride navigating the aisle of the church with a long train streaming behind her. As we have pointed out, this was precisely where Fuller's ideas failed. Despite all his emphasis on the new, conceptually he thought of tanks as being just like the heavy cavalry of 1800, and with about the same logistical needs. Morgan's staff replicated the failure in its plan.

The point here is not to blame these planners, but to point out that this in fact was the basic problem that the Allies simply never solved—how to mount mechanized offensive operations at a continuous pace without the tanks running out of fuel. In North Africa, Rommel at least had the excuse that fuel supplies weren't getting through to him. Allied planners in 1944 had no such excuse, and yet they signally failed to master the basic logistical problems involved, starting with the original invasion plans for Normandy, which, conceptually speaking, had as their model a sort of medieval cavalry charge: The foot soldiers would open the gates (the beachhead) and the knights (the armored forces) would thunder out and trample the enemy.

This leads to the second flaw, the narrow front. Although the planners defended the narrow-front idea by claiming, quite truthfully, that they hadn't been given the resources to plan for a broad-front offensive, what is striking is that such an idea could even be contemplated. That anyone sat down and seriously planned it suggests the extent to which the Allies were still locked into the idea of the narrow thrust that they believed had characterized the correct deployment of armored and mechanized forces.[4]

The proof that the flaw was institutional rather than forced on them by circumstances is seen easily enough. After the Germans began their great retreat from France in August 1944, the major Allied generals promptly began a dispute about which great thrust would be the best way to end the war. In so doing they simply replicated the same way of thinking that had marred the original COSSAC plan for Normandy.

Whether Eisenhower was a great military genius or not, when, at the end of 1943, as the man who would be the supreme commander, he first saw the COSSAC plan, he realized that it was, in his words a quarter of a century later, "too weak in numbers and frontage, if there were con-templated a heavy and rapid buildup with the purpose of smashing through the defending front at an early date. I had Beetle Smith come in with me during the examination and we decided, off the cuff, that a five-division attack was far more desirable."[5] Lt. Gen. Walter Bedell Smith, interviewed three years after the fact, had the same reaction, and put it even more strongly: "I nearly fell out of my seat. After all we had more than that in all our landings."[6] Left unsaid was the obvious: Given the difficulties that the Allies had encountered in their earlier amphibi-ous assaults, an attack aimed at the European heartland would need to be stronger, not weaker.

On December 27, 1943, therefore, Eisenhower, as the about-to-be appointed supreme commander, met with Montgomery, who would be the overall ground commander of the operation. Montgomery was of the same mind as Eisenhower. Although much has been made of the British general's contempt for his American superior, in this instance Montgomery behaved exactly as the situation warranted. Knowing that Eisenhower saw the basic flaw of the COSSAC plan, Montgomery, as commander of the ground forces that would actually do the fighting, set down the specific objectives that had to be met. The invasion would be on a much wider front. If the beachhead secured was wide enough, the Germans should not be able to smother it to contain the attacking forces in a confined space, as had happened at Anzio. This was the application of the same basic principle that the Germans and the Russians had been using: a broad-based attack that overloaded the defenders and would bring about a rupture in their position.

Montgomery also aborted one of the more potentially disastrous features of the COSSAC plan. Morgan was proposing that when the successive waves of invasion troops landed on his three-division front, in order to get into combat they would have to pass through the units already there, and in the COSSAC plan, American divisions would have to work their way through already-landed British forces in order to get into combat. This was a repetition of the deployments of the First World War, when the Allies envisioned moving new units through the positions of existing ones in order to get them into action. The French general (later marshal) Fayolle had observed in his diary as early as 1915 that passing one army through another is no easy task, and the Allies had not done it with much success in their offensive operations.[7]

Finally Montgomery insisted that in order to make the invasion front appear even larger than it was, airborne divisions would be deployed on both wings of the actual landing zone. This would not only confuse the German defenders into thinking that the attack was on an even more broadly based front than was the case, but the airborne units, no matter how dispersed their landings were, would be able to disrupt the defensive responses. The German defensive doctrine was that airborne landings had to be contained within twenty-four hours, so local German commanders could therefore be expected to put all their energies into prompt countermeasures, and would thus be diverted from the real invasion, which was amphibious.

Montgomery was clearly right in his extensive revisions, and right to insist on them. Although there was broad agreement about what was required, it was Montgomery who set the specific parameters, and in that sense the plan was his. It is equally clear that in Eisenhower's mind this was a good thing. By the end of 1943 the British were painfully aware that they were slowly but surely becoming the junior partners in the alliance. The bulk of the Allied manpower was American. Most British tanks were American tanks. What the British did possess—in their own minds anyway—was a superior sense of organization and planning. It was better for the plan to appear to be Montgomery's, and hence British. Moreover in Montgomery the British possessed a major asset. He was the only senior commander who had indisputably beaten

the Germans in a straight fight. Whether they liked it or not, he was
their major command resource.

Or so it would seem. The problem in the Second World War, as in the
First, was that modern armies required large staffs, and these staffs were
generally composed of experts who knew everything about how to fight
the war except how actually to fight it. In the First World War, the
French General Staff had done everything in its bureaucratic power to
stifle Pétain, and the situation with Montgomery was not far different.

In fact Churchill's staff tried to prevent Montgomery from actually
seeing the COSSAC plan and forming his own evaluation of it, insisting
that he should be allowed to go over it only in the presence of the
COSSAC planners, who, on their own turf in London, would presumably be able to smother his objections. Bureaucracies, of course, never
present their objections in such clear language. Instead the claim was that
"it is most undesirable that Monty be given an opportunity of criticizing
the plan before he has discussed it with the people who prepared it.
They alone can explain the reasons which have led to the adoption of
the plan in its present form."[8]

But if the COSSAC plan was unacceptable to Eisenhower, what
would be accomplished by beating Montgomery into acquiescence?
The obvious answer is that this would put the Americans in the
uncomfortable position of rejecting the British plan without one of
their own to offer in its place. Presumably the idea was that, since the
Americans were notoriously unprepared in the planning area, COSSAC
would either win by default, or—Churchill's clear preference—be
shelved altogether.

However, while Churchill had his own strong preferences for how to
run the war, he was above all determined to win it, and this meant letting Montgomery critique the plan on his own. And that is precisely
what happened. Montgomery flew to Marrakesh, where Churchill
was—together with the COSSAC plan. The prime minister let him see
it, and the next day Montgomery wrote his appreciation. Like Eisenhower and Smith, he had little use for the COSSAC idea. In January,
back in London, he began to prepare his own plan.

Instead of COSSAC's three-division narrow-front landing, Montgomery proposed an offensive that would land on a seventy-five-kilometer
section of the coast between Oustreham (at the mouth of the Orne
River, just north of Caen) and Ravenoville. The core of the assault
would be five divisions (two British, two American, and one Canadian)

landed amphibiously, while three airborne divisions would be dropped farther inland, on the flanks, to block the German reactions (the American 82nd and 101st ahead of the Americans, the British 6th ahead of the British).

Instead of COSSAC's complicated pass-through operations, Montgomery proposed to divide the landing zone between a British and an American army, each operating separately with its own supply zone. The units that landed would not only secure the beachhead, they would expand it, moving out and broadening the bulging front, which would mean that subsequent waves of troops would move directly into combat positions without having to pass through other units.

Tactically the aim was this: The Americans, landing on the right flank, would seize Cherbourg and the Cotentin Peninsula. This would give the Allies a major port and a staging area for the breakout. If they could clear the immediate bridgehead, the American armored and mechanized divisions would be able to operate on favorable terrain and strike southeast into France proper. The British, by seizing the area around Caen and advancing inland, would be able to block any German offensives that would otherwise catch the Americans on their left flank as they moved inland. Unmentioned was the fact that this plan allowed the two Allies to make use of their strengths: the great mobility of the Americans and the excellent combat skills of the British.

Unfortunately for his subsequent reputation, Montgomery had a tendency to appear to rewrite his ideas so as to make whatever superb improvisation he had thrown together a part of his initial script.[9] His clear intention in January and February 1944 was to get as much armor ashore as quickly as possible and drive inland.

So both Montgomery and Eisenhower realized that if the initial Normandy landing was on too small a front, the Germans would simply overwhelm it. This decision was what might be called a decision based on the classical military principles of the First World War, when Joffre had realized that the only way to break the Germans was to mount an offensive operation on such a large scale, and on such a broad section of the front, that the Germans would not be able to take advantage of their superior mobility and move troops into positions where they could sew up the rupture.

And, as we have seen, the Germans themselves had used this same principle quite successfully in the opening offensives of the war: They had attacked Poland from three sides, and in May 1940, despite the mythologies of the offensive that were rapidly created by Allied apologists and Hitler's propagandists, they had attacked all along the front.

While this was not possible in northern France, the Allies could nonetheless achieve two things. On the one hand they could vastly expand the actual landing. Montgomery basically doubled the landing zone frontage, which with the airborne drops at either end, in effect tripled the initial strike zone. On the other hand the Allies could pretend that they had the intention of landing elsewhere along the coast, so that when the actual invasion began, the Germans would hesitate, uncertain as to where the main effort actually lay. In the first instance, then, the triumph of the Montgomery-Eisenhower conception marked the victory of traditional thinking over the new enthusiasms.

"Traditional" in this context is perhaps misleading. Fuller, Douhet, and their fellow travelers and apostles, had all heaped scorn on the "traditional" military view, seeing their own ideas as more progressive and more scientific. As we have seen, despite being able to chase Rommel out of Africa and defeat his army, Montgomery was criticized as being unable or unwilling to understand the proper deployment of armor. As preparations for the actual invasion continued, Montgomery seemingly confirmed this view.

Montgomery realized that an offensive delivered by seaborne troops— an amphibious assault—had another requirement as well, however, and this was to get out of the beachhead and move inland. This was not something the Allies had thus far consistently been able to do, and so Montgomery, in his orders to the Allied divisions scheduled to hit the beaches in June 1944, correctly emphasized the necessity of a speedy drive off the beaches and inland.

This was common sense: Everyone realized the necessity for a rapid deployment off the beach. But Montgomery took the plans one step further, and made them realities, by reversing the general order of the assaults. The order of these was by now firmly set: After an intensive air and naval bombardment, which, it was hoped, would either destroy the defensive positions or force them under cover, the infantry would go ashore and seize the needed ground. Then, in a complex and carefully orchestrated sequence, everyone else would land, and the armored columns thus disgorged would set out, rapidly expanding the lodgment area with great sweeping thrusts. The Allied problem was that everyone on the broad front had to get off the beach and move inland.

Allied planners had given great attention to almost every detail of this invasion but one: how the infantry would actually occupy the beaches once they were ashore. For the Americans the answer was simple enough. The infantry would simply storm out of their landing craft and assault the positions, taking them by a *coup de main*. Montgomery had a fundamental distrust of this idea in principle. Instead of infantry, the first thing to disembark would be armor. In the Montgomery plan, tanks would storm ashore first, followed by the infantry.[10]

Not ordinary tanks, but a variety of purpose-built vehicles the British had been experimenting with for years, it having occurred to them a heavily armored vehicle was ideal for, among other things, clearing a path through minefields.[11] To that end the British had fitted a sort of giant flail on the front of a tank. As the tank advanced, the flail revolved, the penetration of the steel chains into the ground igniting the mines.

An armored vehicle with a powerful gun was also an ideal weapon for destroying a fixed emplacement or bunker; indeed, that was the idea behind the German *Sturmgeschütz*, or assault gun, a hulking, low-profile vehicle that could get within close range of any gun position and, it was to be hoped, destroy it. Tanks were also useful as traditional debris clearing devices: mount a steel scraping blade on the front of a tank, and it could perform more or less the same function as its agricultural or industrial counterpart.

The immediate problem, however, was that tanks of this period didn't float, they weren't designed to operate underwater, and their fording capabilities were extremely limited. But here British ingenuity came into play. They designed a system that enabled a tank to float, at least for a limited time, enough to allow it to make it onshore.[12]

So Montgomery planned to have the first wave of his amphibious landing consist of just such special-purpose vehicles, which would both clear a path for the assault troops and provide them with the cover the combat engineers in particular needed if they were to clear the beach sufficiently for the remaining waves of vehicles to disembark.

By the spring of 1944, despite the extent to which Montgomery was disliked by many British commanders, his reputation in Great Britain was such that he could do as he wished, and so his ideas about the deployment of armor were accepted, despite the obvious objection that this was a complete violation of what experience had shown was the only sensible use of armor. What Montgomery was proposing was to use it in "penny packets" in conjunction with the infantry, to do nothing more than enable them to go about their job. Clearly, for the Rommel supporters, this was yet another sign that Montgomery simply didn't understand how to use armor.

Consequently, when Montgomery offered a third of the British collection of special-purpose armor to the Americans, Bradley's staff demurred:

> Bradley and his staff eventually accepted the "DDs" [tanks with flotation devices] but did not take up the offer of . . . the rest. . . . Their official reason was that there was no time to train American crews to handle the Churchill tanks in which most of the special British equipment was installed, but their fundamental skepticism about its value was shown when they rejected even the "Crabs" [for mine clearing] which offered few training difficulties, since the "flail" device was fitted to the standard American tank. The terrible consequences of this short-sightedness were only too apparent on Omaha [Beach] on D-Day.[13]

As Chester Wilmot saw decades ago, this was a dodge. What the Americans preferred was to let the infantry storm ashore, then the tanks would be unloaded, and a great mailed fist would be deployed deep into France.

Bradley is invariably thought of as the enlisted man's general, but now, in acceding to the prejudices of his staff, he condemned his infantry to the ordeal of Omaha Beach, an ordeal that could have been greatly ameliorated by the use of the special armor the British had assembled for the invasion.

Nor was this the only American deficiency. In the final plan the basic idea (hotly contested afterward) seemed clear enough. The British would seize the area around Caen and in effect pin down the German counterattack, which would allow a powerful American right hook (the Americans were on the right of the British)—the proverbial mailed fist—to penetrate deep into France. Despite the slow going in Italy, the Americans were confident that this powerful armored thrust would end the war in short order.

This idea was based on the belief that if the armored thrust developed quickly enough, the Germans would be unable to counter it with their own armor, thus enabling the Americans to use tanks as American theorists had decided they should be used: not to fight other tanks but to spearhead breakthroughs.[14]

The belief that a quick deployment would work had two chains of reasoning behind it. The Allies knew that the German defenders were themselves divided about the best way to stop an amphibious invasion of France. Rommel, the ground commander, believed that the only way to stop an invasion was on the beaches. His experiences in North Africa had sensitized him to the devastation wreaked on ground units by tactical airpower when it was allowed to operate unopposed over the battlefield. By 1944 it was clear that German ground troops in France would be facing the same situation: the Allies would have air supremacy. So if armored units were held back, they would never be able to reach the defensive line—they would all be destroyed by tactical air bombing. If an invasion was to be stopped, it had to be stopped on the beaches.

But the other German commanders did not agree with Rommel. On the one hand none of them had ever been in combat in the situation that prevailed in North Africa. As a result they did not grasp what it would be like to try to move troops into action in the face of an intensive and uncontested aerial assault. In this sense Rommel was right and everyone else was wrong.

On the other hand, however, Rommel's appreciation of how to conduct a defense was not particularly useful. In northern France the lines of communication all radiated out from Paris to the major port cities. Land travel from one city to the other—lateral lines of communication running parallel to the coast—were conspicuous by their absence. If an armored unit was in Dunkirk when the invasion forces landed at Cherbourg, it would be, practically speaking, impossible to get it into action in timely fashion. Basically it would have to entrain for Paris and then move back up to the coast.

Given the shortage of mechanized units available for the defenders, von Rundstedt, the overall ground forces commander, felt that the only sensible approach was to hold them far enough back so they could respond to an invasion anywhere along the coast. Unlike the Allies, who, having broken the German codes, had a very good idea of what the Germans were doing, the Germans were almost completely in the dark when it came to the Allies: They had no real idea where an invasion would occur.

Complicating the German situation was Hitler's belief that the prepared coastal positions were so strong that invaders would all be massacred on the beaches. After North Africa, Hitler was inclined to believe that Rommel was one of those talented officers who had an unfortunate tendency to lose his nerve at critical moments. His trust in him was therefore highly conditional. But in one key aspect Hitler's trust in Rommel was quite high. Hitler had never trusted the senior German generals. He felt—correctly—that they resented and disliked him. The tensions had been papered over with a string of victories. But now that there were only reverses, the senior military leaders were becoming more and more restive. Rundstedt was arguably the army's best senior general—but this was a factor which counted both for and against him in Hitler's mind.

By having both Rommel and Rundstedt in France, Hitler therefore had resorted to the sort of divisive system he had always employed. Rommel would make use of his privileged status to appeal directly to Hitler, which would force von Rundstedt to do the same, the result being that all important decisions would be made directly by Hitler himself. So when Rommel attempted to have the armor released directly to him, Hitler temporized: Some was, some wasn't, but the end result was that the geographical location of the German mechanized units was of little importance. Effectively they could be moved only with Hitler's approval, which might or might not be given, depending on how he personally read the situation.

This gave the Allies a major advantage. It was one they would need, the Americans in particular, because the whole notion of a prompt armored breakout from the landing area flew in the face of the actual terrain over which the tankers would have to operate. But this of course was part of the Fuller legacy: When he talked about the invincibility of armor, he never mentioned the difficulty of running complex mechanical devices over sand, through swamps, in subzero temperatures, or, for that matter, over an urbanized landscape.

From the point of view of an armored commander, this landscape was nightmarish. Norman farms were separated one from another by a combination of stone walls and thick hedges (the infamous *bocage*). Roads were narrow, and often appeared to be sunken, with stone or earth embankments on either side. These roads passed through small villages consisting of tightly clustered houses. Although this last was a typically European feature which the Allies had already encountered in Italy and Sicily, Norman buildings were if anything much sturdier, the villages even denser, closer together.

The combination of hedgerows, stone walls, sturdy buildings, and sunken roadways would enable any competent infantry commander to re-create the sort of defensive position that had characterized the German lines in the First World War—and without having to do any digging: The defenses could be created as fast as the infantry could reach them. Yet the Americans were acting as though once ashore, their armor would simply motor on into France.

How could this be? There were by now hundreds of thousands of French soldiers on the Allied side who knew Normandy. There were British officers who had fought there, British tourists who had vacationed there, British landscapes that mirrored the Norman one. There was extensive aerial reconnaissance. What was missing was not the data or its availability. What was missing was an understanding of the data and how that affected the planned objectives.

This curious blindness could of course be traced to the backgrounds of the American commanders and their staffs. The last great maneuvers of the U.S. Army had taken place mostly in north and central Louisiana, which was rolling country with few towns of any size, and the experiences in Sicily and Italy were perhaps too recent to have been thoroughly assimilated. Or perhaps the American commanders were simply inexperienced and overconfident.

They were certainly overconfident. Although the evidence is anecdotal and suspect, it would appear that American tankers were as surprised by the German tanks they met as the Germans had been by the Red Army's T34 and the Grant and the Sherman. And in fact, as we have seen, if there is one consistent thread running through any serious discussion of armor versus armor it is the extent to which each army, as it went into combat, was totally surprised by the tanks of its adversaries.

By 1944 only the British seemed to have any serious institutional awareness of the power and toughness of the new generation of German tanks, the proof being that British engineers had managed to shoehorn the potent seventeen-pounder gun into the turret of the Sherman tank.[15] The resulting vehicle, which the British called the Sherman Firefly, was the only tank the Allies would send into action in 1944 that had any chance at all of prevailing on the battlefield against the high-velocity 75- and 88-millimeter guns that were now the staple of the German tank force.[16]

American tank doctrine in 1944 looked as if it had been penned by Fuller himself. The role of tanks was the breakthrough, not a tank versus tank battle. The Sherman was poorly armored and badly armed, but it was a fast and reliable vehicle, exactly the sort of tank that Fuller had seen dominating the battlefields of Europe.

It was inconceivable to the American commanders that once ashore, their tanks would be unable to operate in accordance with their theories. And in this they had the growing acquiescence of Montgomery's North African critics, who were vocal in their complaints that the man knew nothing about armor. Moreover the Americans believed that the absolute air superiority the Allies would enjoy over the battlefield would cancel out any problems.

The Stall

That the Normandy landings were a major success, perhaps the greatest Allied victory of the war, is beyond dispute, and their success was not— as is sometimes argued—because of German failure. As we noted earlier, although Rommel was correct in his understanding of the impact of tactical airpower, he had no real solution to the problem. Moreover, although he had devoted a great deal of energy to constructing beach-front defenses, these defenses were brushed aside, easily in the case of the British, and less so for the Americans at Omaha Beach.

But the sacrifices of the American infantry there, although to a certain extent unnecessary (had the Americans taken advantage of the British offers of special-purpose armor) were crowned with success. Although they lacked some of the right tools for the task, the Americans did have one potent weapon: close support from naval vessels. In the Pacific, flat-trajectory fire frequently did little damage to the Japanese defenders on what were essentially flat islands: They simply dug themselves in. But the cliffs overlooking the landing area rose up high enough for naval gunnery to be extremely effective, which suggests that von Rundstedt's instincts to let the Allies land and then begin the battle, as had been the case at Anzio, may well have been correct.

The heavy American casualties should not blind us to the fact that by the end of that first bloody day, the Allies were ashore, they were ashore in great numbers, they were off the beach, and they were debarking on such a broad front that there was no real possibility of their being dislodged.[17]

Where the problem came in was in the weeks—and months—after the initial victory. Essentially the powerful American armored thrust never developed, choked off by the hedgerows of Normandy, which, among other things, turned all the existing roads into land canals, while the sturdy Norman villages and farmhouses were simply so many forts. This revealed the fundamental error in the American idea of mechanized warfare: it was a doctrine that took no account of the terrain. Consequently the Americans found themselves engaged in a sort of combat for which they were totally unprepared.

On their left Montgomery was marginally more successful, in that his army was able to tie down the bulk of the German armor. But his troops had been unable to secure the area around Caen in the first few days, as the original plan called for, and the fighting there degenerated as well. Moreover Montgomery was now operating with a great handicap: the British army, with substantial combat forces tied down in Italy, did not have enough manpower available to replace its infantry losses. The only way to keep infantry regiments at combat strength was to disband existing units and combine them.[18]

The Allied air commanders, habitually skeptical about the idea that a war could be fought and won on the ground in the first place, had opposed almost every aspect of the invasion, and immediately on the first checks, they promptly proclaimed there was a crisis on the battlefield. Curiously—and this reveals quite clearly what their overall aims actually were—having proclaimed a crisis, they grew strangely shy about using airpower to solve it. Eisenhower's headquarters, on the other hand, was champing at the bit for a series of great breakthroughs. They were as wildly aggressive as the air barons were timid and reluctant.

Montgomery, in overall command of the ground forces, was thus being pressured from three sides. Like a good many senior commanders, Montgomery's personality was basically sociopathic. A brilliant commander—the only senior Allied officer who possessed true military genius in all the senses of the word—he had a fatal tendency to insist that everything was going according to his plans, regardless of what the situation appeared to be.

In the face of two apparent stalemates, each of the Allied sides blamed the other, and as Montgomery had already incurred almost universal dislike from his fellow British and American commanders, his alleged failure to take Caen became the scapegoat for the stalemate.[19] When the Americans finally broke out, and the German front simply collapsed, they felt that it was no thanks to Montgomery, who, for his part, claimed that he had done exactly what he had set out to do.

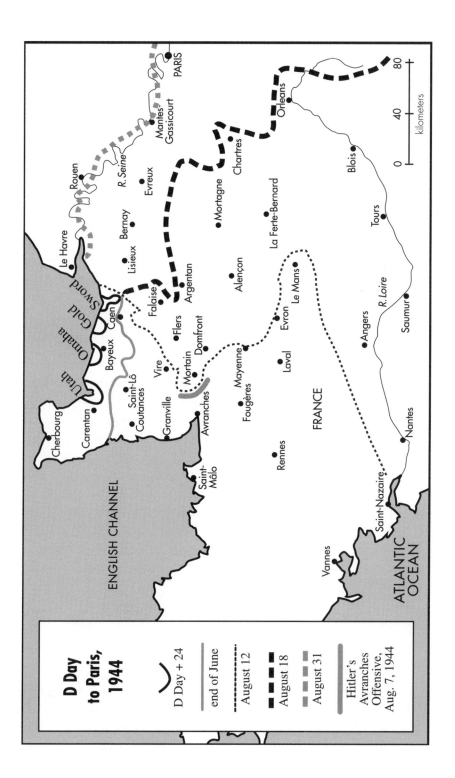

D Day to Paris, 1944

D Day + 24
end of June
August 12
August 18
August 31
Hitler's Avranches Offensive, Aug. 7, 1944

ENGLISH CHANNEL

Cherbourg
Carentan
Utah
Omaha
Gold
Sword
Caen
Bayeux
Saint-Lô
Coutances
Vire
Granville
Saint-Mâlo
Avranches
Mortain
Domfront
Flers
Falaise
Argentan
Alençon
Mortagne
Chartres
Évreux
Lisieux
Bernay
Rouen
Le Havre
R. Seine
Mantes-Gassicourt
PARIS
Orléans
Blois
Tours
La Ferté-Bernard
Le Mans
Évron
Mayenne
Laval
Fougères
Rennes
Angers
Saumur
R. Loire
Nantes
Saint-Nazaire
Vannes
Orléans

FRANCE

ATLANTIC OCEAN

kilometers
0   40   80

The real reason for the stall, however, had little to do with Montgomery's supposed failures. The Allies had invested their planning efforts
in the task of securing a landing area. This was a formidable problem to
solve. Both Eisenhower and Montgomery had grasped the flaw of the
COSSAC plan, and Montgomery had altered it in such a way as to
ensure its success. The fundamental problem, however, remained: Almost
the entire planning effort had been devoted to getting ashore. The landing zones had been intensely scrutinized, special equipment had been
developed—little or nothing was left to chance.

Logistically the operation was a triumph. Despite the problems at
Omaha Beach, The Allies had managed to get more than 150,000 men
ashore by the end of the first day. Half a million men had come ashore
within two weeks, a million men and nearly two hundred thousand
vehicles ashore within a month.[20] But surprisingly little was done with
regard to the actual course of the land operations themselves, other than
Montgomery's confident prediction that the Allies would be in Paris
ninety days after D day.[21]

In hindsight it is easy to see the defect. It would probably be more
accurate, however, to see the problem as being partly a function of
administrative strain: The logistics of the landing were vastly more
complicated than anything that had been done before, and there was
clearly a shortage of competent planners to begin with, or an inexperienced officer like General Morgan would not have been given the
job.

But at bottom, what the situation really reflected is the unquestioning
belief in theory. Given that the planning took place in the spring of
1944, one would suppose that the Allied armies had begun to assimilate
the lessons of the Italian and North African campaigns, and certainly the
most basic of those lessons, that in fighting the Germans there would be
no easy victories.

But both the Americans and the British persisted in trying to develop
unsupported thrusts of armor. Here is Col. Hans von Luck describing an
attack by the British Eleventh Armored Division against his ad hoc
combat group during Operation Epsom in July:

> As almost always with the British, they carried out their tank attacks
> without accompanying infantry; as a result, they were unable to elim-
> inate at once any little antitank nests that were lying well camou-
> flaged in woodland or behind hedges. The main attack broke down

under our defensive fire, although on the flank British and Canadian infantry were able to force their way into the Western part of Caen.[22]

By contrast German doctrine since 1942 had attempted to instill into armored officers that "when there is no infantry follow-up, an armored thrust is useless," and "a tank attack is really only worthwhile if there is an infantry unit to cover the flanks and immediately clear the country once it has been passed through."[23]

More than a century before, Goethe had remarked that when a man subscribed to a particular school of thought, his adherence to those beliefs blinded him to accurate observations—Goethe's way of trying to account for the fact that it often seemed to him that the more people knew, the less they were able to observe.[24] That being the case, it is hardly surprising to find that the devotees of Fuller and Douhet were unmoved by the facts of the war thus far.

As we have seen, the American surveyors trying to evaluate the success of the strategic bombing campaign at the end of the war concluded that it was not until the last half of 1944 that the campaign began to achieve results. As we have also seen, this conclusion is a doubtful one, but let us accept it for the moment. It then follows that up until July 1944, the bombing campaign had not achieved its goals. However, rather than changing their tactics, senior air force commanders insisted not simply that the campaign was successful, but that strategic bombing alone would win the war. American tank experts back in the United States likewise resisted requests for tanks with guns powerful enough to counter their German adversaries: Like the bomber barons, they knew better.

The Breakout

Instead of breaking out of the beach area in June, the Allies did not advance appreciably until August. They had planned to take Rome in 1943. Instead they entered that city on June 4, 1944, months behind schedule. As in Italy, each partner in the alliance blamed the other. In France the blame became more complex. A sizable contingent of British officers joined with the Americans in blaming Montgomery, whose caution and arrogance, it was alleged, were the reason for the slow progress. Montgomery—and his supporters—blamed Eisenhower, who was increasingly inclined to treat the American divisions under Bradley as a separate (American) army operating independently of Montgomery.

Certainly it was the Americans who were making progress. On June 18 American troops had cut across the base of the Cotentin Peninsula and reached the Atlantic Ocean, and by June 27 they had seized the port of Cherbourg. By contrast—or so it seemed—Montgomery's two offensives, Epsom and Charnwood, failed to dislodge the Germans from their positions around Caen. Montgomery's lack of progress, and his increasing caution, were now firmly established.

But this was unfair. Montgomery's British and Canadians had to fight more Germans than did the Americans: Eight infantry and six armored divisions were blocking his way, as opposed to the nine infantry and two armored divisions opposing the Americans. Part of the reason for the imbalance was the terrain, but it was also true that the Germans shared Montgomery's appreciation of the importance of the area around Caen. If he broke out there—as had clearly been his original idea—the whole front would implode.[25] If Montgomery made some disastrous mistake, and his front broke in the face of the counteroffensive with which the Germans invariably responded to any Allied error, the whole position could collapse.

There was another, more serious problem, which, although routinely noted by analysts, is rarely given its due: The British army was running out of infantry. Less than three weeks after their successful landing, they were already confronting the fact that the only way they could maintain their infantry strength in France was by breaking up existing units and reassigning the men as replacements. Thanks to American largesse the British army had plenty of tanks, and thanks to British ingenuity it had tanks capable of holding their own against German armor.

What Montgomery needed in Normandy was the excellent Commonwealth (and French and Polish) forces Churchill's insistence on attacking the "underbelly" had doomed to the long and costly fight in Italy. Because now the crucial theater of operations was France, and as the Americans poured more and more men into Normandy, the pressure not only mounted for independent American armies, but there was less and less inclination to listen to what the British had to say. Thus did Churchill's strategic ideas and the jealous gossip of the British army combine to diminish the weight of their country in the crucial phase of the war.

What made this all the more galling was that the American progress was contributing nothing to the fundamental needs of the Allied armies. The rationale for seizing Cherbourg was that it was a port, and the Allies needed ports. But three weeks after the landing gave the Germans time to destroy the port facilities completely, and the port of Cherbourg was only barely operational by the end of September. And in any case, it was too far away from the front to be of any great value.

Nor has it ever been clear that securing additional ports was an important military objective. As the Allied advance developed in late July and August, the bottleneck was not at the ports: The bottleneck was moving the needed supplies, fuel, food, and ammunition across northern France. Unlike the Germans, who always worried about the destruction of the transportation structure ahead of their planned advance, the Allied high command had simply let their air forces bomb bridges, railroads, and highways virtually at will. Apparently no one considered the negative impact this would have on efforts to keep the million-man Allied army moving. But now that the Allies had landed, those same logistics dictated zones of operation. There was no effective way to shift American troops into the British sector, where they could provide the needed manpower for offensive operations.

In July, Montgomery tried again. His idea—which had met with great resistance—was to use the weight of Allied airpower to obliterate the German positions ahead of him. So on July 18 Goodwood, as the operation was called, began with RAF Bomber Command dropping fifteen thousand bombs on the German positions, and this was followed by a tactical air force strike that dropped another thirteen thousand bombs. The air force commanders had been reluctant to divert efforts from what they considered to be the decisive part of the war—the strategic bombing campaign—but they assumed that after such an intensive bombing the fighting was essentially over.

To everyone's surprise the German defenses were largely intact, and after two grueling days of bitter combat, Montgomery had to bring Goodwood to a halt. As good as the British army was, it was simply unable to defeat its German adversaries, and the bombing attacks had been of no significant help.

The Allies had, however, come to the conclusion that the only way out of Normandy was to destroy the German positions with high explosives, and at the end of July, Bradley decided to rely on Montgomery's idea, the chief difference being that the American ground offensive would be on a very narrow front of about seven kilometers. In two days of bombing, Allied strategic and tactical bombers killed 136 American soldiers, including Lt. Gen. Lesley McNair, and wounded 621 others; German losses were said to be "considerable."[26]

But the American ground attack was successful. The Germans opposite were thinly stretched, and had few if any reserves to bring into play to stem the assaults. So Cobra, the code-name of the operation, was judged a success, and almost every historian dates it as the beginning of the "breakout" from the Normandy beaches. And indeed there was a breakout. The Americans captured Coutances, and on July 30 they seized Avranches: impressive gains, and clearly the whole German defense in western Normandy had collapsed.

That this was the beginning of the breakout will puzzle anyone who looks at a map of northern France. The American forces deploying out of their containment area had broken out, all right, but in the wrong direction. Avranches was sitting on the rugged terrain overlooking the Bay of Mont Saint-Michel, a stretch of water mostly famous for its great tidal surges, and hence problematic for unloading cargo. Even if Allied ingenuity could make use of the bay to unload cargo, there was no real transportation system linking it to the rest of the country.

So to term Cobra a success, and to speak of the breakout as beginning at that point (August 1, 1944) when the operation was formally over, is inaccurate. Although Bradley—and most of his command—were infantrymen, they now proceeded to act like Gen. J. E. B. Stuart at the Battle of Gettysburg, who left Lee to his own devices and conducted his own campaign. Bradley proceeded to direct offensive operations that, in terms of geography, as well as military necessity, were going backward.[27] Although it was true that breaking out in any direction was good, as it gave the enormous mechanized forces room to maneuver, the terrain made it difficult for armored columns to turn around and move in what was tactically the right direction.

From the point of view of strategy Cobra was a mistake, breakout for the sake of penetration. If there was a successful advance, the Americans would essentially be going in the wrong direction, headed northwest, back toward the ocean. If the Germans were successful in conducting a retreat—and given North Africa, Russia, and Italy, they certainly had the experience to do so—they could simply fold their defensive line back so it was roughly parallel with the main highway out of Caen. So long as the Germans had the area around Caen, their defensive line would remain intact.

Hitler and the Loss of France

Hitler had been watching events develop. After the Stauffenberg assassination plot on July 20, his suspicions about the German officer corps crystallized into a hostility that went far past unmasking and punishing the conspirators. "Now I finally have the swine who have been sabotaging my work for years. . . . Now I have proof: the entire General Staff is contaminated," Hitler exclaimed.[28] By coincidence (there had been several earlier planned attempts on Hitler's life) the failed attempt of July 20, and the inexorable reprisals that followed, took place at exactly the same time as the renewed Allied offensive attempts to break out of the Normandy bridgehead.

They thus occurred at the precise moment when Hitler was most determined to assert his control over the army. Convinced that he alone understood the principles of modern warfare, and that his officers had "sabotaged" him, he resolved to destroy the Allies once and for all. It had not escaped his notice that as the Americans had advanced west into Brittany, they had lengthened the front without appreciably deepening it. Moreover the American advance meant that the bulk of the Allied forces, the two American armies, were now drawing away from Montgomery's British and Canadian troops.

To Hitler this demanded a Frederickian riposte: just as Frederick the Great had compensated for his numerical disadvantages by attacking his enemies in detail before they could combine and overpower him, Hitler aimed to launch a massive armored assault aimed at Avranches, which would separate the Americans from the British and force them back into the wilds of Brittany.

Given the fact that the bulk of the American armor was already moving backward, the idea was sound enough. The problem was that by this time Hitler simply did not have the resources available to enable him to contain Montgomery around Caen, block the American probes to the east (there were plenty of American troops still trying to break out toward Paris instead of looping back into Brittany), and also launch an offensive of the size needed to accomplish his aims.

But at the end of July 1944, no one in the German high command was disposed to acquaint Hitler with the realities of the situation in France. Rommel and von Kluge had tried in June, but to no avail, and now Rommel, who might perhaps have been able to prevail in other times, was in the hospital, seriously wounded in an Allied air attack. So it is doubtful that anything could have moved Hitler at this point. As time passed, he had fallen more and more under the sway of his own propaganda, a propaganda for which there was by now plenty of support on the Allied side. Didn't everyone admit that his own army had done precisely the same thing in May 1940? Moreover German tanks and guns were clearly better, their troops more skilled and experienced. And this qualitative advantage would more than offset the Allied advantage in numbers. The Germans had believed the same thing when they were planning the invasion of the Soviet Union.[29]

The only thing that can be said about this plan is that it perfectly mirrored the ideas of the theorists that an armored thrust was unstoppable. Germany's exhausted divisions lacked the armor to carry it out, and they lacked the air support to make it a possibility. Even the commanders of the SS units, in which Hitler placed so much faith, as they were politically committed to him, thought the plan folly.

But who had the courage at this juncture to tell him? Or, more pertinent, what evidence was there that he would listen? None. Consequently Hitler ordered the German armored units holding the line to withdraw, and to form the core of an attack against the Americans. His exact orders, which reached von Kluge on August 2, 1944, were simple enough:

> Army Group B together with all its main armored units will prepare a counteroffensive aiming to break through to Avranches, with the objective of isolating the enemy forces and ensuring their destruction. . . . All the armor available must be transferred from present positions without being replaced. . . . The decision of the French campaign depends on this offensive.[30]

This order was the death warrant of the German army in the west. Its battered units had been hanging on now for months, relying on their superior training, on the terrain (ideally suited for defensive warfare), and on their powerful weapons. In what was essentially an infinite number of small-unit conflicts, these advantages were crucial. But the German commanders had by now recognized that the Allied troops opposing them were not the green and inexperienced soldiers of 1943 or earlier. To go over to the offensive would mean that the attacking Germans would forfeit their advantages, which would now accrue to the Allies.

Moreover the German units were barely holding on. Cobra had not, as expected, broken through the defensive positions as had been intended—a great wall of water bursting through a dike or levee and washing away everything it had protected. What it had done, however—to continue the metaphor—was to pierce numerous small holes in the dam. The Germans, despite their growing panic and frustration, were very good at plugging such holes. But it was at this precise moment that Hitler deprived them of the ability to plug those holes. Everything was to be directed into this grand offensive.

The spearhead would be a roughly twenty-kilometer thrust conducted by the XLVII Armored Corps, which consisted of no less than four armored divisions. One of these, the First SS Armored, was one of the two armored divisions in Sepp Dietrich's I SS Armored Corps. The transfer of this division was the nail in the coffin for the German army: Dietrich, an experienced armored commander, had been holding off Montgomery around Caen, but only by the skin of his teeth. Cutting his armored component in half meant that if Montgomery mounted another determined attack, the crucial right flank of the German position would collapse—unless other divisions could be rushed in.

But Hitler's order demanded that those other divisions were to be committed as well. Supporting the XLVII Corps to its right would be Bittrich's Ninth and Tenth SS Armored Divisions, which, together with the Twenty-first Armored, constituted the entire German tank force in Normandy.[31] Everything was to be staked on this one offensive.

Given the overwhelming Allied strength in Normandy, everything the Germans had in France was hardly sufficient to make even a dent in their position. By the end of July the Allies had 1.5 million men in Normandy, and, as noted earlier, their only real shortage was infantry, not armor. Moreover Hitler now made the same sort of error the Allies had been prone to make: Seen on a map the assault looked promising. Seen on the ground the assault looked well-nigh impossible, given the rugged terrain. Brittany was if anything worse country for armor than Normandy, and German armored divisions were no more prepared to fight there than the Americans had been. Indeed, by now—the first week in August—they were considerably less so, as the ingenuity and enterprise of local armored commanders—and enterprising American soldier-mechanics—had led to a number of improvised solutions (such as bulldozer blades brush-clearing teeth mounted on tanks) to the problem posed by the *bocage*.

The German commanders charged with carrying out this offensive were well aware that they were executing the death warrant for their units. On August 3, von Kluge phoned Jodl at the German high command to give him the final details of Hitler's plan. "Plan approved," Jodl said. "Plan useless," von Kluge retorted.[32] Clearly the plan would fail, and to no one's surprise, when the German attack began on August 7, it stalled out very quickly to the north of Mortain. The German penetration was minimal, but Hitler insisted the offensive continue.

As an assault Hitler's August drive for Avranches was so ineffective that it simply faded into insignificance as yet another German counterattack. And as it was sandwiched between what was by now an almost continuous series of Allied breakout offensives (Montgomery's penultimate one, Totalize, had begun a few days earlier), the Allied commanders can be forgiven their assumption that the German lines broke owing to their offensive operations.

It was Hitler's Avranches offensive that brought about Germany's greatest military defeat. For now (August 9) the Allied commanders began to realize that the German attack could be pinched off, and the core of the entire German force in the west entrapped. The resulting moves became known as the Battle of the Falaise Gap, but this is actually to misrepresent the situation considerably, as it makes it appear that the attacking Allies managed to break through the German defenses so quickly that they were almost completely surrounded before they had time to withdraw. The reality was that the German thrust weakened their defensive line to the point that it simply collapsed on both sides. The reason for the German predicament was that they had driven straight into a cul-de-sac, as Hitler had demanded, with the results his generals had predicted.

Although the Americans to the south of Mortain reacted more quickly than the British and Canadians around Caen (mostly because the American units were more heavily mechanized), both American and British commanders saw the opportunity to surround the German force and annihilate it. As North Africa and Siciliy had demonstrated, however, it was extremely difficult to catch the Germans in such a trap. Moreover, in August 1944, they simply abandoned any concept of a fighting withdrawal and raced for the safety of the Netherlands and Alsace.

Although the Allies promptly began a bitter game of blaming one another for the fact that the entire force was not trapped, the ability of the Germans to save at least a portion of their army is hardly surprising.

Although reliable and fast, the Sherman was poorly armored, and the 75-millimeter gun was inadequate. The British remedied this problem by cramming their excellent, high-velocity 17-pounder into a modified turret. The model shown here has a late-model 76-millimeter gun, which was not notably better than the gun it replaced. (*National Archives*)

Mechanization enabled a routed army to retreat far more quickly than its opponent could advance, particularly since the retreating men simply abandoned the less mobile vehicles, while the advancing and victorious army was forced to supply its own tanks with fuel.

This basic fact was obscured by the controversy over whether or not the Allies could have inflicted even worse destruction on the Germans than they did. Although Montgomery subsequently claimed that the Allies had taken 123,000 German prisoners since the start of Cobra, the consensus seems to be that the Allies took about 50,000 Germans prisoner, that at least 10,000 German soldiers were killed in the August fighting, and that at least 20,000 (maybe 40,000) German soldiers escaped entirely.[33] Part of the confusion stems from the obvious fact that once the retreat began, it quickly became a rout which extended all across northern France, but even the highest estimates suggest that the whole controversy over the closure of the alleged gap is misplaced.

It is no exaggeration to say that in August 1944 the German army suffered the worst defeat in its history. Strategically it was worse even than Stalingrad—and the number of divisions involved was about the same.[34] Although the army suffered heavier losses in personnel in the Soviet defeat, its military strength was surprisingly untouched. The German army on the Eastern Front was hardly a spent force after Stalingrad. It still had the capability to launch powerful offensive operations (Citadel) and to hand the Red Army some horrific defeats (Kharkov). But when the front in France collapsed, the German presence in France was finished.[35]

Given the tenacious German defense, the American charge backward, and the slow progress made by Montgomery's men, it is logical to wonder how Normandy would have turned out had Hitler not demanded his great offensive. But this is to miss a fundamental point about Hitler. After the initial successes of 1939–40, his only prescriptions were to hold the ground at all costs and then go over to the attack. He was convinced that his ideas were correct and that it was only the behavior of his generals that had stopped further German victories. It was, in other words, completely impossible for Hitler to sit by and let his officers conduct defensive warfare aimed at wearing the Allies down and making them—perhaps—inclined to seek a negotiated peace.

Since this plan—and the others that followed—were all failures, it is tempting to see Hitler's strategic thinking in purely negative terms. But this is a misjudgment. Hitler realized, far more perceptively than those who had survived the retributive terror that began on July 21, 1944, that this war would in no way be a repeat of the last, when the army, faced with impending defeat, had requested—and gotten—an armistice. This time the Allies would follow on a grander scale the pattern established by General Grant in the American Civil War: Surrender would be complete and unconditional. Germany's only hope was to secure enough of a victory on the battlefield to enable either breathing space or a negotiated peace. His gamble was desperate, but the situation in Germany was even more so.

At some point the populations of the Allied nations would realize the enormous numbers of perfectly innocent people that had been killed at Hitler's orders. By the summer of 1944, the entire Jewish population of the occupied lands had for all practical purposes been murdered, leaving aside for a moment the uncountable numbers of Poles, Russians, and Ukrainians who had also been killed.[36] This was not a war that could end in a draw. Not unless Hitler could destroy the Allied armies in the field so totally that they would have nothing left to fight with. It was about this time that Hitler began to express openly to his intimates the idea that Germany would either triumph or perish. This was not a rhetorical statement. There were already men in the U.S. government who were envisioning a postwar Germany that would resemble nothing so much as Carthage at the end of the Third Punic War. So he drove his armies to failure, and his generals obeyed him.

The price of the failure in early August was high. Hitler had committed everything available to his offensive. No other reserves existed. The German defenses, maintained at such great cost and with such great skill in June and July, now crumbled, and crumbled rapidly. All the survivors could do was retreat, and the retreat quickly became a rout that was only finally reversed when the armies reached the Netherlands (and Alsace) at the beginning of September.

To say that the Allies were surprised by the collapse is an understatement. Montgomery, never one to underestimate his adversary, had envisioned an orderly advance on Paris. He had forecast that Cherbourg would be taken eight days after the landing, and in fact it did not fall to the Allies until twenty-two days after they had landed. All his early projections were equally amiss. After the initial checks there was considerable doubt as to whether his objectives would be met. However, he had forecast that the Allies would be in Paris three months after the day they landed, that is to say, on about September 5, 1944.[37] In actuality by that date the Americans had not only advanced past Paris, but Patton's tankers had crossed the Meuse River and were moving on Metz; to their north, the British and the Canadians were deep into Belgium.

Amazed by the rout, fundamentally misunderstanding the reasons for it, and intoxicated by their sense of impending victory, the Allies hastily began to plan for how to bring about an early end to the war. Like Hitler's schemes, theirs were fatally flawed.

NOTES

1. Eddy Florentin, *The Battle of the Falaise Gap*, trans. Mervyn Savill (New York: Hawthorne Books, 1967), 339.

2. There are two outstanding studies that focus on Normandy. John Keegan's *Six Armies in Normandy* (New York: Viking, 1982) is the best military history Keegan has written. Carlo D'Este's *Decision in Normandy* (New York: Konecky & Konecky, 1983) is likewise a classic of modern military history. Among the many other accounts, the first 188 pages of Russell Weigley's *Eisenhower's Lieutenants* (Bloomington: University of Indiana Press, 1981) is perhaps the classic brief summation, which has the advantage of putting the campaign in the context of the rest of the war. But the list is a long one: The more significant are referred to below in the course of this narrative.

3. Quote from Nigel Hamilton, *Master of the Battlefield: Monty's War Years, 1942–1944* (New York: McGraw-Hill, 1983), 272.

4. It may also be a function of Morgan's lack of command and combat experience (see note 3 above). As we shall see, both of the British commanders involved in the September 1944 Market-Garden were also curiously inexperienced: Gen. Frederick "Boy" Browning, commander of the Allied airborne forces earmarked for the operation, was from the Grenadier Guards and had no substantive combat experience. Maj. Gen. Robert Urquhart, who commanded the British First Airborne Division, had combat experience but not with airborne units—he had never made a drop.

5. As quoted by D'Este, *Decision in Normandy,* 55.

6. Ibid.

7. On June 1, 1915, General Fayolle confided to his notebook, "It is not sufficient to open a breach, it is necessary that the breach be many kilometers wide, otherwise one cannot expand to the right and left. It is necessary to make that breach with one army and have another one ready to pass through it. It is not simple." Taken from [Marshal Marie Émile] Fayolle, *Carnets secrets de la grande guerre*, ed. Henry Contamine (Paris: Plon, 1964), 109.

8. As quoted by D'Este, *Decision in Normandy,* 57. In the second volume of his biography of Montgomery, Hamilton has a much more thorough discussion of this; see *Master of the Battlefield,* 495–507.

9. This is doubtful, hence the word "appear." See the discussion in chapter 8 on North Africa.

10. Wilmot's brief exposition of this can hardly be bettered. See *The Struggle for Europe,* 181–85.

11. The best succinct account of the development of the British special-purpose

armor in David Fletcher's *The Great Tank Scandal* (London: Her Majesty's Stationery Office, 1989), 119–37.

12. See the technical specifications listed in Chamberlain and Ellis: *British and American Tanks of World War II*, 131–32. There is an excellent brief discussion of the amphibious tanks in Ford, *The Sherman Tank*, 78–80. As usual Wilmot has the best precis of the situation: Wilmot, *Struggle for Europe*, 195–96.

13. Wilmot, *Struggle for Europe*, 265. As he notes (note 2) his account is based on an interview with General Hobart, the presiding genius of special armor, done on November 10, 1946.

14. See the trenchant summary in Weigley, *Eisenhower's Lieutenants*, 10. Weigley rightly assigns much of the responsibility for this fundamental misconception to Maj. Gen. Lesley McNair, who emphasized mobility over firepower, because of his belief that "tanks should not fight tanks anyway."

15. This modification is surprisingly misunderstood, with one Sherman authority going so far as to say that the seventeen-pounder was mounted in the turret without any recoil absorption mechanism (Ford, *Sherman*, 34). As I had never seen a Firefly, I asked the curators of the Imperial War Museum, who assured me of what I had deduced from basic physics: The seventeen-pounder (76.2 millimeters) certainly had a recoil mechanism—or else the impact would have blown the turret off. What the British did was to mount the gun sideways, welding on an extension to the turret and rearranging the internal storage of the tank.

16. The notoriety of the German 88-millimeter gun, and the havoc wreaked by those German armored vehicles mounting it has to a certain extent eclipsed the excellence of the later versions of the German 75-millimeter weapon, which had by 1944 become the standard German gun mounted both on tanks and other tracked vehicles such as tank destroyers. The Allied problem was not just that they had no tank to match the German Panthers and Tigers (and their tank destroyer variants), it was that they had no tank which could match the much more numerous German Mark 4F2 or G with its high-velocity 75-millimeter gun.

17. Readers whose most recent knowledge of D day comes from popular films may find this surprising, but it is true nonetheless. And American casualties, although heavy, were substantially less so than in land-based assaults made during the First World War. The largest American military cemetery in France is not at Normandy, but at Montfaucon-sous-Romagne in the Argonne.

18. There is no dispute about this situation, but there is no satisfactory explanation for it either. In the First World War, Great Britain's appalling losses had created a similar situation, and army supporters, notably Charles à Court Repington (the military correspondent for *The Times*) had charged that this was because too many men were being

held back for "essential" jobs. But in the Second World War, Great Britain—whose population had hardly shrunk in the intervening decades—sustained vastly fewer casualties, and yet the army was running out of infantry at an alarming rate. After examining the various reasons being given, what emerges is that in this respect too, the dependence on theory was at fault: in Fuller's view, infantry were hardly necessary. And, unlike the Germans, the British and the Americans were in practice strangely reluctant to create infantry by dragooning service troops—one reason why, as we shall see, that the Allied intelligence estimates of German strengths in the Netherlands were so erroneous. When the German army was in difficulties, it simply shanghaied naval and air force personnel and used them as combat infantry. On an individual, or anecdotal, basis, this resulted in some bizarre examples: On September 9, 1944, for example, the Irish Guards captured an indignant German soldier who was actually a naval diver. But overall the German idea worked. Whatever the British problem was, it is at bottom responsible for the increasing caution of British commanders in 1944. The Irish Guards example taken from Alexander McKee, *The Race for the Rhine Bridges* (New York: Stein & Day, 1971), 121–22.

19. The basic reason for the failure was simple enough: The Germans had positioned an armored division there (the Twenty-first Armored) before the invasion. Allied intelligence knew this, but no one seemed to be overly concerned, probably because they assumed that it would be destroyed in the aerial blitz. Just as the Germans in France wildly underestimated the effects of tactical airpower, the Allies were inclined to err in the opposite direction. D'Este provides the basic information on this unpleasant development: *Decision in Normandy,* 119–25.

20. The many excellent detailed studies of the invasion sometimes obscure the enormity of this achievement as they concentrate on an hour by hour recapitulation of the fighting. See the brief overview in Murray and Millett, *A War to Be Won,* 423.

21. The arguments surrounding the so-called position lines Montgomery set forth on the maps of northern France, indicating the stages of the Allied advance, are probably symptomatic of this: the confusion about what was meant, and what was done, suggests the extent to which the attentions of everyone involved was directed at the landing effort itself.

22. Hans von Luck, *Panzer Commander* (New York: Praeger, 1989), 150. Although in this example the situation involves British armor, this is not to suggest that the Americans were doing any better, or were any less slavish devotees of theory: von Luck simply happens to be the most succinct and precise explanation of the problem.

23. These two quotations are taken from internal German reports identified in Rudolf Steiger, *Armor Tactics in the Second World War: Panzer Army Campaigns of 1939–1941 in German War Diaries,* trans. Martin Fry (Oxford, England: Berg Publishers, 1991), 41. The contrast with Patton's speech to his officers when the Third Army became

operational is interesting: "Forget this goddamned business of worrying about our flanks." As quoted by Florentin, *Battle of the Falaise Gap,* 18.

24. Johan Peter Eckermann, *Goethe's Conversations with Eckermann (1823–1832),* trans. John Oxenford (1850; reprint, San Francisco: North Point Press, 1984), 223.

25. There is considerable controversy on what Montgomery intended. D'Este establishes clearly that his original idea was to seize Caen and move inland. But, as we noted earlier, like any great general, Montgomery had alternative plans in his head—if the initial thrust failed, he would pin down the bulk of the German armor and let the Americans break through. When, as time passed, the American breakthrough did not occur, Montgomery tried a third option—big-scale traditional offensives with massive air support that, he hoped, would break the German line (the July operation known as Goodwood). Lost in the criticism is the point that by the time this operation was launched, the Allies were in a state of near panic over their failure to break out of the containment area. Someone had to do it, the Americans so far had been unable to achieve any penetration, and so Montgomery did the obvious thing. Thus is genius mistaken for inconsistency.

26. Numbers of American casualties, together with the adjective "considerable," taken from Murray and Millett, *A War to Be Won,* 429.

27. That the "breakout" was going backward is increasingly realized. See the comments in Murray and Millett, *A War to Be Won,* 430. A contrasting view is that of D'Este, *Decision in Normandy,* who makes the activation of Patton's Third Army (which occurred when Avranches fell) the climax of a successful campaign (see, especially, 406–7). The problem is that when Patton was finally unleashed, he too went the wrong way, back into Brittany—as he had been ordered. Kershaw's claim—that the "taking of Avranches" led to the "opening not only of the route to the Brittany coastal ports, but also to the exposed German flank towards the east, and to the heart of France" is typical of postwar attempts to fictionalize actual events. In point of fact at Avranches the Americans were much farther from Paris than the British were at Caen. The quote is from Kershaw, *Hitler 1936–1945,* 718.

28. These investigations went far beyond the actual groups of conspirators, to include those who allegedly knew about the various plots or had in some way, however vague, given indications of support. Von Kluge, commander of the German forces in the west until August 15, when Hitler summarily replaced him with Walter Model, shot himself outside Metz on the way back to face what he saw as disgrace and a certain death. Although most of the executions and forced suicides occurred within the first few weeks after the failed plot attempt, the repercussions continued for months. On October 14, Rommel, who had been injured in an Allied strafing attack on July 17, was forced by Hitler to commit suicide, although the evidence against him seems in retrospect—as

Fraser has argued—to range from the insubstantial to the clearly mendacious. Rommel's real "sin" was his open breaking with Hitler in June over Hitler's handling of the defensive operations in France, and it was probably this that led to his forced suicide. See the discussion in Fraser, *Knight's Cross,* 535–52. Although Kershaw's treatment of these matters comes later, he seems unaware of Fraser's analysis of the evidence against men like Rommel, and therefore accepts their "guilt." (For example, Kershaw, *Hitler 1936–1945,* 733).

29. See Guderian's remarks about Soviet armor in *Panzer Leader,* 147.

30. As quoted by Florentin, *Battle of the Falaise Gap,* 28. He concludes by observing that "Von Kluge had the foreboding that this order was the death warrant of the German forces in Normandy."

31. See the excellent large-scale map in Wilmot, which shows how these armored units were deployed (*Struggle for Europe,* 384). Kluge had been promised that one armored division would be sent up from the south, and another, the Panzerlehr, was in reserve (momentarily) south of Domfront.

32. This interchange is recorded by Florentin, who also reports the equally bleak comments of the other senior German officers (*Battle of the Falaise Gap,* 37–38).

33. D'Este has a good discussion of the basic data in *Decision in Normandy,* 498–500.

34. Surprisingly the numbers of divisions engaged were about the same: twenty-two German divisions at Stalingrad and eighteen divisions in Normandy. Over the years the Stalingrad estimates have varied wildly. The best estimate seems to be that the Germans lost about 75,000 soldiers killed and missing, another 100,000 were prisoners of war, and about 25,000 were successfully evacuated. See Manfred Kehrig's *Stalingrad* (Stuttgart: Deutsche Verlag-Anstalt, 1974) for a balanced discussion of the generally inflated figures. Since twenty-two divisions would never have been more than four hundred thousand men, figures showing losses in excess of that are clearly bogus.

35. The German defensive position finally stabilized in Lorraine and Alsace—places the Germans regarded as historically German, not French. Although the French would dispute this claim, what matters is what the German defenders themselves thought—that they were defending German territory, and had abandoned France proper entirely to the enemy—a fact overlooked in the accounts of the collapse.

36. For example, by this date it would appear that most of the Jewish population of Poland had already been murdered, as the killing camps involved had been closed down. See the extensive discussions in Yitzhak Arad, *Belzec, Sobibor, Treblinka: The Operation Reinhard Death Camps* (Bloomington: Indiana University Press, 1987). Although the Germans continued to murder the people they had incarcerated right up until the very end of the war, the point here is that by July 1944 the majority of the killings, which had begun on a grand scale only in the summer of 1941, were completed; in that sense the Germans

were already far along a road with no turning back, which was perhaps not necessarily the case in the summer of 1940.

This must be borne in mind when judging the comments made by the surviving generals, particularly since many of them seemed to be remarkably naïve about what was going on. In 1943 Rommel suggested to Hitler that the best way to counter the growing foreign perceptions about Germany's treatment of the Jews would be to appoint a Jewish *Gauleiter.* In 1943? Although this example is perhaps the most extreme, it does suggest the extent to which the officer corps was out of touch with the realities of Hitler's regime. This incident reported by Manfred Rommel and recorded in Fraser, *Knight's Cross,* 132.

37. There is some controversy about the intent of Montgomery's "phase lines." See the map and analysis in Hamilton, *Master of the Battlefield,* 585. Hamilton's remark that Montgomery's projections were in the main correct seems a bit of a stretch.

10.

The Breakthrough Failures:
Arnhem, Metz, Bastogne

But what started as a military success would end in streams of blood. Today the cemeteries of that region speak loud and clear of what awaited our troops.
—LUDWIG LINDEMANN, TWENTY-SIXTH VOLKSGRENADIERE[1]

When the Allies had considered what they would do after they had made a successful landing in France, the options seem few and sensible. They would advance on a broad front to the Ruhr, thus choosing an area which the Germans would have to defend and could not abandon, as it was the main center of Germany's industrial might. So Berlin, the capital, was not actually an objective, although there was no question that it would eventually be occupied, as would all of Germany. The plan was not precise. Anthony Kemp rightly calls it an "outline," not a plan.[2]

However, it was worse than that. Rather than a plan, we should refer to it as a direction, a preference for a point of entry. Part of this vagueness was a function of the fact that in the spring and early summer of 1944 the Allied high command envisioned the war as proceeding very slowly. Given the slow pace of the advance up the Italian peninsula, this was realistic. So it was assumed that it would not be until late spring of 1945 that the German army would have been driven back into Germany, which would give the Allies plenty of time to work out a new set of objectives.

The struggles in Normandy during June and July if anything hardened this assumption. Consequently, when the German front suddenly dissolved, as it did in August after the failure of Hitler's Avranches offensive, the Allies were caught by surprise. For the retreat, once it began, rapidly became a precipitous withdrawal. Suddenly the Allies were on the very approaches to Germany, eight or nine months ahead of their projected schedule. The time they had thought they would have to plan had vanished.

There was a further complication. Thus far, in their offensives the Allies had used one supreme commander, Eisenhower, who presided over a mix of British and American force commanders. Technically, for Normandy, Montgomery had been in charge of the Twenty-first Army Group, which comprised the British Second Army under Lt. Gen. Miles Dempsey and the U.S. First Army under Bradley. Montgomery was therefore the commander of the Allied ground forces.

But the number of American troops in Europe was growing rapidly. The plan was that when the U.S. Third Army was created, commanded by General Patton, it would become part of the Twelfth Army Group, commanded by Bradley, with Montgomery still technically the overall commander of the ground forces. Despite the problems Montgomery caused Eisenhower, at this point he was clearly the best of the Allied commanders. From a purely military point of view, therefore, he should have remained as overall commander of the ground forces.

Politically this was impossible. Montgomery was a wildly popular figure in Great Britain, but not in the British officer corps. He was disliked generally by the Americans, who felt the American contribution to the war effort was now such that there should be an overall ground commander, and he should be American.

Nor was Eisenhower unreceptive to the idea. The goal of a general— a real general at any rate—is to command an army, not to herd cats, which was essentially what he had been doing as supreme commander. The obvious solution was for him to assume overall command of the ground forces, and on September 1, 1944, this is what happened. So in effect Eisenhower now had two jobs. He was supreme Allied commander and also commander of the Allied ground forces in Europe.

Whether or not this was a good decision, Eisenhower as overall commander had one apparent major defect: He had not been able to develop a grand plan to end the war. By contrast, while he had been herding cats as supreme commander, Bradley, Montgomery, and Patton had all developed their own ideas on how to defeat Germany. Each in fact had the same basic plan: Give him all the resources required, and he would strike through into the heart of Germany.

Montgomery even had a name for his, he called it the "Von Schlieffen Plan in Reverse." Thus the original idea of a steady push all along the front, which had been the original assumption, was replaced by the spectacle of three excellent commanders each pushing his own patent remedy for ending the war.

Each plan was unworkable, and for a simple reason—the same reason that had led Montgomery to expand the original Normandy invasion area. No matter how powerful the Allied force was, it could not develop an attack on a broad enough front to overload the German defensive system; it would simply be overpowered as the Germans moved their resources to meet the offensive thrust. Moreover, as the Germans were forced back closer to Germany, their defenses became denser, their interior lines of communication better, so they could shuttle forces around more easily.

All this was classical military doctrine, understandable by even a general from the last war. It had escaped the three best Allied generals because they were seduced by the prospects beckoning them in the light of the sudden German retreat. It had also escaped them because it was only just at the end of August that the basic Allied planning failure was becoming known.

Quite simply this was the failure to comprehend the enormous appetites of mechanized forces for fuel and supplies. In their attempt to keep the Germans from bringing in reinforcements to Normandy, the Allied air forces had totally wrecked the French railroad system and destroyed most of the bridges. Opening up the nearest ports was a time-consuming process, but the biggest bottleneck was not the port problem, it was the difficulty in getting supplies from the ports to the troops operating at the front.

In a sense the Germans had wrecked the Allied plans by their rapid retreat—more or less the same thing the Russians were alleged to have done in 1941. In both cases the retreats were forced on them, but the result was curiously similar, and the Allied situation was in a way worse, because the German army had never been really mechanized, and Allied armies advancing on Germany were highly motorized. So when each Allied commander called to be given all the resources and turned loose, he was in effect asking that other war efforts be shut down to supply his offensive.

This is a necessary prelude to understanding why Eisenhower continued with the original idea of an advance on a broad front. No matter what each commander thought he could achieve, in reality he was going to be limited by what was available to him in the way of logistical support. So to that end each commander was encouraged to do what he could with his share of the resources available.

It is often said that Eisenhower's decision was motivated mostly by politics, that, for instance, he couldn't divert all the resources to Montgomery because that would have left the Americans unable to operate. But in reality the decision was militarily correct. No one army would be able to win the war on its own, but the combined pressure they would exert would slowly force the Germans back.

By now each senior commander clearly had his eye on posterity and was rewriting the campaigns as they progressed, Bradley no less than Montgomery or Patton—or Eisenhower.[3] This being the case, however, Eisenhower apparently never brought up the most cogent defense of what he was about. In Normandy the Allies had pushed and pushed, until finally Hitler, in a fury, had stripped the German armor bare and thrown it at the Americans in a mad gamble at breakthrough. When that had failed—as his own commanders knew it would—the whole German defensive position in France had collapsed.

Whether he knew this or not, Eisenhower's strategy was—perhaps unintentionally—an extremely shrewd shot into Hitlerian psychology. There was no way Hitler could let himself be pushed backward without attacking. Push hard enough, and he would risk everything on one bold offensive stroke once more. And this time the Germans would have no place to retreat to, they would find themselves on the wrong side of the Rhine in short order. Eisenhower's strategy, then, whether he knew it or not, was precisely the strategy calculated to make Hitler ruin himself. And so it did, but not until Eisenhower's two best senior commanders had demonstrated that they were just as seduced by the idea of breakthrough as their opponent.

The Airborne Carpet: Montgomery and Market-Garden

In their planning for the offensive of May 1940, the German high command had aimed to overwhelm the Netherlands by a dispersed set of air landings that would seize all the key airfields and bridges, thus allowing the ground troops to advance into the country. Such a tactic was a necessity because the Netherlands is crossed by a major system of waterways, rivers, and canals. On September 16, 1944, the position of Montgomery's forces could be roughly defined as running along the Meuse-Escaut (Maas-Schelde) Canal, which formed an arc between Antwerp and the Meuse River with the apex of the curve roughly at the town of Neerpelt.

As we have seen, the German airborne assault on the Netherlands had hardly been an unqualified success. The act that almost immediately brought about the Dutch surrender, the bombing of Rotterdam, happened by mistake; the paratroopers that landed suffered heavy casualties, and the Luftwaffe lost most of its transport fleet.[4] But in the mythology of the war that had already developed, the Germans had used their paratroopers brilliantly, and the Allies had been anxious to follow suit. If anyone had studied the series of accidents and catastrophes that befell the Germans in May 1940, there is no evidence to that effect.[5]

But, leaving aside the matter of casualties, the basic comparison was misleading. The Germans in 1940 were fighting a small, poorly trained, and badly armed force with no combat experience and no way to receive reinforcements. In September 1944 the Allies would be fighting one of the best armies in the world, an army whose weapons were as good or better than anything the Allies possessed, and, above all, an army able to receive reinforcements from its base.

Allied planners got around what in retrospect seems an insurmountable objection by the expedient of claiming that there were only a few small groups of demoralized and poorly trained Germans in the areas along the invasion road, and so the objectives could all be secured before the Germans could react. The best explanation for the optimism was that after the collapse of August 1944, the Allies simply assumed that the Germans were on the verge of quitting the war. On August 25 the Allied intelligence appreciation contained the following: "The end of

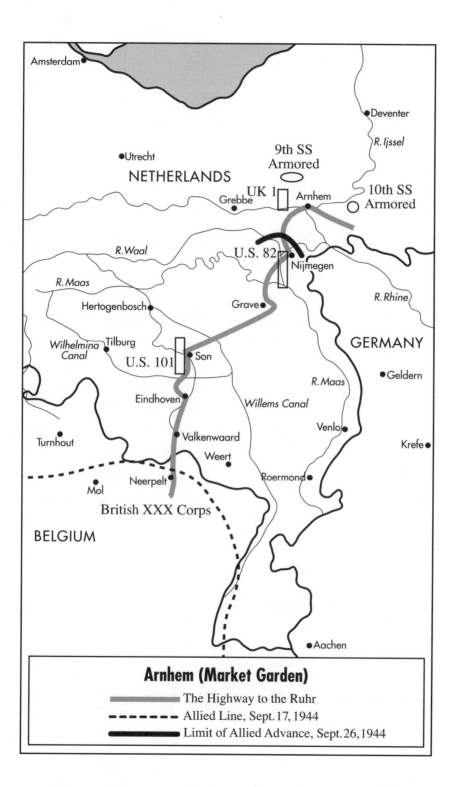

Amsterdam

Deventer

R. Ijssel

Utrecht

9th SS
Armored

NETHERLANDS

UK 1

Grebbe   Arnhem

10th SS
Armored

R. Waal

U.S. 82

Nijmegen

R. Maas

Hertogenbosch

Grave

R. Rhine

GERMANY

*Wilhelmina
Canal*

Tilburg

U.S. 101   Son

Geldern

R. Maas

Eindhoven

Willems Canal

Venlo

Krefe

Turnhout

Valkenwaard

Weert

Mol

Neerpelt

Roermond

British XXX Corps

BELGIUM

Aachen

Arnhem (Market Garden)

The Highway to the Ruhr

- - - - - - Allied Line, Sept. 17, 1944

Limit of Allied Advance, Sept. 26, 1944

the war in Europe [is] within sight, almost within reach. The strength of the German armies in the West has been shattered."[6]

The plan, Market-Garden, was simple enough. From the British position on the Meuse-Escaut Canal to Arnhem is roughly 150 kilometers. Arnhem, with its bridge across the Rhine River, is the gateway to the industrialized area of the Ruhr, which Montgomery felt was the base of the German war effort. The Rhine is a formidable river to cross. As we saw earlier, both French and German planners in the 1920s and 1930s thought of it as being essentially uncrossable in the face of any defensive activity. But if the Allies could drive north through the Netherlands, at Arnhem they would in effect be in a position to outflank the Germans: Seize and hold the Arnhem bridge, and they would be poised to strike into the heart of Germany's war industry.

So Montgomery and his planners envisioned a two-part operation. A three and a half division airborne force of Americans, British, and Poles—more than thirty thousand paratroopers—would land alongside the highway between Son, where the road crossed the Wilhelmina Canal, and Arnhem. This operation was called Market. The paratroopers would seize all the bridges, and hold them until British ground forces, attacking up the highway from Neerpelt, could give them relief. This was Garden, and the execution of it was entrusted to the British XXX Corps, whose spearhead would be the Guards Armored Division. Lt. Gen. Brian Horrocks, the XXX Corps commander, planned to move twenty thousand vehicles along the road in sixty hours.

If there was ever a plan in the Second World War that epitomizes the ideas of the theorists, Market-Garden was that plan. The Allies would use their command of the air to deliver a surprise blow, and then launch a massive armored thrust deep into enemy territory. To revert to the words of General Patton to his Third Army officers in July 1944, there would be no worrying about the flanks, only pushing ahead until the objective was taken.

Montgomery's plan was not a success. In the popular mind, its failure is summed up in the phrase "a bridge too far," but this is a distortion. The objective of the whole operation was to seize the chain of bridges and connecting roadways leading to the prize: the bridge across the Lower Rhine at Arnhem. This was the "last bridge," the bridge that gave the Allies the access to the Ruhr that was the reason for the whole operation.

Market was the largest airborne operation of the war, and, since troops are now increasingly deployed by helicopter rather than by glider and parachute, it will probably remain the largest airborne operation ever mounted. Airborne units were the elite of the war, and any operation involving their deployment attracts a great deal of attention. The failed operations of such units are even more subject to attention, and in this case it would seem there is no shortage of suspects.

There was a general intelligence failure all the way down the chain of command. Reports of two SS armored divisions refitting around Arnhem, the presence of a formidable airborne army holding the line ahead of the Allies, and the reappearance of the survivors of the German Fifteenth Army, who by rights should have been trapped on the coast—all were either missed entirely by everyone or resolutely ignored. The prevailing wisdom was that the Germans had been beaten decisively. Allied intelligence decided that there were no forces near enough to the landing zones to impede the paratroopers from taking and holding the bridges, or to stop the British tankers from advancing up the highway to relieve them.

However, as is well known, by the time the operation was actually scheduled, there was a small but significant flow of contradictory information reaching both American and British intelligence officers. The situation was in fact strangely reminiscent of Normandy, when intelligence had reported the presence of a German armored division around Caen, but the information had simply been discounted.[7]

Although it is customary to see this failure to comprehend the intelligence data as a command failure, what it suggests is a failure that runs far deeper than the simple denial of information that contradicts one's ideas. Neither the British nor the Americans had grasped the institutional toughness of the German army, its ability to reorganize scattered troops and meld them into effective combat forces, and the rapidity of the response of those forces. "Every war has its routes," General Doumenc had observed in May 1940 when the first reports came in to French headquarters of the German crossing at Sedan.[8] What he meant by that remark was that it was the task of any competent commander to react accordingly.

The war was nearing its end, and the Allies had still not grasped a basic lesson about their adversary. The men who failed to understand this were neither incompetent or closed to ideas. On the contrary: Montgomery was the most successful general his country had produced. He loathed incompetence and had angered dozens of British officers by insisting that his army be run only by men he regarded as capable.

The failure in Market-Garden was not a simple failure of intelligence, or the failure of commanders to listen to what their intelligence officers were telling them. It was a failure based on a functional misunderstanding about their adversary, and a fundamental misunderstanding about modern warfare. Given the magnitude of the German collapse in August 1944, no one on the Allied side believed that the routed armies could be put back together again—perhaps not at all, but certainly not in a few weeks. In Montgomery's experience, once he had beaten Rommel in the field and the Germans had started retreating, they had never stopped, had never recovered from their defeat. As no one could dispute the magnitude of the German rout in August, it seemed unthinkable that a coherent defense could be assembled by the middle of September.

There was also the fact that by September 1944 it was simply a given that an operation like Market-Garden would succeed, because it conformed so perfectly to the theories of how battles were won. This mindset goes far to explain why, even under the intense scrutiny given the operation retrospectively, attention is focused almost entirely on the failure of the airborne units to seize and hold the bridges that were their objectives.

It is true that the airborne operations were far from trouble free. At the highest level there was a repeat of the COSSAC problem. It will be remembered that General Morgan, who had been responsible for the development of the Normandy invasion plans, had no substantive experience either in command or in combat. General Browning, in command of the airborne forces, was a Guards officer with little combat experience. Maj. Gen. Roy Urquhart, the British First Airborne Division commander, had combat experience, but he had never made a drop. He was not an airborne officer. This may explain why he let a drop zone twelve kilometers from the Arnhem bridge be forced on him by the Allied air forces.[9]

On the ground it emerged that the British radios were either defective or inoperable, so the airborne units were mostly out of touch with one another. Urquhart, who went trying to find his widely dispersed units, was out of touch with all of his commanders for the first thirty-six hours of the battle. He had not made the chain of command clear to his subordinates (again, a failure that speaks to his lack of airborne experience), so there was confusion about who was to take charge in the event he was missing, and a general lack of coordination as to who was to do what once the troops on the ground began to discover that there was serious opposition.

Although there were operating ferries along the Rhine south of Arnhem, photographs of which had at least been shown during the briefings, British commanders proceeded as though they had no knowledge of these ferries, one of which, at Diel, could easily have been used to reach the German side of the bridge.

All that being said, however, the failure of Market-Garden had surprisingly little to do with the airborne side, although, lamentably, it was the airborne troops, principally the British, who paid the price for the failure. Much is made of the presence around Arnhem of two SS armored divisions. But these divisions were little more than regiments. They had seasoned personnel but next to nothing in the way of equipment.[10] The main armored attack on the Arnhem bridge was carried out by no more than two dozen vehicles, mostly lightly armored scout cars, half-tracks, and even trucks, not by tanks (this was hardly surprising, Capt. Paul Gräbner, the commander of the attack, was in charge of the Ninth SS Armored Division reconnaissance battalion). The British paratroopers easily defeated this attack, and Gräbner was killed.[11] A couple of dozen half-tracks and armored cars is not much of a showing for an armored division, but the truth was that neither unit had much in the way of equipment to deploy within the first twenty-four hours, when German doctrine stressed that it was imperative to stop an airborne assault.

And set against all these problems must be recorded the very real successes of the paratroopers. Despite the distant landing site, British paratroopers did seize the south side of the Arnhem bridge. It is far from clear that the course of the battle would have been changed had the British airborne troops gotten to the bridge earlier. Their problem was not getting to the bridge (which is not to belittle their heroic struggles in accomplishing this) but how to hold it in the face of a determined ground attack.

Behind them, the Americans did seize most of the bridges. The plan had foreseen the destruction of many of these intermediate bridges, and British engineers were able to reconstruct the main ones that had been destroyed. The appalling losses sustained by the British First Airborne (there were more than 7,500 casualties out of a drop force of 10,000 men) was caused not by the fact that the British had bad intelligence or landed in the wrong place but by the fact that they were forced to hold on to their positions without relief. So too for the much lower losses of the two American airborne divisions: Most of these men were killed or wounded trying to make up for the failure of the ground operations. The failure of Market-Garden was not an airborne failure, it was the failure of the ground forces.

The reason why is simple enough. On September 16, 1944, the Allied line ran along the Meuse-Escaut (Maas-Schelde) canal. From Neerpelt, in Belgium, the highway runs due north, and then northeast, going to Arnhem. The Allied plan called for the mechanized forces of the British XXX Corps to run up this highway to Arnhem and get there in basically two days, as it was reckoned that the airborne units could not hold out longer than that.

The crucial section of this highway was from Neerpelt to Eindhoven, because this was the only stretch with no bridges. So the British plan was to break through the German defensive line and be in Eindhoven in a matter of hours, as the Dutch town was roughly twenty kilometers from the British line. Above Eindhoven the bridge issue comes into play. But above Eindhoven there is more than one road for the armor to deploy on.

The problem, basically, was that the highway from Neerpelt to Eindhoven is not simply the main road, it is the only road. In fact it is the only passable route going north for many kilometers in either direction, because the ground on either side of the highway was (and still is) mostly a sandy marshland forest, cut by numerous steep ditches and small canals. In places the road was bordered by an actual earthen embankment about two meters high, with soft spongy ground—and trees—beginning on the other side.

Just at the point where the ground begins to clear up, about twelve kilometers from Eindhoven, there is a town, Valkenswaard. Then as now it was a dense cluster of brick town houses, with the main highway going right through the center. Although many European towns that cluster around the main road have alternative roads around them, Valkenswaard does not simply sit astride the highway to Eindhoven, it blocks it entirely. The only way the British tanks were going to get to Eindhoven was through this town. In 1944 most buildings faced right on the highway itself (the church still does).

So here was the British plan: to run tanks down a straight, eight-kilometer two-lane highway running through a forest, a highway with no parallel side roads, a highway that emerges abruptly into a compacted urban area. The soil on either side was too spongy to support armored vehicles, and particularly the narrow-tracked Sherman tanks. But it was not too soft for antitank guns, and the forest gave them, and their crews, perfect air cover. An attack up this highway was an attack straight into a trap, a series of ambushes, in which the advancing vehicles and infantry would receive direct fire from three sides.

Clearly, the only chance an attack like this had was surprise. Overwhelming force was no factor, because the effective breadth of the armored attack was essentially the width of the highway. The British knew this, because on September 15, two scout vehicles from the Household Cavalry had made a dash to Valkenswaard and then back (somewhat incredibly, one would think), and their commander, Lt. A. R. J. Buchanan, had reported the road to be heavily defended.[12]

However, the ground-attack plan called for an intensive bombardment of the area, followed by the use of ground-attack aircraft called in on a case by case basis to deal with enemy strongpoints. This both alerted the defenders and forced the attacking armor to wait until the air corridors from Great Britain to the Continent had been cleared of transports so their ground-attack aircraft could arrive.

But this merely exacerbated the whole timing problem. The first wave of the airborne assault would not land until the early afternoon. So the planners had decided that the ground assault could not begin until the airborne troops were landing safely. That meant that the bombardment phase of the ground attack did not begin until 2:15 in the afternoon. But by September 17 we are approaching the equinox: The hours of day and night are almost equal, so the British had given themselves only three hours or so of daylight to get to Eindhoven.

The disaster that followed can easily be imagined. The tanks started down the highway, the German gunners (unscathed by the bombardment) waited until the column of armor was strung out, and then opened fire, disabling twelve tanks in as many minutes, and stopping the advance cold. So the British infantry had to dismount and fight their way through the forest, clearing the way for the armored advance.

No one can fault the courage and competence of the infantry and armor: By nightfall they had broken through the German defensive positions and were in Valkenswaard. They then stopped for the night. The advance to Eindhoven did not begin until 9 A.M. the next day.[13]

Although failure in combat is never the function of one single factor, the events of the first twenty-four hours, both in planning and execution, put the ground attack almost a day behind the schedule required if the airborne troops were to be relieved. When to this delay was added the type of delay that could reasonably be expected in an operation like Garden, overall failure followed quickly enough.

During the June and July fighting, the British had consistently been critical of what they saw as the failure of the Americans to break out as evidence of the superior British mastery of battlefield tactics.[14] American gossip invariably went back to what was perceived as the inability of the British to respond quickly enough to the fluidity of the battlefield. Whether the failure of the British ground forces in the Netherlands was a function of this or not, the armored thrust toward Arnhem is the epitome of the failure of the breakthrough idea, including of course the usual caveat—that the tanks were not deployed properly, as the front was too narrow.

But this objection illustrates the whole fallacy: The tactics and the technology have to be adapted to the terrain. Since the eighteenth century, soldiers have not generally had the luxury of picking the area on which they would do battle, instead they had had to do battle wherever was needed. Clearly no armored commander wants to fight in an urban area, in a forest, in a swamp—or in the hedgerows of Normandy. Unfortunately his opponents, who know this, would love to force him to fight there. So his tactics must be adapted accordingly.

Inevitably there will never be a complete agreement about the causes of the failure. What is beyond dispute is how costly a failure the operation was. Allied casualties for Market-Garden were substantially higher than on D day: 17,200 as opposed to some 10,000-odd casualties in the first twenty-four hours of the amphibious assault. Very roughly the Allies lost about the same percentage of their airborne force as the Germans had in 1940. Sadly both operations caused a high number of civilian casualties: The postwar death toll for the Rotterdam bombing in 1940 came to about nine hundred, known civilian casualties in 1944 were about five hundred, but it is widely believed in the Netherlands that the real total was two or three times that.[15] After the war Prince Bernhard of the Netherlands remarked to the war correspondent Cornelius Ryan that his country could "never again afford the luxury of another Montgomery success," a wry and bitter quip that cuts right to the heart of the matter.[16]

Montgomery, never one to back down, insisted until his dying day that the plan was a sound one, and that it failed only because he hadn't been given enough support. Presumably what he had in mind in saying this was that the Allies were unable to land the entire airborne force on the first day, owing to a shortage of transport planes and also gliders.

But this idea is based on the assumption that the German reaction to the plan was immediate—that it failed because the paratroopers were unable to get to their objectives soon enough and in enough strength. In reality, however, the operation caught the German command completely off guard, and their reaction time was surprisingly slow. The real slaughter of the airborne troops, and especially of the British division, began only when the Germans finally began to react. And had the armored thrust been close to its schedule, these counterattacks would have failed. The idea that more lightly armed paratroopers would have enabled the airborne units to fight off German armor simply does not stand up. But then when Montgomery made his complaint, he had his mind fixed on the airborne part of the operation, which had been the problem with Market-Garden from its inception: It didn't make any difference how many tanks XXX Corps had, they could still only run them up that narrow highway no more than two abreast.

Metz: The Patton Myth

At one point in *A Bridge Too Far* Cornelius Ryan has German general Günther Blumentritt worrying about how to stop Patton's Third Army drive to the Saar, where the Germans had some of their best troops: "These forces might delay Patton, but they were not strong enough to stop him," and Blumentritt then posits a whole series of great Allied advances into Germany stemming from the drive into the Saar.[17] As one reads any account of Montgomery's failed offensive, one is always conscious of the thundering armor of Patton's Third Army in the background, and it sometimes seems that by this point the war was simply a contest of egos.

But if General Blumentritt thought Patton was advancing to the Saar he was sadly out of touch with what was happening. Although almost universally ignored in accounts of the fall of 1944, Patton's Third Army, which had reached the Meuse River by the end of August, remained stalled around Metz until the end of November. The corps diary records that on August 31, 1944, "the Fourth Armored Division advanced to the high ground east of the Meuse river in the vicinity of Saint-Mihiel, where General Patton had fought and almost bled to death from machine-gun wounds in the First World War."[18] Eighty-three days later, the diary records that "of this date [November 22, 1944] all resistance at Metz ceased. The city called the Bastion of the East was captured by assault by General Patton's Third Army . . . after a two months' siege."[19]

This is an excellent example of an official report putting the best possible face on one of the worst failures of the war. The basic German garrison in Metz, Fortress Division 462, consisted of troops deemed unsuitable for any other task. It was reinforced by such diverse units as the 1010th Security Regiment, an officer candidate regiment, and men in NCO training. As the fighting developed, this motley crew was reinforced by actual combat units, but these were all greatly understrength. There was no comparison with the hastily formed German units in the Netherlands that Montgomery's men faced. Whatever its publicists claimed, Third Army was facing the dregs of the German military.

The reason for the stall was simple. Between 1871 and 1914 the Germans had surrounded the high ground to the west and south of the city of Metz with a ring of powerful fortifications, making it in some measure the German equivalent of Verdun. So although the Americans had forced the Germans back against Metz in September 1918, they had not mounted any further offensives in Lorraine. After 1918 the French had modified some of the forts, but they were already formidable positions. Moreover, the east bank of the Moselle was substantially higher than the west bank. In effect the Americans would be attacking steadily uphill, against an enemy whose vantage points would make it extremely difficult for any sort of surprise attack to develop. The forts were powerful—and difficult to attack—and the terrain to the south of the city, and all along the Moselle River, was ideally suited for defensive warfare. Indeed one section of the Moselle below Pont-à-Mousson is known (locally) as the "Switzerland of Lorraine."

Patton had of course been an officer in that war, he had fought at Saint-Mihiel, and he was by all accounts one of the most well read of any American officer of his generation. If there was anyone who should have been familiar with the difficulties of assaulting the area around Metz, both by experience and education, it was Patton. But since the day Third Army had been activated, Patton had been straining at the leash. He was convinced that he could bring the war to a rapid conclusion by striking up into Germany through Lorraine, and the rapid advance of

Third Army during August apparently convinced him—as it did many journalists at the time—that he alone possessed the key to the new armored warfare.

At one level the debate (or disagreement) between Patton and Montgomery mirrored a similar division in the Allied commanders in the summer of 1918. The British were convinced that the only way to win the war was to attack Germany through Belgium. Pétain and Pershing were of the opinion that the attack should be through Lorraine. In the event, the war ended with the Allied armies still in French (and Belgian) territory, so the point was moot. But the same division had now reared its head, and, as we have seen, Eisenhower, like Foch, the supreme Allied commander in the First World War, opted for the same decision that Foch had ordered: Attack everywhere on a broad front.

So Patton's strategic analysis of the invasion route into Germany was certainly valid.[20] His ideas foundered, however, for two reasons. First, the great dash across France that had established him as the tanker par excellence had been accomplished without any real opposition. As we have seen, once Hitler's offensive failed, the Germans simply turned and bolted. They retreated through France faster than the Allies could advance behind them. The swiftness of Patton's advance was a function of lack of opposition more than any military virtue he or his men possessed.[21]

The other problem was that the Third Army was not equipped to attack Metz. It lacked the heavy artillery, the engineers, and, above all, enough trained infantry. Patton, like most of his colleagues, believed that tactical air support would compensate for such deficiencies. But as we have already seen, this was not really true. The German defenders along the Neerpelt-Valkenswaard highway were largely unscathed, and even with close tactical air support the British infantry still had to clear the wooded areas on each side of the road—and the infantry took casualties in the process. At Normandy there had been similar problems. There were also major successes, but it should have been clear that the simple fact of tactical air, like the fact of air supremacy, did not mean that the infantry could simply occupy the ground or that armor could drive through it.

Part of the mythology of airpower was that fortifications were worthless in the face of high explosives dropped from above. In 1940 the Germans had discovered that this was simply not true. They had subjected the easternmost position of the Maginot Line, Schoenenbourg, to intensive aerial bombardment with the heaviest bombs they possessed. The resultant damage can still be seen—an irregular pattern of craters in the earth, the rusting steel turrets of the fort rising up among them like so many mushrooms.[22] Other than relocating an enormous amount of earth, the bombing had no effect whatsoever on the position.

The Metz forts were older, and their surface area above ground was more extensive. Consequently they were easier to hit from the air. But this made little difference. These seventy-year-old structures had been built at the beginning of the great age of high explosives. They were largely impervious to bombs. The German defenders would have to be flushed out of each position by Patton's infantry, which by September 1944 was in short supply.

To make matters worse, the ground between the Moselle and the Meuse Rivers, the area out of which Patton's troops would have to attack, alternates between forested hills and swamps. There is little flat terrain. Given a rainy autumn, the Woëvre Plain, as the area is called, was historically regarded as impracticable for military operations by the French.[23] In September 1914 the Germans, in a surprise attack, had captured the entire area. The French, in trying to regain it, had suffered one of the worst defeats of the war. This terrain was one reason why it had been argued in 1918 that operations coming out of Lorraine into Germany were not feasible.[24]

Like Montgomery with the Netherlands, Patton apparently believed that the German defenders around Metz were so demoralized and broken that he could be across the river and around the fortified belt before they could react—or receive reinforcements. Once again this proved to be an illusion.

Following the failure of two weeks of assaults of Patton's XX Corps to break the German defensive positions, on September 25 the Americans tried to reduce one of the main forts, Jeanne d'Arc, with heavy artillery. But Patton did not have any truly heavy guns. For this barrage the heaviest weapons available were 240-millimeter howitzers, and the 25 rounds fired at the fort did no serious damage; likewise with the 107 rounds from 155-millimeter guns fired on Fort Kellerman. "The only result was chipped concrete. Metz was rapidly becoming a frustration to both Twentieth Corps and Third Army Headquarters," is how the official diary puts it.[25]

Slowly the Americans fought their way across the Moselle and began an advance to the east, pushing the line out around the city of Nancy. But this advance was more or less the same sort of advance that Bradley had made in Normandy: It was going in the wrong direction. Just east of Nancy are the Vosges Mountains, a formidable obstacle in and of themselves. The main route through the mountains and on to the French side of the Rhine River valley runs through the city of Strasbourg, which, like Metz, the Germans had girdled with forts. An advance to the Vosges might look impressive, but, like Bradley's right turn to the Channel, it was of no real military value. There was no possibility of any breakthrough across the mountains.

The only practicable route into Germany, the only approach with any military value, was to the north, and the fortifications at Metz had been designed by German engineers after 1871 specifically to block such an advance. Until the area was cleared, Patton's drive would be bogged down.

Alarmingly, as time passed, the Germans were able to reinforce their positions, just as they had done in the Netherlands. So although Third Army was a powerful combat force, with each passing week, it encountered stronger German units, and thus the stalemate of late September and October. Slowly the American situation improved. Despite Patton's repeated complaints about supplies, Third Army was a potent combat force, and by late October, American bombing had wreaked enough havoc on the German transportation system to the immediate rear of the line that the Americans had quantitative and qualitative superiority.

There was never any doubt that eventually the Germans would be surrounded, reduced to individual pockets, and either destroyed or forced to surrender. And they were, although, incredibly, isolated detachments in the forts were still holding out weeks after Patton proclaimed the "fall" of Metz.[26] A vastly outnumbered German force consisting of the debris of a dozen divisions of dubious quality, fighting out of fortifications built half a century before, had held up one of the U.S. Army's most distinguished armored commanders for nearly three months. It was a sobering commentary on the effectiveness of fortifications and the weakness both of armor and airpower.

Hitler's Final Offensive in the West

If the Second World War was a drama of the sort that often seems to appeal to military historians, it would have ended in the afternoon of

December 8, 1944, when the last defenders of the Metz forts were flushed out by exhausted American infantry throwing phosphorus grenades. Dramatically it was a perfect end to a war in which by all accounts fortifications had been rendered totally obsolete by armor and airpower, and the only test of a general's competency was whether or not he knew how to deploy armor correctly—that is to say, in enormous massed thrusts.

The actual war itself would drag on into May 1945. But the war of ideas we have been describing came to a double conclusion at the end of 1944. On December 8, around Metz, and then, a second time, at the Belgian town of Bastogne, on December 27, 1944, when the advancing American forces relieved the besieged airborne troops and ended forever the chance of a German breakthrough to Antwerp.

Hitler had been planning this operation since September 16, 1944. Apparently undeterred by the failure of his Avranches offensive, he now planned for an even more ambitious one: a great armored thrust developing out of the German Eifel that would strike through the Belgian Ardennes, split the Allied armies in two, and capture the vital port of Antwerp. It would also, Hitler believed, destroy the will of the Americans to fight—as well as present them with the prospect of a much longer and more arduous struggle. This prospect, he apparently believed, would lead to a negotiated settlement with Great Britain and the United States, enabling him to fight the Soviet Union.

At the grand strategic level Hitler's belief was mistaken.[27] The Allies had planned for a long and arduous struggle, so they could hardly be expected to quit now. But tactically, if one believed that wars were won by grand thrusts of massed armor, Hitler's idea was imaginative, and the few generals to whom he revealed his ideas had mixed reactions. Whether they liked it or not, however, the idea was now firmly fixed in Hitler's mind. Planning began, and by October 21 preparations were well under way. Overall commander of the operation, which Hitler named Wacht am Rhein, would be Rundstedt. For the offensive a new army would be formed, the Sixth, commanded by Sepp Dietrich, who had started his career with Hitler as the man in charge of his bodyguard, but who had established himself as a first-rate combat officer.[28]

The attack was scheduled for November 1, when, Hitler believed, the weather would preclude the Allies' using their most formidable weapon, tactical airpower. Moreover, in the heavily forested regions chosen both

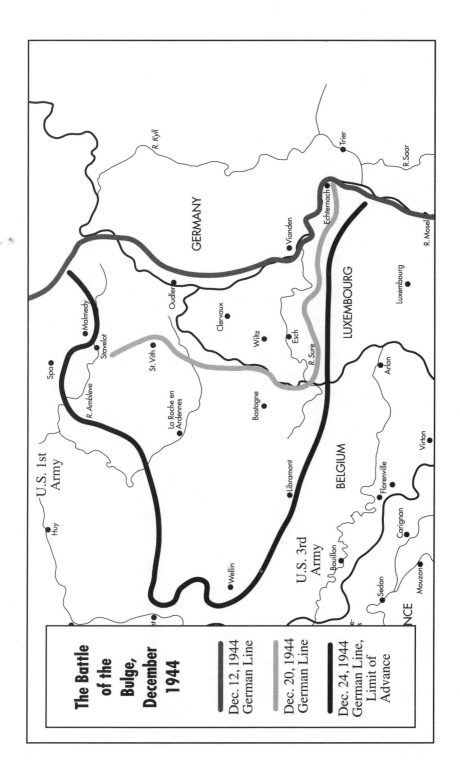

The Battle
of the
Bulge, December
1944

━━━ Dec. 12, 1944
German Line

━━━ Dec. 20, 1944
German Line

━━━ Dec. 24, 1944
German Line,
Limit of
Advance

GERMANY

LUXEMBOURG

BELGIUM

U.S. 1st
Army

U.S. 3rd
Army

FRANCE

R. Kyll

R. Saar

Trier

Echternach

Vianden

R. Mosel

Luxembourg

Oudler

Clervaux

Wiltz

Esch

R. Sure

Arlon

Malmedy

Stavelot

St. Vith

La Roche en
Ardennes

Bastogne

Spa

R. Amblève

Huy

Librament

Wellin

Bouillon

Florenville

Carignan

Virton

Sedan

Mouzon

for assembly and attack, mechanized columns could easily be concealed. November came and went, with the Germans still trying to contain the Red Army and build up enough of a force to make Hitler's offensive a reality. Initially the plan had called for a force of thirty divisions, eighteen of them armored. This was an impossible aim: By the time December arrived, the forces earmarked for the offensive had dwindled from thirty divisions to twenty divisions and an armored brigade. Basic logistics problems continued to impede the deployment of the divisions needed: Two of the armored divisions reached their positions only hours before the assault, two more arrived too late to be of any use (and were diverted in to the Alsace), and several others went into action without all their component units.

The force was less than half the size originally envisioned, and it was particularly weak in infantry. In this Hitler's plan was Normandy in reverse. There, an operation using far too few resources had been expanded into a massive amphibious assault, the size of the force used more than doubling. Here the reverse took place: The massive thirty-division thrust was basically cut in half—but the objectives remained the same. Cognizant of this, alternatives were put forth by Hitler's restive senior commanders, all of them scaled-down versions of Wacht am Rhein. But Hitler had fixed on this plan as his masterstroke, which would turn the situation in the west decisively in his favor.

The area chosen was a fifty-kilometer stretch of the now stabilized front in Belgium, essentially running from a little to the north of Saint-Vith to a point south of Bastogne. Hitler now made precisely the same error that the Allies had made earlier. He assumed that the American divisions in line (from south to north, the 28th, 106th, and 99th infantry, with the Fourteenth cavalry between Malmédy and Saint-Vith) were so weak, so understrength, and stretched so thinly along the line that his powerful armored thrust would break right through them and be across the Meuse River before the Allies could react.

This assumption—like the Allied assumption that the road from Neerpelt to Arnhem was basically unguarded and that Arnhem was undefended—was a most necessary one if the operation were to have any hope of succeeding. The problem was that in order to break through into the rolling open ground northwest of Bastogne, the Germans had to cross a series of small rivers. The first of these, the Ours, forms the boundary between Germany and Luxembourg. Immediately behind it, in the direction of Belgium, however, was a second river, the Clervé

(Clerf), and overlooking the river crossings from the north was a strategically important outcropping, the *Schnee Eifel*.

If Manteuffel's Fifth Panzer Army was to break through north of Bastogne, shielding Dietrich's Sixth Army as it thrust toward the Meuse
between Liège and Namur, his tankers were going to have to cross both
rivers, take the *Schnee Eifel*, and cross over an irregular ridge that lay just
east of Clervaux. The Germans had done this before, of course, in May
1940. But in December 1944 there was a new and troubling problem.
The tanks that formed the core of the two panzer armies no longer
consisted of vehicles like the Mark 2 or 3, whose combat weight was less
than twenty metric tons, but Panthers and Tigers, weighing in at anywhere from forty to seventy metric tons. Even the relatively light Mark
4 series G tank weighed twenty-five tons, and the assault guns and tank
destroyers were all big, heavy vehicles.

In his planning Hitler had brushed these difficulties aside. So too
with the American defenders, whom he believed would be swept aside
within a few hours. He believed his tanks, particularly the new Tiger 2
vehicles, were unstoppable. In his mind, apparently he felt that only the
Allied mastery of the air (together with the treachery or lethargy of his
commanders) had doomed his Normandy offensive. The weather would
fatally cripple any airpower, and he was by now confident that his generals would do as he wished.

In addition to modifying the Mark 4 tanks, the Germans eventually came up with
entirely new designs. The Panther tank, which went into service in 1944, embodied
all the latest developments in design—a sloped armor, wide-track vehicle with a
high-velocity 75-millimeter gun capable of destroying any Allied or Soviet vehicle.
But the tanks were too big, and too few were produced. (*John Mosier*)

In other words Hitler envisioned a plan that was almost pure Fuller. There was no terrain unsuitable for tanks: hence armored thrusts were unstoppable, and could strike far behind the enemy's defenses, destroying his ability to wage war. Clearly this was a fantasy, but no more so than the idea that thousands of armored vehicles could speed along a narrow two-lane highway and reach Arnhem, or that tactical airpower could destroy the massive concrete fortifications of Metz. Like Patton and Montgomery in September 1944, Hitler planned his operation with a sort of indifference to the terrain and with a sublime contempt for his adversaries.

In the popular accounting the offensive failed for a number of reasons. Most Americans believe that it was the heroic resistance of the airborne units at Bastogne that stalled the advance. The British apparently believe that it was only the prompt intervention of Montgomery that saved the day when the Americans broke and ran. Airpower enthusiasts attribute Hitler's failure to the shifting weather, which allowed the Allies to make use of their tactical airforces. More sober analysts believe the plan was fatally flawed from the start and had no chance whatsoever of any real success.[29]

There is some truth in this last position, since Hitler simply overlooked the obvious difficulties of both the terrain and an effective defense. However, to say that the plan was doomed from the start is to fall into the same trap that we have seen before: The fact that one side has a marked advantage in men and equipment, or that the battle will be fought over unsuitable terrain, does not automatically mean it will fail. Wacht am Rhein was no more of a gamble than many earlier operations.

In retrospect, however, Hitler's obliviousness to the terrain was probably the decisive factor. Getting the new monster tanks across even relatively narrow streams was no easy engineering feat, and when the offensive was launched, at 5:30 A.M. on December 15, the task proved much more difficult than had been envisioned. As with Market-Garden, these initial delays would prove fatal.

So too with the unexpectedly stiff nature of American resistance. Wacht am Rhein, like Market-Garden, went wrong almost from the beginning, when the American 110th Infantry Regiment mounted roadblocks along the main road out of Clervaux. The German problem, then, was that although there were plenty of places where they could break through, none of these places happened to be roads suitable for the passage of heavy vehicles. Moreover, although it was winter, much of the ground was still soft, so that when tanks went off the road, they would simply break through the earth and have to be towed out.

What Hitler had therefore envisioned as a great armored thrust promptly degenerated into a series of infantry assaults and combats between mixed units of armor and infantry. As with Market-Garden, Hitler's plan was predicated on breaking through the defenses in the first twenty-four hours, so the armor could speed toward the Meuse unimpeded. But on the seventeenth the Germans were still engaged in desperate assaults on the American positions. Although, as in any battle, there were isolated instances of panic, overall the Americans were putting up a stiff resistance and slowly retreating.[30]

To emphasize the fact that they were retreating is to miss the point. The German offensive couldn't possibly succeed if the best it could do was to slowly beat the Americans back across eastern Belgium. Although the Allied command, like the Germans earlier at Arnhem, was initially slow to react, after the first twenty-four hours had elapsed, every day that passed saw more Allied forces moving into position, either to block a possible German breakthrough or to attack the struggling German forces. The fact that there was still heavy fighting on the seventeenth and the eighteenth (and on successive days afterward) meant the German assault had failed. As the British had discovered at Arnhem, three or four days can be an eternity.

Wacht am Rhein was the final chapter in a series of armored failures. The underlying thread that binds them together was the mistaken notion that armor could operate without regard to ground conditions. The first tanks had been envisioned as true cross-country vehicles, designed to cross the shell-cratered terrain between the trench lines, break through the barbed wire, and cross the trenches. Basically they were too underpowered to be able to perform this function with much success, and the Germans in particular were right to place a premium on speed and mobility in their own tank designs.

But as the tank became bigger and heavier, it lost whatever true cross-country capabilities it might have possessed. If the ground was firm enough, if the obstacles were small enough, a tank could operate without benefit of roads. But in northern Europe, those were substantial qualifiers. As we have seen, in almost every place the armies fought, some aspect of the terrain made it unsuitable for the deployment of armor. Nonetheless both the Allies and the Germans persisted in the contrary notion, and with dismal results.

On the other side Hitler's last offensive revealed a shrewd understanding of the limits of airpower. His idea was that his armor could,
through superior speed and mobility, break through to its objective
without being destroyed by tactical airpower, because in December the
weather was simply too bad for it to be a dependable weapon. Of course
once the armored thrusts stalled out because of delays and determined
American opposition, there was enough clear weather for there to be
some tactical air support.

However, some of Dietrich's Sixth Army's tanks had thrust all the
way into Celles, about 10 kilometers from the Meuse at Dinant, and
were still largely intact, a point which perhaps neutralizes criticisms of
the Allied airpower failures of May 1940. After the fact, the Allied failure
to destroy the German armored columns advancing through Belgium in
May 1940 is seen as a grave error, the idea being that the British and
French should have challenged the German control of Belgian airspace
more vigorously, with an eye to destroying the German armor before it
could move into action. But was this actually possible? How much of a
difference did command of the air actually make? In December 1944,
the Allies had almost complete mastery of the air over Belgium, but
German armor was still able to sweep across the eastern part of the
country unscathed. Even with air supremacy the Allies simply were not
reliably able to destroy armored divisions on the move.

This of course has to be qualified. It had taken the German Second
Armored Division more than a week to travel roughly one hundred
kilometers from its start line, despite meeting light resistance. The
armored divisions on either side had essentially been stalled out by the
Americans, and were out of fuel. All it could do was dig in and wait for
the inevitable American envelopment. Its end came not through air
strikes, but through ground attacks.

Wacht am Rhein also established, together with Market-Garden,
some real limits on tactical surprise. In September the Germans had
been astonished—and caught off guard—by the airborne blitz. Although
it is usual to say that their surprise was a function of personality (the
German commanders thought that Montgomery, a cautious commander, would do no such thing) at bottom this is to turn a professional
judgment into a personal one. In 1940 airborne assaults had a chance:
They were new, and those attacked were overwhelmed by the novelty of
the attack. Moreover the high proportion of automatic weapons German airborne soldiers carried gave them a decisive advantage in encoun-

ters against infantry armed with bolt-action rifles. But by 1944 the novelty element had vanished, and airborne troops now had no advantage of
any sort in armaments.

Market-Garden was a surprise, but only because the Germans had
difficulty believing any competent commander would sacrifice almost all
of his airborne troops so recklessly and for so little. The same thing could
be said about Hitler's offensives. The Allies were surprised because it
never occurred to them that the Germans, who excelled at defensive
operations, would throw away their advantage and squander all their
reserves on some grand offensive scheme. Whatever temporary successes
were achieved were vastly overbalanced by the cost.

Long after the war was over, the defenders of Patton and Montgomery have continued to argue that their general could have won the
war if only Eisenhower had let him. But as we have seen, any objective
accounting of these failed campaigns makes clear that neither general
possessed the necessary ideas to win the war outright. The marooned
German Second Armored Division around Celles at Christmas 1944 is
eloquent testimony to what happens when operations are planned in
accordance with the best theories but without regard for military realities. Had it not been for Eisenhower's prudent refusal to support the
grandiose breakthrough operations proposed by his commanders—a
prudence usually described as vacillation and indecision—those stalled
German tanks could easily have been British or American. The heroic
last stand of the British First Airborne Division at Arnhem could well
have been replayed over and over again on the Allied side.

If history conformed neatly to our ideas of the dramatic, the Battle of
the Bulge would be a perfect end, and in a book devoted to tracing
failed ideas, the subsequent reputation of that battle as a close-fought
engagement, as an example of something that Hitler almost managed to
accomplish, is singularly appropriate. The Bulge owes its importance to
the fact that it was an offensive launched in accordance with the theory
of how armor should be used. Consequently it had to be taken seriously,
and so it has been.

But Hitler's failure was not his final failure. Nor was it the end of the
war. Although clearly in one sense his Ardennes offensive had destroyed
the last reserves of his army, he persisted in directing still more breakthrough operations. In a desperate attempt to salvage Wacht am Rhein,

he decided on a new offensive, directed toward Strasbourg, which, he hoped, would halt the American counterattacks. There were two prongs to this attack. One, to the north of Strasbourg, aimed at breaking through the Saverne Pass and thus into Lorraine. The other, personally directed by Heinrich Himmler, aimed to break out at the other end of the Vosges mountain chain, around Colmar.

At the same time there would be a massive aerial assault by what was left of the German air force, which would neutralize the Allied mastery of the air over Belgium. This would be synchronized with renewed attacks around Bastogne, which had now been relieved by American ground troops. For the Alsace attack Hitler had scraped together eight divisions. But there too the offensive was simply unable to penetrate American forces. Nor were the Germans able to make any progress around Bastogne, although the fighting there in early January was actually worse than in December.

Moreover, in his attempts to overwhelm the Americans in Belgium and Alsace, Hitler had shifted his resources too far south, so when Montgomery launched his response to Wacht am Rhein on January 3, 1945, the Germans had no choice but to abandon the Bastogne operations and withdraw in order to keep Montgomery from trapping them in his drive to the south.

Nor was that the end. It was true that by January 16, 1945, Hitler was prepared to order troops back to the Eastern Front, but instead of using them as a strategic reserve to block the advance of the Red Army, Hitler decided to throw the debris of Dietrich's Sixth Army into an offensive aimed at securing Hungary against the Soviet advance. Guderian, whom Hitler had belatedly brought back as chief of the General Staff, protested bitterly. He argued, probably correctly, that their correct use was to try to attack into the flanks of the advancing Soviet forces moving out of Poland and East Prussia, thus slowing their advance.[31] But Hitler would have none of this, and so whatever was left of Germany's powerful armored force was dispatched to Hungary. The Germans fought their way to Budapest (thus dooming the city to virtual destruction along the lines of Stalingrad), but to no real purpose. By now (the spring of 1945) Hitler had no more forces to throw into great offensives; German defensive efforts had degenerated into a series of local operations in which each commander concentrated on defending whatever stretch of ground he and his men controlled.

The Final Assault

Whether because of luck, ignorance, or sound military advice, after 1941 Stalin never subscribed to the idea of one great armored breakthrough. Whatever his ideas had once been, Finland had apparently cured him of modern theories about armor. The Red Army fought the Germans in pretty much the same way the Czarist armies had fought them in the First World War—that is to say, all along the front. In fact most Soviet offensives were simply recapitulations of General Brusilov's famous assault in the summer of 1916, the only difference being that increasingly the Red Army was much better equipped than Brusilov's forces had been, thanks to lavish support from the West.[32]

Brusilov's idea had been an attack all along a great swath of the front, so that the defenders would simply be overwhelmed and pushed back. In 1916 this idea had worked extremely well. In fact in terms of territory gained and enemy losses, it was the only real Allied victory of the war. Gradually the Red Army evolved in the same direction, and by January 1945 it was attacking all along the entire Eastern Front, from Kurland (now part of Latvia) in the north to Lake Balaton (in Hungary) in the south, with subsidiary offensive operations in Yugoslavia as well.

By February 1945 Eisenhower was of the opinion that all that was required in the west was one last broad-front push across the Rhine, and Germany would collapse. Predictably this was still problematic for most of his commanders, and particularly for the British. Gen. Sir Alan Brooke, the chief of the Imperial General Staff, objected that the Allies simply didn't have the force necessary to mount such an operation, and that all resources should be thrown behind a thrust into the Ruhr. Militarily this was clinging to failed ideas with a vengeance. Politically the British were astute: They were concerned that the Red Army would overrun northern Germany (as far as Schleswig and, quite possibly, Denmark) while the Allies were trying to fight their way across Baden and the Palatinate.[33]

British concerns about Stalin's intentions were probably well founded: Regardless of what Stalin said—or what he was perceived to agree to in high-level meetings with Roosevelt and Churchill—the pattern was clear enough: The territory the Red Army seized it had no intention of giving up, and once in place, the Red Army became the stalking horse allowing communist sympathizers, exiles, and party mem-

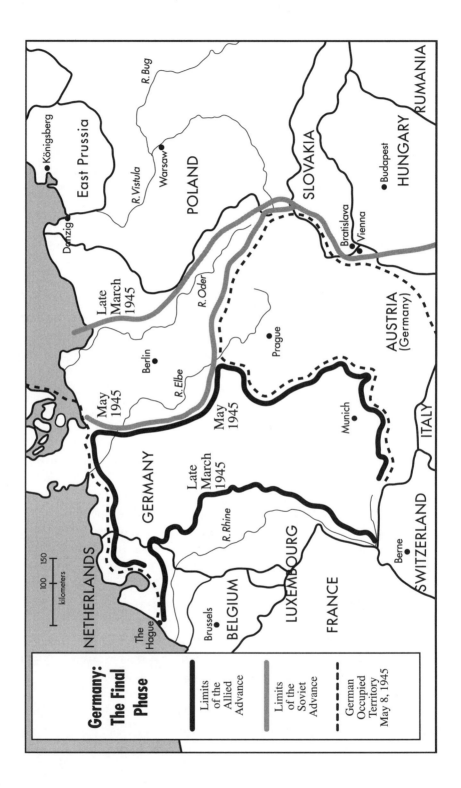

Germany: The Final Phase

Limits of the Allied Advance

Limits of the Soviet Advance

German Occupied Territory May 8, 1945

NETHERLANDS

The Hague

Brussels
BELGIUM

LUXEMBOURG

FRANCE

Berne
SWITZERLAND

ITALY

GERMANY

Late March 1945

R. Rhine

May 1945

Munich

AUSTRIA (Germany)

Late March 1945

May 1945

Berlin

R. Elbe

Prague

R. Oder

POLAND

Warsaw

R. Vistula

R. Bug

East Prussia

Königsberg

Danzig

SLOVAKIA

Bratislava
Vienna

Budapest
HUNGARY

RUMANIA

100 150
kilometers

bers to establish a new government that would ensure that the country was subservient to Stalin's aims.[34]

But there were many more valuable objectives—politically speaking—than the Ruhr and Schleswig-Holstein: Berlin, for example. On this point Brooke was curiously mute. But then his position in the alliance was steadily eroding. By now the British component of the Allied forces in the west was hardly greater than that of the French: By February 1945, there were four American, one British, one Canadian, and one French army operating, and this considerably overstates the matter: The British and Canadian forces were all in the Netherlands, while the four American armies had the entire front stretching through Belgium, Germany, Luxembourg, and France.

Eisenhower's preference was for a series of phased attacks to develop, going from north to south. Thus Montgomery and the British (supported by the American Ninth Army) would have the first chance to mount their offensive. If they were successful they would cross the Rhine and, if they moved quickly enough, occupy the northern German plain before the Red Army got there. Once this attack began, the other American forces would attack as well, hopefully driving deep into Germany.

Despite the widespread feeling that Montgomery was far too slow and cautious a general, in actual fact, his careful planning paid off here as it had in North Africa. The British simply overwhelmed the German defenses and pushed rapidly on to the north. Once Montgomery's offensive began, it was followed in rapid succession by attacks directed by Bradley (into the Palatinate) and Patton (into Bavaria).

The extent to which the operations of March and April 1945 were true victories has been to a great extent obscured by the claim—which has a good deal of merit—that the Germans were surrendering in the west and fighting hard in the east. However, this is to overlook the obvious point that one reason the German soldier felt this way was that he was now facing an adversary whose superiority was overwhelming—one moreover to whom it was safe to surrender.

The Allies were successful, in other words, not because they mastered some new method of warfare or because of superior tactics or equipment. Germany fell because the Allies invaded the country on all sides with such overwhelming force that its armies were beaten in the field. They then forced those armies to surrender unconditionally, occupied the capital, and incarcerated the surviving leaders. These were concepts employed by Ulysses S. Grant in the American Civil War. Indeed, the final assaults on Germany could have been conducted by Scipio Africanus: The Romans of the Second and Third Punic Wars understood these principles well enough. The only real lesson to be derived from the Second World War is that advances in technology do not really change the basic principles of warfare.

NOTES

1. As quoted by Michael Tolhurst, *Battle of the Bulge: Bastogne* (Barnsley, South Yorkshire, England: Leo Cooper, 2001), 46. Although Lindemann is speaking of the fate of the German soldiers who attacked in December 1944, his comments are equally applicable to the American, British, Dutch, and Polish soldiers who fought at Arnhem and Metz.

2. Anthony Kemp, *The Unknown Battle: Metz, 1944* (New York: Stein & Day, 1981), 5.

3. Thus Bradley spoke of a great advance that would overrun "the fortifications of Metz and the Maginot Line," even though at the time those sentences were allegedly expressed, he had no real idea that Metz was fortified. See the discussion in Kemp, *Unknown Battle*, 6–7 (quotation is on 6).

4. See the discussion in chapter 7. To the reader who feels that the bombing was deliberate and not a mistake, it should be pointed out that this hardly vitiates the main argument: The Dutch quit not because the airborne assault had succeeded but because the German air force had destroyed one of their cities.

5. This is the case even with Cornelius Ryan, who apparently believed that the total German airborne casualties in May 1940 came to 130 men. See *A Bridge Too Far* (New York: Simon & Schuster, 1974), 38. In reality about one out of every three soldiers in the Twenty-second Air Landing Division, which was only one of the German units deployed, was a casualty during operations around The Hague. "The landing operations around The Hague must be regarded as a failure," was how the divisional history put it. Data taken from McKee, *The Race for the Rhine Bridges*, 65.

6. As quoted by Kemp, *Unknown Battle*, 6.

7. The movie *A Bridge Too Far*, based on Ryan's book, makes this point rather eloquently but misses saying why the reports were discounted. For Ryan's own take on the situation see *Bridge*, 131–32.

8. As quoted by Beaufré (who was there and heard him say it), in *The Fall of France*, 182.

9. In the view of the American airborne commanders, this was suicide. When Gen. James Gavin, commander of the Eighty-second Airborne, found out where the British planned to land, his reaction was "My God, he can't mean it." Gen. Stanislaw Sos-

abowski, commander of the Polish Airborne Brigade, told Browning that the mission was suicidal (both reactions recorded by Ryan, *A Bridge Too Far*, 141–42). These were the only senior airborne commanders with any experience of actual combat insertions into enemy territory. Another problem is that the various components of the British First Airborne division had never fought together as a unit. Moreover the British troops would be carried (mostly) into combat by American transports. In Sicily this had been more or less a disaster, but then it would seem that airborne operations are really not the place to try to mesh different services from different countries: One great advantage the Germans had in May 1940 was that everyone involved in the operation was in the same branch of the service.

10. Robert Kershaw, *It Never Snows in September: The German View of Market-Garden and the Battle of Arnhem, September, 1944* (New York: Sarpedon, 2001), 42–53, has the definitive accounting of the sad state of these divisions.

11. The attack was subsequently made famous for being one of the highlights of the film *A Bridge Too Far*. The movie, however, does not make clear that one key factor in the defeat of the attack was the artillery that had been landed by glider. Kershaw has a lengthy discussion of Gräbner and his attack—which apparently mystified his fellow German officers (*It Never Snows in September*, 87–97).

12. McKee, *Race for the Rhine Bridges*, 126.

13. The reason supposedly was the fog; operations were supposed to begin at dawn, i.e., about 6 A.M. Half a century after the fact, it is difficult to understand why (*a*) the existence of ground fog in September in northern Europe would have been a surprise, and why (*b*) it would have been an impediment to British soldiers in particular. But then it is a characteristic of these affairs that the apologists feel that the fact of giving a reason is sufficient to ensure immunity to the operation being excused. While there is a reason for fog delay, it is, like the reason not to begin the bombardment until the afternoon, entirely insufficient in the face of what was supposed to be a lightning thrust of armor through the Netherlands. When the German armored division attacked on December 15, their jump-off hour was 5:30 in the morning—well before dawn. Apparently only the British were concerned about darkness and fog.

14. Russell F. Weigley, *Eisenhower's Lieutenants* (Bloomington: University of Indiana Press, 1981), 120–21, for example.

15. Ryan quotes estimates as high as ten thousand. I have heard the figure of eighteen hundred over the years, offered with no evidence, but the persistence of figures in the low thousands is significant—it certainly makes clear that the loss of civilian life was about the same in both engagements.

16. Montgomery insisted that the idea was sound, and that had it been "properly backed from its inception" it would have been successful. "I remain Market-Garden's unrepentant advocate," he wrote in *Montgomery of Alamein* (London: Corgi, 1974), 267.

When I turned to the final page of Ryan's book, I was surprised and delighted to find that he had included this quote, along with Prince Bernhard's (*A Bridge Too Far*, 597).

17. Ryan, *A Bridge Too Far*, 53. As a war correspondent, Ryan covered Patton's press conferences. See p. 72 where he recounts being present and hearing Patton's famous "if Ike stops holding Monty's hand and gives me the supplies, I'll go through the Siegfried line like s★★★ through a goose."

18. Charles M. Province, *Patton's Third Army: A Daily Combat Diary* (New York: Hippocrene, 1992), 33. As the bibliographical material makes clear, this is simply a printed version of the actual war diary.

19. Ibid., 96. Like many of the entries in this official document, this one is extremely misleading. The last Germans manning the forts did not in fact surrender until December 8, 1944 (see the *Diary* entry for that date), and Patton had to keep an entire regimental combat team on duty there in siege operations.

20. Basically it has been discounted for the same reason it was discounted in 1918—that the terrain made it impracticable. But in both wars there was no easy way to cross the Rhine, which suggests that the Lorraine option was a realistic one. The same unfortunately cannot be said for Bradley's preference, which forced his infantry to come solidly up against the prewar German fortification belt (known to the Germans as the *Westwall*) as well as some of the French fortifications from the Maginot Line (notably at Bitche). As in Brittany, Bradley's staff simply had no conception of the ground over which they were planning to fight. See, for example, among the many photographs of the terrain now on file in the National Archives, SC111 (WWII), Box 52, picture 197774; Box 61A, pictures 203387, 202879, and 202955.

21. McKee, one of the relatively few analysts to point this problem out, argues that where Patton's genius lay was in finding the weak spot through which to send his armor (*Race for the Rhine Bridges,* 123). Perhaps, but in the chaos of the German retreat, it was hardly difficult to divine such weak spots. All that was needed was a decent road map.

22. The superficial damage can still be seen today, as the forward positions are accessible (by foot) from the highway. There is an extensive discussion of the bombardments of Schoenenbourg by its commanding officer, René Rodolphe, in *Combats dans la Ligne Maginot*, rev. ed. (Lausanne: Association Saint Maurice, 1981).

23. In Province, *Diary,* 96, Third Army complained that the flooding had been "the worst in twenty years," and that bad weather had precluded much of the tactical air. Patton, like the other commanders, excelled at making excuses, but these suggest that a reevaluation of his constant complaints regarding lack of fuel and supplies is in order.

24. The news that Nancy, fifty kilometers to the south of Metz, was liberated on September 15, 1944, obscured the basic geographic realities of Lorraine: The only practicable route into Germany was north of Metz, and the Allies weren't even able to recapture Strasbourg until November 23—after the reduction of the Metz fortifications.

25. Province, *Diary*, 54. In 1918 the French had proposed using really heavy guns to bombard the Metz forts. Such weapons, mounted on railway cars, might well have done serious damage, as most fortifications of this vintage could only withstand shells up to 450 millimeters. But in 1944 the Allies put their faith in airpower. Even when the weather permitted, the air strikes against the forts were not successful. Ironically the German defenders possessed some truly heavy weapons: On October 24 three rounds from their 280-millimeter guns narrowly missed Patton's headquarters (ibid., 74). Although tactical air managed to destroy these weapons, that they were firing (in late October!) suggests the seriousness of the American problem.

26. See the accounting in Kemp, *Unknown Battle*, 225. The last Germans surrendered on December 8, 1944.

27. This does not mean, however, that the idea was totally wrongheaded, or that Hitler had retreated into some fantasy land, as Dupuy, Bongard, and Anderson come perilously close to saying in *Hitler's Last Gamble*, 12–13. Hitler was no more mistaken in his belief that he could end the war on his terms through this offensive than Montgomery had been about Market-Garden, or Patton or Bradley in their claims for their projects.

28. Interestingly enough, for this important operation Hitler was entrusting the execution to men he knew to be critical of him—von Rundstedt and Dietrich. Dietrich in particular was outspoken. The stories may be apocryphal, but they are no less memorable for that. Dietrich, on hearing that there had been an assassination attempt on Hitler on July 20, 1944: "Who was it, the army or the SS?" Exasperated by the way his Waffen SS division was being slowly annihilated on the Russian front, Dietrich and his officers allegedly put their Hitler regalia into a bucket, urinated in it, and sent it to his headquarters (this division was the original SS bodyguard unit for Hitler). Whether this is true or not, it reveals a bizarre and little-noted aspect of Hitler: his tolerance for dissent at certain levels. Now, at what he regarded as the key moment in the war, he turned to men who were skeptics, not toadies.

29. As noted above (note 27) this last is the basic position established in Dupuy, Bongard, and Anderson, *Hitler's Last Gamble*. Earlier analysts had the tendency to see the failure as rooted entirely in Hitler. See, for example, Wilmot's comments in *The Struggle for Europe*, 609: "The frustration of the drive to the Meuse cannot be blamed entirely on Hitler and his strategic miscalculations." The most curious "legend" of Bastogne is that current in Great Britain, where it is popularly believed that American troops simply broke and ran in the face of the German attack. Several British correspondents who wrote me complaining bitterly about my account of the British army in *The Myth of the Great War* (New York: HarperCollins, 2001) concluded their missives by saying that it was the height of impertinence for an American to be critical of the British Army. What about Kasserine? What about Bastogne? Apparently these incensed gentlemen had never heard of the Battle of New Orleans. Kasserine did not surprise me, but Bastogne certainly did.

30. The idea that there was a massive panic is another one of those myths. In *The Struggle for Europe*, Wilmot disposes of the idea deftly: "It is undoubtedly true that there were cases of panic and that some service units, anxious to save their equipment, took to the roads in default of orders. Many others, however, organized their areas for defense and stayed to fight" (588).

31. Guderian's account of this is to be found in *Panzer Leader*, 392–93. Its accuracy has never to my knowledge been challenged; for example, see Ian Kershaw, *Hitler 1936–1945* (New York: W. W. Norton, 2000), 757.

32. The classic account of the war in the east in 1914–1917 is Norman Stone, *The Eastern Front 1914–1917* (New York: Charles Scribner's Sons, 1975); for a briefer account of the Brusilov offensive, see my *The Myth of the Great War* (New York: Harper-Collins, 2001), 248–52. The amount of military aid shipped to Stalin is both staggering and generally unappreciated—not least by Stalin's disciples and supporters in the West. But the British alone shipped 5,218 tanks, 4,343 wheeled vehicles, 2,560 tracked carriers, and 7,411 airplanes. To these enormous totals must be added equipment shipped by the United States: 7,537 tanks, 51,503 jeeps, 375,883 trucks, and 14,795 aircraft—and this is to omit such "incidentals" as 1,981 locomotives and one battleship. The idea that the Soviet Union fought and won its war against Germany entirely (or mostly) on its own is one of the more fantastic myths of the war—made all the more so by the extent to which it is widely believed. For the lists of equipment, see Joan Beaumont, *Comrades in Arms: British Aid to Russia 1941–1945* (London: Davis-Poynter, 1980), 204–8. Typically the crucial data—only a small part of which is listed above—are buried in the middle of an ideologically motivated attack on British postwar critics of the policy of aiding the USSR.

33. See the sympathetic treatment by Wilmot, whose account can hardly be bettered, despite its age (*Struggle for Europe,* 665–66). Well and good, one might say, but if Brooke was so politically sophisticated, once it was realized that Eisenhower was serious about a broad-front advance, he should have devoted his efforts to persuading him of the necessity for taking Prague, Dresden, and Berlin rather than letting the Red Army occupy those cities.

34. Thus the Romanians, who had thought that by breaking with Hitler and becoming an ally of the West (in August 1944) they would preserve their autonomy, discovered that the Soviet Union regarded them the same way it did Hungary and Bulgaria. The Red Army simply did as it pleased, and it was many years before the last Soviet troops left. See the extensive analysis in Constantin Hlihor and Ioan Scurtu, *The Red Army in Romania* (Portland, Oreg.: Center for Romanian Studies, 2000). So in this sense Brooke was quite right to be concerned about Soviet intentions, quite right to distrust their promises, and quite wrong to do nothing about it.

11.

Conclusion: The Persistence of Failed Ideas

It was their ignorance about how the Germans had fought World War I that prevented the majority of French, British, Dutch, and Belgian leaders from adequately preparing for the German attack.
—BRUCE I. GUDMUNDSSON[1]

I t is often opined that truth is the first casualty of war. On the contrary it would be more accurate to say that truth is the first casualty of the theories of war. History is formed by a complex sequence of events. It is not easy at the time to perceive what patterns have emerged, or are emerging. The vision of hindsight is invariably perfect.

Two conclusions seem clear enough, however. The theorists who spun out fantasies of future wars won or lost in the air, and massive armored breakthroughs on the ground, were wrong. Even the most cursory examination of what had happened in the First World War would have shown their errors. That tanks and planes played a major part in the Second World War is indisputable; the error lies in assigning to these two instruments of war, together with the ideas about their employment, the chief or primary responsibility for the course of the combat. Tanks and planes, armor and airpower, were implements, not ends.

Airpower was a major factor in all the campaigns we examined, an observation which seems to confirm the views of the airpower enthusiasts. Aviation was a major factor, but not the strategic bombing campaign postulated by Giulio Douhet and, more or less independently, by his fellow preachers in America and Great Britain. Where airpower was decisive was when it was used tactically, that is, in support of objectives set for the ground forces, and that is what the Germans pioneered in 1939 and 1940.

But even there the claim must be carefully qualified. Tactical airpower failed the Allies in 1940 because they based their ideas on an assumption about the accuracy and effectiveness of level bombing which everyone knew was untenable: It was next to impossible for an airplane flying a level path over a bridge to hit it with bombs. This failure to consider the actual evidence obtained in tests was compounded by a belief in one of Douhet's more ludicrous maxims—that ground-to-air defenses could not stop bombers.

At the same time, although tactical airpower was clearly of extreme importance in the Allied victories over Germany in the summer of 1944, the Germans were remarkably successful in adapting to the loss of air supremacy over the battlefields of France. Even with an Allied air superiority that was well near total over the French air space, the war went on for many months.

Part of this was because the two Allied air forces were determined to conduct the war according to the theories they had developed, and poured their resources into strategic bombing campaigns. But as the postwar data collected out of Germany makes quite clear, these campaigns were of only marginal value until the fall of 1944, at which point many other factors must be considered, not least the complete erosion of Germany's occupied territories and the loss of much of its key industry and resources. It is hardly a coincidence that the marked decline in German production occurred at a point when the mineral resources of France, the Romanian oil fields, and the heavy industries of Bohemia were all either lost or about to be evacuated.

Whatever the modest results of strategic bombing are, they are more than offset by the appalling loss of civilian life that resulted from the inherent inaccuracies of such campaigns. The loss of civilian life during wartime is unavoidable, and the history of warfare demonstrates that

long before there were airplanes. Cities were sacked and their populations slaughtered in the Thirty Years' War—and long before. The idea of
destroying your enemy by devastating his towns and slaughtering his
people was hardly new: By their own accounting the Romans deliberately razed Carthage and sold the surviving inhabitants into slavery. But
the Romans, unlike the Allies, were successful. Nor did they pretend—or
believe—that the damage inflicted on the civilian population was accidental, an unfortunate by-product of a military campaign.[2]

While the bomber barons went on their way, impervious to the
empirical results, and wasting the lives of thousands of airmen to no real
end, the armored apostles busied themselves in a frantic rewriting of the
history of warfare so that everything conformed to their own ideas.
Notably the two great "breakouts" of the war—the Germans at Sedan in
1940 and the Americans at Saint-Lô in 1944—were charges off in the
wrong direction. In both cases the ultimate outcome was victory, and
this has led theorists to assume that it was the armored thrust, the breakthrough, that was responsible.

But as we have seen, in neither case was this true. The German penetration of the Meuse succeeded not because of its intrinsic strength in
armor, but because the BEF then precipitously and unilaterally withdrew
from the field of battle, leaving the Allied front with an enormous gap in
the center, a gap that, by their own witnessing, was filled by Germans
riding in trucks or on bicycles, and by ordinary infantry advancing on
foot, not by hordes of tanks.

The famed Allied breakout in August 1944 succeeded because Hitler
stripped the already overtaxed German defenses bare to mount his own
counterthrust—which, not incidentally, was a complete failure. So was
his Ardennes offensive, even though it certainly conformed to the ideas
of the theorists. But then in reality all the great armored thrusts were
failures, from the attack of the German armored divisions at Gembloux
in Belgium to the great German tank attack at Kursk, which is usually
considered as the greatest tank battle ever fought.[3] In other words the
concept was made to work not only by twisting the facts of the few successes, but by ignoring the many failures, appropriating the numerous
successes won by traditional means, and denying the evidence at hand.

So the armored theorists were no less foolish than the airpower
enthusiasts. The difference is that their concepts did no real damage.
Indeed, insofar as Hitler came to believe in them himself, and believed
his armor could smash through the Allied lines in August and December

1944, thus prolonging the war indefinitely, they may actually be said to have brought the war to a more rapid conclusion.

Militarily it is customary to explain the German successes of 1939–41 by invoking the idea of a new and previously untried form of warfare, which in this book has been termed *breakthrough*. The idea passed on by most historians of the war is that the Allies were initially unprepared for this new form of warfare, but as time went on, they were able to master it and thus defeat the Germans.

But no analyst is content to leave it at that. After an aborted initial attempt to blame the Belgians, the responsibility for the Allied defeats of 1940 is usually laid squarely at the feet of the French, who, it is alleged, were completely unprepared to fight a war and completely unequipped to fight a modern one. As we have seen, however, this is hardly the case. Nor does there seem to be any real evidence to support the idea that the war involved dramatically new concepts or equipment. Tanks and planes had been used in the First World War. Of course by the end of the Second World War new and revolutionary weapons were in use. Leaving aside the atomic bomb, the war concluded with the use of jet aircraft, intercontinental ballistic missiles, and ground- and air-launched rockets, and high-velocity weapons (and explosives) that used new and little understood principles (shaped charges and tapered guns, for example).

But that should not blind us to the fact that in September 1939 the war began with both sides relying almost entirely on equipment conceptually familiar to the soldiers of the past war. Indeed, in more than a few cases it was literally the same equipment. Nor, as we have seen, was it used in some particularly novel way.

The German use of airborne troops was new, but the novelty must be carefully qualified: the use of paratroopers had been foreseen before May 1940. *Life* magazine had run photo essays on actual massive airdrops as early as 1937. That they would be used in a future conflict was hardly a surprise, and in any event is essentially the sole exception to a war that began with the use of equipment and tactics developed decades earlier.

It is perhaps this realization—that the war did not commence with the use of the new and untried—that has led many of these same analysts into intangibles such as the claim that France was defeated quickly in 1940 because of some great moral weakness. From 1940 on this has proven to be an idea popular with British historians, and also with the Gaullists, who had their own reasons for promoting the idea of a corrupt and morally enfeebled country. But France in 1940 was no more badly governed or corrupt than it had been in 1914. And as the death lists make clear, its soldiers were no less courageous.

Nonetheless it is hardly surprising that France lost a war with Germany. From 1900 on the French leaders, whether military or civilian, virtuous or corrupt, had all subscribed to a simple truth: There was no way that France alone could beat Germany. An alliance with one—and preferably two—major military powers was necessary. To that end the leaders of the Third Republic had laid aside their distaste for the czars and entered into a military alliance with Russia. But in the 1930s, as we have seen, there was no serious possibility of such an alliance being revived. France therefore had to place even more emphasis on its alliance with Great Britain and, somewhat unwillingly, a dependence on a reasonably competent and well-armed neutral, Belgium. Regardless of the necessity of the situation, when the British began to evacuate their expeditionary force, thus trapping the Belgian army along the coast, France was lost.

Conversely there was no way that Hitler's Germany could beat Great Britain, the Soviet Union, and the United States. This had been as true in 1914 as it was in 1941. So the interesting question is simply this: Why did the war go on so long? By the middle of 1941 whatever German superiority there had once been in armor no longer held true. Both the British and the Russians had better tanks, and more of them. There would be exceptions. In Italy and France the Germans consistently outgunned their opponents. But the superiority was hardly overwhelming, and the situation was highly fluid. Moreover, to a great extent, any superiority in weaponry the Germans had was more than offset by the Allied control of the air.

Although the Germans enjoyed air superiority in the east for most of the war, they lost it almost immediately in North Africa and from then on the German forces in the west never regained command of the air. As far as command of the air went, the situation of the German army after the summer of 1941 was pretty much the same as that of the Polish army in 1939.

Why, then, did the German army hold out for so long? Or, to put it another way, if its superiority did not lie in better weapons and new tactics, why was it so successful? Certainly it had nothing to do with any quantitative superiority. Except for 1939 the Germans hardly ever had the advantage of numbers, and even in Poland the two sides were surprisingly even in terms of simple manpower. Rommel's situation in

North Africa was more the norm than the exception, a fact that makes the German army's ability to fight on and on all the more amazing.

The German army did more than fight on; it was consistently successful on the field of battle, regardless of the specifics of the engagement. This superiority is not subjective. The American researcher Trevor N. Dupuy quantified it as long ago as 1977, discovering that, on the average, 100 German soldiers were the equivalent of 120 American, British, or French soldiers.[4] Although there were engagements in which Allied soldiers were as effective as their adversaries, Dupuy found that the 1.2:1 ratio was generally true throughout the war, while on the Eastern Front (which he computed separately), the ratio of combat effectiveness was much higher: 100 German soldiers were as effective as 200 Soviet soldiers.

There are two basic reasons why this was the case. Germany possessed a much larger cadre of experienced officers and noncommissioned officers than did its opponents, and its methods of training were much more efficient. Both of these crucial superiorities go back to the decade before the First World War. They were swept aside by analysts eager to rewrite the history of that war, and consequently have been largely unremarked, but they are no less true.

In the years before 1914 both Germany and France planned to field enormous armies if a war broke out. Although France had a smaller pool of eligible males, it conscripted almost all of them, while the Germans were much less thorough. As a result both countries had peacetime armies of about the same size, around nine hundred thousand men. Once the war began the standing army would be rapidly expanded into a much larger force: Both sides intended to put roughly two million men in the field.

This equivalence of numbers has generally blinded historians to an important difference between the two countries—the number of officers and noncommissioned officers in each army. In 1913 the German army had 42,000 officers and 112,000 noncoms, while the French army had 29,000 officers and 48,000 noncoms.[5] In other words there were almost precisely two German officers for every French officer. But this dramatic imbalance actually underestimates the difference. On mobilization both the French and the German officer corps expanded as their armies doubled in size. But Germany had over twice as many reserve officers available as did France: In August 1914, by its own accounting, the mobilized French army was short more than eight hundred lieutenants.[6] The French problem, then is quite clear: an incredible shortfall of trained officers when the war began. The situation for Great Britain was even worse: In 1900 the country had only a budgeted strength of 10,800 officers and 254,100 men—a woefully insufficient base from which to create an army of millions.[7]

To understand how this German advantage had an impact on the next war, we must turn to a different set of numbers—the casualty figures for the combatants. There too the data reveals a striking German advantage. Over the course of the war the German army lost many fewer men than its opponents. This was as true for officers as for ordinary soldiers. In fact, it appears that the ratio of dead officers to dead soldiers in the German army was lower than in the French and British armies.[8]

So, since the Germans entered the war with a leadership cadre twice as large as the French cadre, and since over the course of the war that cadre suffered fewer losses than did the French, at the end of the war the German army had a much larger leadership cadre with battlefield experience than did any of its potential opponents. The commanders of 1939–45—Patton, Montgomery, Rommel (to name only the most famous) were all men who had been commanders in 1914–18, so the implication of these figures is simple enough: The German army simply had more officers with combat experience than anyone else did.

This advantage was reinforced by one of the more curious features of the Treaty of Versailles. The victorious Allies imposed a limit on the size of the postwar German army. It was restricted to one hundred thousand men. This gave the Germans an enormous advantage. The German high command simply purged its ranks, keeping the Guderians and the Rommels and demobilizing their less capable colleagues. Gen. Hans von Seeckt, the architect of the new army, thus created a leadership cadre with skills out of all proportion to the numbers of men actually in uniform.

By contrast the French and the British appear in retrospect to have gone out of their way to retain the less capable and encourage the more talented to leave. So the Germans, who had a larger leadership cadre when the war had begun in 1914—and had lost less of that cadre in combat—acted systematically to distill their leadership advantage in the 1920s. The French in 1940 reckoned that their soldiers were better trained than German soldiers, and they were probably right.[9] The German army of 1940 was not nearly as good as the army of 1914—and most German officers were vocal in drawing attention to the decline. But its leadership cadres were better, and in 1940 this advantage was multiplied by the experience of combat in September 1939.

There is another phenomenon, even less discussed, contributing to Germany's combat effectiveness. Hans von Seeckt was undoubtedly a brilliant peacetime leader. But he was an unabashed aristocrat who preferred officers with aristocratic backgrounds. The size and social attractiveness of the old German army's officer corps had to a surprising extent made it more egalitarian or democratic than is usually perceived. Under Seeckt, however, the officer corps became enormously more aristocratic.[10]

But Hitler's ascent to power provided an alternative route for men uncomfortable with von Seeckt's aristocratic and traditionalist social ideals. The formation and expansion of the two explicitly National Socialist branches of the military, the Luftwaffe and the SS, enabled Germany to make use of the services of men who for one reason or the other did not find the traditional German army congenial.

The truly horrifying thing about the Waffen SS is not just its record of brutality and war crimes—those were an integral part of Hitler's regime—but its military competence. Unfortunately for the Allies, SS generals like Sepp Dietrich and Wilhelm Bittrich were not isolated examples. We would like to believe that men in uniform who are guilty of war crimes are bad soldiers, and not simply wicked ones. But the Germans in the Second World War shattered this idealistic myth as well as many others.

Simple numbers, however, do not reveal the whole picture. Before 1914 British observers had estimated that the Germans could train soldiers more effectively than either the British or the French, and during the war, the top French commanders gloomily confirmed those estimates. Thus General (later Marshal) Fayolle confided to his secret diary in 1916 that German infantry was better than his own because French officers were "mediocre" and "ignorant."[11] In early 1918, reflecting on his experiences as one of France's leading generals, Fayolle summed up the situation in his usual succinct manner: "The great superiority of the German Army lies in its instructional methods and in its organization."[12]

So the main reason for the toughness and success in combat of the German Army in the Second World War was the same as in the First World War, when it had been noted by one of the German army's best opponents. Unfortunately Fayolle's conclusions were buried in the avalanche of falsehoods systematically propagated by British propagandists. Even before the war there had been an English prejudice to the effect that the Germans were simply automatons, incapable of independent action, and that their officers were feudal relics unsuitable for modern warfare.[13] Once the war began this idea quickly became an unchallenged—and unchallengeable—assumption, as it has been ever since. But the idea is purely and simply mythical.

One practical consequence of a better-trained and -educated army is decentralization, and this in turn is a direct cause of faster reactions on the battlefield. Better trained and led soldiers are able to quickly turn from defense to offense, from retreat to attack. Instead of waiting for orders from on high, local commanders are able to respond immediately to the changing battlefield situations, improvising their responses in the field.

As our account of the various campaigns has made clear, the Germans were consistently able to do precisely those things. The dramatic reorganization of the German army after its precipitous withdrawal in August 1944 is perhaps the best example, but again and again the Germans proved themselves able to disengage from combat, stage an orderly retreat, and then begin the fight anew.

The German army was, as we have noted, the least mechanized of the major armies. But it was the most mobile; not because of its vehicles but because of its brains. The Allies do not appear to have understood this at any point during the war. The Americans routinely criticized the British for what they saw as inordinate delays to refit and regroup. As our account of Market-Garden makes clear, there is some truth to this criticism. On the other hand there is a good deal of truth to the British criticism of the American tendency to rush headlong into battle without engaging in the sort of careful preparation that would minimize casualties: Bradley at Omaha Beach, Patton at Metz. The reality, however, is that neither army really grasped how quickly the Germans could put together offensives, how quickly they could reorganize a shattered position, and how effectively they could use the terrain over which they were forced to fight.

During the Second World War, German commanders frequently lamented the fact that their soldiers were not as well trained as those of 1914–18, and Dupuy observes that by late 1944, German soldiers were not nearly so well trained as they had been in the earlier years:

The average German soldier in the Ardennes campaign was not as well trained as the average American soldier. The fact that the Germans retained an average combat effectiveness superiority, even though at a lower margin than earlier in the war, was due to the continuing high standards of German professional leadership.[14]

At bottom the German army was successful in combat not because it had developed a new and terrifying concept of warfare, or because it was more highly mechanized, or because its leadership understood the proper use of tanks. It was successful because its methods of training were superior, and its doctrines were the result of a careful and accurate understanding of the lessons learned from the First World War. In other words it was simply a better army. Individual units in other armies were as good or better: In September 1944 the Germans were amazed by the skill and energy of the British airborne troops they had to dislodge from Arnhem, and equally impressed by French armored units who fought them at Epinal.

But such anecdotes, true as they may be, should not disguise the fact that the success of the German army in combat had little to do with the new and a great deal to do with traditional military virtues. When, in 1940, a British officer Montgomery had removed from command protested that he had studied diligently for months to master his duties, Montgomery replied that their German counterparts had spent their entire lives mastering those same principles.[15]

For the advocates of airpower, none of this counted. They mystified their failures and invented most of their successes, creating a misleading paradigm as to what airpower could do. That it was a significant factor on the battlefield is unquestioned. But although command of the air over the battlefield was seen as the virtual guarantor of success, the Germans held on to their defensive positions in Normandy for months.

If the airpower enthusiasts had been correct, the German army would have been destroyed in its entirety by the end of June 1944. If the theories of the armored apostles had been valid, the Allies would have been on the Rhine by the end of the following month. Stubbornly the German army fought on, and to a great extent the failure to recognize its successes, and instead to blame the Allies for various failures, is an attempt to sweep away the unpleasant realities of the battlefield.[16]

Strategically and tactically what destroyed the German army was not an Allied breakthrough, it was Hitler's insistence on mounting counterattacks, so that all the German armor in the field would be lost in one desperate gamble. Fortunately for the Allies, Hitler was an early convert to the idea of the overwhelming power of the offense. He was, in other words, Fuller's best pupil.

NOTES

1. Bruce I. Gudmundsson, *Stormtroop Tactics: Innovation in the German Army, 1914–1918* (New York: Praeger, 1989), xii.

2. The strange obtuseness of the bomber commanders is often seen as an example of moral blindness; not so: It is an obliquity of vision caused by an adherence to a theory that for the sake of convenience we may assign to Douhet and call strategic airpower.

3. More tanks were deployed in the ground phase of the Gulf War, but it is not clear that the numbers of tanks actually in combat were greater. Moreover, in both battles there was an extensive use of tactical aircraft and, particularly at Kursk, of antitank weaponry. Although the claim will be hotly disputed, it is distinctly possible that the largest tank-versus-tank engagement of the Second World War was Gembloux.

4. The initial work is *A Genius for War: The German Army and the General Staff, 1807–1945* (Englewood Cliffs, N.J.: Prentice-Hall, 1977). Dupuy appended an updated summary of his work on this subject to Dupuy, Bongard, and Anderson, *Hitler's Last Gamble*, appendix H, 498–501.

5. Jean Feller, Le *dossier de l'armée française: la guerre de cinquante ans*, 1914–1962 (Paris: Perrin, 1966), 36–49.

6. Général Maxime Weygand, *Histoire de l'armée française* (Paris: Flammarion, 1961), 310. See also, Felix Martin and F[elix?] Pont, *L'armée allemande: étude d'organisation* (Paris: Chapelot, 1903), 47.

7. See the analysis in [Sidney Rau], *L'état militaire des principales puissances étrangères en 1900* (Nancy: Berger-Lavrault, 1900), 370–74. But of course Great Britain had not planned to create an army on the Continental scale of between 1.5 and 2 million soldiers.

8. During the war this imbalance was first revealed in the French Chamber of Deputies in 1916, and later confirmed by the statisticians at the British War Office. See Paul Allard, *Les dessous de la guerre révélés par les comités secrets* (Paris: Les éditions de France, 1932), 14–15; for the French testimony, and War Office [United Kingdom], *Statistics of the Military Effort of the British Empire During the Great War, 1914–1920* (London: His Majesty's Stationery Office, 1922), 359–62, for the British calculations. In *The World Crisis,* Winston Churchill used these data, as well as German figures, to argue that the Allies had seriously underestimated the combat effectiveness of the German army. As this idea

contradicted evolving British myths about their military successes during the First World War, the information was ignored or suppressed, and Churchill was savaged. In the 1980s Niall Ferguson and I, working independently, came to the same conclusion: The Germans lost many fewer men and were thus much more effective in combat. See his *The Pity of War* (New York: Basic Books, 1999), 282–317, and my *The Myth of the Great War*, 12. Unfortunately by now, traditional British military historians have become so enmeshed in the mythologies of how the BEF won the First World War that facts are of little value, particularly when the facts involve quantitative reasoning, which seems the Achilles' heel of military history.

9. Well trained is not the same as well led. Northern France is dotted with testimonials to innumerable last stands by isolated groups of French soldiers in May and June 1940. One hundred thousand French soldiers were killed in the fighting, the overwhelming majority of them on the battlefield. The numbers are simply too great for the assumption that the French army broke and ran for cover to be sustainable—and an army that continues to fight on regardless of the outcome must be considered a well-trained army, whether it is well led or not.

10. There is an excellent discussion of the Reichswehr and Seeckt in Fraser, *Knight's Cross*, 88–95; for Seeckt's "unabashed" (to use Fraser's word) preference for men with aristocratic backgrounds, see 89.

11. Fayolle, *Carnets secrets de la grande guerre*, 160. Although little known outside France, Fayolle was one of the best Allied generals of the First World War—he was, for example, responsible for the successful French offensives on the Somme in July 1916: his troops suffered many fewer casualties than did the British and took more territory.

12. Ibid., 271. Or, as S. L. A. Marshall puts it in *Men Against Fire: The Problem of Battle Command in Future Wars* (1947; reprint, New York: William Morrow, 1964, 12): "By and large, our training system and our standard of battle discipline still adheres to the modes of the eighteenth century, although we are working with weapons and profess to be working with the advanced ideas of the twentieth century." This pretty much sums up the German advantage over the Americans and the British.

13. This false notion has been enthusiastically propagated by analysts like John Terraine, who speaks of the "distressingly backward" nature of the German officer corps in *White Heat: The New Warfare 1914–18* (London: Sidgwick & Jackson, 1982), 48–49. An enormous body of evidence exists that refutes such notions. For example, by 1914, the British army had a substantially higher percentage of officers with aristocratic surnames than did the German. See the discussion in John Ellis, *The Social History of the Machine Gun* (New York: Pantheon, 1975), 48–49.

14. Dupuy, Bongard, and Anderson, *Hitler's Last Gamble*, 499. Dupuy's distinction is an important albeit subtle one that resolves several apparent conflicts. We might list it as follows: (*1*) On occasion, Allied soldiers were as competent as their adversaries—which

accounts for anecdotes to that effect in the French, British, and American armies. (2) By the end of the war, Allied troops were, generally speaking, better trained than their German opponents—which explains why both armies felt they had qualitatively better soldiers in the field. (3) But (and again in general) the German leadership cadres were more than able to compensate for the growing parity—which explains why the Allies could believe they were better and still have such a difficult time.

But German excellence does not—as many analysts conclude—allow us to infer that the Allies were inept. Dupuy, Bongard, and Anderson argue that the Germans "were very good, they were the best," but "the Americans fought pretty well in the World War II. We just weren't as good as the Germans" (*Hitler's Last Gamble,* 452). I would agree, observing only that the same comments would hold true for the British, the French, and even the Belgians and the Dutch. One of the more unfortunate aspects of military history has been the tendency to conclude that the losing side invariably lost because it was inept or incompetent. Thus the Austrians, who were beaten by Frederick the Great, Napoleon, and Moltke the Elder, were judged to be militarily incompetent, even though a simple listing of the generals who defeated them demonstrates the inherent fallacy of the idea.

15. As recorded by Nigel Hamilton in *Monty,* 356. It is true that in certain areas German soldiers had better equipment, but the most notable example was an infantry weapon, the shoulder-fired German antitank rocket launcher, the *Panzerschreck,* which was so vastly superior to the Allied weapon that (then) Col. James M. Gavin recorded "As for the 82nd Airborne Division, it did not get adequate antitank weapons until it began to capture the first German panzerfausts [*sic*]. By the fall of 1944 we had truckloads of them." As recorded by Weigley, *Eisenhower's Lieutenants,* 11. The reason for the notoriety of such weapons as, for example, the 88-millimeter gun, was not that it was any better than a British or American gun, but that the Germans deployed it in ways that their Allied adversaries were reluctant to do. Certainly the British seventeen-pounder was as good a gun, and when used aggressively, it was extremely effective.

16. Thus both the emphasis on the professional shortcomings of the senior commanders, and on the various interservice and national rivalries serve to obscure the basic reasons why the Germans were as successful as they were. When I made this same point in *The Myth of the Great War,* several reviewers accused me of "idealizing" the German army. Apparently they were unfamiliar with Dupuy's calculations (see note 4 above), where the combat efficiency of the German army as opposed to their opponents is seen as ranging from 1:2 all the way up to 2:1. In other words, in order to achieve parity on the battlefield, the Allies would need at least one fifth more soldiers than their opponents. What troubles me is that those analysts who bristle at the "idealization" of the German army implicitly degrade the performance of their opponents; for example, the many American and Commonwealth soldiers who finally defeated them in a long and bloody war.

APPENDIX:

Researching the War

To persuade oneself . . . that the resources of documentary research alone can equip one to write an adequate history of recent events is naïve beyond words.
—POLYBIUS[1]

In an earlier book, on the First World War, I attempted to indicate to the interested reader those sources I had found useful. As no English or American writer had made much use of the French research on the subject, I thought a guide would be helpful. I made no pretense of being exhaustive; nevertheless several of my critics seized on certain omissions as proof that I was unaware of some pertinent fact or new interpretation. Had they actually read the book I had written, they would have discovered that those omissions were made out of charity rather than ignorance.

The same is true here: The purpose of this essay is to provide the reader with a critical guide to those works I have found to be useful, not to write a comprehensive critique of what has been written on the Second World War. When works are omitted it is because in my view they contribute little to our understanding of the war, generally because they repeat what has long been known. The only exceptions are works so well known, or so influential, that some brief comment is required. In this regard it should be noted that more detailed comments are often made in the notes, and that works whose overall value is problematic are frequently mentioned there but not here, where the emphasis is on works of general use to the reader.

In writing about the First World War, it seemed to me that the task was to introduce the reader to those sources routinely ignored; here the task seems rather to provide a sort of filter, as almost every part of the war has received exhaustive attention. So the model employed is roughly comparable to that used by John Keegan in his monograph *The Battle for History: Re-Fighting World War II* (New York: Vintage Books, 1996). Keegan's text is recent, his judgments often quite shrewd, and he is one of the few British scholars who seems aware of American work done on the war. Nonetheless it is useful to dissect the subject from a different point of view, and in a few areas much has been written since Keegan's work appeared.

The brief treatments that follow are divided into four unequal groups. The first group consists of those texts that provide us with the basic information we need to understand the war, both technical and personal. The second group consists of those general works that for one reason or the other seem to me indispensable to any understanding of the wider context of the war. The third group, broken down roughly by campaign, is both a guide to further reading and an indication of what seems to me the most useful work so far. The air war encompasses so many different aspects of the struggle that it is discussed separately, in the fourth group.

Basic Data

The Theorists

The body of J. F. C. Fuller's work is spread over a number of books; I cite only those with most direct bearing: *Armored Warfare*, annotated ed. (Harrisburg, Pa.: Military Service Publishing, 1943); *Armament in History* (London: Charles Scribner's Sons, 1946); *The Foundations of the Science of War* (London: Hutchinson, 1925). Fuller's views in *The Second World War* (New York: Duell, Sloan & Pearce, 1962) are of some interest, but clearly

were written too late to have much influence on how the war was actually fought. In treatments of the war, his ideas are ubiquitous, encountered at every turn, and the only study to question the universal yoking
of Fuller, Blitzkrieg, and the German army in 1939–40 is Maj. Rick S.
Richardson's intriguing essay, "Fall Gelb and the German Blitzkrieg of
1940: Operational Art?"[2]

The situation with regard to Giulio Douhet is less clear. British readers were familiar with many of his ideas without necessarily knowing
they were his, and indeed, there seems no reason to doubt the remark of
Robin Higham that Great Britain's airpower theories were home grown
seems true enough, although it begs the question of the extent to which
these mostly unnamed early British writers borrowed the Italian's ideas.[3]
However most American analysts give Douhet the credit, which is why
the standard edition of his works was published under the auspices of the
U.S. Air Force: Giulio Douhet, *The Command of the Air,* trans. Dino Fer-
rari (Washington, D.C.: Office of the Air Force History, 1983). Several
American studies have attempted to resuscitate Douhet, notably: Lt. Col.
Richard H. Estes, "Giulio Douhet: More on Target Than He Knew," and
Col. John F. Shiner, "Reflections on Douhet: The Classic Approach."[4]

Often overlooked is the extremely thorough analysis of the German
military prepared by the War Department. Although there were subsequent issues of this, the most useful is TM 30-450, titled *Handbook on
German Military Forces* (Washington, D.C.: War Department, December
1941).

Equipment

An understanding of the machines used during this war is vital. Curiously it is a topic much neglected by historians, who have largely left the
field to amateurs and enthusiasts, one reason why so much that has been
written on the war is misleading or incorrect. When it comes to armor,
we are fortunate to have two exhaustive works. F. M. von Senger und
Etterlin's *German Tanks of World War II,* trans. J. Lucas, eds. Peter Chamberlain and Chris Ellis (New York: Galahad, 1967), is the basic source for
German armor, and this English translation is greatly to be preferred to
the original. The equivalent for English and American armored vehicles
is by the editors of the German manual, Peter Chamberlain and Chris
Ellis: *British and American Tanks of World War II* (New York: Arco, 1969).

The situation with regard to the armored vehicles of other countries is more complicated. The most comprehensive work on Soviet tank development is still John Milsom's poorly organized and somewhat propagandistic *Russian Tanks 1900–1970* (Harrisburg, Pa.: Stackpole Books, 1971). Although the data are embedded in a general history, André Duvignac, *Histoire de l'armée motorisée* (Paris: Imprimerie Nationale, 1947), is the best single source for data on French armor, followed by the elaborate *Chars et blindés français*, ed. Col. E[mile] Ramspacher (Paris: Charles-Lavauzelle, 1979). The best single source for the armor of other countries is Werner Regenberg, *Captured Tanks in German Service: Small Tanks and Armored Tractors* (Altglen, Pa.: Schiffer Publishing Company, 1993), and its accompanying text *Captured Tanks in German Service: Small Tanks and Armored Tractors* (Altglen, Pa.: Schiffer Publishing Company, 1998).

The U.S. Army has an enormous (badly maintained and slowly rusting) inventory of weapons and armor at its Aberdeen Proving Grounds, in Aberdeen, Maryland. Partial inventories of the equipment have been printed in two volumes as *Tank Data*, eds. E. J. Hoffschmidt and W. H. Tatum (Old Greenwich, Conn.: WE Press, 1969).[5]

Less satisfactory but still crucial are the listings of weapons found in Terry Gander, *German Anti-tank Guns, 1939–1945* (London: Almark Publications, 1973) and Peter Chamberlain and Terry Gander, *Anti-tank Weapons* (New York: Arco, 1974).

There are a good many—perhaps too many—studies of individual pieces of equipment. I refer here only to those which contain data otherwise difficult to come by, the most notable example being Horst Scheibert's monograph on the Soviet T34 tank, originally published as *Der Russische Kampfwagen T34* (Friedburg, Germany: Podzun Pallas Verlag, 1989); and available in English as *The Russian T34 Battle Tank* (Altglen, Pa.: Schiffer Publishing Company, 1992).

The aircraft of the war are not treated in the same systematic way as the weaponry discussed above. Two reliable and comprehensive works by William Green are the best available: *War Planes of the Second World War: Fighters* (Garden City, N.Y.: Doubleday, 1960); *Famous Bombers of the Second World War* (Garden City, N.Y.: Hanover House, 1959). See also Owen Thetford, *Aircraft of the Royal Air Force since 1918* (New York: Funk & Wagnalls, 1968).

Fortifications

This area is perhaps the most poorly understood part of the war, although extensive work has been published. There are numerous accounts of every aspect of the development of the French fortifications, I cite here only some of the most useful: Emmanuel Bourcier, *L'Attaque de la Ligne Maginot* (Paris: ODEF, 1940); *Roger Bruge, Histoire de la Ligne Maginot I: Faites sauter la ligne Maginot* (Paris: Librairie Fayard, 1977) and *Histoire de la Ligne Maginot II: On a livré la Ligne Maginot* (Paris: Librairie Fayard, 1975); Paul Gamelin, *La Ligne Maginot: images d'hier et d'aujourd hui* (Paris: l'Argout, 1979); Jean-Yves Mary, *La Ligne Maginot: ce qu'elle etait, ce qu'il en reste* (Paris: SERCAP, 1980), André Gaston Prételat, *La destin tragique de la Ligne Maginot* (Paris: Berger-Levrault, 1950); J. J. Rapin, *Une organization exemplaire: l'artillerie des ouvrages de la Ligne Maginot* (Lavey, Switzerland, 1977); Michel Truttmann and Alain Hohnadel, *La Ligne Maginot* (Paris: Tallandier, 1989); Jean-Bernard Wahl, *La Ligne Maginot en Alsace* (Steinbrunn-le-Haut: Editions du Rhin, 1987).

Research on other areas is less exhaustive, but there is an excellent account in English: J. E. and H. W. Kaufmann *Maginot Line Imitations* (New York: Praeger, 1997), greatly to be preferred over Anthony Kemp, *Maginot Line, Myth and Reality* (London: Frederick Warne, 1981). Prewar German fortifications are mostly dismissed by historians, that this is a capital error can be seen simply by referring to Dieter Bettinger and Martin Büren's voluminous two-volume work, *Der Westwall* (Osnabrück: Biblio Verlag, 1990), which gives the specifications and locations for virtually every concrete structure built. Based on the photographic evidence, it would seem that the Germans incorporated Czech techniques into their work. Post-1990 a considerable body of work has emerged in the Czech Republic on this subject. See, in particular, Emil Trojan, *Betonová Hranice: Československé Pohranič ni Opevně ní 1935–1938* (Prague: Oftis, 1994), which has the most complete set of photographs. For those who read Czech, Eduard Stehlik and Martin Vaňourk, *Osmnáctí Hranič áŕ i* (Mohelnice: [unknown], 2001), and Jiří Novák's four-part series *Opevně ní na Králicku* (Prague: Princo, 2000) are most helpful; even for those without understanding of the language, the extensive photographs are of great value: Although the Czechs borrowed the bunker concepts from the French, their extensive use of antitank obstacles is remarkable—and attested to by photographs taken at the time.

Intelligence

Who knew what when—and how that affected the war—has long been a popular subject. The standard compilation of essays is to be found in Ernest R. May, ed., *Knowing One's Enemies: Intelligence Assessment Before the Two World Wars* (Princeton, N.J.: University Press, 1984). The strength of May's account of May 1940 lies in his dissection of the intelligence agencies involved: *Strange Victory* (New York: Hill & Wang, 2001). See also Douglas Porch, *The French Secret Services* (New York: Farrar, Straus & Giroux, 1995).

The extent to which the Allies were "reading" German signals has by now been thoroughly integrated into every account, and is hardly a separate area of inquiry. What has not been fully understood, however, is the intercept traffic going from communist agents through Stalin and then back to the Germans in the period before June 1941—a logical result of the Hitler-Stalin pact, but not one much noted. But then the whole issue of communist penetrations in the West is almost a taboo subject. There was however a clear and disturbing pattern. See Nigel West's account in his abstracts of the intelligence documents in *Venona* (London: HarperCollins, 1999), and the complementary work of Herbert Romerstein and Eric Breindel, *The Venona Secrets* (Washington, D.C.: Regnery, 2002), supplemented by Harvey Klehr, John Earl Haynes, and Fridrikh Igorevich Firsov, *The Secret World of American Communism* (New Haven, Conn.: Yale University Press, 1995).

The Arms Race

How much money was spent, on what, and by whom, has always been the Achilles' heel of historians of this war, whose interpretations in some instances are probably driven as much by politics as by ignorance. The conventional view of a defeated and disorganized France, an aggressive and determined Germany, and an almost passively defeatist Great

Britain, the sort of view advanced most eloquently by writers such as Alistaire Horne in *To Lose a Battle* (London: Penguin, 1969), is hardly borne out by the numbers. For the decades up to the immediate pre-war period, the data worked up by Quincy Wright, *The Study of War* (Chicago: University of Chicago Press, 1939) is indispensable.

The only historian actually to examine the situation with regard to France and Germany in detail is Russell Henry Stolfi, whose Ph.D. dissertation, "Reality and Myth: French and German Preparations for War, 1933–1940," Stanford, 1966, is one of the few unpublished dissertations to contribute anything substantive to any field. For exhaustive enumerations of what sort of arms were actually built during this period, see the sources in the section above ("Equipment" and "Fortifications").

Personal Experience Accounts

One great difference between the two wars is that after 1945, a talented group, mostly British, interrogated all the surviving German generals, who in several cases then went on to write about the war themselves. The evidentiary value of this is problematic. On the one hand some of the men who asked questions, notably Basil Liddell Hart, were clearly looking for answers that would support their ideas about what had happened in the war. On the other hand the senior generals were all keenly aware that at least some of their colleagues and superiors were regarded by the Allies—quite justifiably—as criminals.

Understandably, then, their accounts have a certain bias built into them—protestations about opposing Hitler, for example, should be taken with a large dose of salt. The general principle here, it seems to me, is to use the same procedure any competent lawyer would employ: Statements made that are not necessarily in the best interest of the witness are probably true, offhand remarks that have no bearing on the issue at hand may well be true, those that portray him favorably are probably misleading.

Taking this into account, Basil Henry Liddell Hart's *The German Generals Talk* (New York: William Morrow, 1953), is an indispensable source, and there is much of value in the four great German personal experience narratives: Heinz Guderian, *Panzer Leader,* trans. Constantine Fitzgibbon (New York: Da Capo Press, 1996); Erich von Manstein, *Lost Victories,* ed. and trans. Anthony G. Powell (New York: Regnery, 1958); Walter Warlimont, *Inside Hitler's Headquarters 1939–1945,* trans. R. H.

Barry (Novato, Calif.: Presidio, 1964); and Albert Speer, *Inside the Third Reich,* trans. Richard and Clara Winston (New York: Macmillan, 1970). All these have to be read carefully: The comments of the German generals in particular are often disingenuous.

French accounts must be read with equal caution, as they come to us through a sort of double filter: the need to find someone to blame for the defeat of 1940, and the need for each writer to exculpate his own actions during that defeat. The two that make the best reading are the most unreliable, but for all that they are probably the two best essays of this type to emerge from the war: Marc Bloch. *Strange Defeat: A Statement of Evidence Written in 1940,* trans. Gerard Hopkins (New York: W.W. Norton, 1968); Jean Dutourd, *The Taxis of the Marne,* trans. Harold King (New York: Simon & Schuster, 1957).

Three personal experience accounts which are written as though they are histories are also of considerable value: Andre Beaufré, *The Fall of France,* trans. Desmond Flower (New York: Alfred A. Knopf, 1968); Gen. [François Pierre Raoul] D'Astier de la Vigerie, *Le ciel n'etait pas vide* (Paris: Juilliard, 1952); René Rodolphe, *Combats dans la Ligne Maginot,* rev. ed. (Lausanne: Association Saint Maurice, 1981).

Although it touches only marginally on the concerns of this book, the two installments of Nikita Khrushchev's dictated memoirs are indispensable to understanding key events in the war: *Khrushchev Remembers,* trans. Strobe Talbott (Boston: Little, Brown, and Company, 1970); *Khrushchev Remembers: The Glasnost Tapes,* trans. and ed. Jerrold L. Schecter with Vyacheslav V. Luchkov (Boston: Little, Brown and Company, 1990).

Since 1920 or so, it has been the fashion for military historians to depend heavily on the accounts of eyewitnesses in their recreations of battles. As Jean-Norton Cru demonstrated rather conclusively in 1929, however, these accounts must be interpreted carefully and subjected to a good many checks if one is to take them as authentic or accurate.[6] The most basic check is simple: was the person actually present at the events he describes.

Unfortunately, the conclusions of the few researchers who have investigated this suggests that this is by no means a foregone conclusion. In *Stolen Valor* (Dallas: Verity Press, 1998), for example, Bernard Gary Burkett found that the great majority of Americans who claimed to be Vietnam veterans were either lying outright or egregiously misrepresenting their records. Although Burkett did not attempt a systematic investigation of the veterans of early wars, the few examples he provides suggest that the pattern is hardly restricted to Vietnam.[7] In fact, there are remarkable similarities between Burkett's investigations in the 1980s and 90s and Norton Cru's work in the 1920s.

The net result of this is no less disturbing for its simplicity: Eyewitness accounts in which the witness's bona fides have not been verified are worthless, and this can be exceedingly difficult. Although British and American infantry divisions, for example, had a nominal strength of around fifteen thousand only about two-thirds of those (and this is a conservative estimate) would actually be in the combat component. Moreover, even if the witness was actually present, either his story must be corroborated or his veracity as a witness confirmed. These are two rather large ifs, and the student of military history will find that the authors who rely on such accounts rarely if ever give any indications that this has been done.

Archival material, the lifeblood of historical research, is similarly suspect. Hans von Luck records how Maj. Gen. Edgar Feuchtinger, commander of the Twenty-first Armored Division, turned "this defensive success of ours into a victory report: 'with the combined fire of the artillery and our few antitank guns we were able in a very short time to destroy more than forty enemy tanks.' "[8]

Journalists

In the First World War, journalists were carefully manipulated, hardly ever allowed near any fighting, and strictly enjoined as to what they could say; as a consequence they said little of any interest. In the Second World War the situation was quite different. Moreover, for the first twenty-six months of the conflict, American journalists were technically neutrals, and could say pretty much what they pleased. It is remarkable the extent to which the coverage in *Life* magazine after 1936 provides an accurate and comprehensive context for the struggle, and how its early reportage bears an eerie resemblance to many later accounts. Conversely the prewar reporting in the *Manchester Guardian* reveals a considerably more sophisticated understanding of Central European politics than most of the accounts written by academic specialists postwar.

Even in situations where there was heavy censorship, there are surprising insights. William L. Shirer, *"This Is Berlin," Radio Broadcasts from*

Nazi Germany (New York: Overlook Press, 1999), is probably the best of these, but it is notable that one of the very best accounts of the European war—still—was written by a journalist from New Zealand: Chester Wilmot, *The Struggle for Europe* (New York: Harper & Brothers, 1952).[9]

General Works

Biographies

There is no major figure without a substantial biography—and many lesser figures have equally hefty treatments as well. The treatments of Churchill, Eisenhower, DeGaulle, Roosevelt, and Mussolini are well known and need no further comment.[10] In recent years there have been two extraordinary accounts of Stalin's life published, both written by Russians, and both of great interest—taken together they make obsolete all earlier work: Edward Radzinsky, *Stalin*, trans. H. T. Willetts (New York: Doubleday, 1996); Dmitrii Antonovich Volkogonov, *Stalin: Triumph and Tragedy*, trans. and ed. Harold Shukman (New York: Grove Weidenfeld, 1988).

It must be said, however, that no one of these is particularly satisfactory when it comes to a consideration of matters of strategy in the war itself, and the same must be said of a host of other works, regardless of the contributions they make to biography as a form, the most recent example being Ian Kershaw's tortuous *Hitler 1936–1945: Nemesis* (New York: W.W. Norton, 2000).[11] The only biography of a major political figure that offers serious illumination on the war is Roger Keyes's *Outrageous Fortune: The Tragedy of Leopold III of the Belgians* (London: Secker & Warburg, 1984).

In this regard, for instance, the brief account of Churchill and Hitler in John Lukacs's *The Duel: 10 May–31 July 1940: The Eighty-Day Struggle Between Churchill and Hitler* (New York: Ticknor & Fields, 1991) is much more helpful. So too with Norman Gelb, *Ike and Monty, Generals at War* (New York: William Morrow, 1994), a much better account of Eisenhower at war than is to be found in the standard biographies. Where Gelb falls down is in his hostile and unsympathetic treatment of

Montgomery. Fortunately Great Britain's greatest modern general has been the subject of one of the very best modern biographies, that by Nigel Hamilton: *Montgomery*, three vols. (New York: McGraw-Hill, 1981). Montgomery's supposed rival (at least in the biographical mythology of the war), Patton, is equally fortunate: Carlo D'Este, *Patton: A Genius for War* (New York: HarperCollins, 1995).

The Prewar Context

In this century if not before, history has often meant diplomatic history, and the literature on the immediate background of the war is rich to the point of surfeit. Unfortunately, although researchers in Great Britain worked over the documentary evidence in great detail, they were for various reasons handicapped in their discussions of the Soviet Union; consequently much of what they wrote must now be discounted almost entirely, from A. J. P. Taylor's provocative *Origins of the Second World War* (Greenwich, Conn.: Fawcett, 1965) to Donald Cameron Watt's convoluted apologia for British foreign policy, *How War Came: The Immediate Origins of the Second World War* (New York: Pantheon, 1989).

There is a fair summary of Taylor's position in the opening pages of Geoffrey Roberts, *The Soviet Union and the Origins of the Second World War* (New York: St. Martin's Press, 1995). Basically Taylor put forth a benign interpretation of Stalin's negotiations with Hitler consistent with initial Communist Party formulations: the provisions of the treaty, which were both defensive and tactical, essentially bought time for Stalin and were forced on him by the unreasonable anticommunism of the British and French governments. As even Roberts is obliged to admit, Taylor's thesis had been the official Soviet line for many years after the war.[12]

A useful and authoritative corrective to the various attempts to sanitize Stalin's acts is François Furet, *The Passing of an Illusion: The Idea of Communism in the Twentieth Century,* trans. Deborah Furet (Chicago: University of Chicago Press, 1999). Furet's *La passé d'une illusion*, published in France in 1995 by Robert Laffont, is the definitive essay on the subject, written by the man who was (he died in 1997) France's great authority on the French Revolution. The recent biographies of Radzinsky and Volkogonov (cited in the section "Biography") are also quite useful in this regard.

Although they reveal the stereotypical British contempt for the

French, two British accounts of the immediate prewar period are indispensable: Brian Bond, *Britain, France, and Belgium* (London: Brassey's, 1990), and Roy Douglas, *The Advent of War* (New York: St. Martin's Press, 1978). Both should be supplemented not only by the works on Stalin and communism just listed, but also by works on Central Europe that give more objective accounts of what transpired. The most important of these is unfortunately not available in English: Henry Bogdan, *De Varsovie à Sofia: Histoire des Pays de l'Est* (Paris: Editions de l'Université et de l'Enseignement Moderne, 1982).[13]

General Histories

As wars have become more complex, the omnibus history that attempts coverage of the entire war seems to me to be less and less useful, and nowhere does this seem more true than in the case of the Second World War. Although in theory there is a case to be made for the consistency that results, as well as the virtue of a unified perspective, in practice neither objective is met. Two exceptions should however be noted. Basil Henry Liddell Hart's *History of the Second World War* (New York: G. P. Putnam's Sons, 1970) is a special case. Liddell Hart was intimately involved in the development of military theory and history after 1920; he writes from a unique perspective. Moreover, his is, I believe, the only omnibus history that has useful and original insights. In *A War to Be Won* (Cambridge, Mass.: Harvard University Press, 2000), Williamson Murray and Allan R. Millett attempt—admirably in my view—to confine themselves to a history of military operations and nothing else.

Campaigns

Poland and the Blitzkrieg

Keegan (*Battle for History*, 68) notes with a certain disdain that "for a general treatment [of Poland] we still depend on Robert Kennedy's semiofficial account written for the U.S. Army and on Nicholas Bethell's later and more impressionistic *The War Hitler Won* (New York: Holt, Rinehart & Winston, 1972)." This is hardly the case, although it is certainly true that Robert M. Kennedy: *The German Campaign in Poland (1939)* (Washington, D. C.: Department of the Army, 1956) is indispensable, and Bethell's account is largely vitiated by his ignorance of it. Two valuable Polish accounts (in English) are Lt. Gen. Mieczyslaw Norwid Neugebauer, *The Defence of Poland*, trans. Peter Jordan (London: M. I. Kolin, 1942), and Andrzej Suchcitz's monograph distributed to the Polish Ex-Combatants Association in Great Britain in 1995 to commemorate the fiftieth anniversary of the end of the war. J. W. Kaufmann and H. W. Kaufmann, *Hitler's Blitzkrieg Campaigns* (Conschocken, Pa.: Combined Books, 1993) has a good basic narrative of what happened. Both Guderian and von Manstein have interesting things to say about this campaign, as do the authors of the various studies on the Luftwaffe (cited in the next section).

Finland and Norway

In *The Battle for History*, Keegan says that "we lack an accessible account of the next episode of the war in Europe, the Soviet attack on Finland. Thomas Rics's *Cold Will* (London: Brassey's, 1988), a recent English study, is the best substitute" (68). A few sentences later he says that "François Kersaudy tells the story [of the Norway campaign] inspiringly from the Norwegian point of view." Both comments are incorrect. The most thorough account of the Russo-Finnish war is William R. Trotter's excellent and detailed *A Frozen Hell* (Chapel Hill, N.C.: Algonquin Books, 1991). Although the account is superficial, there is much important data in Eloise Engle and Lauri Paananen, *The Winter War* (New York: Charles Scribner's Sons, 1973). Väinö Tanner's *The Winter War* (Palo Alto, Calif.: Stanford University Press, 1957) is an important account by a member of the Finnish government who played an important role in the conflict. As all these studies were published in the United States, Keegan presumably is unaware of them. The Tomas Ries book to which Keegan refers is a more general account of Finland's military history after 1919.[14] Despite Keegan's description of it, Kersaudy's *Norway 1940* is hardly written from the Norwegian point of view. It is in fact by a French historian and stands as an example of what any history of a campaign should accomplish.[15]

May 1940

For many decades after the war, general accounts of the events of May 1940 differed little from the propaganda of the time, for example, Alistaire Horne, *To Lose a Battle: France, 1940*, (Boston: Little, Brown, 1969) and Colonel [Adolphe] Goutard, *The Battle of France*, 1940 (New York: Ives Washburn, 1959). This was the case even in France, where all accounts of the war were seen through the prism of Gaullism, communism, and the similar isms that dominated French intellectual and political life.

Although specialist studies, particularly on the Maginot Line [see above, *Fortifications*], had begun to chip away at these distorted accounts, there was no overall attempt to discuss what had actually happened in any serious detail until recently, the most notable being Jean Paul Pallud's *Blitzkrieg in the West* (London: Battle of Britain Prints, 1991), which was more or less ignored by historians as it was a lavishly produced book with excellent photographs and the first thorough account of the fighting.

This was followed, eventually, by a more academic study that stands as a useful corrective to the classic accounts: Ernest R. May's *Strange Victory* (New York: Hill & Wang, 2001). It is Pallud, however, who gives the most detailed accounts of what actually happened, and his accounts of the specific phases of the fighting are only supplemented by the specialist texts below (and by May, when he discusses them).

Belgium and the Netherlands

There is a surprising literature on the airborne invasion of the Netherlands. From the German side, the basic text is Franz S. A. Beekman and Franz Kurowski, *Der Kampf um die Festung Holland* (Herford, Germany: Verlag E. S. Mittler und Sohn, 1981). From the Dutch side there is Lt. Col. P. L. G. Doorman's *Military Operations in the Netherlands* (London: Allen & Unwin, 1944), followed by the more narrowly focused *De Krijgsverrichtingen op het Zuidfront van de Westung Holland*, originally written during the war by Capt. M. R. H. Calmeyer, and subsequently expanded by V. E. Nierstrasz ('S-Gravenhage: Staatsdrukkerij en Uitgeverijbedrijf, 1963).

The basic Belgian account of the war is J. Wullus-Rudiger, *La défense de la Belgique en 1940* (Villeneuve-sur-Lot: Alfred Bador, 1940), together with the anonymous Belgian government publication, *La campagne de mai 1940* (Bruxelles: Les Presses de l'Institut Cartographique Militaire [May 1945]), Roger Keyes's biography of King Leopold III (see above, "Biography") is the most authoritative recent account, and indispensable to an understanding of the war.

The authoritative account of Col. James E. Mrazek, *The Fall of Eben Emael* (Washington, D.C.: Luce, 1971), is not likely to be equaled, and stands as the model of what such a monograph should achieve. Brian Cull, Bruce Lander, and Heinrich Weiss, *Twelve Days in May* (London: Grub Street, 1995), provide a competent account of the air campaigns in both countries (particularly when supplemented by the works enumerated below in "Airpower").

The Fall of France

There are numerous specialist accounts of the significant but almost unknown battles of this campaign in French. Some of these are buried in narratives of the specific branches of the military: for armored engagements, see *Chars et blindés français*, ed. Col. E[mile] Ramspacher (Paris: Charles Lavauzelle, 1979), while there are also battle narratives in Michel de Lombarès, *Histoire de l'artillerie française* (Paris: Charles-Lavauzelle, 1957).

There is an excellent and detailed account of the fighting in the French Ardennes by Gérald Dardart, *Ardennes 1940* (Charleville-Mézières: Editions Ardennes 1940, 2000), and also in Robert Leclercq's *Les combats de Stonne-Tannay-Oches-Sammauthe* (Vouziers: Imprimerie Félix, 1997). Nor should the first-person narratives and biographies mentioned above ("Biographies," "Personal Experience Narratives") be overlooked. René Mathot, *Au ravin du loup: Hitler en Belgique et en France* (Bruxelles: Editions Racine, 2000), contains much of interest that generally goes unremarked either by Hitler's biographers or chroniclers of these campaigns.

Other than the biographies enumerated above, little has been contributed in recent decades by British analysts to an understanding of these campaigns. L. F. Ellis, *War in France and Flanders* (London: Her Majesty's Stationery Office, 1953), provides the basic details of the BEF, and Arthur Durham Divine, *The Nine Days of Dunkirk* (New York: W.W. Norton, 1959), is a surprisingly well-done study, one of the first accounts to question the established mythology of May 1940. Other than May's book (above, "May 1940") even less has been done by traditional American analysts; although J. W. Kaufmann and H. W. Kaufmann, *Hitler's Blitzkrieg Campaigns* (Conschocken, Pa.: Combined Books, 1993), have little that is new to say about the specifics of the campaigns, as usual they have compiled a great deal of information not readily available elsewhere.

North Africa

A number of works previously cited deal with some aspect of the North African campaign: obviously any work detailing Montgomery or Rommel does so. For many years the standard account has been Corelli Barnett's *The Desert Generals* (London: Kimber, 1960), which fortunately has been superseded. For what happened before Rommel arrived in 1942, the most penetrating account is that of Barrie Pitt in *The Crucible of War: Western Desert 1941* (London: Jonathan Cape, 1980). The best short account of the entire campaign is Samuel W. Mitcham Jr.'s somewhat misnamed *Rommel's Desert War* (New York: Stein & Day, 1982). Although at first blush it appears to be a sort of amateurish photo album, Walter J. Spielberger and Uwe Feist, *Armor in the Western Desert* (Falbrook, Calif.: Aero Publishers, 1968), contains much information not seen elsewhere.

Italy

A number of recent studies have brought the disastrous Italian campaign into focus. Fortunately, the three most valuable of these supplement one another. Dominick Graham and Shelford Bidwell, in *Tug of War, The Battle for Italy: 1943–1945* (New York: St. Martin's Press, 1986) attempt the classical analysis of the campaign, albeit one marred by their overt hostility toward Americans. One comes away with the impression the authors would have preferred to be fighting with the Germans as allies rather than as adversaries. A certain ingenuousness toward Hitler's army is a common feature in many British accounts—as indeed it was in many British generals during the war itself. Richard Lamb's account of the atrocities and barbarisms inflicted by those same German commanders makes his *War in Italy* (New York: St. Martin's, 1993) an indispensable antidote. The introduction (pages 1–10) should be required reading for anyone seriously interested in the war. In *Circus of Hell, The War in Italy 1943–1945* (New York: Crown, 1993), Eric Morris offers a more ground's eye view of the war, giving a traditional account, but one compellingly done.

The Eastern Front

This topic lies outside the scope of our study, but in the interest of comprehensiveness, I list the following texts that I have found quite useful: John Erickson, *The Road to Stalingrad: Stalin's War with Germany* (London: Weidenfeld & Nicolson, 1975); *The Road to Berlin: Continuing the History of Stalin's War with Germany* (Boulder, Col.: Westview Press, 1983); Earl F. Ziemke, *Stalingrad to Berlin: The German Defeat in the East* (Washington, D.C.: Office of the Chief of Military History, U.S. Army, 1968); Christopher Duffy, *Red Storm on the Reich: The Soviet March on Germany, 1945* (New York: Maxwell Macmillan International, 1991). Probably the best short study of the war was done by James Lucas, deputy head of photographs at the Imperial War Museum (London): *War on the Eastern Front* (New York: Stein & Day, 1980).

One of the best-kept secrets of the war was the extent of Allied aid to the Soviet Union. See the exhaustive inventory of this in Joan Beaumont, *Comrades in Arms: British Aid to Russia 1941–1945* (London: Davis-Poynter, 1980), which lays to rest many myths still held about how Stalin fought the Nazis all by himself. Alexei Tolstoy, in *Stalin's Secret War* (New York: Holt, Rinehart, & Winston, 1981), gives an estimate of the true focus of much of Stalin's wartime activities, while Allen Paul, in *Katyn* (New York: Charles Scribner's Sons, 1991), analyzes a practical example in detail.

A small but steadily growing body of work traces the unknown wars of Hitler's mostly reluctant allies: Charles K. Kliment and Bretislav Nakládal, *Germany's First Ally: Armed Forces of the Slovak State 1939–1945* (Atglen, Pa.: Schiffer Publishing, 1997); Franz von Adonyi-Naredy, *Ungarns Armee im Zweiten Weltkrieg: Deutschlands letzter Verbundeter* (Neckargemund, Germany: K. Vowinckel, 1971); Mark Axworthy, *The Romanian Army of World War 2* (London: Osprey, 1991). Although this last is ostensibly a book on Romanian army uniforms, in actual fact it is the only succinct account of that army's role in the war.

Indispensable to any understanding of this conflict, and by far the best personal experience narrative to come out of the war: Milovan Djilas, *Wartime*, trans. Michael B. Petrovich (New York: Harcourt Brace Jovanovich, 1977). Indispensable for a different but equally compelling reason: Radu Ionid, *The Holocaust in Romania* (Chicago: Ivan R. Dee, 2000).

Normandy

John Keegan has said that Chester Wilmot is the man who showed him how military history should be written, a statement that speaks well for Keegan's perceptions.[16] Wilmot's account of the last year of the war, *The Struggle for Europe* (New York: Harper & Brothers, 1952), remains the classic account. Surprisingly little has been discovered since Wilmot wrote to make us revise in any substantial way his portrait of the fighting. Of the numerous biographies of the major figures involved, only Hamilton's study of Montgomery sheds new light on any particular issue.

In addition there are two outstanding studies that focus on Normandy itself (Wilmot goes through until the end of the war). John Keegan's *Six Armies in Normandy* (New York: Viking, 1982) is the best military history Keegan has written. Carlo D'Este's *Decision in Normandy* (New York: Konecky and Konecky, 1983) is likewise a classic of modern military history. All subsequent writers have depended heavily on the contributions of Martin Blumenson in *Breakout and Pursuit* (Washington, D.C.: Office of the Chief of Military History, 1961), part of the U.S. Army's history of the war. Russell F. Weigley's *Eisenhower's Lieutenants* (Bloomington: University of Indiana Press, 1981) is misleadingly titled; its subtitle describes the subject of the book, albeit in a peculiar way: *The Campaign of France and Germany, 1944–1945*. In reality the text is an excellent reference work as well as an insightful account of the American Army's struggles in France and Germany. There is one French text that seems of great value in looking at the whole struggle from a different point of view: Eddy Florentin's *The Battle of the Falaise Gap*, trans. Mervyn Savill (New York: Hawthorne Books, 1967).[17]

Fall 1944

The campaigns of fall 1944 are invariably covered in a variety of different texts, ranging from general histories of the war to biographical studies. What follows is restricted to studies of one specific campaign. For the Allied airborne offensive in September 1944, there is Alexander McKee's surprisingly accurate *The Race for the Rhine Bridges* (New York: Stein & Day, 1971), Cornelius Ryan's popular but well researched *A Bridge Too Far* (New York: Simon & Schuster, 1974), and Robert Kershaw's *It Never Snows in September: The German View of Market-Garden and the Battle of Arnhem, September, 1944* (New York: Sarpedon, 2001).[18]

For the events of December 1944, there is the almost encylopediac account of Hitler's failed Ardennes offensive, *Hitler's Last Gamble*, by Trevor N. Dupuy, David L. Bongard, and Richard C. Anderson, Jr. (New York: HarperCollins, 1994), a work that in scope goes far beyond a simple consideration of the fighting. At the other end of the spectrum—as far as length goes, is Michael Tolhurst's compact *Battle of the Bulge* (Barnsley, South Yorkshire, England: Leo Cooper, 2001). As far as biographies go, we have the excellent study by Carlo D'Este, *Patton: A Genius for War* (New York: HarperCollins, 1995), as well as the concluding volume of Nigel Hamilton's biography of Montgomery, *Monty: Final Years of the Field-Marshal* (New York: McGraw-Hill, 1986). Like the Dupuy study, these are both works that go far beyond the simple limits of the subject.

That being said, there is much of interest in Anthony Kemp's *The Unknown Battle: Metz, 1944* (New York: Stein & Day, 1981) while H. M. Cole's contribution to the U.S. Army history series, *The Lorraine Campaign* (Washington, D.C.: Office of the Chief of Military History, 1950), is notable. In *Panzer Commander*, Hans von Luck notes the disastrous (for the Germans) battles with French armored forces under General Leclerc (172–74) around Epinal in the fall of 1944. It is often forgotten how effective these units were wherever they fought. *Les chasseurs d'Afrique* (Paris: Histoires et collections, 1999), by Jacques Sicard and François Vauviller, traces the combat records of the twelve regiments of these elite troops.

The Air War

Losses

The two basic texts for evaluating the success of the strategic bombing campaign, invariably either ignored or misunderstood, are the two volumes prepared by the U.S. Strategic Bombing Survey: *The Effects of Strategic Bombing on the German War Economy* (Washington, D.C.: Overall Economic Effects Division, October 1945); *Overall Report (European War)* (Washington, D.C.: Overall Economic Effects Division, September 1945). An equally basic, albeit incomplete, source for aircraft losses is W. R. Chorley, *Royal Air Force Bomber Command Losses of the Second World War* (Leicester, England: Midland Counties Publications, 1992); Norman L. R. Franks, *Royal Air Force Fighter Command Losses of the Second World War* (Leicester, England: Midland Counties Publications, 1997). Despite its controversial thesis, David Irving's *The Destruction of Dresden* (London: Kimber, 1966) is an indispensable and well-researched guide to the whole issue of strategic bombing.

Histories

Despite some errors Robin Higham's *Air Power, A Concise History* (New York: St. Martin's Press, 1972) is the most useful general account. However, it is quite weak in its treatment of the early years of airpower and, particularly in antiaircraft defense. Consequently it should be supplemented by Jules Poirier, *Les bombardements de Paris (1914–1918): Avions, Gothas, Zeppelins, Berthas* (Paris: Payot, 1930), a much more comprehensive and theoretical book than its title indicates.

The rise and fall of the Luftwaffe remains too little understood, but there are four excellent works, which, taken together, are quite helpful: Matthew Cooper, in *The German Air Force* (London: Jane's, 1981); Edward L. Homze, *Arming the Luftwaffe* (Lincoln: University of Nebraska Press, 1976); Hanfried Schliepahke, *The Birth of the Luftwaffe* (Chicago: Regnery, 1972); Herbert Molloy Mason, *The Rise of the Luftwaffe* (New

York: Dial, 1973). Uniquely the German Air Force was responsible for the air defense systems. Patrick de Gmeline's somewhat eccentric *Flak: La DCA Allemande, 1939–1945* (Tours, France: Editions Heimdale, 1986) is by far the best discussion of this, arguably the most successful branch of the Luftwaffe.

Numerous accounts of the American and British air forces have been written, most of them so propagandistic as to be of no real value. One might as well read the official histories—that of the RAF makes for entertaining reading: Denis Richards, *Royal Air Force, 1939–1945,* three vols. (London: Her Majesty's Stationery Office, 1953-54).

The account of the German aerial offensive by Richard Hough and Denis Richards, *The Battle of Britain* (New York: W. W. Norton, 1989), is not likely to be bettered. There is a very thorough account of the Allied bombing campaign in Robin Neillands, *The Bomber War* (New York: Overlook, 2001), who makes the best case possible (not a very good one) for its success. Both accounts, though written very much from the British point of view, are nonetheless valuable.

When we turn to French aviation the situation becomes muddy. The conventional wisdom has long been that France had no air force to speak of, or anyway no "modern" air force. But anyone who reads Antoine de Saint-Exupéry's *Flight to Arras* (London, Toronto: W. Heinemann, [1943]), as I did as a child, will be skeptical of this idea. The reality is much more complex. For one thing, naval aviation was ignored. A serious error: see the monograph by Vice-Admiral R. Vercken, *Histoire succincte de L'aéronautique naval* (Paris: ARDHAN, 1993). See also the monograph by Claude Abzac-Epezy, *L'armée de l'air des années noires* (Paris: Economica, 1998). The most serious treatment of the subject, however, is a manuscript by Lt. Col. Faris Kirkland, "The French Air Force in 1940: Was It Defeated by the *Luftwaffe* or by Politics?" Kirkland provides ample documentation for the relative strength and modernity of France's air force, and his argument seems to me conclusive.[19]

Postwar, the U.S. Air Force commissioned numerous studies, drawing freely on the expertise of ex-Luftwaffe officers. The most valuable of these is Gen. Paul Deichmann, *German Air Force Operations in Support of the Army,* ed. Littleton B. Atkinson (New York: Arno Press, 1962). Other studies were commissioned as well. I found Adam L. Gruen, *Preemptive Defense: Allied Air Power Versus Hitler's V-Weapons* (Washington, D.C.: Air Force History and Museums Program, 1998) to be the most useful for the practical light it sheds both on what airpower could do and for the light it sheds on the refusal of the commanders of the two air forces to be deterred from their obsession with strategic bombing.

NOTES

1. Polybius, *The Rise of the Roman Empire*, trans. Ian Scott-Kilvert (London: Penguin, 1979), 443 (book 12, para 25e).

2. This essay was written for the School of Advanced Military Studies, U.S. Army Command and General Staff College. My understanding is that it is freely available by application to the college, which is located at Fort Leavenworth, Kansas (document identification: 19991109 062). How the Germans themselves perceived armored warfare is best seen by examining Rudolf Steiger, *Armor Tactics in the Second World War: Panzer Army Campaigns of 1939–1941 in German War Diaries*, trans. Martin Fry (Oxford: Berg Publishers, 1991). Most studies of Blitzkrieg are simply uncritical summaries written by adherents of Fuller. See the most recent, Charles Messenger, *The Art of the Blitzkrieg*, 2nd ed. (London: Ian Allan, 1991), for an uncritical point of view, although Messenger's opening chapter is a clear exposition of the various theories—and particularly those relating to the air.

3. Higham, *Air Power*, 70. See the parallel remarks of McKee, *Dresden 1945*, 13.

4. My understanding is that copies of these essays, prepared as part of the U.S. Air Force's Air University, are available at http://www.airpower.maxwell.af.mil/.

5. No authors are given for these volumes; the names of the editors were taken from the information supplied in volume 2.

6. His is the classic work: *Témoins* (Paris: Les Etincelles, 1929); it has subsequently been reprinted by the University of Nancy (Nancy, France: Presses universitaires de Nancy, 1993).

7. During 1999, for example, the Associated Press reported as credible an account of U.S. Army atrocities in the Korean War, only to discover later that the key witness had not actually been anywhere near the incident he claimed to be reporting. Typically those accounts using the now debunked story as evidence of Korean War atrocities are still in circulation, which suggests the root of the problem: Such stories are believed because they meet the preconceptions of a segment of the audience, not because they meet any investigative standard.

8. Luck, *Panzer Commander*, 176. But who, one might ask, has attempted to verify the accuracy of Luck's account, depending as it often does on letters written forty years after the fact? Typically we are asked simply to accept all these recollections on faith—in this case because an eminent historian found him impressive and charming and became

a friend of his (xvii). But if Stephen Ambrose made any attempt to verify the accuracy of Luck's account at any level, he fails to mention it in his introduction.

9. John Keegan, writing in 1995, observed that "he showed me how military history should be written" (*Battle for History*, 36).

10. These are Gilbert, *Churchill;* Stephen Ambrose, *Eisenhower* (New York: Simon & Schuster, 1983); Forrest C. Pogue, *Marshall,* four vols. (New York: Viking Press, 1963–87); Kenneth Sydney Davis, *FDR: The War President, 1940–1943: A History* (New York: Random House, 2000).

11. Biographies of the major figures of the Third Reich are particularly unhelpful, for example, David Irving's *Göring, A Biography* (New York: Morrow, 1989). In *The Battle for History*, Keegan (51–53) has high praise for Irving's *Hitler's War* (New York: Viking Press, 1977), which seems to me simply more of the same. One often has the feeling that works about the Third Reich are cultivated to titillate rather than to inform.

12. Although (American) historians have always seen Taylor's interpretations as tilted (to use Teddy Uldricks's word), this relatively benign portrait, which consigns Stalin to the background of the conflict, has had surprising resonance. See the discussion in *The Origins of the Second World War Reconsidered: The A. J. P. Taylor Debate After Twenty-five Years*, ed. Gordon Martel (Boston: Allen & Unwin, 1986), and especially Teddy Uldricks, "A. J. P. Taylor and the Russians," 162–87.

13. After 1945, most historians were unable or unwilling to untangle the complex situation in Central Europe, making serious factual errors in their accounts. As a result works dealing with what had actually happened were simply not published by mainstream presses in the United States (which accounts for the peculiarities of the publication data in the list that follows). For some useful correctives, see J. M. Kirschbaum, *Slovakia, Nation at the Crossroads of Central Europe* (New York: Speller, 19[60?]); Charles J. Hokky, *Ruthenia, Spearhead Toward the West*, trans. Alexander Gallus (Gainesville, Fla.: Danubian Research and Information Center, 1966); Edward Chazar, *Decision in Vienna: The Czechoslovak-Hungarian Border Dispute of 1938* (Astor, Fla.: Danubian Press, 1978).

14. His correct name is Tomas Ries, not, as Keegan has it, Thomas Rics. Presumably a typographical error.

15. The book was first published in France (Paris: Editions Tallandier, 1987); subsequently Kersaudy did his own translation of the French text, which was published in Great Britain (London: William Collins Sons, 1990) and in the United States (New York: St. Martin's Press, 1991); in paperback (Lincoln: University of Nebraska Press, 1998).

16. Keegan, *Battle for History*, 36.

17. The Florentin study was originally published as *Stalingrad en Normandie* (Paris: Presses de la Cité, 1964).

18. Kershaw's work was first published in England in 1990—Keegan singles it out as the best of the various accounts of the fighting (*Battle for History*, 78), but although this

commendation is warranted in the sense that the book is well done, it is misleading. Kershaw's work is a compilation of German eyewitness accounts; it does not give the reader a general overview of operations.

19. My understanding is that copies of this essay, prepared as part of the U.S. Air Force's Air University, are available at http://www.airpower.maxwell.af.mil/.

INDEX

Page numbers in *italics* refer to illustrations.